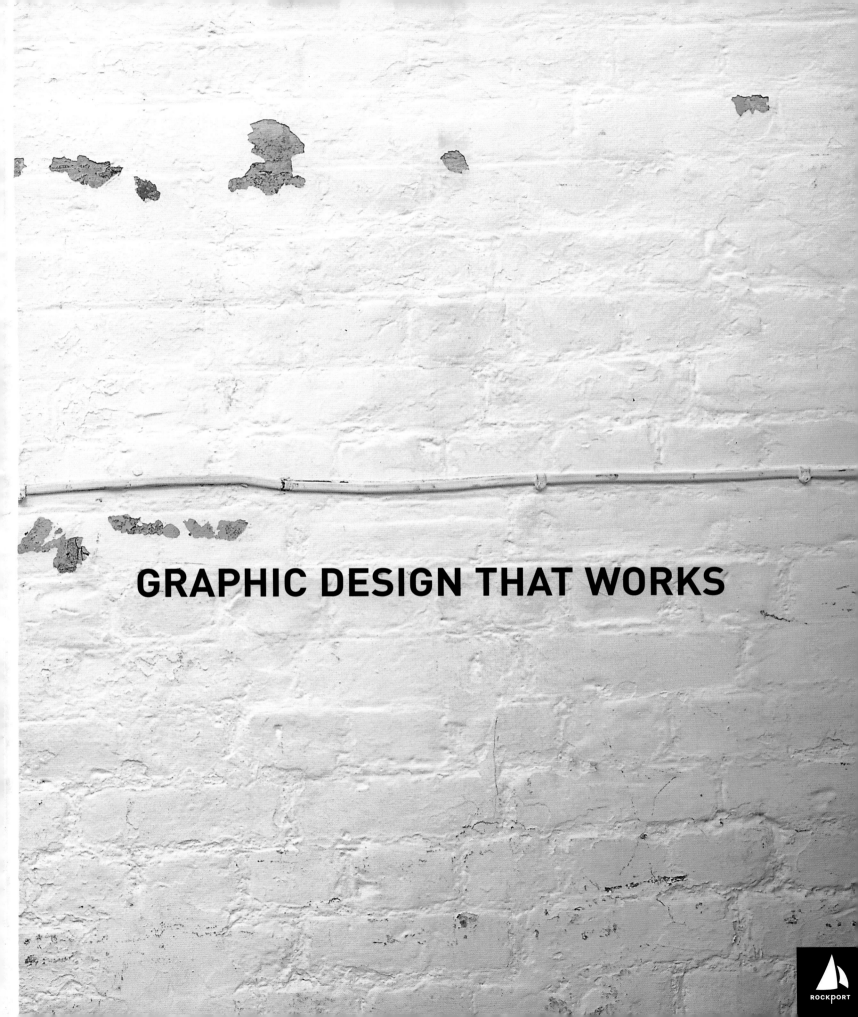

GRAPHIC DESIGN THAT WORKS

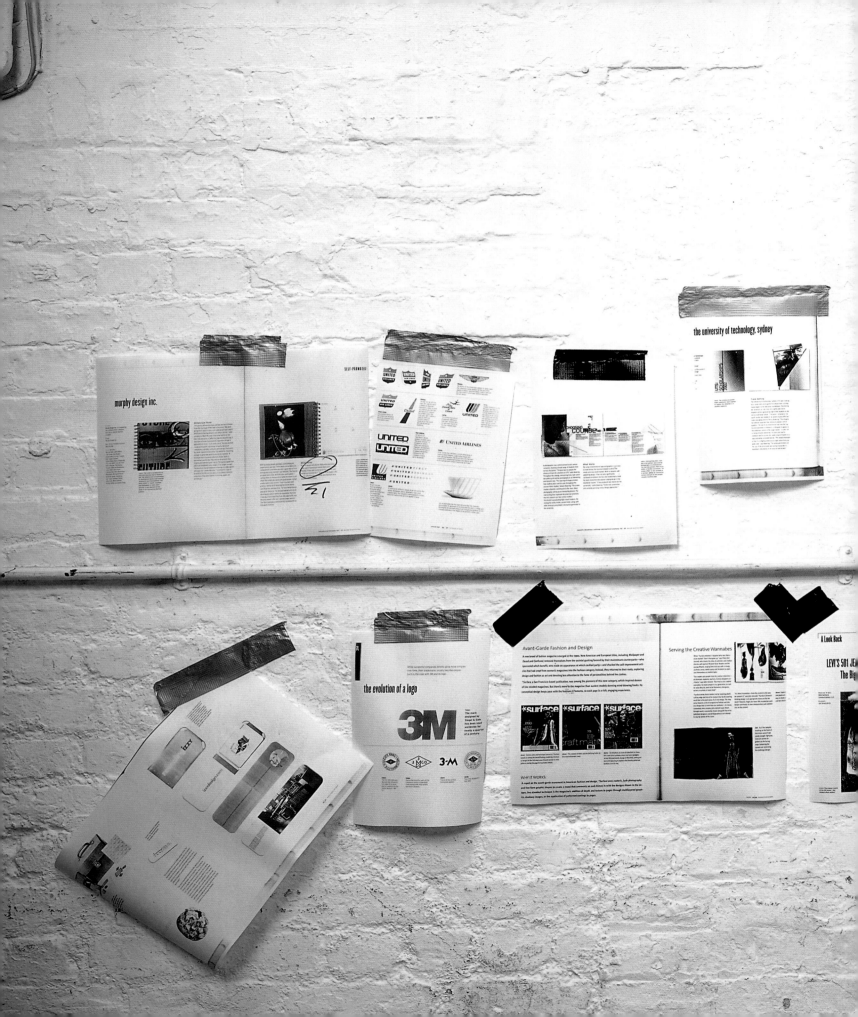

GRAPHIC DESIGN THAT WORKS

Secrets for Successful Logo, Magazine, Brochure, Promotion, and Identity Design

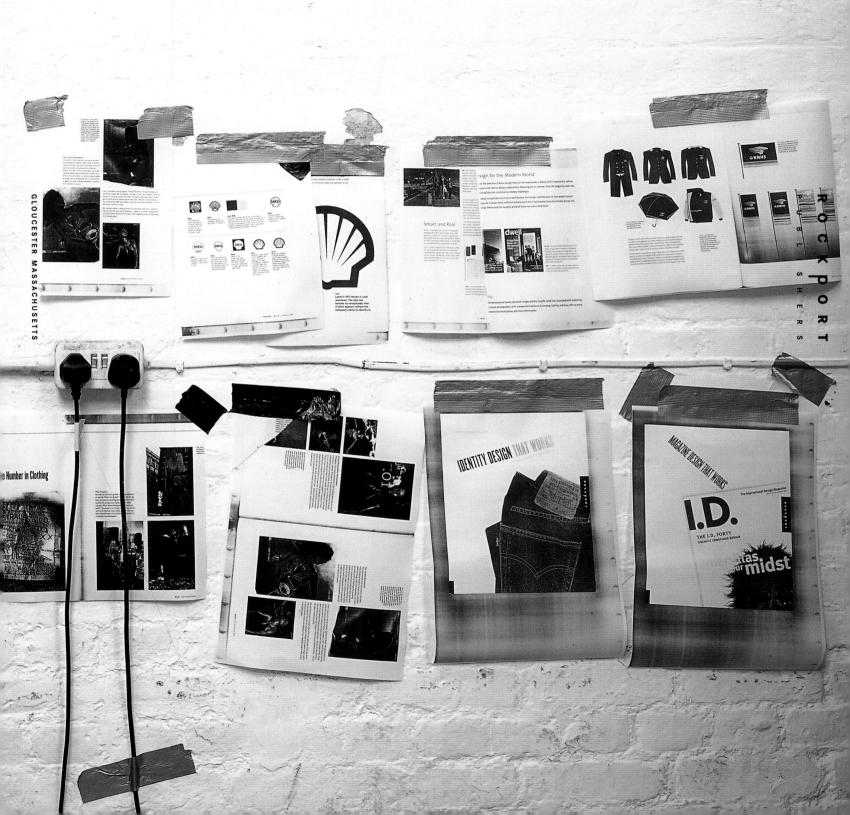

GLOUCESTER MASSACHUSETTS

ROCKPORT PUBLISHERS

First published in the United States of America by
Rockport Publishers, Inc.
33 Commercial Street
Gloucester, Massachusetts 01930-5089
Telephone: (978) 282-9590
Fax: (978) 283-2742
www.rockpub.com

Library of Congress Cataloging-in-Publication data available.

ISBN 1-59253-084-2

10 9 8 7 6 5 4 3 2 1

Special acknowledgment and thanks is given to Cheryl Dangel Cullen for her work on pages 276–309 from *Promotion Design That Works* and on pages 312–347 from *Identity Design That Works*; to Lisa L. Cyr for her work on pages 180–273 from *Brochure Design That Works*; to Stacey King for her work on pages 90–178 from *Magazine Design That Works*; and to Lisa Silver for her work on pages 10–88 from *Logo Design That Works*.

Cover Design: plan-b studio limited
Cover Image: Fredrika Lokholm plan-b studio
Production: Leslie Hames

Printed in China

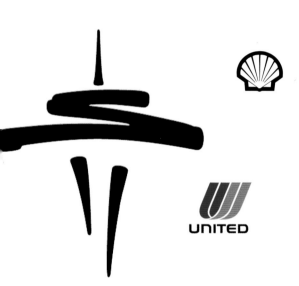

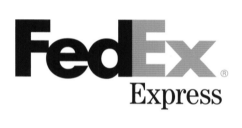

Express

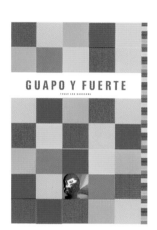

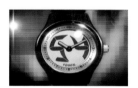

GUAPO Y FUERTE

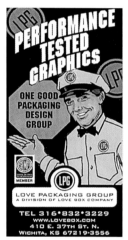

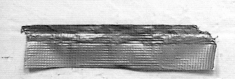

Contents

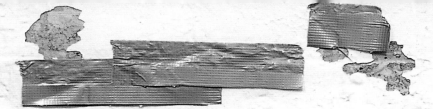

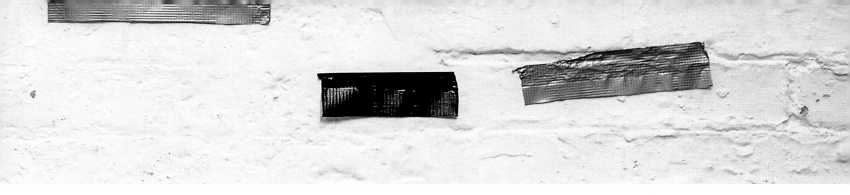

Logo Design

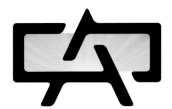

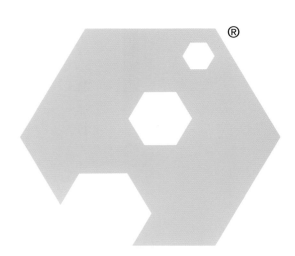

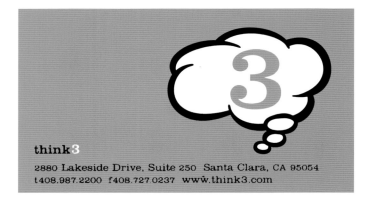

think3
2880 Lakeside Drive, Suite 250 Santa Clara, CA 95054
t408.987.2200 f408.727.0237 www.think3.com

a l i b r i s ™

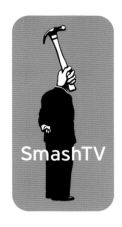

SmashTV

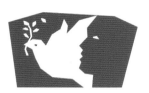

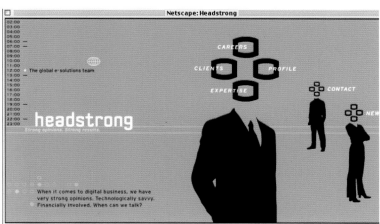

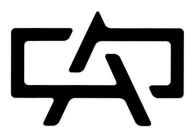

Client
Adams Outdoor Advertising is an Atlanta-based company specializing in billboard advertisements.

CREATIVE DIRECTOR
Kevin Wade

DESIGNER
Martha Graettinger

FIRM
Planet Design Company

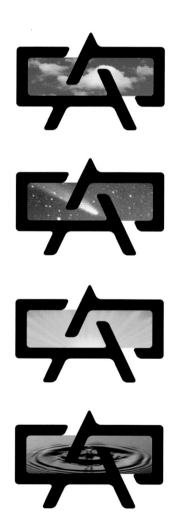

Process
The biggest challenge in developing the logo was finding a way to combat the negative stereotypes surrounding the billboard advertising industry, says Kevin Wade, a principal at the Madison, Wisconsin-based Planet Design. "Billboards tend to be a medium used only after a company has decided to use television, print, or radio advertising," he explains. "Adams wanted to change perceptions, and one way to do that is to develop an identity that is different from the industry norm." And since the norm in the billboard industry has traditionally been nondescript type treatments, Wade's team decided to do the opposite and develop a symbol. The team began by sketching designs based on a capital A, the first letter of the client's name. One direction transformed the A into a monumental object seen from below, an allusion to a billboard viewed from a passing car; another approach flipped the A onto its back, transforming it into a road disappearing into the horizon. From these experiments evolved the idea of an A as an easel displaying a blank canvas, a concept, says Wade, that seemed to lend a kind of "blue sky, anything's possible," quality to the client's product. Pursuing the easel concept, Wade's team refined a design in Illustrator, opting for bold outlines so that the mark would be legible both in very large sizes, as in billboards, and very small, as in business cards. Next, the team searched through stock photography for images to place inside the logo's central rectangle. The four images that were ultimately chosen—a blue sky, a sunrise, a pool of water, and a shooting star—imbue the final mark with an aspirational quality, a message that is further emphasized by the company's tagline: "Out There. Thinking."

What Works
The primary logo, a capital A bisected by a horizontal rectangle, visually references a billboard. The logo's four variations, each of which features a different photographic image in its center, stress the flexibility of billboards as an advertising medium.

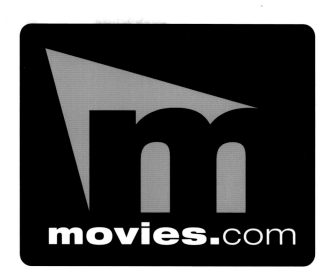

Client

Movies.com is a website that provides information about feature films to a general audience.

Designer

John Smallman

Firm

Movies.com

Process

Knowing the Movies.com site aimed to reach a wide audience, designer John Smallman set out to create a logo that was general enough to appeal to a range of age groups, cultures, and aesthetic tastes. He began by sketching designs based on film reels, but felt they were too similar to other movie websites. Next, he shifted his focus to the site's tagline, "Don't get left in the dark," and explored different designs based on spotlights. Literal illustrations, however, seemed too cliché to Smallman so he tried a more abstract approach using type. In Illustrator, he created a triangular-shaped spotlight, then placed a reversed-out m at its base. After experimenting with different typefaces, he chose Helvetica Neue Heavy Extended, as its bold, sans serif forms were easily readable within the spotlight shape. He chose a lowercase m because the curved strokes suggest a row of movie theater seats.

What Works

The logo, a lowercase m cut out of a triangular shape, evokes the spotlight created by a film projector shining over a row of seats in a darkened movie theater.

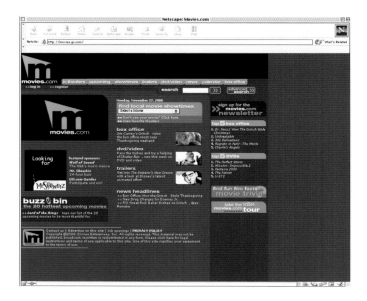

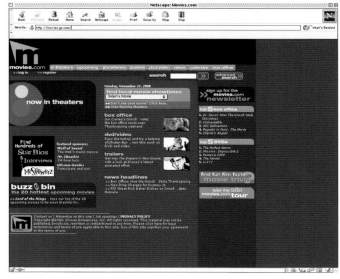

While successful companies tend to grow more complex over time, their trademarks usually become simpler. Such is the case with 3M and its logo.

the evolution of a logo

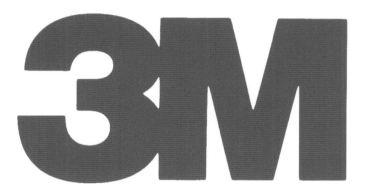

Today:
The mark designed by Siegel & Gale has been used worldwide for nearly a quarter of a century.

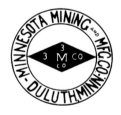 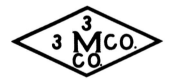 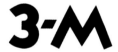 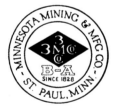

1906:
The first 3M trademark features the company's full name, its location, and, in a diamond at the center, the term "3M Co."

1926:
During the first fifty years of the company's history, trademarks come and go with little fanfare and much variation.

1937:
Traces of the current monogram appear.

1938:
Then they disappear a year later.

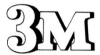

1942-1948:
The monogram reappears, sometimes with a hyphen, sometimes without.

1950:
An oval design debuts. Who created this mark and why is unknown, but soon it is in general use.

  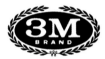 PRODUCT OF
3M
RESEARCH

 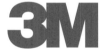

1951-1960:
With no standards manual to guide usage, variations of the oval design flourish. In some cases the oval appears as an outline. In others, as a colored solid. Sometimes the oval disappears altogether. When 3M celebrates its fiftieth anniversary, laurel leaves are added.

1961:
3M hires the design firm Gerald Stahl & Associates to create a definitive logo that will unite the corporation and all its business units under a single mark. The result is a boxy, serif 3M, whose industrial look earns it the nickname "Plumber's Gothic."

1961:
With the new logo design comes a standards manual that contains four approved variations of the logo. This one is based on the geometric paintings of the Dutch artist Piet Mondrian.

1977:
When variations of the 3M logo multiply due to differing needs of company divisions, the design firm Siegel & Gale embarks on a redesign to solve the problem. The result is a monogram simplified to the bone: Serifs vanish; so do taglines. Even the space between the 3 and the M is stripped away. For color, red is chosen to convey a sense of power.

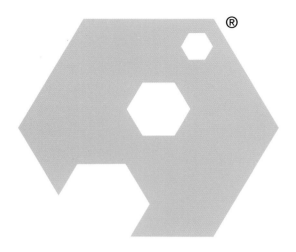

Client

Lightflow is an online company that provides help in using the Internet.

CREATIVE DIRECTOR
Carlos Segura

DESIGNER
Tnop Wangsillapakun

FIRM
Segura Inc.

Process

From the beginning, the notion of simplicity drove the design process. In part, this was due to practical reasons, says designer Carlos Segura, who led the project: Since the mark would be used on the Web, its form had to be streamlined in order to work well across a range of computer platforms and to allow for the possibility of animation in the future. Simplicity was also important for conceptual reasons, says Segura, as it reflected the client's mission of making Web navigation easy. Working within this parameter, the design team searched for ways to visually represent light and hit upon a hexagon, a form that carries a range of associations with light—prisms, sunspots, and camera apertures come to mind—and whose simple geometry easily adapts to the Web. Next, to suggest the movement of light, three more hexagons, diminishing in size as they bisect the larger hexagon, were added. For the logotype, the clean, straightforward Helvetica Neue was chosen; for color, a pale blue to evoke a sense of calm.

What Works

The logo, a solid hexagon bisected by a diagonal line of three smaller hexagons, visually represents the process of light flowing through a multifaceted prism, which in turn reflects the client's mission of "shedding light on," or helping to solve, problems arising from the Internet.

lightflow®

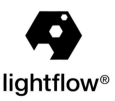

lightflow®

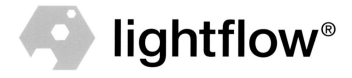

Client

New Leaf Paper manufactures and distributes paper made from recycled material.

Art Director
Jennifer Jerde

Designer
Nathan Durrant

Firm
Elixir Design, Inc.

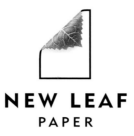
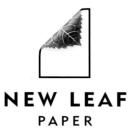

Process

To reflect its intention of becoming a big player in the paper industry, New Leaf Paper wanted a logo that felt corporate. And yet, to distinguish itself as being more environmentally responsible than its competitors, the client also hoped for a logo that had a natural feel. With these parameters in mind, designer Nathan Durrant created sketches based on the double meaning of the company's name: "leaf" refers both to plants and to pages. From these sketches emerged the idea of combining both meanings into a single image of a turning leaf. But Durrant was not satisfied with the illustration-based renderings that followed, feeling they were not corporate enough. So he shifted his attention to photography. He began searching for a leaf that had clearly visible veins, so that an image of it would be readable at reduced sizes, and had edges that met at a right angle at the tip so that it could later be inserted into a rectangle. He eventually chose a hydrangea leaf, photographed it with a digital camera, then scanned the image into a computer and retouched it in Photoshop, adding highlights and shadows to create the sense of a curling leaf. The result is a logo that is at once slick and elegant and, as Durrant puts it, "enviro-groovy." However, like all photography-based logos, this one does present challenges in reproduction. To ensure it works well in different sizes and media, Durrant created a variety of versions, ranging from micro-versions where the leaf has wider veins and fewer scalloped edges to outline versions for black-and-white applications.

What Works

The logo, a white rectangle whose upper corner curls downward to reveal a photo of a leaf, is based on both the client's product and its mission. While the logo's shape suggests a sheet of paper, and the leaf the paper's recycled content, the mark's curled edge evokes the phrase "turning over a new leaf," which in this case refers to switching from non-biodegradable products to environmentally friendly ones.

Perhaps the strongest example of "less is more" is the Bayer cross. Beginning life as an intricate heraldic shield, the logo became instantly recognizable only after its design was pared down to bare essentials.

the evolution of a logo

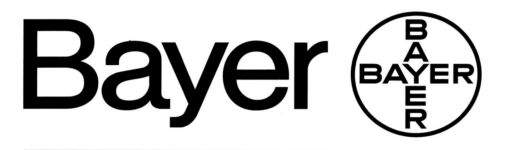

Today:

The Bayer cross has remained virtually unchanged for nearly 75 years.

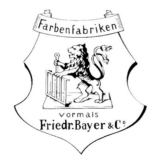

1861:
Bayer's first logo, which depicts a lion and grid, pays tribute to the coat of arms of Elberfeld, the Germany city where the company was founded.

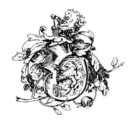

1886:
The logo becomes more intricate. Numerous heraldic elements are added to project a heroic company image.

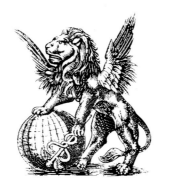

1895:
Bayer introduces a new logo featuring a lion holding a caduceus, the symbol of physicians, and resting one paw on a globe, an indication of the company's self-confident and international intentions. Later, when public taste shifts away from such heroic designs, the Bayer lion is retired.

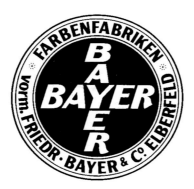

1900:
Hans Schneider, an employee in Bayer's pharmaceutical department, sketches the company's name in a cross-like configuration. Four years later, his design becomes an alternative trademark.

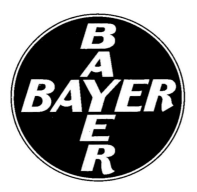

1904:
In the European market the Bayer cross is used with the lion; abroad, the cross is used alone.

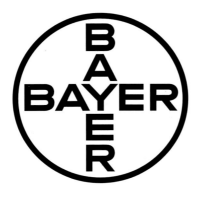

1929:
The Bayer cross is given its present-day appearance. Pared down to bare essentials, the design works equally, stamped on tiny aspirin tablets or lighting up the night sky, as it does in the giant illuminated sign atop the Bayer plant in Leverkusen.

While the United logo today is instantly recognizable worldwide, it underwent a number of distinct changes before reaching its present form.

the evolution of a logo

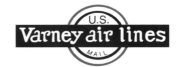

Today:

The present logo

1926-1933:
Each of United's four predecessor companies had its own logo.

When United became the management company for those carriers, it established a bar-and-circle logo with the bar containing the words "United Airlines" and the circle housing each of the four carrier's logos.

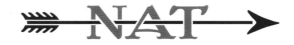

1934:
The bar-and-circle logo is modified. The circle now contains a map of the United States inscribed with lines denoting air routes.

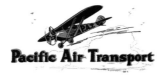

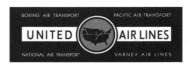

1936:
In an attempt to standardize its logo, the company adopts a red, white, and blue shield.

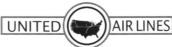

1934-1940:
With no standards manual to guide usage, logo designs flourish. Each one varies radically from the others.

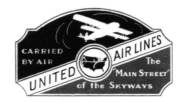

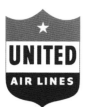
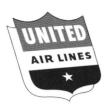
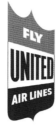
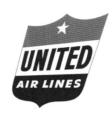
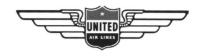

1940s:
Variations of the shield logo appear. In some cases the company's name appears at the top of the shield; in others, centered below a star. In still others, the shield is stretched, slanted, and even sprouts wings.

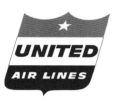

1946-1958:
This slanted version of the shield logo becomes the most commonly and consistently used.

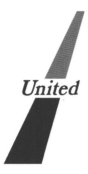

1960s:
Though not an official logo, this slanted spire, created by designer Raymond Loewy, is used on United's aircraft tails and begins to replace the shield. Later, the bold, sans serif typeface used to spell out United's name is replaced by the more delicate Bookman typeface.

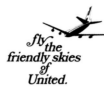

1970:
The shield logo all but disappears. Without a new logo, United's identity becomes tied to its "Fly the friendly skies" slogan.

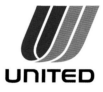

1973:
United commissions the designer Saul Bass to develop a logo that will convey leadership and innovation in air travel. The result is a stylized red and blue U symbol—later nicknamed "the tulip"—and a custom logotype featuring bold, sans serif letters.

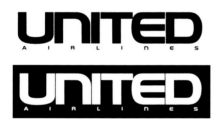

Mid-1980s:
Variations of Saul Bass's design appear. In some cases, the word "airlines" is dropped; in others, letters are squeezed together. Occasionally, the official logotype is scrapped altogether, replaced by the company's name set in Bookman.

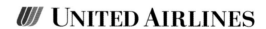

1992:
After surveying customers, United determines it needs a more elegant, understated image with international appeal. The design firm CKS Partners retains the U symbol but replaces Saul Bass's sans serif logotype with a more traditional serif face.

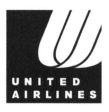

1997:
As part of a new branding campaign, Pentagram Design updates the United logo. It introduces new, cropped versions of the U symbol, creates a bolder typeface for the company's name, and drops the word "airlines" from the logotype.

1998:
To distinguish different classes of service within the airline, Pentagram Design develops a new color scheme. Here, the company's name appears in black, while the name of the services appear in gray.

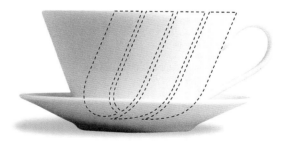

So recognizable has the mark become that the company encourages its designers to incorporate the logo's U shape and 68-degree tilt into everything from navigational buttons on the company website to the shape of the airline's coffee cups.

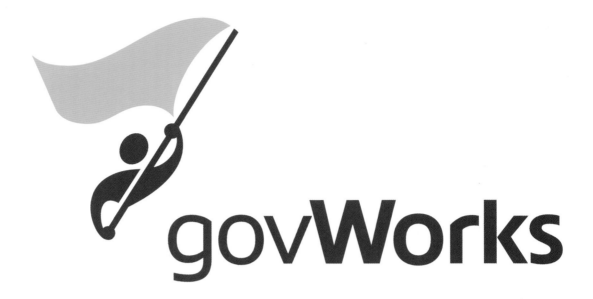

Client

GovWorks is an online portal connecting local governments and constituents.

Designers

Carlos Sanchez, Craig Stout

Firm

St. Aubyn

Process

As an international company that provides a link between local governments and constituents, GovWorks hoped for a logo that was simple enough so that it could be translatable across a wide variety of cultures. And yet, as a start up, GovWorks also hoped for a logo that somehow conveyed the new company's values and goals. With these two parameters in mind, the design team at the Manhattan-based firm St. Aubyn began by researching the client to come up with a visual that succinctly described GovWork's core message. "We found that the message at the heart of the company was one of passion and idealism, a commitment to a new way of doing things," says Maria V. Nunes, a partner at St. Aubyn. To visually convey this message, the team explored different kinds of imagery in hopes of finding a symbol that would be recognizable worldwide as representing passion and idealism. The solution, says Nunes, was the standard bearer. "Whenever a really important human accomplishment has occurred—whether it be the discovery of new lands or walking on the moon—it tends to be marked by the planting of a flag," she explains. "So that's what we sought to translate into a visual identity." Composed in Illustrator, the mark evolved into a pared-down stick figure holding a flag, a design whose simple lines ensure easy reproduction across a range of applications. Next, the company's name was set in a modified Verdana, but the final step, color, presented a bit of a challenge, says Nunes. "There were a number of colors that we didn't want to go near," she explains. "A white flag means surrender. The environmental movement owns a green flag. A red flag, to some people, signifies Communism, while a black flag recalls a brand of mosquito repellent." The team decided to use orange, a color that conveys a sense of vibrancy and energy and is not linked to any one particular country or political movement.

What Works

The logo, a stylized stick figure holding a flag, is meant to symbolize leadership, unity, and positive change.

classic logo

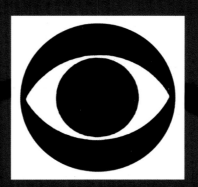

The CBS eye, the pictographic logo par excellence, suggests both the aperture of a camera lens and the eye of the TV viewer. Designed by CBS creative director William Golden and based on the "eye of God" symbols Amish farmers paint on their barns to ward off evil, the logo first appeared on television on November 16, 1951, as a black-and-white symbol overlaid on a photograph of a cloud-filled sky. Since then, the logo has become colored and animated, but its basic shape has not changed in fifty years.

Since first appearing in the early 1900s, the Shell pecten logo has become increasingly stylized, reflecting the trend towards simplicity in graphic design over the past several decades. Today, with its bold shape and distinctive colors, the logo works in any size and in any medium, whether it be a small patch stitched on a serviceman's cap or a mural-sized icon painted on an oil tanker.

the evolution of a logo

Today

Loewy's 1971 design is used worldwide. The logo has become so recognizable that it often appears without the company's name to identify it.

1904:
In the beginning, Shell's logo depicts a realistic rendering of a pecten, or scallop shell. Subtle modeling highlights the shell's ridges.

1915:
The modeling soon disappears making the logo easier to reproduce.

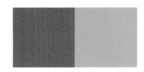

circa 1915:
Color appears when Shell builds its first service stations in California. Red and yellow are bright, which helps Shell stand out, but they are also the colors of Spain, the birthplace of many early Californian settlers. By displaying Spanish colors, Shell hopes to create an emotional bond with customers.

1925:
The word Shell is added to connect the emblem to the company it represents.

1930:
The shell's ridges all but disappear, making the company's name easier to read.

1951:
In the days before fax machines and the internet, many logos included subtle details such as modeling. Today, this logo would become blurred when faxed.

1963:
Seeds of the present-day logo appear. Single lines efficiently convey the shell's ridges; two triangles describe the shell's base.

1971:
Raymond Loewy, famed for his design of the Coca-Cola bottle, redesigns the logo. He simplifies the shell's scalloped edges into a smooth semi-circle, reduces the shell's ridges from thirteen to seven, and adds a bold, red outline.

1976:
While the company's European divisions adopt Loewy's design, American divisions use a modified version: lines denoting the shell's ridges are thinner; the two outer ridges join at the base.

classic logo

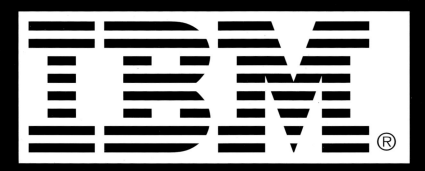

Debuting in 1956 and designed by Paul Rand, the original IBM monogram featured three solid letterforms set in a modified version of City Medium, a geometrically constructed slab-serif typeface created in 1930 by the German designer Georg Trump. In 1962, however, Rand embarked on a redesign, feeling the monogram in solid form exuded an aura of heaviness that didn't reflect the company's progressive aspirations. As a remedy, Rand added stripes to the logo to unify its three letterforms and give it a high-tech feel by evoking the scan lines on video terminals. The mark's simple, flexible style has allowed it to remain virtually unchanged for nearly forty years and to move with ease from print to fax to broadcast to the Web.

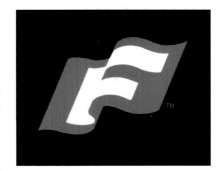

Client

Fisher Companies is a group of milling, broadcasting, and real estate operations.

ART DIRECTORS

Steve Watson, Ray Ueno

DESIGNER

Steve Watson

FIRM

The Leonhardt Group

Process

When Fisher Companies Inc. came to the Seattle-based consultancy The Leonhardt Group, the ninety-year-old company was seeking to unite all of its separate entities—which included flour mills, radio and television stations, and real estate properties—into one company with one corporate identity. In terms of logo design, this meant coming up with a mark that would be flexible in style, to effectively represent all of the company's different entities, and in functionality: the mark needed to work well in a range of sizes and media, from tiny symbols printed on business cards to huge signs painted on building exteriors. To the design team at TLG, the solution was an image of a rippling flag, a symbol that connotes strength, unity, and passion, and whose shape is simple enough to function well in various sizes and media. For the logotype, the team chose Bembo as a base due to its classic, straightforward look and feel. For color, red was selected to project a message of boldness and energy.

What Works

The logo, an image of a rippling, rectangular flag with a reversed-out F at its center, conveys a sense of the power, strength, and unity that is associated with a large corporation with a long history.

Designed to function well in a range of sizes, the Fisher logo has been applied to everything from company flags to business papers.

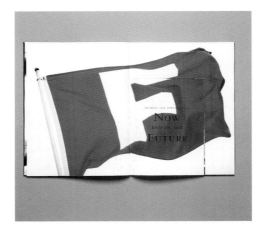

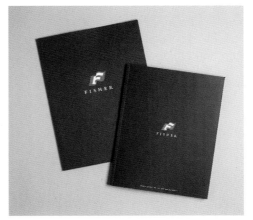

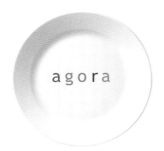

Process

For art director Sarah Dinnick, the biggest challenge of the project was convincing her clients that a sunflower logo would not work. "They had their hearts set on a sunflower, but I'd seen sunflowers used a zillion times before," she says. "In addition, sunflowers have a seasonal aspect to them. They suggest summer, and the restaurant is open all year round." While Dinnick did create a sunflower logo for her clients, she also developed an alternative approach, which, in the end, the clients happily adopted. Dinnick began by photographing a white plate. (Bought at Ikea, the plate's mass-produced perfection made it "a modern icon and a powerful graphic form," says Dinnick.) Using Photoshop and Illustrator, she next experimented with different typefaces for the logotype, ultimately choosing Trebuchet, a sans serif font that feels modern due to its clean, simple letterforms, but also friendly and warm, owing to the jaunty little upsweeps that end many of the strokes. The colors—warm oranges, reds, and mustards—match the colors of the gallery walls that lead to the restaurant, as well as hint at the colors of the clients' beloved sunflower.

What Works

The logo, a pristine, white plate with the restaurant's name spelled out across it in Trebuchet, is based on the idea of an artist's palette: Just as a palette holds paint, so a plate displays food. The analogy heightens the value of Agora's cuisine as well as links the restaurant to its location in a modern art museum.

Client

Agora is a restaurant located in the Art Gallery of Ontario.

Art Director
Sarah Dinnick

Designer
Samantha Dion

Firm
Dinnick & Howells

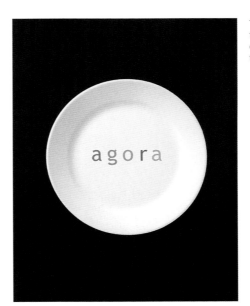

The clean and simple feel of Agora's logo is echoed in the design of the restaurant's menu.

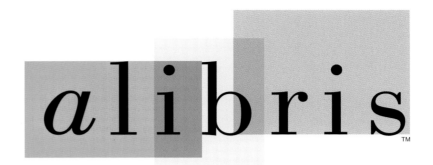

Client

Alibris is an online retailer of hard-to-find books.

ART DIRECTOR

Kit Hinrichs

DESIGNER

Jackie Foshaug

FIRM

Pentagram Design Inc.

Process

Though Alibris is an online company that uses cutting-edge technology to function, the company's actual product, books, is centuries old. This mix of old and new became the starting point for Pentagram's San Francisco office when it set out to design Alibris's logo. "We wanted to create a visual representation that looked modern and fresh but also harkened back to classic book design," says designer Jackie Foshaug. Inspiration came from letterpress books of the 1950s, designs that today feel both modern in that they incorporate simple typography and geometric shapes, as well as old as they were produced in pre-computer days. For the logotype, Foshaug chose Bodoni. "Bodoni is one of those great faces that has roots in history but has a contemporary look because of its square serifs and geometric forms," says Foshaug. Next, she added three overlapping rectangles, elements that echo the color bar forms found in 1950's book design. Unlike the color bars of old, however, a more muted palette of orange, olive, and blue was used to give the mark a more contemporary feel. As a final touch, the first letter of the company's name—libris means book in Latin—was set in italics to aid pronunciation. The italicized a, which resembles the "@" symbol of Internet addresses, also serves as a visual reminder that the company conducts business online.

What Works

The logo, which consists of the company's name set in a modified Bodoni against three translucent, overlapping rectangles, is based on letterpress book design. The rectangles also suggest a stack of books or a series of pages.

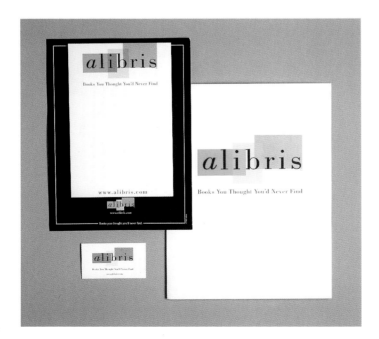

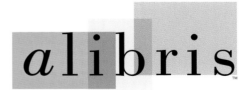

Books You Thought You'd Never Find

A new logo for a nonprofit group begins with a series of literal illustrations and ends with a sophisticated abstraction.

rough drafts/final drafts

An early approach features stylized finger-prints. Though intended to illustrate GLAAD's impact on society, it also suggested FBI Most Wanted posters and Seger shifted his focus elsewhere.

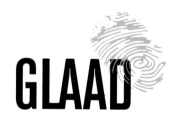

To reflect the client's role as an advocacy organization, Seger created designs featuring pointing hands, but deemed them too strident for a group hoping to build partnerships with media insiders.

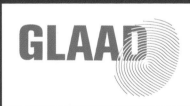

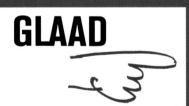

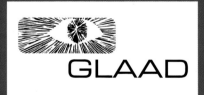

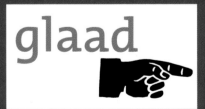

Another approach, an eye peering out of a television set, illustrates GLAAD's role as a media monitor, but Seger felt it wasn't distinctive enough.

Seger altered the logo-type. He chose Thesis, a Dutch typeface reminiscent of old typewriter fonts, to suggest the client's role as a media watchdog group, and replaced the stern looking capitals of earlier designs with friendlier lowercase letters.

Client

GLAAD, which stands for Gay & Lesbian Alliance Against Defamation, is a nonprofit organization that promotes fair and accurate representation of gays and lesbians in the media as a means of combating discrimination.

What Works

As a group that analyzes the media, GLAAD knows the power of bold images to attract attention and therefore wanted a logo that was simple. But as a nonprofit organization that values complexity in discussions, GLAAD also hoped for a logo that encouraged multiple interpretations. Both qualities appear in the group's new logo, designed by Sven Seger, which features two rows of circular shapes that gradually merge together and meet at a single point. Though its form is bold and simple to reflect the organization's seriousness of purpose, its meaning is intentionally complex: Does it illustrate a minority group's integration into mainstream life, or does it represent a series of options—ranging from independence to integration—that members of communities can choose from? "Both," says Seger, who wanted to leave space in the design for the viewer to decide. "Within GLAAD there are some people who want integration into mainstream American life and others who want to maintain separation. That's why we went with this particular direction. It causes discussion and that's what GLAAD is all about."

STRATEGY
Ron Capello

CREATIVE DIRECTOR AND DESIGNER
Sven Seger

FIRM
Enterprise IG

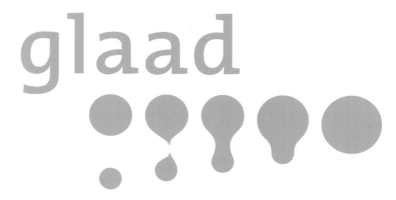

The final Logo
The abstract form represents GLAAD's focus on change.

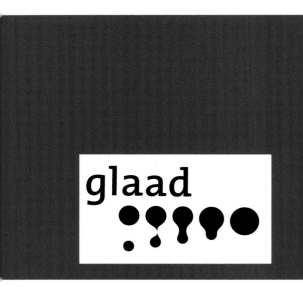

Unsatisfied with literal illustrations, Seger turned to abstraction in hopes of creating a design that evoked GLAAD's focus on change. Experiments with photograms, created by dropping different fluids onto photographic paper in a darkroom, lead to a logo of fluid-like forms.

memory starts with an image

Since GLAAD lacks the budget for four-color printing, Seger limited the color palette to two colors. "Mixed together, yellow and gray allows for a whole range of different, almost earthy, beige tones," says Seger of his choice. This two-color brochure illustrates this point.

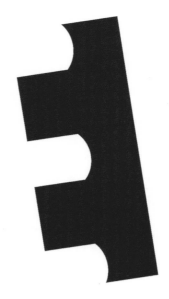

Client

The End is a production company that specializes in television commercials, music videos, and feature films.

Designer

Buddy Morel

Process

The project began with the client requesting a logo that looked fresh and current, yet gave the impression of belonging to a long-established company. To designer Buddy Morel that meant creating a mark whose visual power lay in its simplicity. As a starting point, he asked the client for a roll of 35-millimeter film, then made sketches based on it. "I played with it for about a month, doing everything you can imagine to it," says Morel, who adds, "all of it was junk." So he started over, this time with a pair of scissors rather than a pencil. "I started cutting the piece of film into little pieces," he says. "I was pretty much winging it. I didn't pre-visualize the concept." The pieces he cut were tiny—less than a quarter of an inch long—but when Morel laid them out on a piece of paper, he noticed that one contained a crude E, created by the negative space between two film sprockets. After scanning the film piece into a computer, he used Illustrator to modify the form, making the E more legible, while at the same time making sure the solid form still read as a piece of film. Next, he added a slight tilt to the mark's orientation, to create a spontaneous feel and suggest a snippet of film strewn on a cutting room floor. The result is a logo that serves both as an illustration of the company's services, as well as a monogram that refers to the company's name.

What Works

The logo presents a visual puzzle to the viewer. While the colored form reads as a snippet of film, which refers to the type of service the client provides, the negative space surrounding the form reads as an E, the first letter of the company's name.

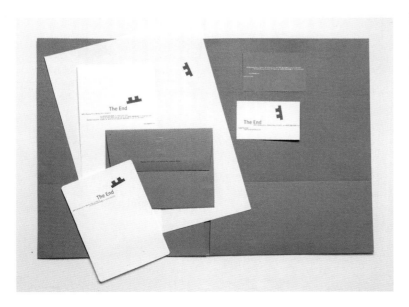

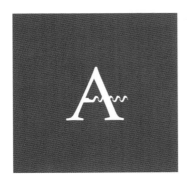

Client

The American Sommelier Association is a nonprofit organization for wine experts.

ART DIRECTOR/DESIGNER

Jon Rohrer

FIRM

Flux Labs

Process

In developing a logo for the American Sommelier Association, designer Jon Rohrer hoped to create a mark that instantly communicated the idea of wine and had a classic, almost old-fashioned feel to it. An idea came almost instantly. Using Illustrator, he experimented with a capital A, the first letter of the client's name, replaced its cross bar with a corkscrew, then selected the typeface Adobe Garamond for its elegant, sophisticated feel. Next, he experimented with logotypes. "I didn't want to just center the client's name under the symbol because that seemed too trite," he says. Instead, he created what amounts to a secondary logo: the client's name set in a configuration reminiscent of a label, with the word Sommelier in the center, and the words American and Association laid out in arcs above and below it. For color, Rohrer chose a burgundy to suggest the color of wine.

What Works

The logo features a capital A set in Adobe Garamond. The cross bar has been replaced with a corkscrew, which reinforces the subject's identity as an organization for wine experts.

Tim Kilcullen
Chairman: Ways and Means

100 Old Gulph Road
Gulph Mills, PA 19428

T 610.526.9300
F 610.520.2045
mctk1@aol.com

rough drafts/final drafts

As a starting point, designer Philip Kelly turned to the client's writings about termite mounds. Though blind, groups of termites are able to build two separate structures that are virtually identical to one another by releasing chemicals called pheromones that serve as a form of communication. The client used this three-dimensional model, which shows the pheromone activity between two termite mounds, as a basis for her design of an African spa. Kelly, in turn, used it as a basis for the client's logo.

Kelly created sketches for a logotype based on a plan view of the three-dimensional diagram of termite pheromone activity.

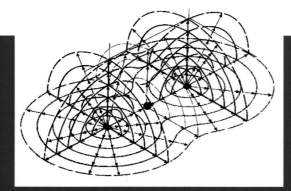

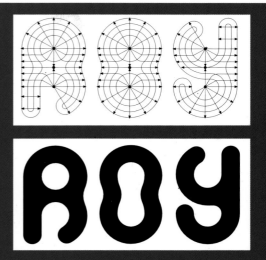

After filling in the letterforms, Kelly deemed the result too fluid for a mark representing an architect.

Client

Lindy Roy is an architect and critic best known for her design of an environmentally friendly spa in Botswana, which was inspired by the structure of termite mounds.

What Works

The logo features the client's last name set in Trade Gothic, which has been modified so that the last letter, a Y, is an upside down version of the first, an R. As a result, the mark becomes a visual demonstration of symmetry, a basic principle in the client's field of architecture.

Designer

Philip Kelly

Firm

pk(des)gn

Next, Kelly experimented with Trade Gothic, a typeface whose strong, sans serif strokes echo architectural forms. He noticed that when the R is turned upside down, it resembles a Y.

The final Logo

Because the client's offices are located in Manhattan's meat packing district, Kelly chose a color—a burnished red—that suggests dried blood, and used French Paper's Butcher Paper stock for the stationery system.

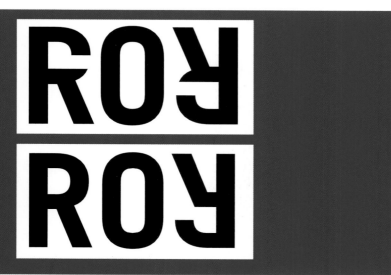

The final National Campaign Against Youth Violence logo began as an afterthought. Five minutes before faxing seven other ideas to art director Joel Templin, designer Felix Sockwell thought of one more: combining a dove with a hand. His last-minute scribble evolved into the final design.

rough drafts/final drafts

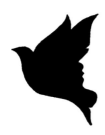

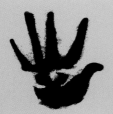

Searching for a concept, designer Felix Sockwell sketched several possible directions, including designs that use doves to symbolize peace, a hand to communicate "stop violence," faces to represent families, and stars and stripes to reflect the campaign's national aspect.

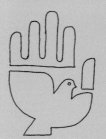

Flipping through an old clip-art book, Sockwell came across a dove created in the 1950s by Eugene Grossman for the Mitsubishi Bank Group. Sockwell sketched a logo design based on it.

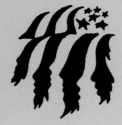

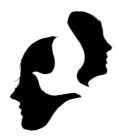

Client

The National Campaign Against Youth Violence (NCAYV) is a White House initiative whose aim is to educate parents about teenage violence.

What Works

The urgent nature of the anti-violence campaign is suggested in the logo through two bold images: a dove and an upraised to hand, reversed-out of two rectangular shapes in red and black. Designed to look as if it were hastily cut out of paper, the logo recalls the visual power of protest posters from the 1950s and 1960s.

AGENCY
Foote Cone & Belding

DESIGNER
Felix Sockwell

ILLUSTRATORS
Felix Sockwell, Erik Johnson

FIRM
Templin Brink Design

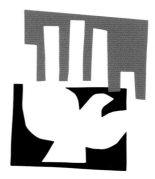

The final Logo

For color, black and red are selected to convey a sense of urgency.

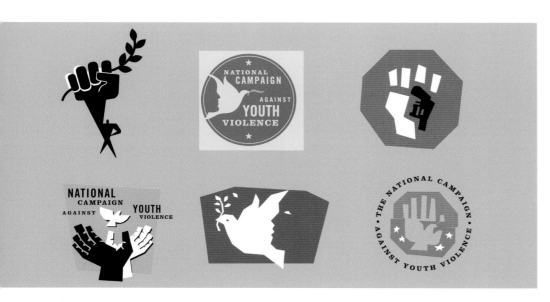

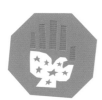

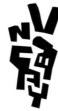

Rough sketches are fleshed out and refined in Illustrator. Sockwell later feels the designs incorporating guns are too negative. And though he likes the design that features a blue circle with silhouettes of a face and dove "for its 1950's, Boy Scout-y feel," he prefers the boldness of the hand-dove approach.

classic logo

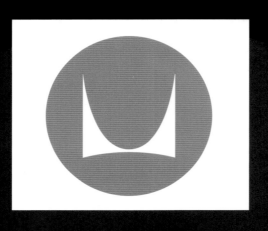

The first Herman Miller logo, a stylized "M" meant to represent the first letter of Miller, appeared in 1946. Since then, a circle has been added to the mark, but otherwise Irving Harper's simple design has remained virtually unchanged for nearly half a century.

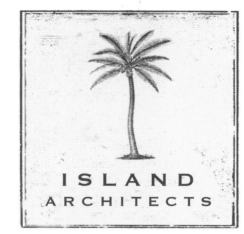

Client

Island Architects is an architectural firm that specializes in high-end residential buildings.

ART DIRECTOR/DESIGNER

David Lecours

ILLUSTRATOR

Mariko Kitano

FIRM

Lecours Design

Process

When Island Architects came to Lecours Design looking for a logo, the architectural firm was hoping for a mark that would reflect the location of its offices—in La Jolla, California, and the U.S. Virgin Islands—as well as appeal to an upscale, sophisticated audience. For designer David Lecours that meant creating something that had "an Old World colonial feel to it." Inspiration came from looking at nineteenth-century etchings depicting the palm trees, sand, and sea of the Virgin Islands. "We did several explorations based on these prints, but we seemed to keep coming back to the palm tree," says Lecours. "As a symbol, a palm tree can refer to an island or to coastal California so it seemed an appropriate image for this particular firm." After a palm tree was created in Illustrator, Lecours added the company's name beneath it, opting for Copperplate as a typeface, as its serif letterforms echo the typography found in Old World prints. Next, he encased the tree and logotype within a square and added texture. "We wanted the final mark to have a bit of a distressed, weathered texture so that it would feel like something from the past," he says. For color, he chose off-white, to suggest a piece of paper slightly yellowed with age, and a muted blue-green to evoke the sea and sky.

What Works

The logo, a square containing a drawing of a palm tree and the company's name set in Copperplate, borrows imagery from nineteenth-century travel prints to create a sense of Old World sophistication.

Client

Netflix is an online service that offers DVD movies delivered free to customers' homes.

ART DIRECTOR

Jill Savini

FIRM

MarchFirst

Process

When Netflix came to the design consultancy MarchFirst, the DVD movie company already had a logo—a yellow and black wordmark featuring the company's name in lowercase letters—but was hoping to replace it with one that better communicated movies in general and the positive emotions associated with movies in particular. "We wanted people to look at the logo and experience feelings of warmth, nostalgia, and excitement. And yet because we are a modern service, we wanted the logo to have a contemporary feel as well," says Leslie Kilgore, Netflix's Vice President of Marketing. To Jill Savini, a MarchFirst creative director, that meant concentrating on classic designs rather than edgy ones and type treatments rather than symbols. "We wanted to avoid imagery like film reels or video screens not only because they are over-used, but because they don't convey any sense of the romance and thrill of watching movies," says Savini. Instead, her team focused on designs that would somehow conjure up the 1940s, a time when a trip to the movies meant grand theaters with red velvet curtains and wide screens. For inspiration, the team turned to vintage movie posters and began developing marks based on their typography. The result was a streamlined type treatment featuring the company's name set in all capitals with drop shadows behind each letter and arranged in an arc. "The sans serif capitals convey a sense of strength and power, and the arc communicates a sense of grandeur," says Savini, who adds that the letterforms, being vertical, hard-edged, and devoid of curves, reinforce this sense of grandeur. For color, red and black were chosen to prompt associations with the red carpets, seats, and curtains found in movie theaters of old.

What Works

The logo, which consists of the company's name set in capital letters and arranged in an arc, prompts several associations with movies, including vintage movie posters and the famous Hollywood sign perched in the hills above Los Angeles.

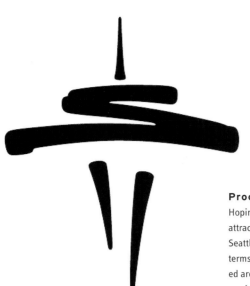

Client

Originally built for the 1962 World's Fair, the Space Needle is a popular tourist attraction located in Seattle, Washington.

ART DIRECTOR

Jack Anderson

DESIGNERS

Jack Anderson, Mary Hermes, Gretchen Cook, Andrew Smith, Julie Lock, Amy Faucette, Belinda Bowling, Elmer De LaCruz, Holly Craven, Ensi Mofasser, Cliff Chung, Alan Florsheim

FIRM

Hornall Anderson Design Works, Inc.

Process

Hoping to increase tourist attendance to the Space Needle while at the same time attract return visits from locals, the owners of the Space Needle commissioned Seattle-based Hornall Anderson Design Works to create a new brand for the site. In terms of a logo—just one element in a far-reaching branding campaign that included architectural signage, merchandising graphics, and business papers—this meant coming up with a design that somehow conveyed the Space Needle's historical importance while at the same time emphasizing its modern-day appeal, says HADW co-founder Jack Anderson. "The original logo the company had before coming to us was a very literal, almost photographic depiction of the Space Needle in full view. It was clear that the logo stood for the Space Needle, but it didn't have any spirit or vitality," says Anderson. To remedy this, the HADW team explored a range of different possibilities, from streamlined wordmarks to abstract symbols. One early design was simply a circle, intended to suggest the 360-degree view the Space Needle provides; while another depicted rectangular planes meant to suggest a horizon. However, these designs were soon abandoned in favor of an illustration. "For merchandising reasons, we determined that the logo needed to depict the Space Needle's architecture," Anderson explains. "But we didn't want the depiction to be literal. We wanted to it to have a gestural, energetic quality to it." To this end, the team experimented with designs that featured only the top of the Space Needle and omitted the monument's base and struts. "The top of the Space Needle is where the real personality lies," says Anderson. "On a foggy day, that's what you see: the Needle's spire and the flying saucer-like shape of its observation deck." To render the mark, the team chose to use four gestural, almost calligraphic strokes, to give the mark an energetic feel, says Anderson. The result, he adds, is a mark "whose imagery references the past but whose style celebrates the future."

What Works

Composed of brush-like strokes, the logo features a stylized illustration of the Space Needle's silhouette as well as the letter S, the first letter of the attraction's name.

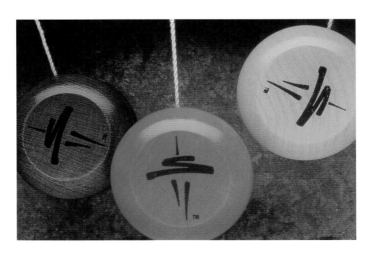

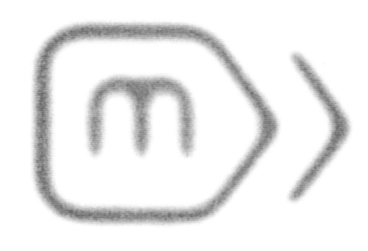

Client

Media & Beyond is a retailer specializing in high-end technological products and services.

ART DIRECTOR
Bob Beck

CREATIVE DIRECTORS
Daniel Fortin, George Fok, Marc Serre

FIRM
Epoxy

Process

To distinguish itself from its rivals in the crowded category of technology retailers, Media & Beyond decided to forgo hard-sell marketing tactics and focus on high-end quality instead. To reflect this business decision, designers at the Montreal-based firm Epoxy hoped to create a logo "that didn't rely on bells and whistles, but rather was minimal and sophisticated," says designer Marc Serre. The team began with customized type treatments of the company's name, which evolved into a pared-down monogram. To connect the mark to the client's business, the designers circumscribed the M within a square with rounded corners so that it would resemble a computer key, then added an arrow, also based on a computer key. The result was an anagram of the company's name. Next, the mark was blurred to temper the potentially cold, streamlined forms with a softer, more low-tech feel. The team chose green for the logo's color, both for its connection to old-fashioned computer screens and as a way to stand out among the ubiquitous blues and reds of other technology firms.

What Works

The logo is an anagram of the client's name. The M stands for "Media"; the arrow, for "Beyond." And while the logo's streamlined forms reflect the client's products and services—cutting edge technology—the blurred treatment, which recalls the low-tech look of early computers, lends a non-threatening feel to the client's identity.

MEDIA & BEYOND 49 mercer street new york new york 10013 usa t 212 965 2600 f 212 965 2626 e info@media-and-beyond.com

MEDIA & BEYOND 49 mercer street new york new york 10013 usa t 212 625 1863 f 212 965 6206 e info@media-and-beyond.com

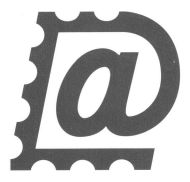

Client

AmazingMail.com allows customers to create customized postcards on the Web. The company will then print, stamp, and send the results through the mail.

Art Director

Russ Haan

Firm

After Hours Creative

Process

For designer Russ Haan, the biggest challenge in the AmazingMail.com project was finding a way to visually convey what the company does. "If a client has a hundred-million-dollar-a-year advertising budget, it doesn't matter whether its logo communicates anything because meaning can be built through advertising," he says. "But for businesses that don't have that kind of money, I believe a logo should communicate something right away." In the case of AmazingMail.com, Haan decided that "something" should be the online nature of the business as well as a the mail-related service that the company provides. As for the style, Haan strove for a bold simplicity so that the design would work well across a range of computer platforms and browsers. His team began by exploring postal imagery, creating sketches of mailboxes, packages, and postal trucks. "But none of these conveyed the digital side of the client's business, so we moved on," says Haan. Next, he added digital components to the postal imagery, creating one design, for example, that featured a mailbox turning into a series of pixels. Out of these experiments arose the idea of combining a postage stamp with an A, the first letter of the client's name. When Haan set the A in lowercase, he noticed it suggested the @ symbol, an instantly recognizable reference to the Internet. Scanning these sketches into Illustrator, Haan refined the design, adding a jaunty tilt to the mark to give it a friendly feel. For color, he chose blue and red not only for their bold appearance, but for their connection to the palette used by the United States Postal Service.

What Works

The logo is composed of two recognizable icons: an @ symbol and a postage stamp. While the @ suggests a company that conducts business on the Web, the mark's scalloped, stamp-like outline communicates "mail."

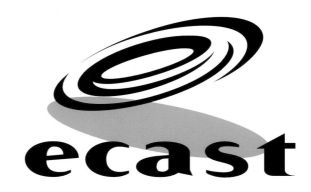

Client

Ecast is a San Francisco-based technology company specializing in jukebox systems that allow patrons to download music and games directly from the Internet.

CREATIVE DIRECTOR
Julie Tsuchiya

ART DIRECTOR
Mark Sloneke

DESIGNER
Andrew Harding

FIRM
Extraprise/Tsuchiya Sloneker Communications

Process

In developing what would become the Ecast logo, designers at the San Francisco-based Extraprise/Tsuchiya Sloneker Communications hoped to create a mark that felt both corporate, to position the client as an established, national company, and fun and approachable, to appeal to potential customers not necessarily familiar with cutting-edge technology. As a starting point, the design team looked at vintage jukeboxes from the 1940s and 1950s as well as the client's modern-day model, a system whose sleek, curved lines reminded creative director Julie Tsuchiya of "a spaceship version of a jukebox." The team experimented with different ways to visually represent both the old and new jukeboxes in a single mark, eventually coming up with the idea of a single record: as a symbol, an old-fashioned LP evokes the non-intimidating feel of a low-tech world, explains Tsuchiya, while as a form, a record's elliptical shape echoes that of the client's high-tech product. The idea was then refined in Illustrator, where curved lines were added to the record to evoke a spinning motion, and a second oval shape was added underneath the first to represent the shadow cast when a record drops onto a turntable. The record was then given a rakish tilt to visually convey a sense of playfulness, and green was chosen for color to help the mark stand out from the blue's found in other technology companies' logos.

What Works

The logo, composed of two tilted ellipses, suggests a spinning record on a jukebox as well as a lowercase e, the first letter of the company's name.

Emily Travis Product Manager
emily@ecastinc.com

Direct 415.659.3101

Ecast. Inc.
650 Townsend Street №375
San Francisco CA 94103
Main 415.659.3260
Fax 415.659.3201
www.ecastinc.com

classic logo

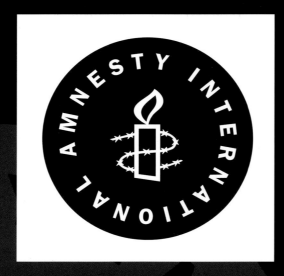

Originally designed by Diana Redhouse and redesigned in 2000 by Simon Endres of Kirshenbaum and Bond, The Amnesty International logo uses an economy of means to convey complex notions: Barbed wire communicates oppression, while a burning candle evokes hope.

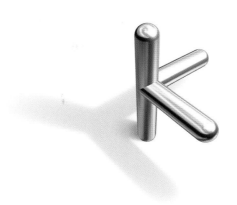

Client

KnowledgeNet is a Scottsdale, Arizona-based IT training company that offers online courses with live instructors and interactive learning.

DESIGNER
Tom Turley

3D RENDERER
Marcus Hoffman

FIRM
t-squared design

Process

When KnowledgeNet came to designer Tom Turley of t-squared design, the IT training company already had a logo—the company's name spelled out in lowercase letters with a globe in place of the o—but wanted to replace it with something that implied global technology in a more distinctive way. "We have a very sophisticated, very tech-savvy customer, so we wanted to be perceived as edgy and hip, but we also wanted to be taken seriously," says Maureen O'Leary, KnowledgeNet's marketing director. "We wanted a logo that instilled confidence, something that conveyed strength but not arrogance." To Turley, this meant avoiding over-used dotcom clichés such as swooshes, orbits, or globes. Instead, he experimented with designs ranging from the purely abstract to the literal, such as ones depicting a big dog to convey leadership to others featuring gurus to reflect the guidance the client offers its students. But Turley was unsatisfied with the results: some didn't communicate global technology, he explains, while others felt too flippant for a serious company. So he shifted courses, this time focusing on designs based on Ks, the first letter of the client's name. As he sketched dozens of Ks, experimenting with lowercase, upper case, solids, and outlines, he noticed that a signpost-like form had emerged, an image that seemed appropriate for a company providing training and direction. To make the signpost more legible, while at the same time making sure the mark remained readable as a K, Turley's team explored three-dimensional renderings. The result was a K with rounded ends, which hint at the broadband ("big pipe") technologies used by the client, and a smooth, metallic texture that reflects the client's place in the high-tech industry. Says Turley of the final mark: "Sure, it is abstract and is open to several interpretations, but I like to think about it as having 'positive ambiguity,' which creates interest and makes it memorable."

What Works

The logo, a three-dimensional lowercase k with a metallic texture, prompts several associations with knowledge, including a signpost pointing the way or a rising structure offering a sturdy foundation on which to build.

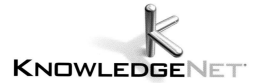

In developing a logo for a company that provides connectivity services, designers explored three different approaches: pictograms, abstract marks, and monograms.

rough drafts/final drafts

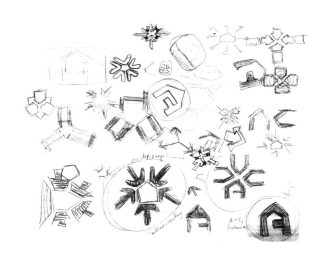

Searching for a concept, the design team begins with pencil sketches exploring images of houses to convey "home services," arrows to suggest "connectivity," and the initials A and C to represent the client's name.

Initial concepts are fleshed out in Illustrator. Designs based on houses are eventually abandoned in favor of a more dynamic design.

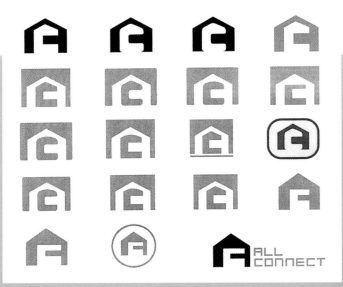

A second approach, abstract designs featuring arrows, is ultimately abandoned in favor of a design with a stronger link to the company's name.

Client

AllConnect is an online company that provides a one-stop resource for comparing, selecting, and ordering home connectivity services such as Internet, cable, and cellular phone access.

What Works

Based on the idea of "connectivity," the logo features a rectangular outline whose form suggests an electrical outlet and which contains a lowercase c plugging into a lowercase a.

CREATIVE DIRECTOR
Michael Taylor

DESIGNERS
Ali Harper, Rebecca Klein

FIRM
Merge

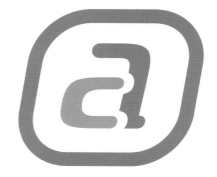

The final logo
Its slight tilt suggests movement. The color blue conveys stability and calm.

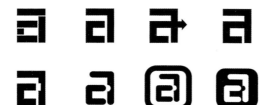

A third approach, based on the company's initials a and c, is deemed the most successful. The design team experiments with different type weights and configurations to visually communicate "connectivity," while making sure the letters remain recognizable.

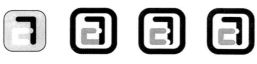

classic logo

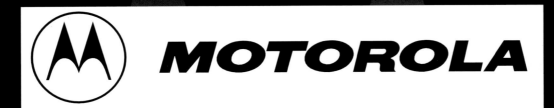

Referred to as the "Emsignia" by the company and "the batwing" by its fans in the design community, Motorola's stylized M monogram was first introduced in 1955. Designed by the late Morton Goldsholl, the original symbol was not surrounded by a circle, but instead appeared with a variety of different design elements such as squares and ellipses. In 1965, however, the M monogram and the circle became inseparable. Since then, other than refinements to its configuration and prescribed usage, the Emsignia has remained virtually unchanged for nearly fifty years.

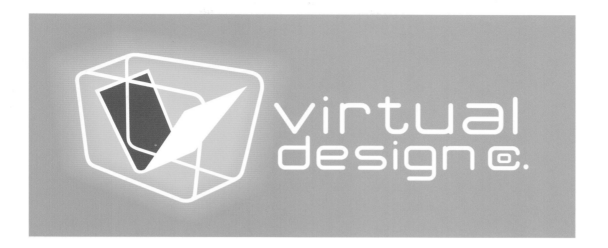

Client

Virtual Design Company is a California-based computer design firm.

ART DIRECTOR
David Lecours

DESIGNER
Van Duong

FIRM
Lecours Design

Process

To reflect the three-dimensional, interactive structures that the client creates, designer David Lecours hoped to devise a logo that suggested both depth and movement. "From the beginning we were thinking about how the logo would work both as a static image and as a moving one," says Lecours. "We wanted a viewer to be able to enter the logo and, in a sense, interact with it in the same way that viewers can enter virtual spaces and interact with them." Early explorations, which were two-dimensional, centered around the letter V made up of overlapping, translucent planes. Hoping to create more depth, Lecours's team shifted to three-dimensions, incorporating a translucent V into a rectangular outline. "The idea was to visually communicate 3-D space," says Lecours of the final mark. "The fact that the V inside the square is translucent is meant to communicate the idea of a screen through which a viewer can visualize an actual space in the real world." For color, he chose a vibrant orange. "People seem to have a strong reaction to orange," says Lecours. "They either love it or hate it; either way it gets an instant emotional reaction."

What Works

The logo, a letter V encased within a three-dimensional rectangular outline, is based on the client's product: virtual spaces created on the computer.

Linda Brady

www.sageo.com

Sageo LLC, a Hewitt eBusiness
100 Half Day Road
Lincolnshire, IL 60069

tel 847 295 5000
fax 847 442 5350
llbrady@sageo.com

www.sageo.com   Sageo LLC, a Hewitt eBusiness   tel 847 295 5000
                 100 Half Day Road   fax 847 442 5350
                 Lincolnshire, IL 60069

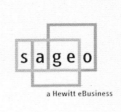

a Hewitt eBusiness

www.sageo.com   Sageo LLC, a Hewitt eBusiness
                 100 Half Day Road
                 Lincolnshire, IL 60069

www.sageo.com

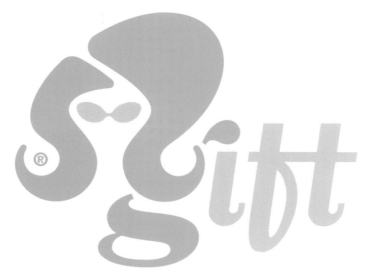

Client

Gift is a line of shirts sold by Molly Enterprises, a company specializing in clothing for teenage girls.

Art Directors
Mike Calkins, David Bates

Designer
Mike Calkins

Firm
BC Design

Process

Because fashion styles change quickly in the teen market, the Gift logo was meant to be a temporary one: used for a season then replaced with another. Thus, the Gift mark did not have to be timeless, but it did have to be stylish, both to reflect the flashy feel of the Gift clothing line and to appeal to the fickle teen market. For inspiration, designers Mike Calkins and David Bates turned to That Girl, a 1970's TV sitcom that starred actress Marlo Thomas as a spunky woman with a penchant for miniskirts and go-go boots. Using the sitcom's stylized logo as a jumping-off point, Calkins created an illustration of a woman in Freehand, paring down the design to just two elements: hair and sunglasses. "I like to think of her as Marlo Thomas's younger, naughtier sister," says Calkins of the result. He chose Matrix Script as a typeface, because, he says, "it has a feminine quality without being fussy," then manipulated the illustration so its outline would form the bowl of a lowercase g. To further tighten the link between type and illustration, he created a teardrop shape to serve as both the ear of the g and the dot of the i. For color, he chose a garish orange and blue to pump up the wordmark's playfully flamboyant feel.

What Works

The logo, which combines a script font with an illustration of a woman sporting a 1970's hairdo and sassy, cat's-eye sunglasses, uses retro imagery to simultaneously evoke glamour and poke fun at it.

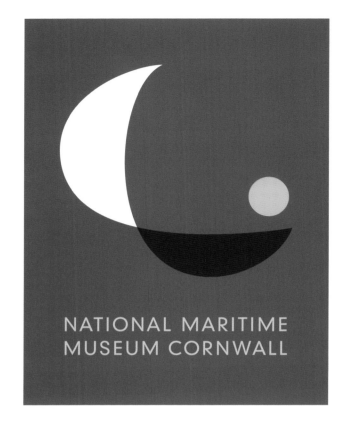

NATIONAL MARITIME MUSEUM CORNWALL

Client
The National Maritime Museum Cornwall
is a British museum devoted to nautical history.

DESIGN DIRECTOR
Mary Lewis

DESIGNER/TYPOGRAPHER
Paul Cilia La Corte

FIRM
Lewis Moberly

Process

Hoping to attract national and international visitors alike, the National Maritime Museum Cornwall wanted a mark that had immediate visual appeal to a wide range of cultures. Paul Cilia La Corte, who was responsible for the design, knew the mark had to refer to the museum's collection of boats, but hoped it would also convey a sense of the museum's location in Cornwall, an area of dramatic cliffs and sweeping views of the sea. One approach involved combining nautical elements into a sea captain's face; another featured a seagull made from a boat's reflection. Neither, however, produced what Cilia La Corte was looking for: a sense of the museum's friendliness combined with the poetry of the sea. Shifting courses, he sought out images of small boats from the museum's collection as well as information about Cornwall's history. "Cornwall has quite a long tradition, not only in boats, but in art as well," says Cilia La Corte, referring to the British art movement that grew out of the artist's colony of St. Ives, Cornwall, in the 1940s. In particular, he was drawn to the work of painter Ben Nicholson, whose spare, geometric abstractions evoke the wide-open spaces of the sea. Using forms similar to those found in Nicholson's work, Cilia La Corte created a design that could be read both as a sailor in a boat and as a scene depicting a cliff, the sea and the sun. The result, Cilia La Corte hopes, gives "a sense of pleasure of being by the sea and messing about in boats. It's intended to be inviting and involving."

What Works

The logo, composed of two curved shapes and a circle, encourages multiple readings. On the one hand, the curved forms suggest a sailboat; the orange circle, a sailor. On the other, the curved forms evoke the silhouette of cliffs and sea; the circle, a setting sun. Both interpretations capture the spirit of sailing celebrated by the museum.

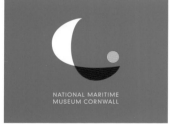

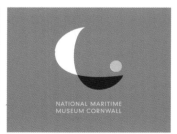

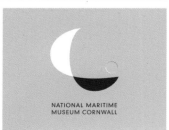

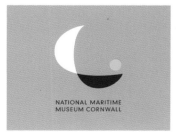

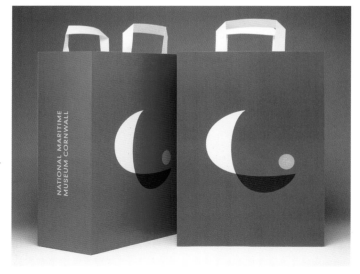

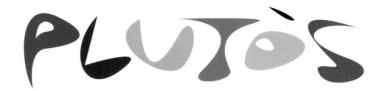

FRESH FOOD FOR A HUNGRY UNIVERSE

Client

Pluto's is a San Francisco-based restaurant that serves healthy fast food.

Designer
Mitchell Mauk

Firm
Mauk Design

Process

The only specific request the client gave designer Mitchell Mauk was to create something "fun," to which Mauk added "but not trendy" so that the logo would not become outdated quickly. With these parameters, Mauk decided on an approach that would mix and match past design styles in order to create a fresh-looking hybrid. Drawn to the biomorphic forms popular in the late 1950s, both for their playful look—"some of the shapes back then got really, really wild," he says—and for their association with food establishments, he used Illustrator to create asymmetrical letterforms, drawn as a single line with a fill. Next, he turned to the 1970s for a palette that would lend a more contemporary feel to the 50s shapes, ultimately choosing a vibrant mix of avocados, oranges, purples, and mustards. Of the result, Mauk says, "We're really conscious of not participating in fads. By coming up with a design that incorporates elements of 50s and 70s design—periods that have already gone out of date at least twice before—I think we've created a design that will endure."

What Works

Just as Pluto's combines two types of food—fast and healthy—to create a hybrid cuisine, so the logo blends elements from two different eras, the 1950s and the 1970s, to convey a contemporary message. While the 1950s-inspired letterforms evoke the friendly feel of roadside diners, the brash palette, culled from 1970s design, adds a playful flash. The resulting logo conveys a sense of friendliness tempered with a dash of irony.

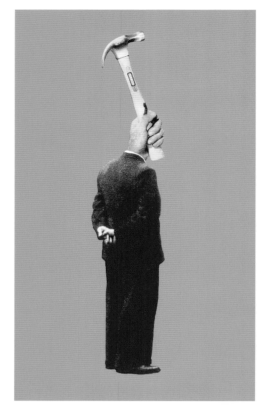

Process

Designer and collage artist John Borruso hoped to create a logo that would reflect the creative energy of the client's services, yet would soften the name, which could be mistaken as aggressive rather than irreverent. He began by creating collages based on old-fashioned television sets. One consisted of a TV set with "SmashTV" splashed across its screen; another depicted a TV surrounded by an eye-popping starburst pattern reminiscent of the hard-sell ads of electronic stores. Neither solution satisfied Borruso, who found them not distinctive enough. So he shifted his focus away from the word "TV" to the word "smash," and began experimenting with ways to visually communicate the act of creative rebellion. In his collection of old tool manuals and vintage magazines, Borruso found a photo of a hand holding a hammer, which evoked the word "smash," and another of a man clad in suit, which suggested a business executive. Using Photoshop and Illustrator to combine them, Borruso found the result to be a bold yet playful illustration of rebellion. "The potential aggression of the upraised hammer is tempered by the figure," says Borruso. "He is prim. His hands are folded behind his back. So the result is humorous rather than aggressive."

What Works

Nicknamed "Hammerhead," the logo depicts a prim, suit-clad man, whose head is a raised hammer. The mark uses wry humor to convey a message of creative rebellion.

Client
SmashTV is a company that creates Web cast programming for children.

DESIGNER AND ILLUSTRATOR
John Borruso

FIRM
John Borruso Design & Collage

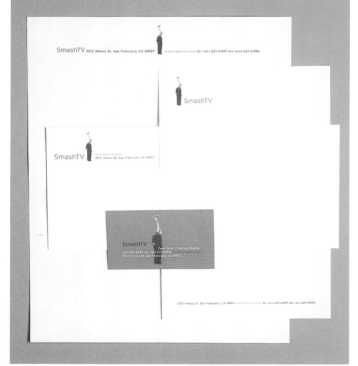

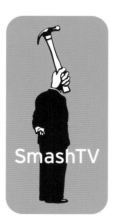

For black-and-white applications, an outlined version is used.

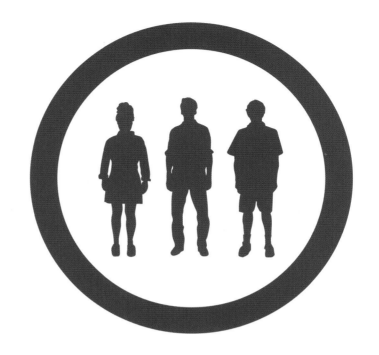

Client

Action Figure is an Austin-based design firm specializing in print and motion graphics.

Designer

Matt Hovis

Firm

Action Figure

Process

Like many design firms, Action Figure had created logos for numerous clients, but had put off designing one for its own business. "We couldn't figure out how we wanted to market ourselves," says Kevin Whitely, a principal of the firm. "We tried different things, got them printed, then threw them away." After months of indecision, he and co-partner Matt Hovis decided "to go dorky," as Whitely puts it. "We thought, 'Look, we're just a couple of dudes. That's all we are. Let's go for something that says that.'" So he, Hovis, and the newly hired Christa Mayre went outside and snapped some Polaroids of each other against a wall. "With Matt and I, we just fuddy-duddied out into the alley and took the pictures," says Whitely, "but with Christa, we got a little artsy. We had her make an extravagant bun." The Polaroids were then scanned into a computer, turned into silhouettes in Photoshop, and converted to vectors in Illustrator. A thick, outlined circle was added to contain the three figures, and a black-and-white palette was chosen to give the mark a 1960's feel, similar to that of the TV show "Mod Squad."

What Works

The logo features a circle containing silhouettes of two men and a woman standing with feet firmly planted on the ground and arms dangling at their sides. A humorous take on the name "Action Figure"—there's not much action, after all, in these figures—the logo reflects the playful approach the firm brings to its work.

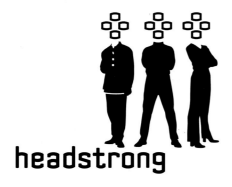

headstrong

Client

Headstrong is an international business consultancy specializing in technology solutions ranging from IT systems to Internet and e-commerce sites.

ART DIRECTORS/DESIGNERS

Steve Watson, Lesley Feldman

FIRM

The Leonhardt Group

For the company's website, the logo's three figures are used as navigational tools.

Process

When Jason Martin + Company approached the Seattle-based firm The Leonhardt Group, the business consultancy was hoping for a new name and visual identity that would better reflect its expertise in new technologies. "In the 1980s, the company was perceived as a bunch of hotshot systems, engineering, and technology guys, but over the years that perception had changed," explains TLG design director Steve Watson. "The company was now viewed as sort of old school and not very exciting." To remedy this, the TLG team began by working with the company to re-position it as a group of consultants with strong opinions, rather than one that simply told clients what they wanted to hear. Next, the team explored names that would convey this new positioning, eventually coming up with "Headstrong," a name that connotes strong brains, intelligence, and a meeting of minds. However, the name did come with risks, says Watson. "Headstrong can also connote bull-headedness and inflexibility, and obviously those are not messages the company wanted to communicate," he says. So when his team set out to design a logo, an important consideration was finding a way to temper the name's negative connotations and emphasize its boldness instead. After creating about 150 sketches of potential directions—from type treatments to abstract symbols to dozens of illustrations of heads—a concept emerged: a design that would combine the company's engineering side with its human side. To visually represent technology, Watson's team experimented with monitor shapes; to convey humans, various renderings of figures were explored. One promising design featured a stylized man whose head was a monitor, says Watson, but it was abandoned "because it looked too much like the Restroom guy." Instead, the team shifted to more realistic renderings, eventually deciding to photograph a variety of people—both professional models and TLG employees—in poses ranging from thoughtful to defiant. After culling through the results, the team selected three, modified them in Photoshop, and replaced their heads with four monitor-shaped forms. Next, a logotype was added which was based on Clicker, a face whose letterforms echo the monitor shapes of the symbol. As a final step, Watson's team experimented with color, but ultimately decided to stick with black and white "to give the figures a kind of chic, Armani-esque type feel," says Watson.

What Works

The logo, which consists of an all lowercase logotype and three human figures with monitor-like shapes in place of heads, suggests both the services the company offers and the way those services are provided: The monitor-heads and mechanical-looking logotype refer to the company's technological expertise, while the figures—two men and a woman—reflect the company's focus on individual ideas and opinions.

classic logo

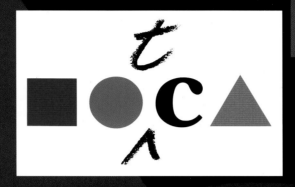

The flexibility of geometric shapes is exemplified by the different yet stylistically consistent versions of the logo for The Museum of Contemporary Art (MOCA). Designed in 1984 by Ivan Chermayeff, the original logo features a blue square, a green circle, a red triangle, and a C set in Baskerville to spell the museum's monogram MOCA. When the museum later closed for construction and opened a temporary branch, Chermayeff created a second version of the logo, adding a hand-drawn carat and the letter t for "temporary." Later, when the temporary branch became a permanent facility and changed its named to the "The Geffen Contemporary," Chermayeff designed a third version, this time reorienting the square, circle and square vertically and adding an abstract purple G, created by cutting the upper-right-hand quarter out of a circle.

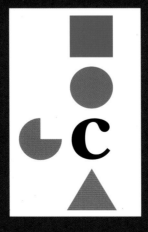

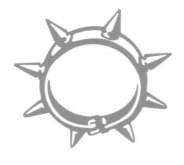

SUNDOG

Client

Sundog Interactive is an intranet and interactive software development company based in Fargo, North Dakota.

CREATIVE DIRECTOR
Dana Lytle

DESIGNER
Jamie Karlin

ILLUSTRATOR
Lin Wilson

FIRM
Planet Design Company

Process

Fearing it was getting pigeonholed as a company that catered solely to conservative corporate clients, Sundog Interactive hoped to adopt a new identity that would suggest the innovative work it was capable of. To the team at Planet Design, that meant coming up with a design that was simple in form, so that it would work well across a range of Web browsers and screen resolutions, but one that also had a playful feel so that it would convey Sundog's forward-thinking attitude. Using the client's name as a jumping off point, the team experimented with different designs depicting dogs and suns, then hit upon the idea of combining the two into one symbol: a dog collar whose radiating spikes suggested a sun. The design was then streamlined in Illustrator where all but the necessary highlights were eliminated so that the symbol would be graphically bold yet remain recognizable as a dog collar. For color, a golden hue was chosen to suggest both a metallic dog collar and a warm sun. In letterhead, the mark appears against a series of blue horizontal lines that can be read either as a sky or as a flickering computer screen.

What Works

The company takes its name from "sun dog," a term used to describe the luminous spots that appear in the sky in sub-zero weather. The logo, however, highlights the term's better-known connotations: a dog collar refers to America's favorite pet, the collar's spikes suggest a radiating sun.

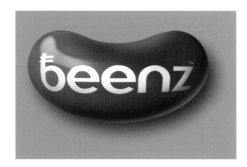

Client

Beenz.com Inc. is a company that offers online merchants a universal, global currency that rewards purchases made on the Web. Headquartered in Manhattan, the company has branches in North America, Europe, and Asia.

Art Director

Nicolas De Santis

Firm

Twelve Stars Communications

Process

In developing what would become the Beenz logo, designers at the London-based firm Twelve Stars Communications worked within several parameters. The mark needed to communicate the idea of money to reflect the client's product. It needed to have a fun, friendly feel to appeal to a young audience. And it had to be understandable to viewers across the globe. As a starting point, the design team explored designs based on a single B, the first letter of the company's name, and eventually came up with a lowercase b with two horizontal strokes across its ascender. As a symbol representing a new form of currency, the mark was deemed successful and was later used as an element in the company's identity system. But as a company logo, the team felt the mark wasn't distinctive enough. "There are too many Bs out there," explains designer Nicolas De Santis, who led the project. "We wanted something that was bolder and friendlier." So the team shifted its attention to the company's name, using Photoshop to create a three-dimensional illustration of a bean. After experimenting with various shapes of beans, the team ultimately chose a kidney-shaped one, a form, explains De Santis, that suggests a smile. The team then added the company's name to the bean, using a custom typeface whose bold, friendly feel is originally based on Frutiger. Next, the team explored color. "Beenz is global so we wanted to find a color scheme that was striking, worked well around the world and would stand out when viewed on a computer screen," says De Santis. The solution was a vibrant red and white, a combination, says De Santis, whose commercial success is proven by none other than Coca-Cola.

What Works

The logo, a three-dimensional representation of a bean with the company's name spelled out across it in a sans serif face, evokes several associations with money. The bright red bean recalls the play money of children's games, while the lowercase b, which features two horizontal strokes across its ascender, calls to mind monetary symbols such as the dollar or yen sign.

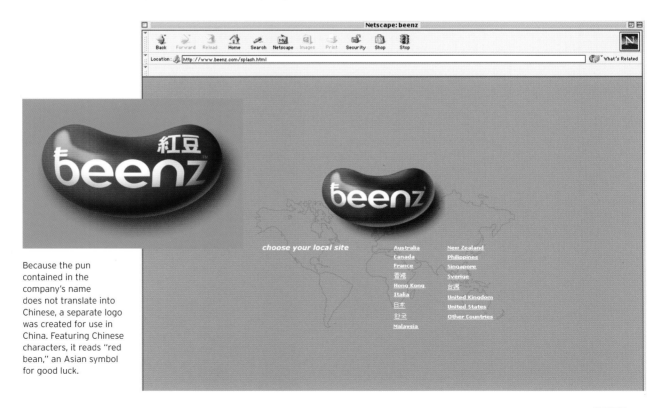

Because the pun contained in the company's name does not translate into Chinese, a separate logo was created for use in China. Featuring Chinese characters, it reads "red bean," an Asian symbol for good luck.

टवfह डफांटह

Client
Cafe Spice is an Indian restaurant located in Manhattan.

Designers
Douglas Riccardi, Kate Johnson

Firm
Memo Productions

Process

In developing what would become the Cafe Spice logo, designer Douglas Riccardi hoped to create a mark that combined an Indian sensibility with an American one. "We felt the mark needed to have an ethnic feel to it in order to visually convey the type of food the restaurant serves, but we also wanted it to feel young and hip to appeal to the college-aged population that lives nearby," says Riccardi. He discovered a solution while thumbing through an Indian penmanship book that he had found on a visit to New York City's Little India. "I started drawing some of the Indian characters and noticed similarities between them and English letters," says Riccardi. "For example, there's an Indian character that looks like an English C, and an accent mark that looks like the dot in the letter I. So I decided to mix the two styles of writing together." Working with a typographer, Riccardi constructed a logotype whose letterforms incorporate both the teardrop shapes found in traditional Indian calligraphy as well as the thick, bold strokes characteristic of modern typefaces. The result, says Riccardi, is a mark "that alludes to Indian culture in a playful, modern way."

What Works

Mixing English script with Indian calligraphy, the logo consists of the client's name spelled out in letterforms that hang from a horizontal bar above them. With its hybrid look, the mark echoes the style of the restaurant it represents: a place where Indian food is served in an American-style setting.

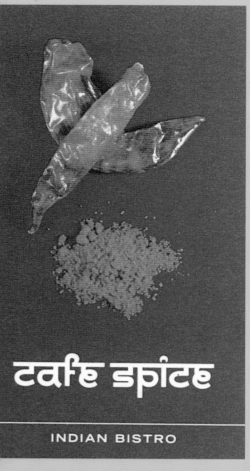

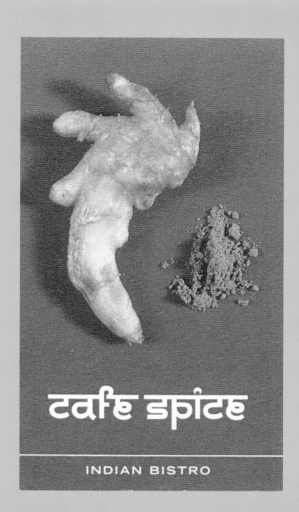

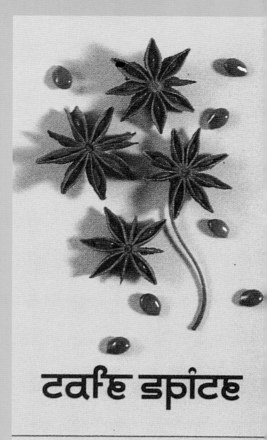

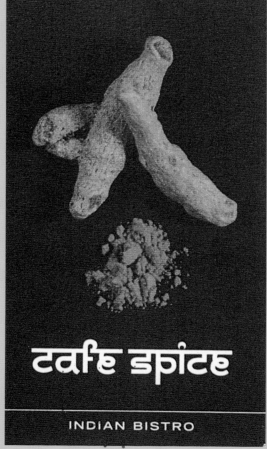

In color applications, the logo appears reversed-out from a palette inspired by Indian spices such as cinnamon and turmeric.

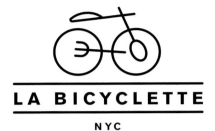

LA BICYCLETTE

NYC

Client

La Bicyclette is a French cafe
and bakery located in Manhattan.

DESIGNER

Felix Sockwell

FIRM

Felix Sockwell Creative

Process

In developing a logo for a new French cafe, designer Felix Sockwell began with a
series of pencil sketches of different types of bicycles in a variety of drawing styles.
Of these, he deemed the designs composed out of the bare minimum of lines the
most successful, feeling they best reflected the simple charm of the neighborhood
cafe. As he further reworked the design, a concept emerged: by replacing parts of the
bicycle's outline with a knife, fork, and a spoon, the mark instantly conveyed the fact
that La Bicylclette was a food establishment. He then refined the drawing in
Illustrator and added the client's name set in Akzidenz Grotesk Bold in a horizontal
line beneath the symbol to suggest a street. And though he experimented with
color—blue and red to suggest the French flag, and red and yellow to convey a
sense of warmth—he ultimately opted for the simplicity of black and white.

What Works

While the mark's imagery, a bicycle composed of two plates and a knife, fork, and
spoon, conveys the fact that La Bicyclette is a food establishment, the logo's simple,
playful style projects a company identity of friendliness and warmth.

Client

PocketCard is an Illinois-based company that offers prepaid expense cards via the Web.

CREATIVE DIRECTOR
Carlos Segura

DESIGNER
Tnop Wangsillapakun

FIRM
Segura Inc.

Process

Since the client conducts its business on the Web, any logo it adopted would need to translate well on a range of different computers and browsers. To designer Carlos Segura, this meant avoiding such details as thin lines, delicate serifs, and subtle color combinations as they might become distorted or disappear altogether when viewed on the Web. "With Web efforts, the design needs to be very clean and stripped down," he says. So he and his team explored different designs based on illustrations of a credit card—a simple rectangular form that works well on the Web—and on monograms featuring the letter P. These two approaches eventually merged into one, resulting in a letter P formed from a graphical representation of a folded credit card. The mark's bold central stripe reads both as a credit card's scan line and as the letter P's counter. As a typeface, the team chose the straightforward Helvetica Bold and selected green as the color to suggest money.

What Works

The logo, a letter P created out of a folded credit card, visually conveys two messages about the client. The mark's imagery illustrates the company's product—credit cards—while its simple, bold style projects a company image of strength and dependability.

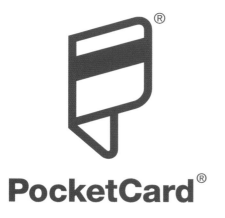

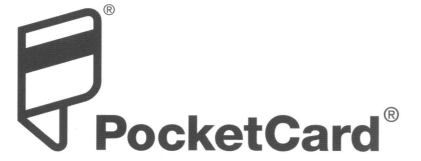

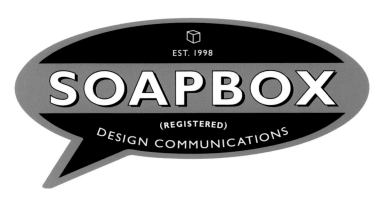

EST. 1998

SOAPBOX

(REGISTERED)
DESIGN COMMUNICATIONS

Client

Soapbox Design Communications is a Toronto-based graphic design firm.

Designers

Gary Beelik, Jim Ryce, Victoria Primicas

Firm

Soapbox Design Communications

Process

The first step in creating the Soapbox identity was finding a way to visually convey the Old World feel of a soapbox. For inspiration, designer Gary Beelik and his colleagues turned to packaging design from the 1930s and 1940s, focusing in particular on soapbox labels. From this research emerged two ideas: creating a logo that was a label or a sticker, and secondly, incorporating some of the graphic elements common in early-twentieth-century packaging design, such as ovals, eye-catching color, and all-capital letters, into the final mark. Next, the team explored different ways to update the vintage designs they had been looking at. "We are a pretty laid back firm, so we wanted to create a logo with a bit of a humorous twist," says Beelik. That twist turned out to be a speech bubble, a symbol that connotes both speech in general and the populist speech of comic books in particular. As a typeface the team chose Gill Sans, a font that was introduced in the 1930s but whose clean strokes lend it a modern feel today. For colors, the team again turned to vintage soapbox labels. "But we wanted to update them slightly," says Beelik. "We made the oranges a little bit brighter and the blues a bit more current." The result is a logo that is playful and modern, but which also carries a sense of history.

What Works

The company's name alludes to the way wooden crates were once dragged into town squares and used as improvised platforms for spontaneous speech. Visually, the logo represents this type of communication: The comic book-style bubble conveys a sense of informal speech, while the attention-getting colors and all capital letters suggest the passion and urgency with which the speech is delivered. And just as Old World soapboxes were easily adaptable to a range of environments, so too is the logo: it varies in size, shape, and color depending on the application.

The logo comes in twelve variations and features six different sayings, including "Choose your platform," which is used for promotionals, and "Try to remain calm," which is applied to invoices.

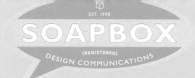
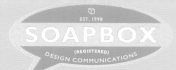
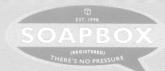
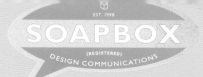

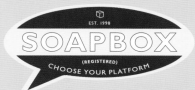
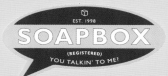
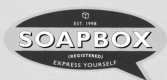
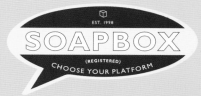

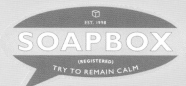
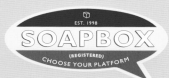
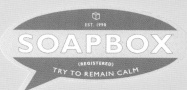
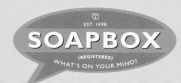

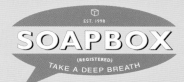
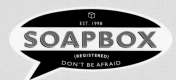
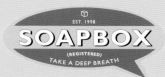
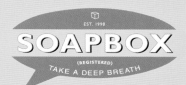

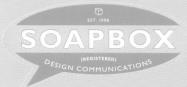
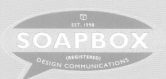
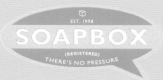
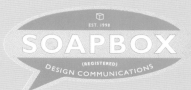

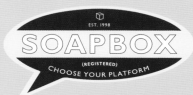
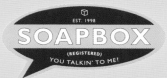
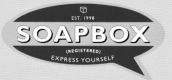
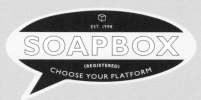

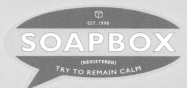
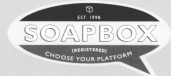
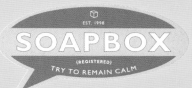
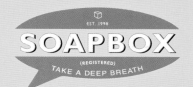

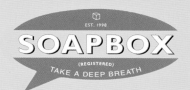
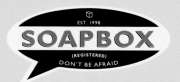
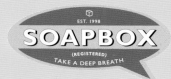
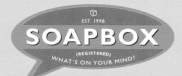

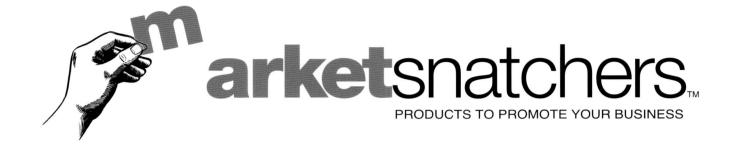

PRODUCTS TO PROMOTE YOUR BUSINESS

Client

Market Snatchers is a provider of logo imprinted products for use in corporate promotions.

DESIGNER

Kevin Hall

FIRM

Kevin Hall Design

Process

When Market Snatchers came to Kevin Hall Design in search of a logo, the company was hoping for a mark that would appeal to small and mid-size businesses and have a friendly, rather than corporate, feel to it. To designer Kevin Hall these general criteria called to mind the phrase "a design with a human touch," and led to the idea of incorporating an image of a hand into the mark. Sketches led to further refinements, resulting in a hand snatching away the first letter of the client's name. To execute it, Hall worked with an illustrator who experimented with different iterations of hands. Some early approaches, such as a hand rendered in a smooth outline, felt too sterile, says Hall, and were later refined by adding cross hatching and shading for a more tactile appearance. For the logotype, Hall opted for the smooth, modern letterforms of Helvetica to provide a contrast to the hand-drawn hand. For color, he chose black and red to lend a bold, aggressive feel to the mark.

What Works

The company's name refers to the act of one business stealing market share away from another. Visually, the logo furthers this notion—and playfully so—by featuring a drawing of a hand plucking away the first letter of the company's name.

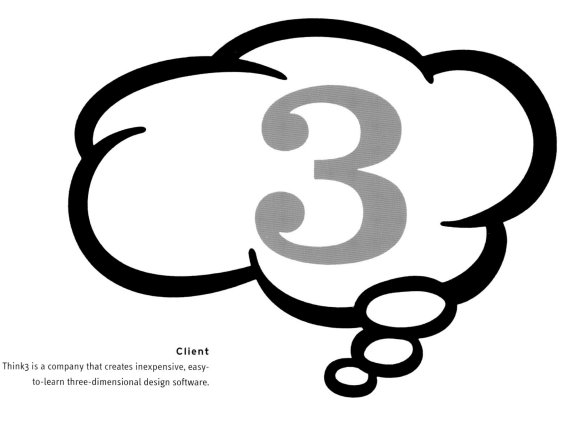

Client

Think3 is a company that creates inexpensive, easy-to-learn three-dimensional design software.

DESIGNER
Keith Anderson

FIRM
Eleven Inc.

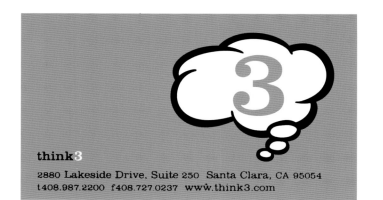

Process

The idea for the logo evolved out of early sketches designer Keith Anderson made of people thinking. Aiming for both simplicity and boldness, Anderson eliminated the people, distilling the design down to a single thought bubble. After scanning his final sketch into the computer and cleaning it up in Illustrator, Anderson experimented with fonts, both serif and sans serif. Some, like Baskerville, Anderson deemed too sophisticated for the feisty, upstart company; while others, like Trade Gothic, felt too technical and cold. Anderson ultimately chose Clarendon, which, with its exaggerated, bulbous serifs, lends a dash of humor to the numeral three. And though Anderson first used red as the logo's primary color, he ultimately decided it wasn't distinctive enough, and opted instead for an intentionally garish orange. "Orange invades you," Anderson says. "You can't turn away from it. By using it in a logo, a company conveys attitude, one that says: Lots of people may not like orange, but, hey, we don't care."

What Works

Rather than illustrating the company's product, the logo focuses on what customers do with it, namely, conceptualize and create three-dimensional objects. With its comic book-style thought bubble and a numeral three seemingly plucked from a grammar school primer, the logo alludes to the product's accessibility and helps create a company identity of playful rebellion and humor.

Before reaching its final form, the Handspring logo underwent over one hundred different iterations. Some changes were major, such as a shift away from a monogram to a stylized figure; others were mere details, such as deciding how big the dot above the letter "i" should be.

rough drafts/final drafts

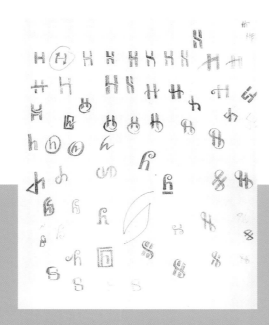

The Handspring logo begins with rudimentary pencil sketches. Here, designer P.J. Nidecker repeatedly draws an H, the first letter of the client's name. A conceptual theme emerges: the H becomes a spring, which refers to the company's use of "springboards," modules that expand PDA's capabilities, and to the company's desired image, one of energy and verve.

Laser proofs reveal different interpretations of the spring concept, all based on the letter H. In the first, the H performs a back flip, while in the second, it transforms into a tightly wound coil.

Client

Handspring is a company that develops handheld personal digital assistants.

What Works

The Handspring logo, a stylized stick figure cart wheeling above a logotype, visually conveys the attitude of youth and vitality.

ART DIRECTOR
Gordon Mortensen

DESIGNER
P.J. Nidecker

FIRM
Mortensen Design

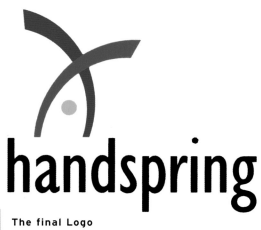

The third approach refers to the spring-like action of a bouncing ball, while the fourth depicts an H composed of cross-sections of springs.

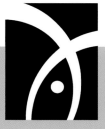

Only the fifth, a stylized character caught mid-cartwheel, moves away from a literal rendering of an H. It is ultimately chosen as the approach to pursue. To stress the mark's humanlike appearance, the figure is removed from the box that once surrounded it.

The final Logo

The chosen mark, which has since been nicknamed "Flip." The colors green, blue and yellow convey a sense of youth and vibrancy.

Client

Y-Not Design is a Cincinnati-based design firm specializing in corporate identities.

Designer

Tony Reynaldo

Firm

Y-Not Design

Process

Though designer Tony Reynaldo had created scores of logos for other companies, he had spent two years struggling to come up with one for his own. "The problem with doing your own logo is that you're super critical of every little thing," he says. Inspiration hit while Reynaldo was on a road trip—"I had plenty of time to think," he explains. He realized that his first name spelled backwards read as Y-not, or "Why not," a phrase that he felt summed up his down-to-earth approach to design and which would therefore make an appropriate name for his firm. To create a mark out of the name, Reynaldo first experimented with rebuses depicting a capital Y and an image of a knot. But when he showed the results to friends, he says, they couldn't decipher it. To remedy this, he added a logotype that spelled out Y-KNOT, but the resulting design was too cluttered, he says. Shifting courses, he abandoned the rebus and returned to his original idea of spelling his name backwards. For a typeface, he chose Futura for its straightforward, modern feel, then encased the letters in a vertical rectangle so that the Y would pop out. To further separate the Y from the NOT, he placed each in a different colored square, then added the word "design" at the base. For color, he chose a vibrant blue and green to convey a sense of playfulness.

What Works

The firm takes its name from the founder's first name, Tony spelled backwards. Visually, the logo reinforces this playful attitude towards design through the use of unadorned typography and bold, eye-popping color.

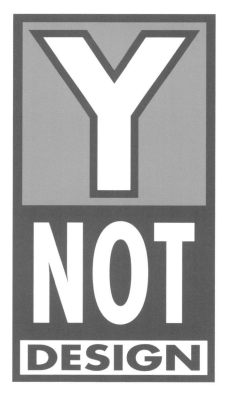

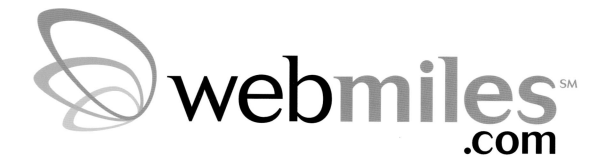

Client

WebMiles is an online service that provides frequent flier miles in exchange for purchases made over the Web.

DESIGNER
Noreen Doherty

DESIGN DIRECTOR
Rick Atwood

FIRM
GMO/Hill, Holliday

Process

When WebMiles came to the ad agency GMO/Hill, Holliday, the company already had a logo—a lozenge shape containing the company's name—but was hoping to replace it with something more distinctive. To the design team at GMO that meant coming up with a design that somehow conveyed airline flight in a friendly, energetic way, says designer Noreen Doherty: "The customers who use WebMiles use them for vacations, not for business travel, so we didn't want the mark to end up looking cold and corporate. We wanted it to be fun and dynamic." The team began by creating a list of five words that could describe the WebMiles brand—Energy, Travel, Personality, Change, and Pro-Active—then developed a round of logos to illustrate each one. One early approach, says Doherty, incorporated illustrations of planes; another featured the WebMiles name in clouds. Both approaches were abandoned however. "They were much too literal and didn't differentiate the company from other travel companies," says Doherty. So Doherty began experimenting with wings instead, sketching designs ranging from mechanical-looking airplane wings to more organic ones based on birds and butterflies. After refining the wing shape in Illustrator, she created two more in smaller sizes, then arranged them in a fan-like configuration to convey a sense of movement. For the logotype, she chose Cosmos as a base, then modified it by adding serifs to convey a sense of forward motion. Next, she experimented with color. "Blue was the obvious choice because it connoted the sky, but in the travel industry, everything is blue so we wanted to find something more distinctive," says Doherty. To this end, the team chose a palette of oranges to suggest sunrises, sunsets, and the warm feelings associated with vacation. Of the final result, Doherty says: "We feel it reflects the excitement of travel while at the same time setting the company apart in a field of blue."

What Works

The logo, which features three wing-shaped forms arranged in a fan-like configuration, suggests movement, flight and the use of orange adds a unique and positive feel.

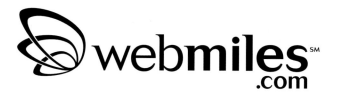

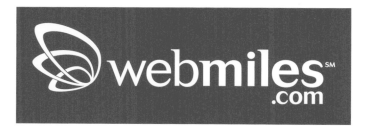

classic logo

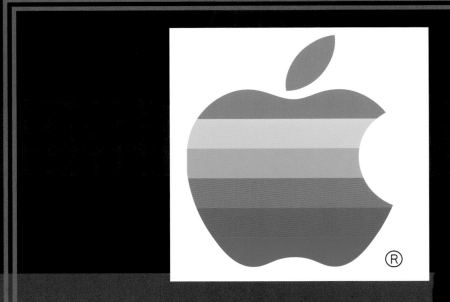

Not only is the famous Apple logo an effective pictograph—the apple being a symbol of knowledge in general; the bite, an allusion to forbidden knowledge in particular—its playful style has had much influence on logo design. Designed by Rob
Janoff of Regis McKenna in 1977, the Apple logo distinguished itself from earlier
high-tech logos by incorporating humor into its design: The rainbow colors were
intended to recall the post-hippie culture in which the company took root; its
stripes, a playful reference to IBM, one of the company's major competitors. Since
then, other high-tech companies have taken Apple's lead, rolling out logos that
communicate a sense of play rather than sheer power.

*ba***zillion**

Client

Bazillion is a telecommunications company providing high-speed voice and data delivery service that combines telephone, cable, and the Internet.

ART DIRECTOR
Ray Ueno

DESIGNER
Katrin Beeck

FIRM
The Leonhardt Group

Process

When Nutel approached the Seattle-based Leonhardt Group, the telecommunications company was seeking a new name and visual identity for its high-speed voice and data delivery service. "The company was moving forward into broader markets and bigger ponds and felt limited by the name Nutel: It didn't stand out from the crowd, plus it sounded like 'noodle,'" says TLG creative director Ray Ueno. To pinpoint what kind of image the company wanted to project, the TLG team began by presenting the client with a variety of names. "We spanned the spectrum from big, scary, corporate-sounding names like 'Octacom,' which sounds like something out of the movie Terminator 2, to friendlier, more feisty names like 'Bazillion,' which has a young, dotcom-ish kind of feel," says Ueno. After the client chose Bazillion—and the message of friendliness and fun it implied—the design team turned its attention to logos. Early explorations ranged from abstract shapes to human figures to type treatments featuring computer icons in place of the A in the company's name. None of them, however, was distinctive enough and all were soon abandoned, says Ueno. Inspiration for a new direction hit when Ueno was driving to work one morning and spotted a flock of sparrows in the sky. Noticing how the individual birds moved together as a group, swarming from one point to another, Ueno thought of Bazillion's delivery system: information is chopped up into bits, bundled into little packets, shot through a cable, then reassembled on the other end so that a receiver hears a voice or sees data on his or her computer screen. Once at the office, Ueno mentioned the swarm concept to his team and they began experimenting with different ways to visually represent the idea. The result was a mass of small bs, dense in the center and growing increasingly sparse at the edges, with a larger b, for Bazillion, reversed-out in the center. Deeming it a strong direction, the team further refined the design by creating a running figure out of the swarm to add a playful touch. Lastly, a logotype, based on Univers, was added. Orange was chosen as a color to differentiate the company from the blues and reds that dominate the telecommunications category.

What Works

The logo, a running figure composed out of a swarm of lowercase bs, visually conveys the movement of millions of bits of data speeding from one place to another.

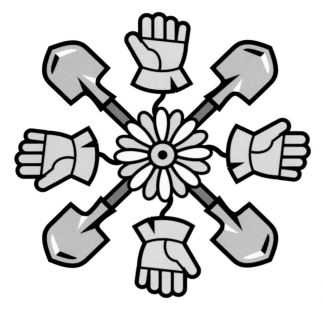

Client

Big Red Sun is a landscape architecture firm based in Austin, Texas.

Designers

Matt Hovis, Kevin Whitely

Firm

Action Figure

Process

As landscape architects, Big Red Sun provides two services: what it calls "softscape," which entails designing gardens, and what it refers to as "hardscape," which involves developing a site so that buildings and plantings work well with each other. To reflect these two services, designers at Action Figure hoped to create a logo that would visually reference both the soft aspects of gardens and the hard aspects of construction. As a starting point, the designers sketched images of suns, daisies, tulips, gloves, and shovels, hoping one could be turned into a symbol representing landscape architecture. But the team found that although the daisies and tulips evoked the gardening side of the client's business, they were too soft to convey the company's construction services. And whereas the shovels suggested construction, they were too hard for gardening. So designer Matt Hovis experimented with different ways of combining the hard and soft elements into a single mark and came up with a radial shape, which, when viewed as a whole, suggested a sun. Next, the team added different symbols to the shape's eight spokes. One design included eight tulips, which the designers deemed too stark; another, a mixture of shovels, tulips, and gloves, was deemed too cluttered. In the end, the team opted for a design that incorporated four gloves and four shovels. Says designer Kevin Whitely, "For us, it was the best marriage of hard and soft."

What Works

The logo features a radial shape whose center is a flower and whose eight spokes are topped with alternating gloves and shovels. Its overall shape evokes a sun, which reflects the client's name, while the mark's individual elements illustrate the tools used in landscape architecture. The logo's style, reminiscent of the bold, playful look of comic books, conveys a sense of a young, vibrant company.

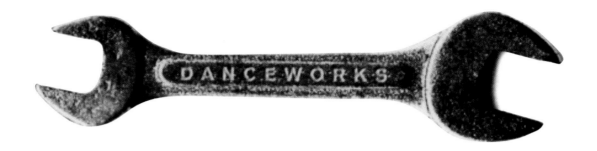

Client

Danceworks is a modern dance company, based in Austin, Texas, that incorporates technology into its choreography.

Designer
Kevin Whitely

Firm
Action Figure

Process

After changing its name from The Sharir Dance Company to Danceworks, the client needed a new logo and hoped for one that would appeal to the college-age population of its home base in Austin, Texas. To designer Kevin Whitely, that meant avoiding the clichés often found in dance logos—leaping people, for example, or dangling toe shoes—and creating something unexpected instead. So he turned away from the "Dance" part of the company's name and focused instead on "Works," concentrating on its use to describe the industrial systems in power plants or factories. To visually convey this idea, Whitely chose a wrench. As a tool, a wrench joins different elements together, a function which echoes that of a dance choreographer. As a graphic form, a wrench is easily identifiable in large sizes or small, making it suitable for a logo. Next, Whitely opted for a photographic image, rather than an illustration, so that the tool's industrial feel would not be lost. He placed a wrench directly on a scanner, entered the image into the computer, then used Photoshop to clean up its outline and add shading, highlights, and drop shadows. For the company's name, Whitely chose Akzidenz Grotesk, a typeface whose unembellished letterforms recall the straightforward lettering engraved on tools. Before adding it to the wrench, however, he modified the logotype by photocopying it multiple times to give it a worn feel that matched the mottled, nicked surface of the wrench. Of the result, Whitely says, "We didn't want to do anything frilly or soft. We were aiming for something hard, something that was the exact opposite of dance. And because there is a touch of humor to the mark, I think it appeals to young people who would never even consider spending a Friday night at a modern dance performance."

What Works

The logo, a photographic image of a wrench with the client's name set in Akzidenz Grotesk across it, serves as a visual metaphor for choreography, equating the rarefied art of creating dance movements to the down-to-earth skills of carpentry or plumbing.

littlefeet

Client

Little Feet is a wireless telecommunications company that develops and manufactures network infrastructure hardware and software.

Art Director/Designer

Denis Zimmerman

Firm

Matthews/Mark

Process

When the newly formed Little Feet came to the advertising agency Matthews/Mark, the telecommunications company was seeking a corporate identity that would somehow reflect the company's innovations in wireless technology. As a starting point, the design team at Matthews/Mark worked with the client to come up with a list of words and phrases that would describe what the company does and how it differs from competitors. From these discussions, the team developed a "brand personality," which centered around four key words: Fresh, Bold, Progressive, and Friendly. The team then began exploring logo designs. "Everything we created held up to the four brand personality words. If a design didn't speak to those four points, it got thrown out," says Matthews/Mark designer Denis Zimmerman. Of the twenty or so possible directions, a sketch that combined an image of a footprint with one of an ear was a standout due to its simplicity and playfulness, says Zimmerman. To render it, he used Illustrator to create an ear shape, basing its form on the ear icons found on computers and other electronic equipment and using a bold outline with rounded ends to give the mark a cable-like feel. Next, he added five circles for toes, and placed a logotype, based on Helvetica Neue Black Extended, below the symbol. To further emphasize the playfulness of the mark, orange was chosen as a color. Of the result, Zimmerman says: "Some people have seen a question mark in the logo, which was unintentional but which seems to work. It reflects the way the company questions the status quo."

What Works

The company takes its name from the small "footprints" of the hardware it develops. Visually, the logo reinforces this name with an image of a footprint, while at the same time referring to communication with an image of an ear.

Process

When the owners of Pumpkin Maternity came to designer Jennifer Waverek in search of a logo, they brought with them a vintage illustration of a pumpkin from an old magazine and suggested a logo based on it might work well. Waverek, however, saw two problems with a vintage-looking logo. For one, any design that was too intricate would not be flexible enough to function well across the range of applications—that a logo for a new clothing line requires; for another, a vintage design would not adequately reflect the modern, simple clothing the company offered. Instead, Waverek opted for a simple approach, a design that would be able to move from hang tags to store signage to the Web with little adjustment required. The result, created in Quark, is an oval-shaped pumpkin ("a circular one looked too much like a balloon or an apple," says Waverek) with the company's name spelled across it in all lowercase Arial. For color, Waverek chose orange and green, a combination, she says "that worked out really well because one is warm, the other is cool, so there's a nice contrast to the mark."

What Works

Client

Pumpkin Maternity is a Manhattan-based company that designs and sells maternity wear.

The company takes it name from the co-owner's nickname, "Pumpkin." The logo not only illustrates the name, but its clean, spare style echoes the simple and casual designs of the maternity wear the company offers.

DESIGNER

Jennifer Waverek

FIRM

General and Specific

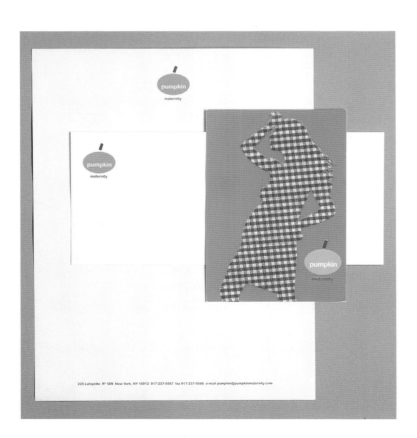

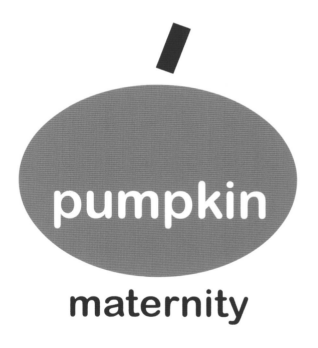

pumpkin

maternity

BLACKSTONE

BLACKSTONE

BLACKSTONE

Client

Blackstone is a San Francisco-based company that creates customized interoffice computer networking solutions.

ART DIRECTOR
Joel Templin

DESIGNER
Paul Howalt

FIRM
Howalt Design

Process

With the Blackstone project, designer Paul Howalt faced two challenges. First, he needed to find a way to visually represent "customized computer networking." Second, he had to come up with a design that would help the client stand out in a crowded business category. To meet the first objective, Howalt focused on the word "customized" and decided to create a "customized logo," one whose basic shape would remain the same, but whose details would change from one application to another. To meet the second objective, Howalt decided to base his designs on fluid, organic shapes—rather than hard-edged, geometric ones—to emphasize the flexibility of the client's services as opposed to the standardized services provided by larger companies. Using Illustrator, Howalt experimented with monograms, basing his designs on lowercase b's, rather than the more closed and solid uppercase ones. Stretching, bending, and distorting the b's ascenders, he created three marks, each one slightly different than the other, yet sharing the same fluid-like form. For color, he selected a pale blue, a color associated with technology.

What Works

The logo, three organically shaped b's enclosed in circles, changes from one application to another, echoing the way the client's customized services change from one job to another. The mark's fluid-like forms reinforce this notion of flexibility.

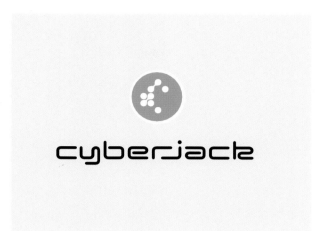

Client
Cyberjack is a London-based Web hosting company.

Designer
Paul Howalt

Firm
Howalt Design

Process

Two design parameters drove the project. First, the logo's form had to be simple enough to be readable on the Web, and second, the logo's look had to suggest the high-tech industry without, both client and designer agreed, relying on over-used clichés such as swooshes or spheres. As a starting point, designer Paul Howalt created preliminary sketches of abstract shapes that he hoped would evolve into a workable design. While continuing to refine these sketches, however, he came across the typeface Dr. No, which was designed by Ian Anderson of the Designers Republic, and noticed that the font's C had the high-tech feel he was looking for. After adding subtle modifications to the letter in Illustrator so that it would work as a stand-alone symbol, Howalt enclosed it in a solid circle and added an outline. For the logotype, he chose Euphoric, a font whose rectangular-based letterforms complement the circles of the symbol. The color, says Howalt, was chosen by the client: "She happens to be the lead singer of a British rock band and orange is the color of the uniforms her band wears on stage."

What Works

The logo's symbol, a solid circle containing eight white dots, can be read in two ways: as a monogram of the company's name (the dots form the letter C) or as a visual allusion to the Web hosting services the company provides in that the cluster of dots suggests a computer jack.

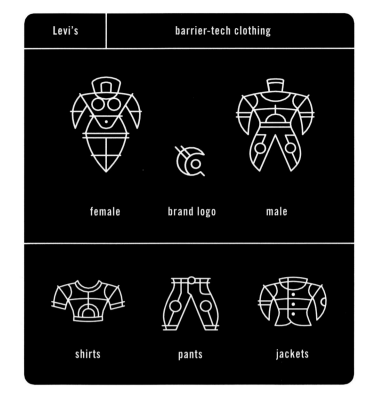

| Levi's | barrier-tech clothing |

female　　　brand logo　　　male

shirts　　　pants　　　jackets

Client
Levi's is a 128-year-old company specializing in
casual wear.

Art Director
Joel Templin

Creative Director
Brian Collins

Designer
Paul Howalt

Firm
Howalt Design

Process

For designer Paul Howalt, the project's biggest challenge was coming up with a visual language for the future, one that felt new but also familiar. For inspiration, he turned to the 1960's sci-fi cult classic *Lost in Space*, a television series about a family marooned in space, and made a series of pencil sketches based on the show's costumes. He then refined the sketches in Illustrator, transforming them into simple, streamlined marks both for stylistic reasons (to create a look that would suggest futuristic computer renderings) and for practical ones (to produce designs that would work across a wide range of applications, from hangtags to the Web).

What Works

Created for a proposed clothing line that would feature futuristic-looking pants, shirts, and jackets, the series of six logos present space-age motifs from the 1960s in the streamlined style of computer renderings. This mixture of past and present results in marks that feel both familiar and new.

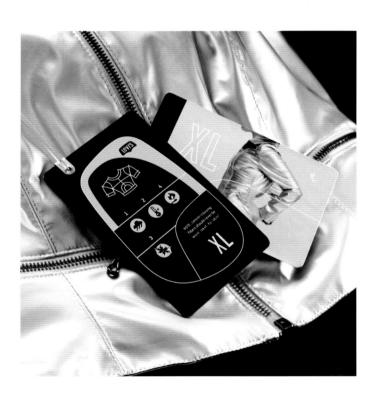

yo5ho ^Y

yo5ho

yo5ho

yo5ho

Client
Yosho is a Web development firm based in San Mateo, California.

CREATIVE DIRECTOR
Carlos Segura

DESIGNER
Tnop Wangsillapakun

FIRM
Segura Inc.

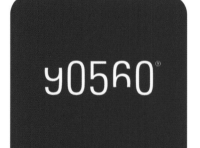

Process

Before coming up with the final mark, designers at the Chicago-based Segura Inc. experimented with several approaches. One was based on the company's name, Yosho, which is a Japanese battle cry, and resulted in cartoon-like logos featuring Japanese super heroes. But although these marks conveyed the energy with which the client approached its work, they didn't address the company's product or industry. So the design team shifted courses, exploring designs based on communication in general and computer-based communication in particular. The resulting sketches featured computer keyboards, scroll bars, and desktop icons, designs that were strong, says Tnop Wangsillapakun, an art director on the project, but that seemed to lack the uniqueness the team was searching for. Brainstorming, Wangsillapakun typed a string of numbers into Illustrator to represent computer code then spent the day rotating and cutting them, until, he says: "It just happened. We discovered that the numbers could be transformed into letters spelling out the company's name." For the final logo, the team chose the typeface Orator, as its geometric and mechanical letterforms suggest computer code. For color, a palette of purple, blue, and green, a combination culled from computer circuitry, was selected. And as a playful finishing touch, the team replaced the customary trademark symbol, a circled R, with a circled Y, the first letter of the client's name.

What Works

The logo, which consists of the name Yosho spelled out in fragments of numbers, is a visual representation of the company's product, namely, the computer code needed to construct websites.

classic logo

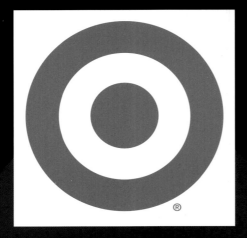

As the design curator and writer Aaron Betsky has pointed out, many of the most successful logos today are circular in form. To Betsky, one of the reasons may have to do with the ancient tradition of the mandala, a graphic device that represents the world and its forces in miniature form, much like modern logos do. The bright red Target bull's-eye is an example of the enduring power of circular marks. Though who designed it and when remains unknown, it has been in use for nearly forty years.

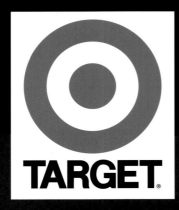

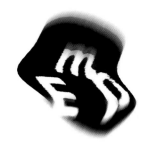

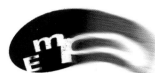

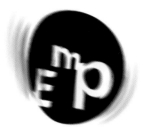

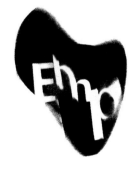

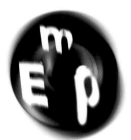

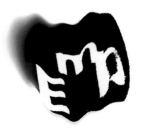

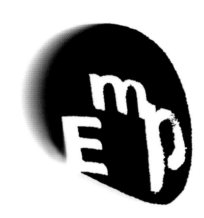

EXPERIENCE *MUSIC* PROJECT™

Client

The Experience Music Project (EMP) is an interactive music museum in Seattle, Washington.

ART DIRECTOR/DESIGNER
Ray Ueno

FIRM
The Leonhardt Group

Process

When Paul Allen, the co-founder of Microsoft, began to develop the Experience Music Project, a music museum devoted to American jazz, R&B, and rock and roll, he commissioned the architect Frank Gehry to design a building for it that would somehow capture the fluid, ever-changing nature of music, and hired the Seattle-based consultancy The Leonhardt Group to create a similarly progressive visual identity for it. To the design team at TLG this meant creating a "kinetic" logo, one whose basic style remains consistent, but whose form constantly changes and evolves, much like a piece of music does. The result was an organic form, which calls to mind both a water drop and a guitar pick, containing the museum's initials reversed-out from black. In addition to this core mark, the team developed a series of different variations, each one distorted and stretched in a morphing program.

What Works

The logo, the museum's initials E, M, and P reversed-out from black, constantly changes form. The mark's fluidity mirrors the dynamic nature of music and reflects the endless interpretations music can invoke in listeners.

While each version of the logo has a consistent style, its variations invite viewers to decide for themselves what the EMP means.

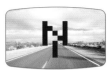

novo interactive

Digital Commerce Architects

Client

Novo Interactive is a Web design and branding firm.

ART DIRECTOR
David Salanitro

DESIGNER
Alice Chang

PHOTOGRAPHY
Oh Boy, A Design Company,
Nonstock, Inc.

FIRM
Oh Boy, A Design Company

Process

As a starting point, designers at the San Francisco-based Oh Boy, A Design Company researched the client's business to find out what differentiated it from its competitors. "There are all kinds of Web design companies out there and all of them offer essentially the same set of skills and products," says David Salanitro, Oh Boy's founder and creative director. "What made Novo Interactive special was its emphasis on design. They had a notion that the computer screen had become a playground where anything could happen." To visually convey this idea, Salanitro's team opted for an evolving logo, one whose open architecture would allow for continual modification and updating. In Illustrator, Salanitro's team created a computer screen-shaped outline, then built a pixilated N and I and placed them inside the outline. Next, the team experimented with different photographic images to add as background. The images that were selected—an open road, a child's hand, a field of grass, taxi cabs, and hands clapping—are based on the five senses. Explains Salanitro: "The aim was to convey the notion that a computer is a portal into a range of real world experiences."

What Works

The logo features the pixilated letters N and I contained within a screen-shaped keyline. To reflect the interactive products the client creates, the logo's design allows for change: different photographic imagery is added to the mark depending on the application.

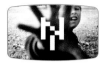

novo interactive

Digital Commerce Architects

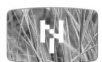

novo interactive

Digital Commerce Architects

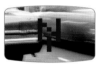

novo interactive

Digital Commerce Architects

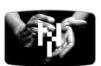

novo interactive

Digital Commerce Architects

classic logo

FedEx Express

Throughout the 1970s, the international shipping service was marketed under the Federal Express brand and had a logotype featuring modularly shaped letters in purple, orange, and white. However, in 1994, the company, hoping to increase the global reach of its brand, commissioned the San Francisco-based consultancy Landor Associates to redesign the logo. Led by art director Lindon Gray Leader, the design team adopted FedEx. The logo design that rose out of this name change—a string of bold, sans serif letters with an image of a forward-pointing arrow formed in the negative space between the final E and X—is today instantly recognizable and moves with ease from one language to another.

Magazine Design

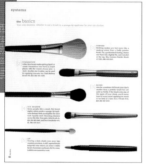

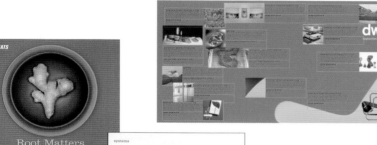

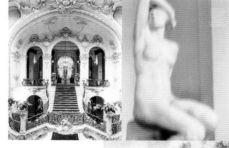

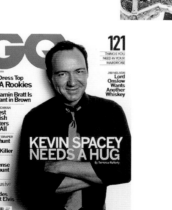

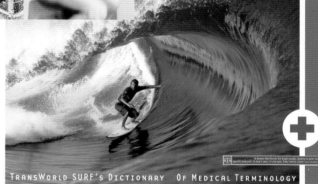

Fashion for the New Affluent Man

Magazines that survive the ages become staples of our culture: *Life, Harper's,* and *Time* among them. These titles are as familiar to us as great film classics and works of literature because they shaped how entire generations have seen the world.

GQ can easily be esteemed as one of the great magazines to weather the turbulent decades. After more than 70 years in circulation, the magazine's title has become synonymous with fashionable, as in, "You look so *GQ.*"

The magazine's design has progressed over the decades to mirror the changing image of the stylish, affluent man. In the era of 20-something millionaires and 30-something retirees, design expresses quality and confidence with a cool, yet reserved, edge.

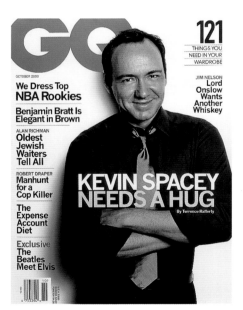

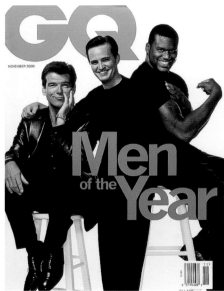

far left Strong, bold cover lines outline a straight-on portrait of Kevin Spacey on the front of the October 2000 issue—an example of the magazine's assertive, confident covers.

left A stunning lineup of stars grace the cover of *GQ*'s coveted "Men of the Year" issue.

WHY IT WORKS:

With few frills, *GQ* is straightforward in its attempt to be a timeless publication, giving a nod to its history while firmly maintaining its stylish reputation. Richly colored photographs and striking type treatment boldly accentuate clean, classic page layout—offering variety but staying grounded with a proud sense of the magazine's identity.

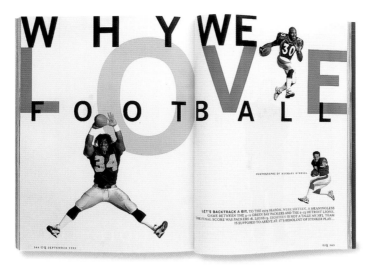

The New Gentleman

Still, *GQ* hasn't avoided becoming "a lot hipper" over the last several years, mainly to appeal to younger audiences who have grown up rather quickly, says design director Arem Duplessis.

"With the economy as good as it's been, we have a more sophisticated audience who's increasingly concerned with overall style," he says. "He dresses for the job he wants, not the job he has."

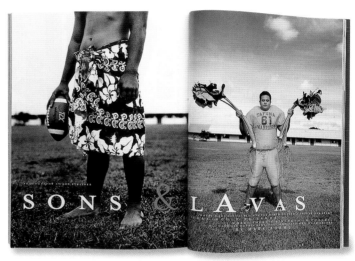

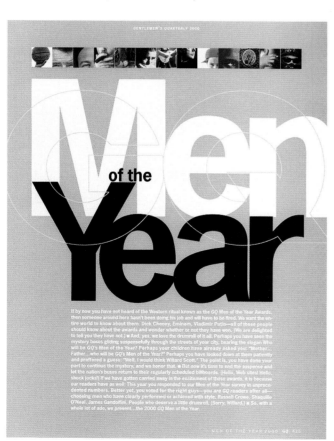

Average readers range from recent college grads to around 40 years old, generally hold advanced degrees, and make between $35,000 and $100,000 a year. Such an age gap may be difficult for other magazines to straddle, but Duplessis says the *GQ* reader responds less to generational messages and more to a prevailing attitude.

"Our readers already know who they are," he says. "We avoid anything over the top and stick to a classic aesthetic, one that has no time period."

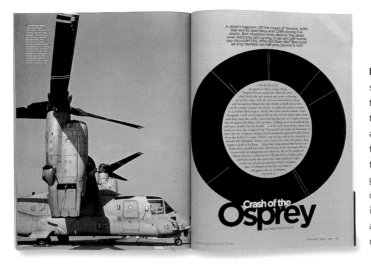

Staying Consistent for Readers' Sake

Much like other publications launched earlier in the century, *GQ* is known for its literary legacy, and editors pride themselves on commissioning talented, recognized writers. But articles also must reflect current issues and appeal to a diverse readership, so the magazine covers broad topics—politics, sports, art, entertainment, as well as fashion.

"Our biggest challenge is staying consistent with all our concepts and reaching as broad of an audience as we have," says Duplessis. Design changes according to the mood of each story, but design elements must tie the book together from front to back.

A strict grid, generally three to four columns throughout the book, plays a role in maintaining coherence. Articles tend to be quite long, but rather than breaking them up with boxes and subheads, designers let them play out in two or three columns, usually with a pull quote or small photograph that acts as an anchor in the gray sea of type.

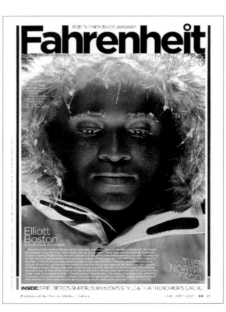

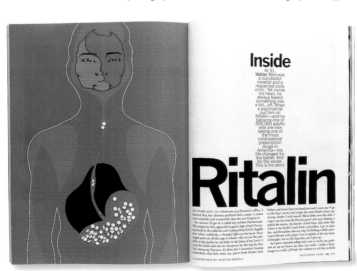

The one place the book strays from this format is in "Fahrenheit," the department in the front of the book that offers short reviews, product snapshots, profiles, and calendars. Colored boxes and heavy black rules break up articles so pages are attractive and delightfully easygoing. "It's a quick read for people who are skimming on the airplane or train," Duplessis says.

The color palette, though subdued, also unites the pages of *GQ*. Heavy blues, grays, and reds guest star in headlines and pull quotes, never taking over a layout but garnishing dense pages of text with just enough color to intrigue and entertain.

Retro Influence on Type

In the same fashion as color, display type gives pages power and pop without detracting from the article's message. Bold headlines contrast handsomely with white pages and tiny body copy, while bold or colored pull quotes, inside shapes or escorted by heavy black rules, break up second or third spreads in articles.

below A bold, all-caps headline, bleeding to the edges of the left page, and the facing photo are a dramatic debut for an article on actor Philip Seymour Hoffman. Yet the pallor of the article is relatively upbeat because of the sharp contrast and demanding type.

GQ's signature typeface, rolled out during a redesign in January 2001, contributes to the designers' goal of consistency as well as to the "modern yet classic" feel of the book. "We hired a typographer to draw a font for us," Duplessis says. "He studied old subway posters from the early 20th century and built a sans-serif font based on the type in those posters." The resulting typeface, with its rounded letters and flat-topped and flat-bottomed ascenders and descenders, graces everything from cover lines to sidebar copy with the geometric character of early Art Deco.

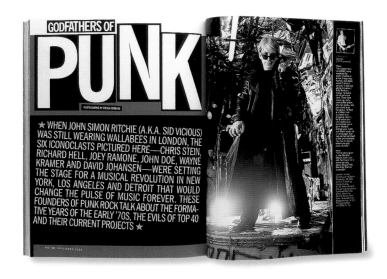

Occasionally, designers experiment with display type somewhat—enlarging it to make a big splash on opening spreads, illustrating it to match the concept of a story, or playing with leading for a "crowded" effect. But even these attempts are somewhat subdued, never venturing out of the realm of expectations or veering too far from the magazine's standard look. Type also rarely strays from the limited palette of colors, taking on some red or blue here or there but more often emphasizing its point with bold, black characters.

The reason *GQ* doesn't get carried away with type treatment? "We don't want display copy to take away from the impact of the photography," Duplessis says.

above In a show of how display type can exploit opening spreads to set a mood, patched together letters and a skewed opening paragraph reflect the iconoclastic mood of the founders of the punk movement.

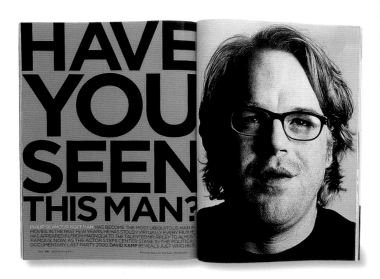

right By contrast, a more shadowy, somber photo of Hank Williams III is surrounded by dark, soft colors, setting a very different mood.

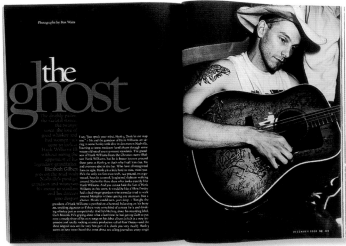

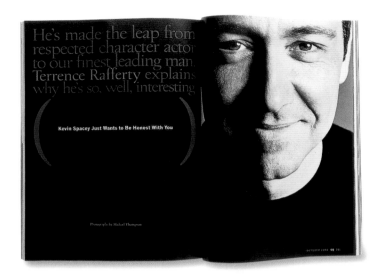

He's made the leap from respected character actor to our finest leading man. Terrence Rafferty explains why he's so, well, interesting

Kevin Spacey Just Wants to Be Honest With You

Photographs by Michael Thompson

OCTOBER 2000 GQ 261

left Opening spreads frequently offer variations on *GQ's* otherwise simple, straightforward layout. For the story on Kevin Spacey, a black page faces the shadowy side of the actor's head shot, while atmospheric gray type makes a tiny white headline stand out even more than it would by itself.

Signature Photography and Illustrations

Photography is a cornerstone of *GQ's* design. Though they change to reflect the tone of the story, images are sophisticated, beautiful, and often lighthearted. Like the pages themselves, colors in photographs often steer toward neutrals—grays, beiges, and blues, with subdued lighting—with occasional explosions of bright colors as accents.

GQ's director of photography, Jennifer Crandall, recently started taking some chances with photographic choices, says Duplessis. "In the past we've always been known for using big-name photographers," he says. "Now we're still using big names, but we're also finding innovators, mixing it up, and doing a lot of experimenting."

The same goes for illustrations, which are another major part of the magazine's brand. Fun illustrations generally accompany fictional pieces or essays that may not lend themselves to photography. Lately,

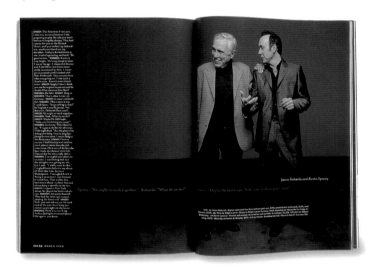

Jason Robards and Kevin Spacey

314 GQ MARCH 2000

Duplessis says, the magazine has been looking at European magazines to find new illustrators and showcase emerging talent. Illustrators must be familiar with *GQ's* look and feel and work within a loose framework—using colors that complement the palette, for instance.

The result of *GQ's* commitment to sophisticated consistency is a refined-looking magazine that feels mature and self-assured—much like the readers who subscribe to it.

above and left The magazine adheres to a suave, yet relaxed and personalized style in its photography. In an article featuring conversations with distinguished actors, soft lighting accentuates the solid characters of the personalities and the sophisticated clothes they wear.

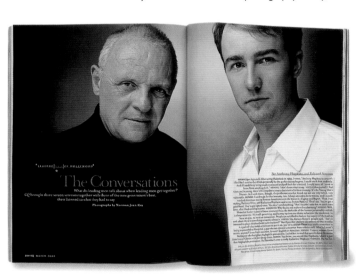

Sir Anthony Hopkins and Edward Norton

"LEADING MEN OF HOLLYWOOD"

The Conversations

What do leading men talk about when leading men get together? GQ brought three screen veterans together with three of the new generation's best, then listened to what they had to say

Photographs by Norman Jean Roy

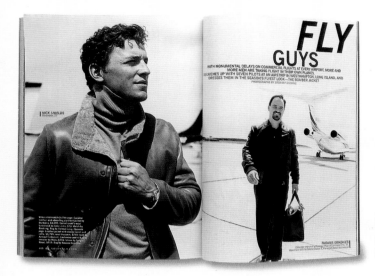

left Combining black-and-white and neutrally colored photos offers a realistic yet rugged feel to this fashion layout involving professional pilots.

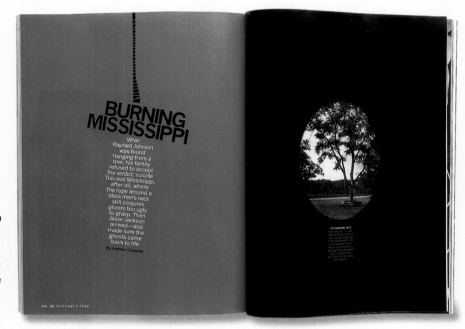

right Reds and blacks are among the boldest shades in *GQ*'s color palette and are often used as accents. Here, however, they've been pulled out to suggest the rage and intensity surrounding an event. A clever use of type and graphics—including a "window" to the scene of the depicted crime—builds the reader's curiosity about a sensitive subject that's difficult to portray visually.

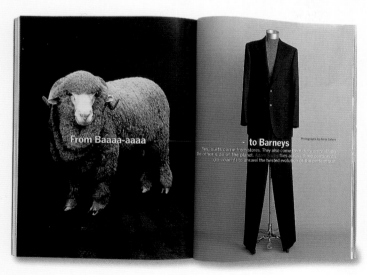

left One of *GQ*'s greatest successes is that no matter how much of a cornerstone of men's fashion it becomes, the magazine never takes itself too seriously. Here, while sticking to its sophisticated neutral palette, facing pages comically link a straight-faced sheep to a highbrow department store suit.

About the Grid

Publication designers love to talk about the grid—why they do or don't choose to use one and, if they do, how much it contributes to their work process every time they sit down to design an issue.

Truth be told, most designers refer to some kind of grid, even if it's a set of simple guidelines rather than a defining framework. Here's a short primer to demonstrate how a grid is used, how designers talk about it, and how it can help create a structure for your magazine.

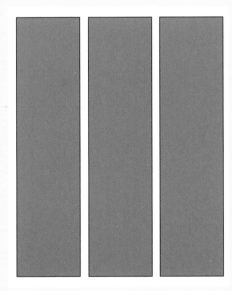

above This simple grid comprises three vertical units and one horizontal unit (a 3x1 grid). Each gray area is a grid unit. The white spaces between the units are alleys; the spaces surrounding the grid are the margins.

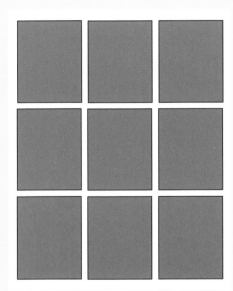

above This slightly more complex (3x3) grid has nine units. Elements should fit neatly within the boundaries of these units, even if they cross over the alleys.

Invisible Frame

As a magazine reader, you never see a grid. It's an invisible set of guides, usually printed on a paper template or set in a template file with a designer's layout software. Quite simply, its purpose is to guide designers in placing text and images.

The grid helps define the format of the magazine—its overall look and feel. It can be responsible for how sporadically or neatly elements are placed on a page, how clean or crowded a page looks, and whether a page is full of illustrations or text.

DESIGNDISCIPLINES

From Graphs to GUIs

by Megan Lane

In an age of media overload, information designers may be our only hope. Content rustlers of the new frontier, they'll tame the information stampede. Do you have what it takes to join their ranks?

The first thing you should understand about information design is that very few people actually call it that anymore. This design discipline that used to encompass charts and maps and diagrams has exploded mainly because of the Internet. So, for example, Aaron Marcus calls what he does "information visualization." And because Nigel Holmes concentrates on explaining things for print publication, he calls it "explanation graphics."

Consequently, it can be very tough to pin down a precise definition of what an information designer does. "You can tell you're an information designer if, when someone gives you a thing to design graphically, you wind up changing words and content structure because you've become interested in the content," says Marcus, principal of AM+A in Emeryville, CA.

DIGITAL DESIGN
Marcus opened his information-visualization studio in 1982 and immediately concentrated on digital design. "If you

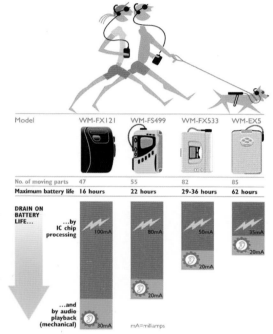

In this infographic for *Sony Style* magazine, Nigel Holmes says he "wanted to combine realistic 'portraits' of the four Walkman models with a different, lighter approach to the people walking their dog." In the lower half of the graphic, a very straightforward bar chart shows each Walkman's drain on batteries.

32 **DECEMBER 2000**

---

above *HOW* layouts exemplify manipulation of a 3x3 grid. Here, text occupies one column and an illustration the other two. The headline and byline form the upper third of the page, the illustration and text the bottom two-thirds.

Understanding the Grid

Grids often define vertical elements—columns—at the very least, and usually also define horizontal structure. The areas where these structures cross are called grid units and are the places on the page where type and images fit. The spaces between grid units are called alleys.

When talking about a grid, designers refer to how many vertical grid units are present versus the number of horizontal units. A grid that contains two columns and three rows is considered a six-unit, or 2x3, grid. One that has three columns and four rows is a 12-unit, or 3x4, grid.

Once the grid is established, columns of text and images can vary in width or length, taking up multiple grid units, for instance, as long as they stay within the confines of the unit borders. This allows designers to be flexible while maintaining order.

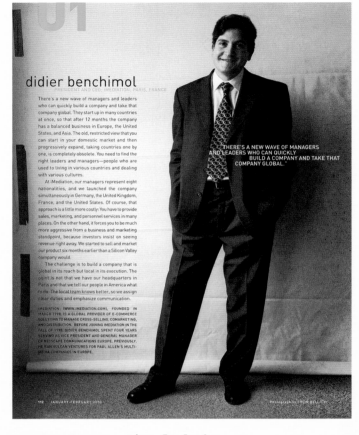

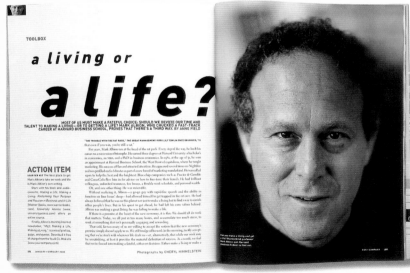

above Two *Fast Company* layouts show two ways to interpret a three-column grid. In the first, the subject of the photograph fills two columns and a column of text defines the third unit.

left In the second layout, body text stretches over two columns while an action item (a small sidebar) occupies the third. The headline and deck expand across all three units at the top of the page.

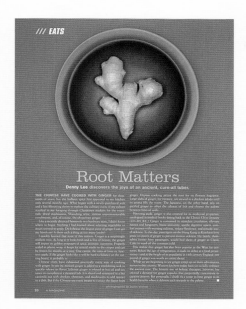

left This *A* layout is an example of flexibility within a simple two-column grid.

From Simple to Complex

Many magazines have different grids for different sections—departments may have a three-column grid with lots of space for small pictures (a 3x6, perhaps), while the feature well has a two-column grid that needs guides only for larger images (a 2x3 grid).

Designers often rely on simple grids and work creatively within them. As a magazine's design becomes more sophisticated, however, some designers build complicated grids with many units—sometimes even units that allow elements to overlap. The rule of thumb is that text-dominated layouts require simpler grids; as more illustrations are added, the grid may become more complex.

right In this *HOW* layout, text is present in all three columns, but one illustration stretches across the upper third of the page and another juts into two columns at the bottom. Note how the image borders coincide with the text borders to reveal the grid outline.

DESIGNDISCIPLINES

This graphic ran as a stand-alone visual story in *Success* magazine. "Since I knew there would be color pictures elsewhere on the page, I kept my palette to a minimum," Holmes explains.

ESTIMATED NUMBER OF AMERICANS INFECTED WITH HEAD LICE

1995 — 9 million
1996 — 10 million
1997 — 12 million

REASONS FOR INCREASE

"An information designer should have an interest in and a tolerance for complexity, an interest in traditional graphic design, a tolerance for technology and systems, and should derive satisfaction from creating systems," Marcus says. His team members have diverse backgrounds, including programming, math and graphic design.

To sell yourself as an information designer—on a freelance basis or in a job interview—you'll have to show more than traditional design work. "It would be helpful to see examples of work that deals with the design of tables, charts, maps and diagrams," Marcus says, "and

of projects that are of a systematic nature, not just a one-shot image." He also looks for projects that emphasize navigation and typography.

Lenk often hires recent RISD grads who have interned at his firm. "We're looking for students who have a good grasp of knowledge, who have a very good liberal-arts education," he says. "We look for people who know how to link facts—how to link a timeline with a map, for example. This is much more important than the ability to visualize."

Some design educators agree with this philosophy. "Design, as we're seeing it, is the intersection of a lot of other

disciplines," says Robert O. Swinehart, professor of design at Carnegie Mellon University's School of Design in Pittsburgh. Carnegie Mellon offers a highly respected design program that emphasizes typography, information design and liberal arts. To educate a more well-rounded designer, the school has shifted its program from one where students take 80% of their classes in the School of Design, to only 62%. The rest of the classes are electives taught throughout the university.

SHOWING YOUR STUFF

If you're past the point of returning to school and have a portfolio filled with traditional design, you can still remake yourself as an information designer. "There's a lot of room in the field," Holmes says. "But the best work comes from dedication. When I worked at *Time* we saw 20 or 30 portfolios a week, and I always thought if I had one simple piece of criticism it was, 'I can't see what it is you want to do.'

"It's easy enough to give yourself assignments," Holmes advises, "Just pick up your local newspaper and look at how they've dealt with some kind of information graphic or map and say, 'Well, I live in this area. What do I really want to know about this map?'"

For example, if a new road is being built, you should ask yourself who will be affected by the construction, what

"This was a perfect chance to take some of the onus of explanation away from the written article and put it into graphic form, with captions written by me as part of the finished piece," Holmes says of the graphic he designed for *Discover Magazine* explaining the life cycle of the lancet fluke. "Much more than half the total time spent on a job like this is taken up by research—the illustration itself is deliberately simple," he says.

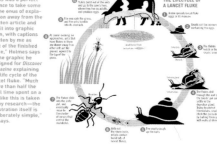

THE LIFECYCLE OF A LANCET FLUKE

42▶

Code

The Style Magazine for Men of Color

Publishing gender-specific fashion titles is a tough business. Some magazines aim to be so general that they water down topics to appeal to as many people as possible. Others wink and nudge with inside jokes that a few people get and other readers dream about someday understanding.

Code strives to change all that. The Los Angeles-based fashion magazine for African American men hit the news-stands in July 1999 and, after a year of tweaking, emerged with a smart, refreshing attitude reflected in its stylish photography and accessible layout.

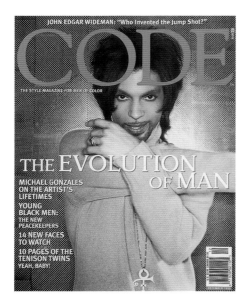
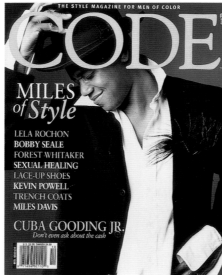

far left *Code*'s designers present photographic sub-jects—even international celebrities—at the reader's level. Here, a black-and-white photo of pop star Prince makes an unimposing, alluring cover. The orange logo is a bold foil to the sensual portrait.

left Decked to the nines, Cuba Gooding Jr. strikes a pose on the October 1999 cover, an image of color and movement meant to draw eyes at the newsstand.

WHY IT WORKS:

Handsome, atmospheric photography and a luxurious color palette combine for a sophisticated, masculine tone. Clean layout, consistent type usage, and realistic subjects in photographs appeal to readers' style and self-image.

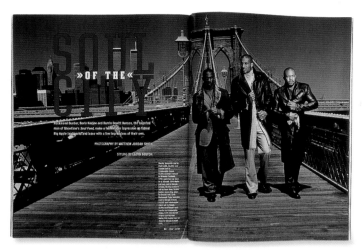

left Often reserving black-and-white photography for serious pieces, designers take a stab at it in a fashion spread. Sepia duotones portray vintage New York as costars of a Showtime drama stroll the Big Apple.

So far, the magazine has reached its target market; 90 percent of readers are African American males, while the remaining 10 percent are Asian and Hispanic men, Robinson says. The magazine is primarily about fashion, though it also covers lifestyle and celebrities, so editors and designers drew from a variety of magazine types—giving nods to titles such as *Nylon, Gear, Interview, Vibe, Elle,* and *Italian GQ* in its design.

Code reaches out editorially to establish a voice with which readers can identify. Realizing that readers appreciate illustrations that mirror their lives, the magazine's designers likewise reach out. Instead of offering traditional haute couture and lofty models, *Code* brings fashion back down to earth.

Smart and Real

Editor in chief Eugene Robinson says the magazine's founding staff strove to create a magazine for a new generation of readers. "As a medium, magazines are dealing with issues that never came up before," Robinson says. "You've got the Web, e-books. It's not the same to do magazines like the ones we dug in our youth."

Editors created a magazine that talked up to its readers, but in a way that was franker and hipper than competing titles. "We presume readers are as smart as we are," he says. "We wanted to make it smart, smart-assed, and funny without resorting to fraternity guffaws or drawing-room chuckles."

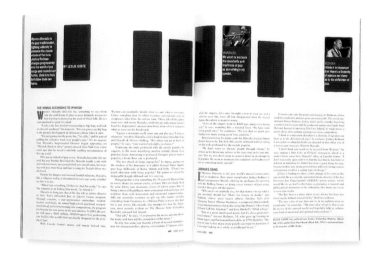

above Hip, jazzy touches, such as these blue boxes floating like musical notes across the top of an article on musicians Wynton Marsalis and Joshua Redman, stand out from the magazine's clean layout.

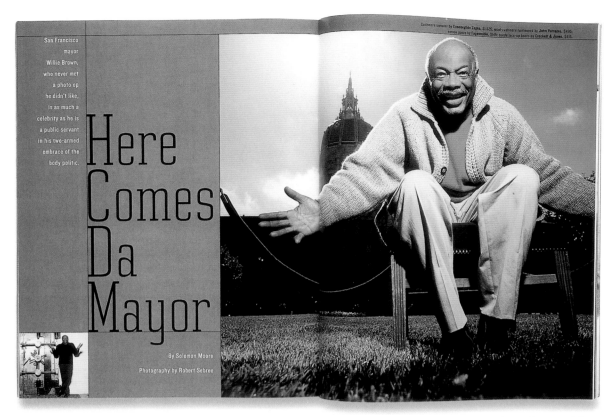

San Francisco mayor Willie Brown, who never met a photo op he didn't like, is as much a celebrity as he is a public servant in his two-armed embrace of the body politic.

Here Comes Da Mayor

By Solomon Moore

Photography by Robert Sebree

Cashmere sweater by Ermenegildo Zegna, $1,525; wool-cashmere turtleneck by John Varvatos, $495; cotton pants by Faconnable, $145; suede lace-up boots by Crockett & Jones, $415.

above Controversial San Francisco mayor Willie Brown is the charismatic subject of this bright and playful fashion layout.

Real Men, Realistic Photos

Photography is obviously the magazine's biggest concentration because of its emphasis on fashion. *Code* raised the bar as it progressed, committing itself to photography at the level of top fashion magazines, says creative director Charles Hess. Four to five photo shoots a month with celebrities and models produce strong, striking images that dominate the book. Designers place importance on working with talented, well-known photographers and illustrators and try to emphasize artists of color.

But recently, the nature of the photography has changed. "The models are depicted as guys the audience can relate to," says Hess. "When readers look at the magazine, they see themselves." This involves not only using more natural light and realistic environments in shoots but also varying the types of models.

For example, a fashion spread in the December 2000 featured six "real working political men" sporting designer suits and posing on the Mall in Washington, D.C. "They were still good-looking, but they're more relatable than models," Hess says.

The magazine also likes to feature celebrities—actors, musicians, politicians, and designers—modeling clothing as well as providing interviews and profiles. On the covers and inside the magazine, these stars have fun with the shoots. They laugh, dance, and strike poses in the gorgeous but practical fashions they model. Even the most elusive or imposing public figures look like friendly, ordinary guys—musician Prince shyly smiling in a baby-soft turtleneck, San Francisco mayor Willie Brown grinning with arms outstretched and wearing a comfortable sweater.

right Fashion shoots take chances with experimental staging. The complexity of featured plaid fabrics is replicated in this photo, with frosted panels creating the same illusion of overlapping layers.

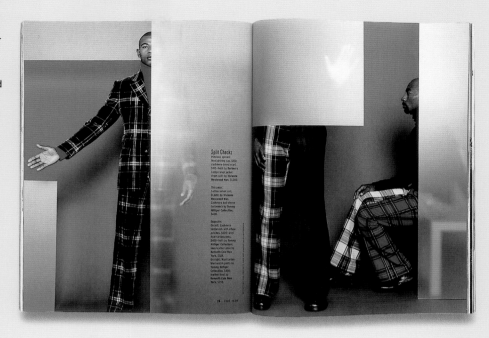

left To stand out from the competition, designers photographed up-and-coming political figures rather than models on the Mall in Washington, D.C. Midnight blue page color suits the nighttime atmosphere.

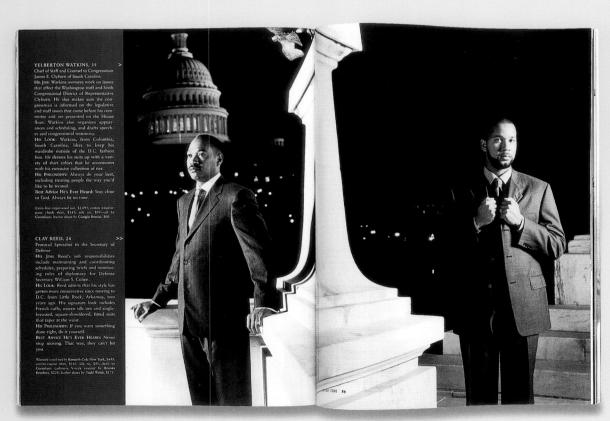

Code of Handsome Colors

An occasional excursion into black-and-white photography gives the magazine a dramatic flair. Sometimes this is reserved for investigative, serious pieces; other times it's an artistic twist on the fashion shoot. Black-and-white portraits even show up on *Code*'s cover on occasion.

An expansive palette of fourteen to sixteen colors sets the tone for the magazine no matter what shades the artwork represents. "The palette is made up of the colors of jewels—deep, rich, and masculine," says Hess. Burgundy red, pumpkin, midnight blue, and deep violet may enhance photographs as beautiful, sophisticated background colors for articles and sidebars.

Light touches of color help department headers stand out in the front and back of the book and make pull quotes diverge gently from the black-and-white formula. But, for the most part, the magazine sticks to simple black type on white pages, especially in departments. "We are trying to establish a recognizable, consistent look with enough variation so that it's not boring," Hess says.

below In an unusually colorful layout, several of the colors from the magazine's palette team up for a commentary on television, specifically MTV.

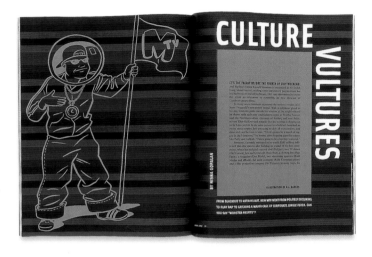

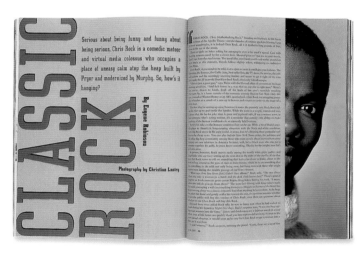

above Though used sparingly, color sets the mood for certain features. A rich pumpkin yellow with burnt orange accents—cheerful but commanding colors—opens an article about the sophisticated comedy of Chris Rock.

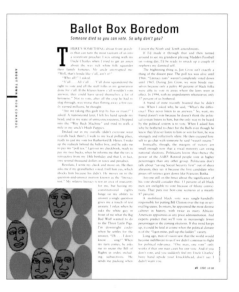

above Front-of-the-book departments usually maintain a consistent format: one piece of artwork and two columns of black type on a white background. However, varying the art placement, as with this lower-corner bleed, keeps readers guessing.

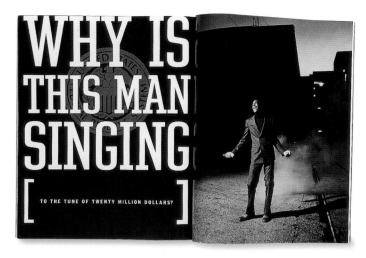

Stylish, Classic Type and Graphics

In that vein, Hess and art director Saralynne Lowrey use a handful of characteristic typefaces to build the magazine's hip personality. The newsprint-style slab-serif Constructa and a sans serif with quirky curves called Solex compete for headlines, decks, drop caps, and pull quotes. Sabon serves as easy-to-read body text; it is less fussy than faces previously used, say Hess and Lowrey.

Another technique meant to give the magazine its distinctive look involves using rules, especially in the back of the book. End departments are given bold, black vertical rules dividing a wide left margin from the left of the page.

In the margin toward the bottom of the page is the article's headline and deck, while at the top is a listing of the back's standard departments. For the article that

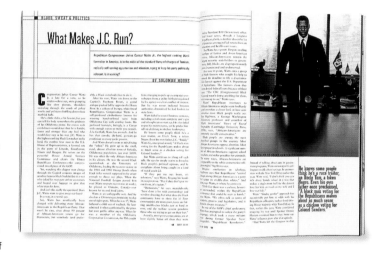

represents a given department, the department name is called out on the other side of the rule. "It's like a mini-table of contents for the back of the book," says Hess. "It works like a file drawer."

Variations on the use of the rule also appear in feature stories. For example, for a themed series of articles on political figures in the November 2000 issue, elaborate maps of double lines and boxes give headlines, rules, bylines, and captions their own playing fields. The orderly lines provide an Art Deco-style ornamental framework on an otherwise simply designed page.

These snazzy but understated design touches express the magazine's commitment to laid-back style, while the surrounding simple design showcases the magazine's friendly, funny articles. Lush but consistent design plays as big a role as editorial content in talking straightforwardly to the smart, sophisticated, style-minded reader.

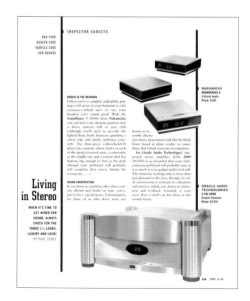

Creative Process

Asking magazine designers how they reach their final layouts is a lot like asking painters, photographers, or novelists how they conceive and produce their masterpieces. They may be able to tell you how they begin or what inspires them, but the actual mental processes involved often remain mysterious—to the artists themselves as well as to the rest of the world.

Some university design programs focus heavily on process. In the real world, however, time for such formalities is rare as designers rush to close issues against strict printer deadlines. The design process is often guided by a helpful grid or patched together miraculously by association, sudden brainstorms, and last-minute tweaking.

Here's a look at how some designers define their own processes, plus a peek inside one designer's mind as he perfects the layout of an important magazine section.

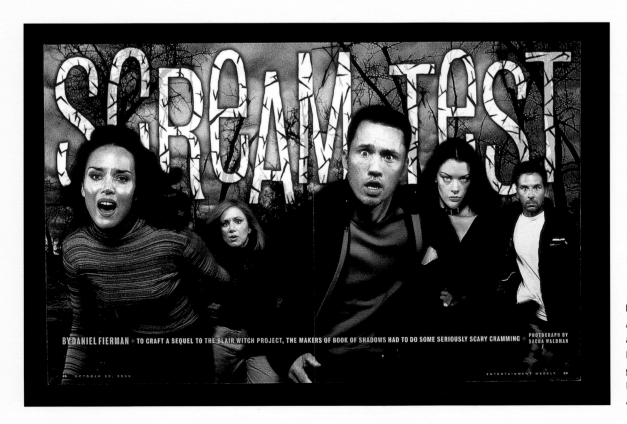

BY DANIEL FIERMAN • TO CRAFT A SEQUEL TO THE BLAIR WITCH PROJECT, THE MAKERS OF BOOK OF SHADOWS HAD TO DO SOME SERIOUSLY SCARY CRAMMING • PHOTOGRAPH BY SACHA WALDMAN

left and opposite page
At *Entertainment Weekly* and *Walking,* designers begin with the photographs or illustrations and let layouts build naturally around them.

Art Is Life

Designers usually start the page layout process with the element that most emphatically sets the tone for the magazine's personality. "Sometimes we'll start a design before the photography is in, but the design always depends on art," says Geraldine Hessler, creative director of *Entertainment Weekly*. "We make a map of the entire feature well. We may cut a page from something else if we have a good photo shoot. We allow ourselves a lot of leeway to play up good art."

An *Entertainment Weekly* layout is "reactionary," Hessler says. "We work with the editors to come up with a headline that works with the art and story." Then designers alter the type to further illustrate the topic or concept. "It's almost like geometry," Hessler says. "There is a certain set of givens, and we have to work with them."

Walking art director Lisa Sergi likewise always waits for an issue's commissioned photographs and illustrations to come in before beginning her work. As for the *Walking* designers, artwork inspires the graphics, headline fonts, layout, and colors that Sergi chooses. From there, she simply launches into a design with a natural feeling of balance and flow.

"It's instinctive," she says. "I just go with what feels right and makes sense. I don't make a huge effort to go through a formal design and review process, though I'll do printouts and look at them to make sure they look the same on paper as on the screen. But I usually go with my gut feeling, trying to put the strong stuff up front and put together a good mix of text-heavy features and sidebars."

DINNER THESE FOUR COMPLETE WEEKNIGHT DINNERS CAN BE THROWN TOGETHER WHEN YOU GET HOME FROM WORK. BY VICTORIA ABBOTT RICCARDI

PHOTOGRAPHY BY LAURA JOHANSEN

PASTA & GARLIC

Believe me, I know how it is: After a hard day of battles, we all want to sit down to a good dinner, one that incorporates today's flavorful, healthful, and exotic ingredients (not to mention a glass of wine or two). That simple pleasure should be our reward for schlepping the kids and enduring downed servers and rush-hour traffic.

But is it doable? If you read WALKING it is. Starting this issue, we've reshaped our food section to make it possible for you to make quick, easy, and affordable weeknight dinners. These are earthy, elegant meals that you can toss together at the last minute, often without even stopping at the store. In each issue we'll present a "dinner package," focusing on a particular food item and building a dinner around it. Next issue, for example, we've got weeknight recipes based on leftover holiday ham and turkey.

Besides main dish recipes, our unique dinner package features complementary side dishes, prep and cooking tips from both Victoria Abbott Riccardi (in the recipes) and Cynthia Salvato (in the new feature Test Kitchen Confidential), nutritional analysis, cost of each meal (something no food magazine does, and who doesn't want to know?), and wine recommendations—worry not, no brand-name wine talk, just a generic, what-best-suits-the-occasion suggestion.

Although we're not talking complicated Saturday night or holiday meals here, each one is a celebration. Monday through Friday we all deserve to sit down and unwind over a great meal. Right, fellow gladiators?

—*John Stark, deputy editor*

SEPTEMBER/OCTOBER 2000 • THE WALKING MAGAZINE   95

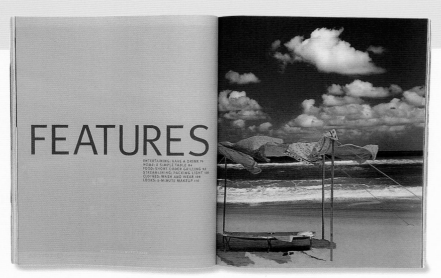

left *Real Simple* layouts spend time pinned on a wall so artists and editors can judge them and make changes.

below When artists share in the editing process, inspired layout concepts emerge. In this layout in *Surface*, designers noticed that several featured products—sofas and benches—had to do with the idea of community, so they grouped the images to complete the theme.

Review and Revision

From the initial concepts onward, all designers have a distinctly personal process for perfecting their final versions. Always perfectionists, some tweak colors, shift text boxes, and add and delete rules in the original computer file right up to the final deadline. Others save versions of files as they make changes, then compare them before submitting the final layout. The image of how the layout should look resides almost exclusively in the designers' heads, and they constantly push themselves until they're satisfied or, more likely, run out of time.

Some designers follow a process that is a bit more formal. *Context* design director Mark Maltais, for example, allows enough time for several revisions of illustrations so art will perfectly complement layouts. "I get tons of sketches from artists," he says. "We go through three to five rounds, from thumbnails to rough sketches." He then begins laying out the story with the sketches in mind to make sure everything works together.

The review process is more democratic at *Real Simple*. "We start by pinning ideas up on the wall and choosing the one we like best," says creative director Roland Bello. Then designers route the initial layout through several stages of approval, from artists to editors. "We might change it three times from the initial layout,"

Bello says. "If we come up with a brilliant idea several steps into the process, we can still implement it."

At *Surface*, the first design review actually takes the form of editing. "Designers help in the editing process," says Riley John-donnell, one of the magazine's publishers and the creative director. "By reviewing the stories and products, we notice design trends before the editor does. Then we use those trends to create a visual dialog" by designing layouts that relate similar concepts.

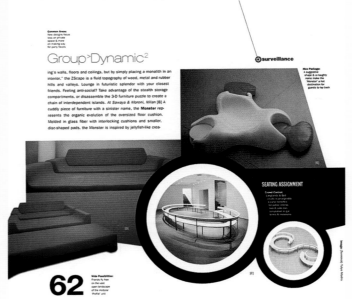

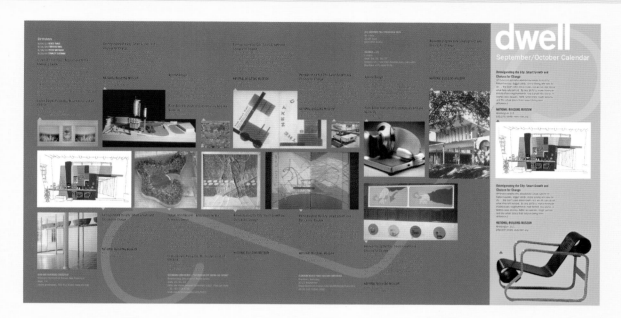

First Draft, Final Draft

Shawn Hazen, senior designer for the San Francisco-based startup magazine *Dwell,* was close enough to the magazine's conception that he could document his design process. Specifically, he recalls how he came to the final version of the magazine's events calendar, a pull-out gatefold piece printed on uncoated stock.

"This format was developed to be a unique addition to the publication and also to have a distinctly different feel than the rest of the book," Hazen says. "The resulting size also makes a more interesting poster than a spread-sized sheet." The idea was that readers could pull it out and pin it on their walls as a reminder of everything going on in the design community.

Editors and designers wanted to make the calendar an important part of the magazine's brand. "Karrie Jacobs, the editor in chief, felt strongly that it should feel like controlled chaos," Hazen says. "I was told to make it a sort of random-access soup. Everyone felt it should be dynamic and kind of crazy."

It took Hazen three issues before he perfected the calendar. "The initial problem to overcome was how to achieve a wild layout that, inherently, is opposed to the modernist tenets upon which we were building the look of the rest of the magazine," he says. Hazen explains the five phases of the project in his own words.

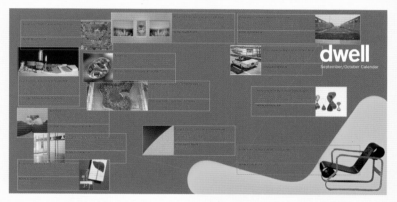

First Sketches

above "I tried a number of things initially—arraying the images in a sort of spine across the page for a horizontal layout or down the page for a vertical layout. Then all the information would bounce up and down or side to side on top of varying images. I also put some saturated colors in the background; color was becoming increasingly important to the magazine. Another early design involved making each entry its own unit, in a box, so each item was clean on its own, but they overlapped each other all over the page. After some quick reviews, both these ideas proved to be too clean—not chaotic enough."

Rethinking the First Sketches

right "I spent time rethinking how I could create a system that, when strictly adhered to, would create interesting relationships on the page. I decided to exploit the strongest design system there is: the grid. I gave each of the six types of entries we were featuring a grid. At this point, the question of what orientation the calendar should have popped up again. Should it be readable horizontally while still in the magazine or oriented vertically for hanging as a tall poster? I decided the type could run both ways. My grids could create interesting horizontal-vertical relationships. This would also limit the number of grids I'd need to use for both the horizontal and vertical orientation. It would look chaotic, but each type of information would have its own system or set of rules that would be consistent. The resulting grid system was cool, kind of a weird plaid when all the different column widths were overlaid."

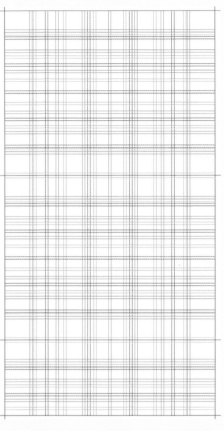

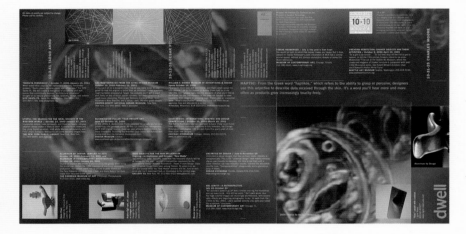

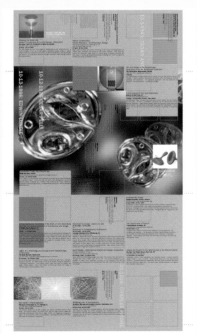

New Sketches

above and left "The next set of sketches followed my plan. Of course, I could take liberties here and there with regard to placement within the grid, but I allowed the intersecting grids to do most of the work. I felt I really had to show the grid selectively in order to visually explain the system—control the chaos visually. The images could fit on any of the same grids as well, and I decided, at this point, to choose just a few illustrations, as the page was becoming dense and active. After review, we realized this was heading in the right direction. I started to think that the feedback about the design being too clean might be due to the strong, solid colors I used in the background. So, in a late-night flurry of designing, I picked out a couple of my favorite images and tossed them in the background as duotones to give a more even, lower-contrast surface for the type. That created a wildly more dynamic page. I developed a subtler way of hinting at the grid—little hash marks, which had a nice architectural feel. And the four-color chunks of the background image that showed through revealed the grid and created an interesting, abstract compositional element."

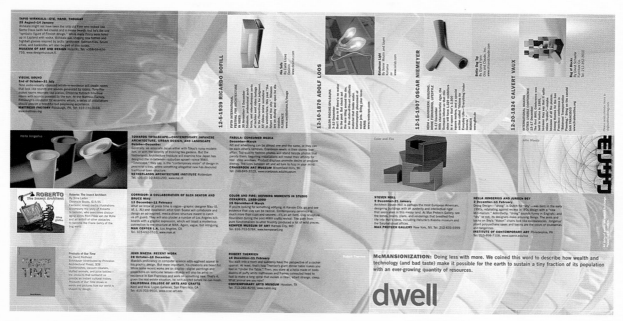

Production Adjustments

above "After the production manager got back from a tough time on press with the calendar for *Dwell*'s first issue, I decided to lighten up on the color scheme so the type could all overprint in 100 percent black or cyan, or at least builds of solid colors like red. The backgrounds would also be easier to control. I also got rid of the four-color portion of the background picture so that I could have more fun with the revealing and concealing of that background image, yet still put type on those areas."

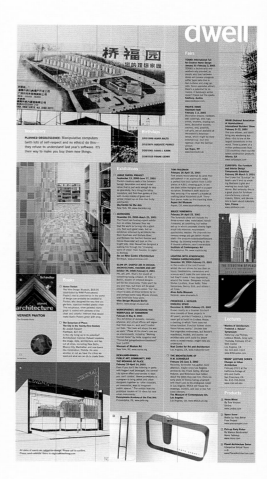

Further Refinement

right "Though we agreed it was 'mission accomplished' with the controlled chaos concept, it seemed we might be making it a little too hard to figure out what was what. I also wasn't convinced that the calendar was working as a poster. The second issue's calendar looked pretty neat when you unfurled it in the magazine, but was anyone really pulling them out? I was already far along with the third one, done in the manner of the previous two, when these realizations came to light. To further encourage their use as posters, I made one that ran all vertically. Thus, I could also clarify the information, more or less keeping each category together. I retained and perhaps strengthened the multiple grid concept by giving each category one or the other of the grids and a binding box of corresponding width, but this time I let both grids show in hairline over all the images. The images also strictly adhered to the grid. The two grids have infinite combinations, so the result still appears loose and organic—but not totally chaotic."

Ideas for Serenity at Home

How many adult women have not lingered enviously—or resentfully—over the grandeur of a room featured in *Town & Country* or *Elle Decor,* or been irked by the resourceful, painstaking creativity of the Martha Stewart franchise? "Sure her house looks like that, and of course she has time to make her own grapevine wreaths, wine, or jewelry," readers may sputter. "She has money, servants, time!"

Real Simple was launched as the answer to magazine consumers' frustrations. A primer on life's practical mysteries—how to buy tools or jewelry boxes, which pants are in style this season, how to put together the perfect barbecue menu—the magazine strives for uncluttered elegance while remaining realistic.

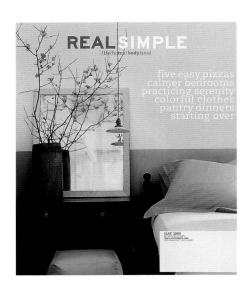

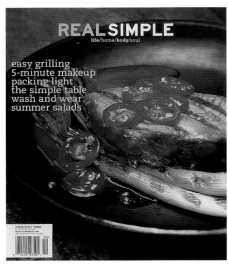

far left Natural, neutral colors with touches of light pink and orange welcome the spring on *Real Simple*'s May 2000 cover. Unlike the home decor and women's magazines saturated with color, minimalist color pops from pale backgrounds.

left Rich, robust colors saturate the front of the June/July issue, whose savory food photography reflects the grilling season. Colors are still subdued compared to the hot pinks and other brights on the newsstand.

WHY IT WORKS:

Generous white space, clean lines, and natural colors fall gently into place on pages, creating an oasis of organization, while photography keeps the magazine sympathetic and true to life.

right One of the magazine's specialties is sorting products into categories to help busy women figure out what they really need. Photographs illustrate each entry, as in this rundown of cosmetic brushes and applicators.

systems

the basics

Your only dilemma: whether to use a brush or a sponge-tip applicator for your eye shadow

[1] POWDER
Nothing makes you feel more like a makeup artist than a fluffy powder brush. For a professional dusting, choose one that's full, slightly flat, and rounded at the top. Shu Uemura Powder Brush #27, $55, 888-540-8181.

[2] FOUNDATION
A flat, firm brush makes getting liquid or cream foundation into hard-to-reach places—like the corners of your eyes—a cinch. Smaller-size brushes can be used for applying concealer too. Trish McEvoy Brush #43, $25, 800-431-4306.

[3] BLUSH
Aim for a medium-full brush (one that's smaller than a powder brush but not quite as fluffy). If the head is the size of the apple of your cheek, you'll never have to worry about applying too much or too little at a time. M.A.C Brush #116, $29, 800-387-6707.

[4] EYE SHADOW
Some people like a small, flat brush (right); others prefer a sponge-tip applicator (below). Both accomplish the same task equally well: blending shadow across the lids. Your pick: Stila Brush #5, $22, 800-883-0400, and Face Stockholm #23, $5, 888-334-3223.

[5] LIP
Tracing a dark shade onto your lips requires precision. A stiff, tapered brush keeps the color where you want it. Bobbi Brown Essentials Lip Brush, $18.50, www.bobbibrowncosmetics.com.

52

Accommodating Chaos

The title from Time Inc., which debuted in April 2000, received a great deal of attention by the media as it struggled to hone its original mission as "a guide to help people simplify their lives," says Roland Bello, the magazine's creative director.

Readers are mostly college educated, affluent, professional women in their 30s and 40s. About 68 percent are married and 62 percent have kids. Whether single or married, they live hectic lives but still want to relax in comfortable, stylish homes, Bello says. Editorially, the magazine offers blurbs about how readers can find easy but graceful solutions to common challenges, including contributions from other readers about their own time-tested tricks.

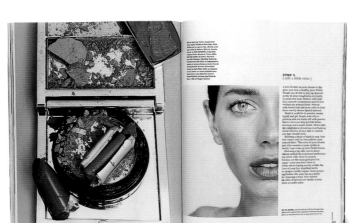

But though it made a splash on the newsstand, the initial format of the magazine didn't quite click with readers. "The idea of simplification was a difficult concept to bring to the mainstream," Bello says. Early criticism was that the magazine was too unrealistic—that there was no such thing as true simplicity. As *Real Simple* evolved with subsequent issues, articles became more comprehensive and substantial.

The magazine's design had to be tweaked along with the editorial concept. "It was too clean to get across the chaos of real life," Bello says. "We wanted to work in more humanity while retaining the integrity of the original idea."

left Amid the magazine's spare and orderly pages are hints of colorful chaos. In this primer on cosmetics, crumpled blush and lipstick smudge an otherwise serene layout.

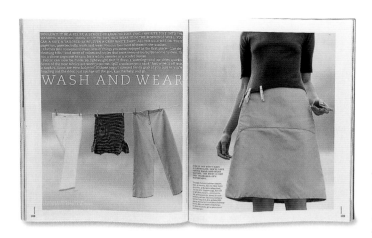

Making Negative a Positive

Simplicity still had to be a major design theme, as it was what the magazine was all about. The challenge, therefore, was to define the difference between simplicity and minimalism. The magazine needed to be straightforward and sophisticated, but not barren or aloof.

White space is one of *Real Simple's* most important tools. "It's such an essential element for communicating the clean and simple factor," Bello says. "More negative space makes type and photos much stronger."

White space doesn't graze freely on pages but rather appears in wide buffers between text and photographs to accentuate each point and picture with poise. Margin size varies between columns of text, surrounding photos, and at the edges of pages. Column alignment, size, and placement are also flexible, so a column may start partway down a page or end partway up it. In the front of the book, which regularly includes features on how to buy tools or appliances, photos of products are crisply outlined against a pristine white background. The spacious pages help the most frenzied reader breathe more easily and begin to sort through the complexities of her life.

Because articles in the magazine thrive on short tips and blurbs to simplify information, all that white obviously doesn't serve the purpose of differentiating text. *Real Simple's* sidebars are often entire corners of pages or floating, borderless boxes filled with subtle beiges and blues. Text sits flush against the left edge of these boxes, which sometimes extend to the edge of the page, leaving a great deal of open space that calls attention to the text at its left.

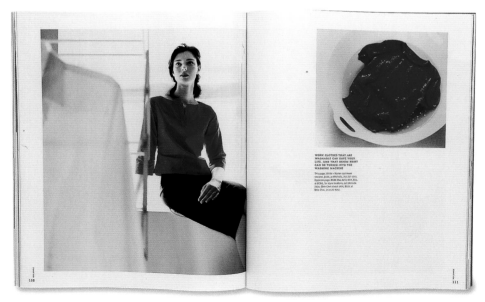

above and left A June fashion article on wash-and-wear clothing is as light as the breeze that dries the featured duds. The wispy blue backdrop and soft lines of fabric, the playful clothespins on the sweater, express the casual nature of the clothing. In startling contrast, an empty white page and a shock of red blouses on the following spread represent the tension of professional life.

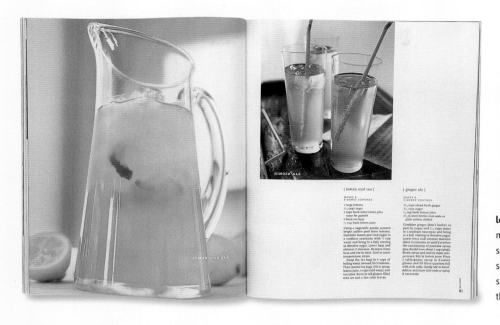

left The pale, complementary shades of these summer drinks and the surrounding negative space team up for a subtle, refreshing layout.

right Shadows speak louder than words in this play on the contrast between light and dark.

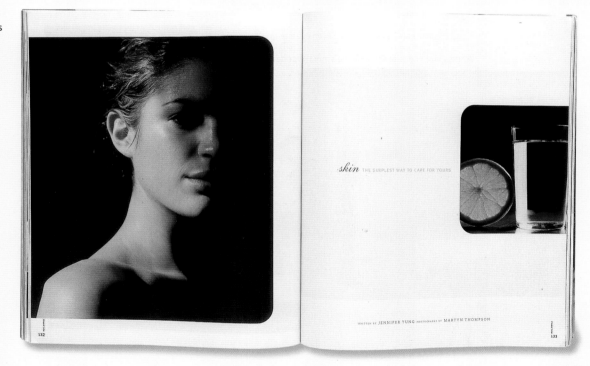

Designing for Success

Q&A with Samir Husni

Dr. Samir Husni has seen his share of magazines come and go. A journalism professor at the University of Mississippi who's commonly known as Mr. Magazine, Husni publishes annual reports tracking the success of new magazines and speaks to hundreds of reporters each year regarding magazines' positions in the market.

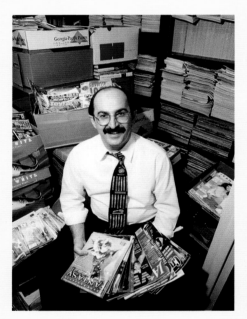

Q: The role of design in magazine publishing has changed a great deal over the years, from a secondary consideration in many categories to top priority for most publications. How has this evolution been influenced by increasing competition on the newsstand?

A: We are a visual society. Everything—not just magazines—is driven by visuals. The magazine industry is no exception. Magazine design has always been one of the major determinants of success of any magazine. However, design, like the magazine cover, helps sell the magazine once; the content is what will help sell it a second time. In a time where potential readers are not willing to give more than two and a half seconds to decide whether to pick up your magazine or move to the next one, design is essential in grabbing the attention of the readers. It must jump at you. That is the main reason why magazine publishers pay so much attention to the design of their books. It is the icing on the cake, and if you have good cake, you better spend some time on the icing so it will be picked up. However, I am quick to add that good design with a bad cake will take you nowhere. You will be able to cheat readers once with design, but that will be the end. Remember, the cardinal rule in magazine design should be "We always sacrifice design on the altar of content." Readers will always forgive a flaw in the design; they will not in content. There are too many options out there.

Q: How quickly must a new magazine's personality make an impression in order to hook and keep a new reader? Does the cover have to say it all, or is the reader searching for something more subtle inside?

A: The cover is the starting point. People buy magazines based on a concept I call the Four Me's: See Me, Pick Me, Flip Me, and Buy Me. Therefore, the visuals on the cover are essential. That is what the reader sees first: the image. They will recognize it more than the name of the magazine, especially if the magazine is new. The image should directly lead them to the main cover lines, or what I like to call sell lines. The cover lines are the pick-me-up lines. This is what makes the reader reach to the stands and pick up a magazine. Next comes the table of contents to reflect the cover and its lines. From there, the reader will flip through the pages to make sure what was promised on the cover and the table of contents is actually there. Then a decision is made to buy or return. It is no longer one thing that sells the magazine. Readers are becoming more and more aware of all the gimmicks, and they can cut to the chase and know what to pick. New magazines must offer a complete package.

Q: How large a role does a brand-new magazine's design play in its survival?

A: Because of the number of new magazines being published each year, design plays a major role in getting your magazine noticed. In all my studies about magazine survival, design was always on the list of the major determinants of success; however, it was always on the bottom of the list. As I mentioned earlier, design is the icing on the cake, and there are plenty of cakes with no icing.

Q: Can you think of an example of a magazine that made it largely because of the way it was designed? How about a magazine that failed because of the way it looked?

A: I wish I could. I do not believe any magazine can survive solely or even largely because of design; neither will it fail because of that.

Q: The early 1990s saw an influx of new magazines in which design was the format—frenetic and somewhat illegible though it may have been. What sparked that trend, and do you think it has been tamed?

A: As with all fads, their time will come and go. Magazines designed for the sake of being hung on the wall at museums will sooner or later lose their audience and fade away. Any magazine that you cannot read is anything but a magazine. So, if you want to produce something that is illegible, just do one copy and hang it at a museum for people to look in awe at your artistic abilities. I firmly believe that some of the best designers are those who help the reader gain more information in less time utilizing less space.

Q: How much tweaking is acceptable with a new publication's design in its first year? How do readers respond to such changes?

A: Change is the only concept in magazine design and magazine publishing. You can—and should—tweak your design all the time. We tend to give readers too much credit when it comes to matters of design, while in reality they are interested in the content of the magazine. Delivering the information in a timely manner for an audience who is willing and capable of paying the price of the magazine is the secret of success. Stop worrying about the design and focus on the content. To paraphrase a presidential slogan, "It's the content, stupid."

High-Energy Sports and Culture

Teenagers—the demographic marketers are trying to tag as Generation Y—are the last untapped consumers, and, these days, plenty of industries are going after the money they earn scooping fries after school. Manufacturers romanticize everything from cell phones and pagers to PCs and CDs to the under-20 population.

There's always been a strong magazine market for the younger set—*Seventeen*-inspired fashion titles for girls, guitar and skateboarding magazines for boys. But one category aimed at this age group takes itself much more seriously. A hard-core subculture with its own international superstars, language, and gear, surfing feeds largely off kids, mostly high school-age boys. Among the titles competing for these die-hards' attention, *TransWorld Surf* stands out for its superior, edgy design.

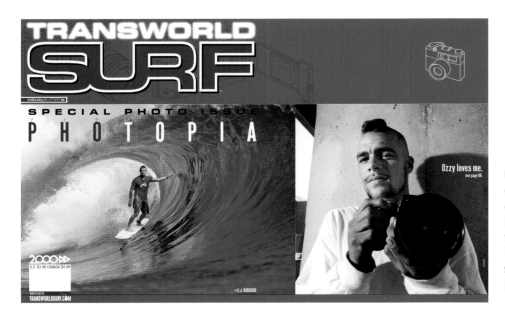

left The October 2000 cover, as usual, featured an action shot surrounded by the vivid border for which *TransWorld Surf* is known. Every cover is a gatefold; here, a surf photographer gears up.

WHY IT WORKS:

Spectacular, fast-action photography and loud backgrounds fuel the magazine's throbbing pulse, while a calculated use of color and type capture the attention of readers whose minds are always trying to tackle the next wave.

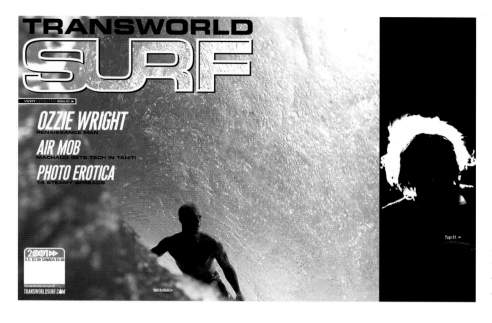

Hooking Young Readers with Attitude

TransWorld Media, the magazine's publisher, has long been known for its design excellence and experimentation—experimental graphic designer David Carson headed up the design for *TransWorld Skateboarding* in the 1990s, for instance.

In the surf magazine's case, the focus on good design was largely competitive. "The design is key in the sense that it's one of the few vehicles we can utilize to visibly differentiate from other magazines," says art director Marc Hostetter. "Like us, our competitors have always and probably will always have great photography. The key to success here is in innovative delivery and design."

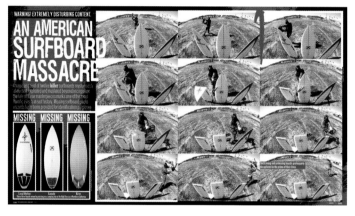

Though *TransWorld Surf* attempts to be sensitive to a broad audience, Hostetter says the magazine's audience is primarily young males, on average around fifteen years old. Readers crave everything they can get about surfing, but they're also immersed in the offbeat culture that goes along with the sport.

So profiles and interviews are heavy with slang, attitude, and prankster features such as "Crank Call"—transcripts of actual prank phone calls to surfers. "Without being too offensive, we try to break as many rules as possible," Hostetter says.

Articles include fashion features, travelogs, contest coverage, and technique, but much of the magazine is about surfing itself. Articles pay tribute to surf professionals known well in the community—high school kids with nicknames like Ratboy—and moves that make readers gasp with envy and respect.

above Repetitive scenes, like in a convenience store security camera, show surfboards being "grotesquely decapitated" for the hilarious treatment of a surfboard product review.

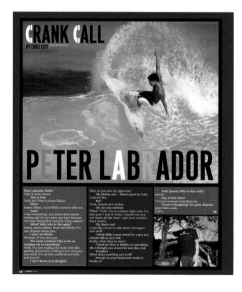

right "Crank Call" is a spoof that prints real transcripts from prank phone calls the editors make to surfers. While Hostetter uses two or three typefaces consistently, different colors make the type visually stimulating.

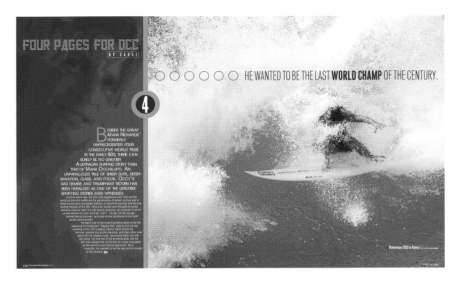

left A silhouette of comeback surfer Mark Occhilupo opens another photo-dominated spread. In this layout, a pull quote skids across the foam in the photo.

below The table of contents is literally a splash page—an exhilarating opening that foreshadows the rest of the issue.

The Rich Blues of Surf Photography

Capturing these moves with photography is the staple of a surf magazine, Hostetter explains. *TransWorld Surf* gives center stage to gorgeous freeze-frame shots of surfers turning, sliding, and punting. High-speed film drinks in every droplet of the spray, every muscle and pose of the boy on the board. Images are examples of masterful, technically perfect photography and surfing at the same time.

"It's definitely meant to inspire, instruct, and, more importantly, entertain," Hostetter says. "*TransWorld Surf*

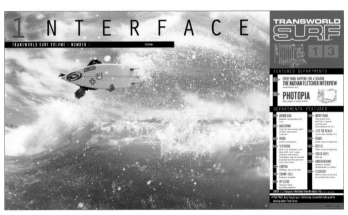

is going to showcase the moves and surfers of the future, not the beauty and purism of the sport. I like to use the analogy that other surf magazines resemble museums and ours is more like a video game."

The magazine makes it a policy not to run a surf photo smaller than one-sixth of a page. Often, main features are made up of several spread photographs or facing full-page photos with small blocks of text. Others include pages divided evenly into repetitive or progressive photos for instruction or effect.

While not all photography is breaking the waves—funny or soulful takes often find their way into fashion spreads and feature profiles—there's so much exotic blue and perfect white foam between articles and ads that, by the end of the book, readers feel exhilarated, if not a little soggy.

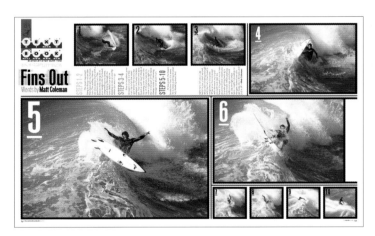

above In addition to entertaining, the magazine aims to teach readers who want to learn from their heroes. The "Textbook" section provides play-by-play explanations of a surfer's technique, with varied proportions for visual effect.

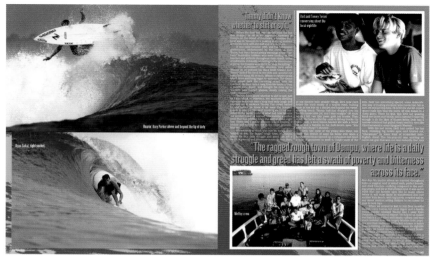

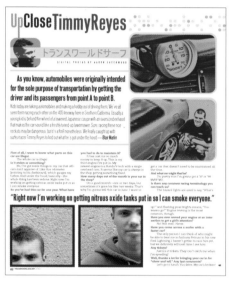

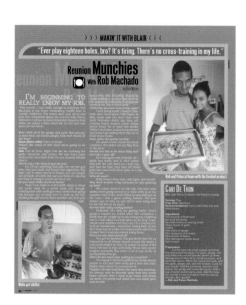

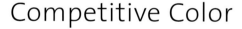

Competitive Color

That's why Hostetter spends so much effort on the design of the pages surrounding photos. "It's hard to be ultracreative and change on a monthly basis with seemingly monochromatic images," he says. "Everything is blue or blue-green in surf photography. Without diluting the photo's impact too much, I wanted to be creative around and at the edges and borders."

This is where color becomes part of the magazine's look and feel. Many of the pages surrounding or facing photographs are filled with background color. Rather than rely on a standard color palette, designers borrow from trendy colors in clothing, sports, gear, and other items popular among teens. The backdrop or rule around a photograph may be the same shades of orange, deep red, or wasabi green seen in swim trunks or boards featured in ads and articles.

Color plays a large role in helping *TransWorld Surf* assert its identity, says Hostetter. "Competing titles seem so married to the white-page, black-text, minimalist mentality," mostly because they're dedicated to the purity of surf photography and don't want to distract from the images, he says.

But Hostetter is careful to use color in such a way that it enhances the photography rather than distracts from it. One technique he applies is to limit contrast in background designs. He uses several shades of red or orange as a pattern or borders within borders, yet is careful not to create too much contrast behind the text so that it remains easy to read.

The effect is one to which *TransWorld Surf's* audience, overstimulated by its visual world, responds well. "It think it's important to acknowledge that kids these days pay more attention to detail and color combos," Hostetter says.

above Background designs help generate the constant buzz and activity that keep readers hooked. To facilitate legibility, Hostetter limits these images to shades only slightly different from the rest of the background color.

left Hostetter finds color and graphic inspiration in gear and clothing. Here, green and yellow merge and divide across the page. A digital dot motif and kanji-like characters—both popular symbols in youth culture—decorate the head.

far left Art director Marc Hostetter applies shades of color to borders to emphasize photos and keep younger readers stimulated. Here, rounded borders mix with right angles to bump and slide readers through the layout.

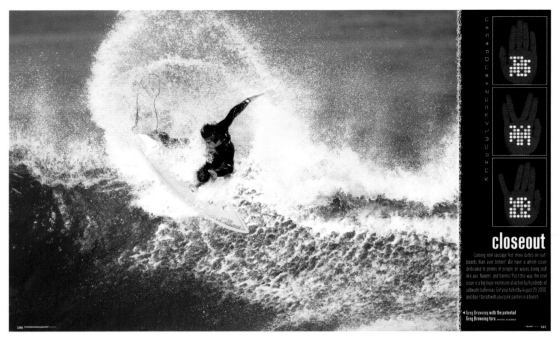

Pounding Energy and Movement

Further charging the buzz created by the magazine's content is the edge-to-edge design. Pages are busy from one end to another, without negative space or spacious margins. Because the magazine runs surf photos so large, designers often must crowd images and blocks of text together into a single layout.

Kids have a short attention span, Hostetter says, so the constant movement and energy in the pages keeps them excited. The audience's wandering minds can also be a negative factor, though; if the pages are too hard to read, the magazine will lose them.

The color combinations are Hostetter's way to create harmony within a layout, therefore making pages more accessible. "I consider each element, including text, an ingredient of a complete graphic," he says. "This method tends to look less intimidating."

Designers also stick to a few consistent typefaces: the serif Caecilia as a body font and sans serifs Optivenus and Eurostile as headlines. "I feel like continuity and simplicity with type styles maintain a critical element of control," Hostetter says. "They also strengthen the magazine's identity."

Measured but energetic design not only sets *TransWorld Surf* apart on the newsstand, it creates page-turners that glorify each incredible surf shot featured in the magazine. The high-impact but consistent and thoughtful layouts go a long way toward hooking young readers—even if they're so lost in the moves they don't realize what's going on around them.

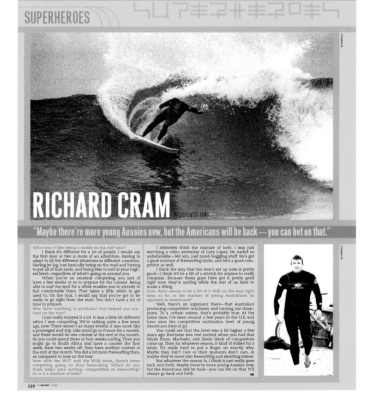

right This profile is another example of the use of bold color with sensible combinations.

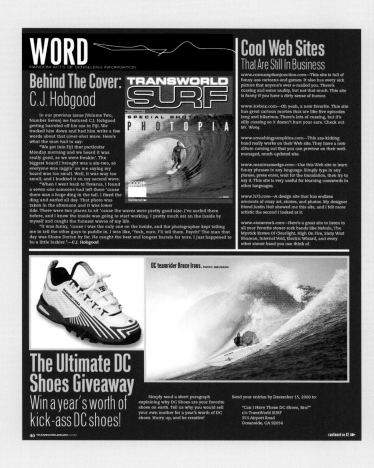

left Rules and borders separate the articles in this department. A nonsensical scribble accompanies the department head to represent the subtitle "Random Acts of Senseless Information."

right Features, such as the tongue-in-cheek "Dictionary of Medical Terminology," are built around spectacular photographic spreads. Readers buy the magazine for the surf shots but stay for the funny writing and sharp design.

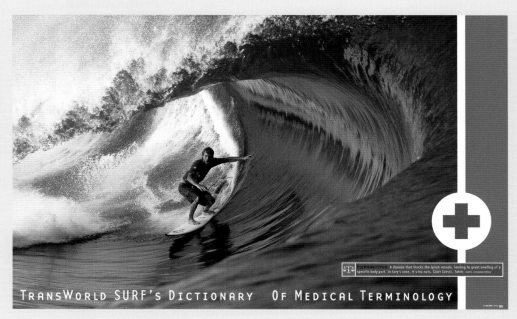

Yoga Journal

Yoga Instruction for the Body and Spirit

America has become hooked on yoga as a relaxation technique, but this centuries-old exercise is just as much about control, balance, and energy as it is about winding down. True to its subject, *Yoga Journal* combines these fundamentals to create a soothing yet fluent design.

In fact, the magazine strives for a reading experience that mirrors the topic it covers. "We want to create the feeling of walking into a yoga studio," says art director Jonathan Wieder. "The look must be one of calm and serenity, but we don't want it to be soporific. There has to be a balance between calmness and energy."

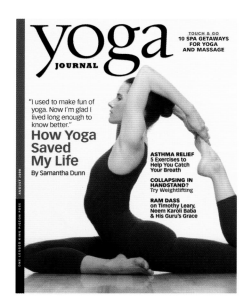

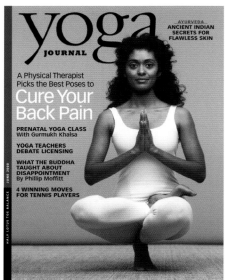

far left The human body forms elegant frames for *Yoga Journal's* covers. Among fitness magazines promising perfect bodies with blaring colors and cover lines, *Yoga Journal* maintains the serenity of its subject.

left The font used for the word *yoga* in the magazine's flag resembles the graceful curves of the body in a yoga position. The logo is a distinct part of the magazine's brand.

WHY IT WORKS:

Handsome, understated layouts and a palette of nature-inspired colors create a serene setting and build a strong, continuous flow analogous to yoga positions themselves. The artists let photographs carry the design, clearly proving their understanding of the magazine's most valuable design asset: the gorgeous human form.

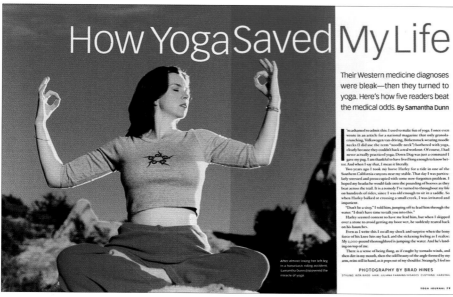

left Yoga poses are not always shown straight-forwardly. Yoga-focused features, such as this one about yoga and health, are accompanied by artistic, emotional photographs that showcase the beauty of positions.

A Yoga-Focused Magazine

the magazine's redesign had to appeal to a broad audience, attracting them to the pages with a look that was familiar, accessible, and attractive.

More people are turning to yoga as a physical exercise rather than a spiritual or meditative one, too, now that magazines and health professionals advocate it as therapy for pain, back problems, and overall flexibility and fitness. So layouts focus more on the physical act of yoga—performing and improving poses—and address their potential effects on specific physical problems. Illustrations of people in yoga poses are used in more issues-oriented articles as well as instructional ones, creating an ongoing challenge for artists to keep each page looking new and interesting.

The magazine has had quite a history. First quite literally a journal for yoga teachers and school owners, it quickly became a special-interest magazine for new-age interests, covering everything from war and poverty to life after death. Yoga itself was the main focus when the magazine started in 1975, but few people were practicing in the United States then, so it moved quickly to the back burner.

With the practice's resurgence in recent years, *Yoga Journal* needed to reinvent itself, so it relaunched in 2000 as a yoga-only magazine and let the technique regain center stage. Articles are instructional, discussing how to succeed at different poses, but also cover benefits and related topics—health, spirituality, and the like.

Who's the reader? "She's me," says editor in chief Kathryn Arnold. The magazine's readership is 80 percent female, Arnold says, and is, on average, 47 years old. Readers generally have high income levels, travel a lot, and are sophisticated, which means they have an eye for fine design.

However, readers vary widely in their connection to and familiarity with yoga. Readership is growing by leaps and bounds and ranges from long-time yoga practitioners who see it as a way of life to people who have just started taking classes at the gym. Therefore,

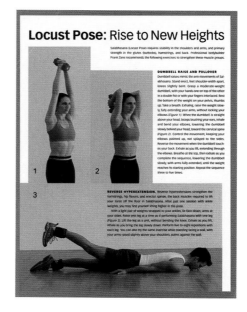

left Some departments are framed with a softly colored border, which sets them apart from other sections and gives them their own personality.

right The shapes of yoga poses dictate the flow of pages. Photographs of poses against white backgrounds divide the page into geometric negative space, a strong feature of the magazine's design.

Flow and Continuity

Luckily, the subjects of the photographs themselves are inherently diverse. The curves and angles of the body in a yoga pose make for interesting negative space, while pointing and leaning bodies give pages direction and flow. Graceful, sensual poses are balanced with ones that are more tense or strenuous, creating a natural ebb and flow. Designers let the provocative shapes alone frame the magazine's covers.

Inside, photography comes in two forms. Instructional photos must be accurate, so readers imitating the poses won't hurt themselves, says Wieder. Editors and

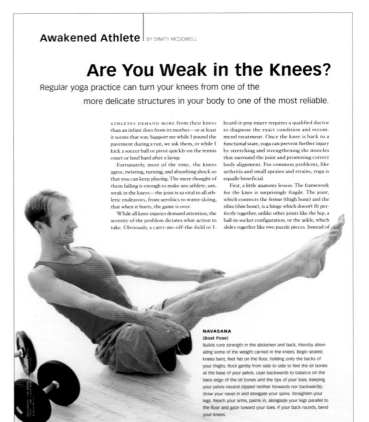

Are You Weak in the Knees?

Regular yoga practice can turn your knees from one of the more delicate structures in your body to one of the most reliable.

ATHLETES DEMAND MORE from their knees than an infant does from its mother—or at least it seems that way. Support me while I pound the pavement during a run, we ask them, or while I kick a soccer ball or pivot quickly on the tennis court or land hard after a layup.

Fortunately, most of the time, the knees agree, twisting, turning, and absorbing shock so that you can keep playing. The mere thought of them failing is enough to make any athlete, um, weak in the knees—the joint is so vital to all athletic endeavors, from aerobics to water-skiing, that when it hurts, the game is over.

While all knee injuries demand attention, the severity of the problem dictates what action to take. Obviously, a carry-me-off-the-field or I-

heard-it-pop injury requires a qualified doctor to diagnose the exact condition and recommend treatment. Once the knee is back to a functional state, yoga can prevent further injury by stretching and strengthening the muscles that surround the joint and promoting correct body alignment. For common problems, like arthritis and small sprains and strains, yoga is equally beneficial.

First, a little anatomy lesson. The framework for the knee is surprisingly fragile. The joint, which connects the femur (thigh bone) and the tibia (shin bone), is a hinge which doesn't fit perfectly together, unlike other joints like the hip, a ball-in-socket configuration, or the ankle, which slides together like two puzzle pieces. Instead of

NAVASANA
(Boat Pose)
Builds core strength in the abdomen and back, thereby alleviating some of the weight carried in the knees. Begin seated, knees bent, feet flat on the floor, holding onto the backs of your thighs. Rock gently from side to side to feel the sit bones at the base of your pelvis. Lean backwards to balance on the back edge of the sit bones and the tips of your toes. Keeping your pelvis neutral (tipped neither forwards nor backwards), draw your navel in and elongate your spine. Straighten your legs. Reach your arms, palms in, alongside your legs parallel to the floor and gaze toward your toes. If your back rounds, bend your knees.

MARCH/APRIL 2000

YOGA JOURNAL 67

yoga spotters usually attend these shoots, and photographs are appropriately straightforward, usually shot at eye level with little background so the lines of the subject are clear and obvious. For features articles, it's less important that the yoga is exact, so portraits tend to be more atmospheric and evocative, shot with various perspectives and lighting to illustrate the feel of each article.

A technique that *Yoga Journal* originally adopted to save money also helps the magazine's overall feeling of continuity. Because the publication relies so heavily on original photography, it's more affordable to shoot a whole year's worth of photos for certain departments,

Bhujangasana

Like many backbends, Cobra Pose is a "heart opener," subtly releasing held emotions within the rib cage to bring greater joy within the body.

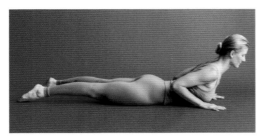

"FEW OF US HAVE LOST OUR MINDS, but many of us have long ago lost our bodies," says transpersonal psychologist Ken Wilber. It is quite common for human beings to live in a disembodied state—for our thoughts to be separate from the experience of our bodies. This loss of the body takes many forms, from not being able to stop the train of thinking mind to catching ourselves hunched over or sick because we haven't paid attention to the many warning signs we were given by our bodies. One of yoga's many benefits is the experience of greater embodiment.

Embodiment is the spreading of one's consciousness throughout the body, from the crown of the head to the toes, the surface to the core. It is learning to listen and understand the language of the body. It is remembering ourselves by exploring and excavating places we are in our own skin. When you begin to take a yoga class or learn from a book or video, the instructor will invite you to move places in yourself that may have been forgotten or never realized.

thigh bones, sternum, and kidneys, as well as places that you may be very aware of due to tightness or pain, such as the lower back or the sides of the neck. The asana that we will explore, Bhujangasana (Cobra Pose), is fundamental not only for embodying your spine but for learning to move as an integrated whole. Bhujangasana is an essential pose for developing the strength and flexibility of the entire back, while toning the legs and buttocks, increasing circulation, and assisting in kidney function. Like many backbends, it is a "heart opener," subtly releasing held emotions within the rib cage to bring greater joy within the body.

Familiar Landmarks
BEFORE WE BEGIN TO DO THE POSE, let's trace some of the important landmarks within the body that are key to activating not only Cobra but many of the

Shiva Rea teaches Cobra Pose to help her students develop strong and flexible backs.

50 YOGA JOURNAL

MARCH/APRIL 2000

left To ensure that models in instructional photos are positioned correctly, a year's worth of photos are shot with a yoga expert on hand. Seeing the same model repeatedly is comforting to readers, designers say.

right Photography illustrating noninstructional features creates a soothing mood and conveys the calm of a meditative environment. This image by Robert Olding uses a short depth of field to portray spiritual chanting in yoga studios.

below Portraits of celebrities and yoga notables offer a departure from routine instruction without straying from the magazine's focus.

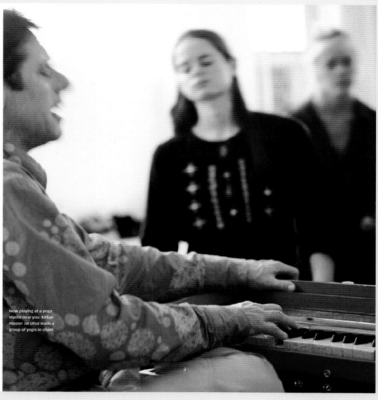

What's old is new again. **CHANTING** is a hot ticket in yoga studios across the country.
By Phil Catalfo

Can You Say Om Namaha Shivaya?

ON A COOL SUMMER EVENING, several dozen people gather in a modest-sized room at Piedmont Yoga, Rodney Yee's bustling studio in an upscale neighborhood near downtown Oakland, California. They doff their shoes and jackets, grab blankets and bolsters, and find places on the floor. But they're not here to do asanas. They've come to dip into the same spiritual well that spawned yoga, only this time they're intent on doing it not through twists, inversions, or backbends, but by opening their mouths and singing in a language none of them speaks.

Along one wall sit three people: a short woman with long hair, waiting quietly before a microphone; a wiry fellow, setting up a pair of tabla drums; and a tall, bearded, bear of a guy popping lozenges into his mouth and taking a few slugs of bottled water. As the crowd settles in, he noodles on a harmonium, a mini-keyboard that generates sound by means of a hand-operated bellows. He pumps the bellows with his left hand while his right hand plays the keys. His name is Krishna Das, and he has come to lead this group in an evening of *kirtan*, devotional chants from the Hindu tradition.

PHOTOGRAPH BY **ROBERT OLDING**

Now playing at a yoga studio near you: Kirtan master Jai Uttal leads a group of yogis in chant.

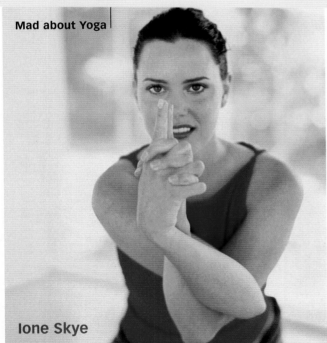

Mad about Yoga

Ione Skye

IONE SKYE, daughter of '60s folk-rocker Donovan, has acted in 25 movies including *Say Anything* and *Gas Food Lodging*. She was first introduced to yoga, at the tender age of 4, by her Jewish, New York City cab driver grandfather. At first she didn't like it very much because he frightened her, especially when he moved into Lion Pose! Now 30, she has tried different classes but "never really got into it" until

a friend invited her to a Kundalini Yoga class in Los Angeles with teacher Gurmukh Khalsa. "I fell in love with doing yoga. The chanting was very deep for me. It was as if I remembered it. It was like a real surrender." Skye, in the midst of her busy life acting (she just finished filming *The Recycler* with musician Beck, to be released next year), painting, and writing a screenplay, always makes time for yoga.

"I like doing a challenging class because it makes me more brave in life. My perception of hardships is now completely different. I'm not whining and moaning inside as much." When she travels, she stays committed to her practice. She especially loves doing Sun Salutations. "Every morning if I go in the sun and do them by myself, it's such protection.... Yoga is a life-saver."—*Dya Englert*

such as the "Asana" section for beginners, in one sitting with a single model, says Wieder. Therefore, faces are the same from issue to issue—as if a reader was returning to a regular yoga class. Readers appreciate the consistency, he says.

Shooting its own photographs also gives *Yoga Journal* some control over colors and patterns used in backgrounds, so they often pick up shades of the magazine's palette. The wood floors or painted walls of a setting often match or complement one of the 30 colors used throughout the book—the muted maroons, pale greens, chocolate browns, maize yellows, and soft grays and beiges that the magazine uses for a unified look. Illustrations also reflect the color choices.

The rich, subdued colors play a major role in creating a sense of calm throughout the magazine, but they're also modern, a reflection of shades universally popular in interior design, fashion, advertising, and other branches of the design world. Therefore, they're familiar and appealing to culturally aware readers.

I decided to go for it and signed up for a stay at the Ayurvedic Institute in Albuquerque, New Mexico.

Ancient Antidote for Stress

THE CONCEPT OF PANCHAKARMA can be a hard one for Westerners to grasp. Those who have heard of it are often quick to assume it's another internal cleansing regimen. But it's more than that. Dr. John Douillard, ayurvedic physician and author of *Body, Mind and Sport* (Crown, 1994), says, "Panchakarma is not a detox program. This is only its side benefit. It is a transformation in consciousness—replacing stress with silence."

> Panchakarma is not a detox program. This is only its side benefit. It is a transformation in consciousness—replacing stress with silence.

An understanding of the principles behind the ayurvedic view of health and disease (the event that panchakarma aims to prevent) helps put the practice in context. Ayurveda explains health as a dynamic balance, the individual living in harmony with natural law. The system takes into account an individual's elemental, unique constitution, called *prakriti*, as well as how far the person has varied from that balance, the *vikriti*. Each person's constitution is described in terms of *doshas*, three distinct energy patterns known as vata, pitta, and kapha. Though all three doshas exist in each of us in different proportion, one is generally predominant. Knowing the ways these doshas coexist in our constitutions can help guide our daily eating and lifestyle choices towards a state of balance—and better health.

When pathology does arise, ayurveda considers it an expression of a person's genetic predisposition, environment, habits, and understanding. Explains Dr. Marc Halpern, director of the California College of Ayurveda, disease starts in the physical body when undigested food and experience create *ama*, a toxic substance that accumulates in the body. Disease then develops through six distinct stages, of which only the last two are recognizable by scientific, evidence-based medicine. Because ayurveda can identify disease patterns before there is clinical pathology, the approach allows a level of prevention unimaginable to conventional medicine. From an ayurvedic perspective, even when physical damage is irreversible, it is still possible to minimize discomfort and arrest further deterioration.

This is where panchakarma comes in. The series of treatments helps the body release toxins and rebalances the doshas. Says Bri Maya Tiwari, Vedic monk, teacher, and author of *Ayurveda, Secrets of Healing* (Lotus Press,

1995). "These are not invasive therapies, but are meant to go deep within to nourish the body and cajole it into releasing its waste, its toxicity. The tissue should not feel a longing for something given up. It should not be traumatic, like candy ripped from a child."

Because ayurvedic physicians view each individual as unique, the customizing of treatment to the patient is central. Therefore, asking physicians trained in Indian ayurvedic schools questions about disease can be frustrating. These *vaidyas*, as they're called in India, don't treat diseases, they treat people. Invariably the response begins, "It all depends on the individual." This is no New Age nod to holism, but rather the very foundation of this approach. (And it's not a lack of sophistication regarding disease, either. Ayurveda recognizes not two, but 20 types of diabetes, for example.)

Indeed, panchakarma—and the broader tradition of ayurveda—are most sophisticated systems. Dr. Vasant Lad, founder of the Ayurvedic Institute, convinced me and an audience of American cardiologists of this several years ago, when I first met him at his presentation to the Department of Cardiology at New York City's Columbia Presbyterian Medical Center. He introduced passages from the *Charak Samhita*, a 5,000-year-old medical text, that outlined symptoms and complications of cardiac disease only recently discovered by Western medicine. Thousands of years before modern science, it seems, ayurveda had gathered this knowledge, without microscope or stethoscope. The result is a deep wealth of understanding that informs the cleansing procedures used in panchakarma to this day.

Deep Relaxation

ONE OF THE FIRST THINGS I discover after signing up for treatment is the emphasis placed on home preparation. I'm told that taking certain steps before the panchakarma treatments maximizes effectiveness, prevents complications, and prepares the body for the profound inner release the sessions will invariably bring. Ayurveda likens the body to a branch that, when dry, will snap under the stress of the various therapies. If the wood has been properly oiled first, however, it will bend beautifully.

To that end, this first phase of panchakarma starts with dietary restrictions: no meat or dairy the week before treatment. That's easy for me. But oleation—the lubrication of the inner body—is a bit harder to swallow.

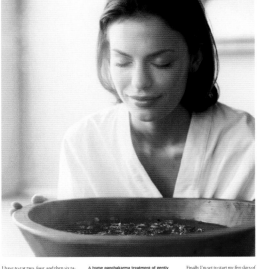

I have to eat two, four, and then six tablespoons of *ghee*, or clarified butter, before meditation for three consecutive mornings. It is strangely filling, and I can barely eat the rest of the day. But according to Lad, the ghee provides internal lubrication, "which is necessary so that the ama or toxins begin to come back from the deep tissue of the gastrointestinal tract for elimination." The third night brings relief...two tablespoons of castor oil. These home therapies help liquefy the toxins at the sites where they've lodged in my body, loosening them and moving them out through the digestive tract.

A home panchakarma treatment of gently steaming water infused with special herbs purifies the skin. The aromatherapeutic experience this practice provides also helps calm and balance the doshas.

Finally I'm set to start my five days of panchakarma. Early Sunday evening, I assemble with four others for an orientation at the Ayurvedic Institute. Besides our daily treatments, we will see Dr. Lad on Monday and Thursday, and check in daily with the panchakarma coordinator. In addition, we can attend yoga classes during the day, sit in on optional lectures, or take a cooking class in the evening. Our food is restricted to one dish, *kitchari*. This easily digestible, lightly spiced one-pot meal of basmati rice and mung dal can be adorned with a little ghee, fresh cilantro leaves (our only vegetable), lime, and a pinch of salt. We are advised to eat according to our

left Articles flow naturally, helped along by unobtrusive callouts and free-floating captions. This easy movement throughout layouts is one of *Yoga Journal's* greatest successes and is instrumental in building the magazine's fluid feeling.

Quiet Flow with Personal Touches

Besides color, matte paper stock adds to a feeling of serenity. Chosen foremost as a more reader-friendly paper that better represents photos, the matte finish gives pages a subtle, poised feeling.

Type plays its own role in giving *Yoga Journal* its unassuming look. Designers chose sans-serif faces of various weights for heads, department headers, cover lines, and some sidebars, offering simplicity and readability. Body text is a small serif font called Journal, a light, elegant face with curves defined by straight lines.

The magazine's logo is a perfect use of type, true to the entire magazine's nature and personality. Designers decided the word yoga should be printed in lowercase letters for a discreet and modern style. It dominates the word journal, which is printed below in all caps. Yoga is portrayed in the font Village—which itself carries the fluid lines and curves of a posing human body. Displayed on top of *Yoga Journal's* cover photographs, the magazine's flag is the essence of yoga.

The magazine achieves continuity from the front of the book to the back, but inside, it manages to allow some pages and sections to assert themselves. The book rarely strays from its three-column grid, but the usual elements are given original twists.

Sidebars defy the box standard, for instance. Some are contained in entire columns with subtle background colors that bleed off the edge of the page. Text sits flush against the left edge of the column. Other sidebars feature floating text separated from body text only by a single bottom rule. Margins and distinctive typefaces act as natural borders, once again communicating the design's quiet confidence.

Another technique is the use of colored borders around certain pages or sections. These indicate regular departments or separate instructional portions of an article from the rest of the text. Borders give sections their own personalities, says Wieder. Because border colors are usually pale, the borders are more comforting than oppressive and help call attention to pages that otherwise might get lost in the flow.

These elements blend to create a reading experience that is calming, complete, and constantly moving. Even away from the yoga studio, *Yoga Journal's* design can inspire the spirit of this physical and spiritual exercise.

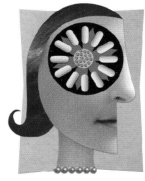

Off the Couch BY MARK EPSTEIN, M.D.

Sitting with Depression

Depressed people think they know themselves, but maybe they only know depression.

A WOMAN NAMED SALLY called me not long ago seeking advice. I had seen her for a single session in consultation months before, and we had talked about a variety of therapeutic and spiritual issues. Like many people with an interest in spirituality, she was suspicious of the role of psychiatric medications in today's culture. It seemed like the mark of some kind of Brave New World to have mood-altering drugs so readily available. But like many others, Sally wondered if there might be a medicine that could help her. She had been plagued with chronic feelings of anxiety and depression for much of her adult life, and despite a healthy investment in psychotherapy, she still felt that there was something the matter with her. When I spoke with Sally the second time, she had been taking a small dose of an antidepressant for several weeks, 25 milligrams of Zoloft, and she was finding that she felt calmer, less irritable, and, dare she say, happier. She was going on a two-week meditation retreat later that month. Something about taking her medication while on retreat made Sally uncomfortable, and that was the reason for her call. "Perhaps I should go more deeply into my problems while I'm away," she said. She worried that the antidepressant would impede that process by making her problems less accessible to her. What do you think? she asked.

Let me be clear right from the start that there is no universal answer in a situation like this. Some people notice when they take drugs like Prozac, Paxil, or Zoloft, antidepressants of the SSRI (Selective Serotonin Reuptake Inhibitor) variety, that they feel cut-off from themselves as a result. They don't feel their feelings quite so acutely and sometimes report feeling numb. Some, both men and women, find that the drugs interfere with their ability to reach orgasm. Many others find that the damping down of their feelings is more subtle. One of my patients notices she no longer cries in movies, for example, but she is willing to accept this because she also no longer worries to the point of exhaustion about things she can do nothing about.

I was relieved to hear that Sally was feeling better. People who respond well to these antidepressants often have none of the side effects mentioned above. Instead they feel restored, healed of the depressive symptoms that they were expending so much of their energy trying to fend off. Less preoccupied with their internal states, they are freer to participate in their own lives, yet they often wonder if they are cheating. "This isn't the real me," they protest. "I'm the tired, cranky, no-good one you remember from a couple of weeks ago." As a psychiatrist, I am often in the position to encourage people to question those identifications. Depressed people think they know themselves, but maybe they only know depression.

Sally's question was interesting not only because of the drug issue but because of her assumptions about

SEPTEMBER/OCTOBER 2000

YOGA JOURNAL 133

left Sidebars contribute color to pages without making them look boxy. One favorite technique is eliminating a margin on one side, running text against the edge of the column.

above Colors in illustrations correspond with the magazine's palette, a selection of quiet, soothing greens, blues, golds, deep reds, and beiges.

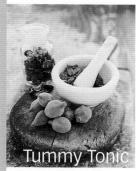

WellBeing

Tummy Tonic

The ayurvedic cure-all triphala can boost sluggish digestion.

IN AN EFFORT TO stay healthy, you probably take strides to keep organs such as the lungs and heart in top form, through practices like pranayama and meditation. But it might pay to set your sights lower.

"Some 80 percent of all degenerative, chronic diseases have their origin in inefficient digestion, assimilation, or metabolism," says Dr. Rama Kant Mishra, an Indian-born ayurvedic physician who is currently director of research and product development at Maharishi Ayur-Ved Products International in Colorado Springs, Colorado. "If we are unable to properly digest and assimilate the food we eat, the body will not receive the nourishment it needs to maintain and regenerate itself. Moreover, digestive dysfunction creates *ama*, a toxic byproduct, which can wreak havoc on normal bodily functioning if allowed to accumulate over time."

To strengthen the digestive fires, ayurvedic physicians traditionally recommend a potent herbal mixture called triphala. A combination of amalaki, haritaki, and bibhitaki, triphala strengthens the digestive process, provides nutrients, and pushes out toxins from the body. With a mild laxative effect, it enhances the health of the gastrointestinal tract by rejuvenating the membrane lining of the intestines and by stimulating bile production. Triphala improves liver function, helps purify the blood, and removes accumulated toxins. It is also high in vitamin C and linoleic oil.

Triphala also helps address a wide range of disorders, from irritable bowel syndrome, ulcerative colitis, constipation, and diarrhea, to anemia, eye disease, skin disorders, yeast infections, and problems related to the female cycle. According to Dr. Mishra, most anyone can benefit from taking triphala, although it is contraindicated for pregnant women, people with chronic liver conditions, and for those taking blood-thinning drugs. In rare cases, if a lot of ama has accumulated in the body, nausea or a skin rash may develop when you first begin taking triphala as impurities are pushed out. If that happens, stop taking the herb and consult with an ayurvedic doctor before taking it again.

Take the herb for about six months at a time, and then take a four-week break before continuing. If you take triphala in powder form, ½ teaspoon every evening before bedtime is recommended. If you take it in pill form, follow the recommendations on the bottle. Monitor your daily bowel movements. If they get too loose, it's time to cut back on the dose.

—*Eva Herriott*

HEALTHWATCH

For the past several years, we've been hearing reports about the benefits of green tea, particularly its role in preventing cancer and other serious conditions. But those who've made drinking it part of their daily routine might wonder: If steeping tea a little releases powerful antioxidants, will steeping it longer produce more of a punch? Probably not, say researchers at the University of Hawaii. In testing the ability of green tea to inhibit colon cancer, the biochemists found that most of the antimutagenic components were released in the first couple minutes of brewing. **Source:** Mutation Research

The aromatic bark of the cinnamon tree has more going for it than just great taste. Microbiologists have recently confirmed the spice's age-old reputation as a versatile food preservative—in this case, as a potent match for *E. coli* bacteria. Kansas State University researchers added a teaspoon of cinnamon to apple juice that contained 100 times the level

of *E. coli* typically found in contaminated food. In three days, the spice had killed off 99.5 percent of the bacteria. Considering that 10,000 to 20,000 of us get sick each year from food-borne illness, it's good to know that we can turn to the most common of kitchen staples for protection. **Source:** Chemical Market Reporter, HerbClip

Could dry cleaning be killing us? That's a question Representative Carolyn B. Maloney (New York City) would like the Department of Health and Human Services to start investigating. A recent study of 1,350 Boston-area women between the ages of 35 and 75 suggested a link between the use of professional dry cleaning and a greater incidence of breast cancer. "Although the study looked at only a limited segment of the population, it raises troubling questions for women nationwide," Maloney says. **Source:** Office of Carolyn B. Maloney, Washington, D.C.

38 YOGA JOURNAL

JULY/AUGUST 2000

Evolution of a Magazine

The way a magazine's design changes over its life can be a sign of the times—a reflection of trendy fonts and colors or developments in printing technology, for example.

But publication insiders know that a magazine's evolution also reflects more personal development. The comings and goings of editors, publishers, and art directors, gradual shifts in audiences' needs, changing ownership of publishing companies, and the magazine's financial growth or decline have a great impact on how each magazine looks from year to year.

Magazine staffers may look back proudly over the work and love poured into their publication over its history, whether it's one year old or 50. But they also may shake their heads in amazement at how far they've come.

Here's a look at three magazines and how they've changed over their lives.

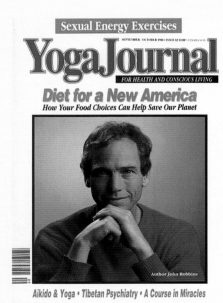

above   Early *Yoga Journal* covers, such as this one in 1988, concentrated on personalities and illustration of new-age issues rather than yoga itself, a reflection of the magazine's editorial mission.

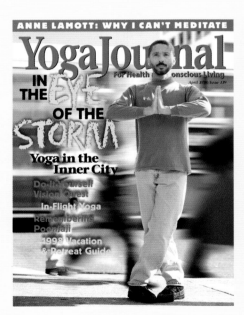

above   As the magazine encompassed a wider range of new-age topics and readership grew, layouts became more high concept. On this 1998 cover, a model poses against a blurred background of moving people.

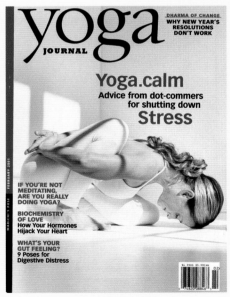

above   After a redesign in 2000, yoga once again took center stage. Photographs of people posed against plain backgrounds create a natural balance and movement for covers.

Yoga Journal

New Age Reader to Slick Consumer Health Magazine

When *Yoga Journal* was launched in 1975, yoga was a fringe practice in the United States, generally reserved for the truly spiritual.

A mouthpiece of the California Yoga Teachers Association for more than 20 years, the magazine was a modest affair in its first decade. Pages were black-and-white and no-frills, laid out in simple grids with little variation in the placement of headlines, photos, and captions.

Because *Yoga Journal* catered to a specialized audience with many common interests besides yoga, however, the magazine's singular focus unraveled. "The subject matter strayed far afield," says editor in chief

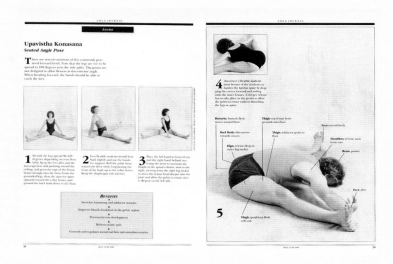

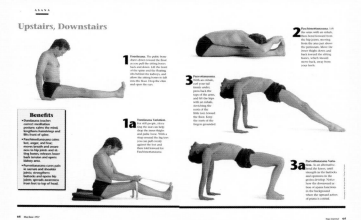

Kathryn Arnold. "It covered new-age topics of all kinds, reaching out to a readership of cultural creatives." As the magazine's topics branched out and attracted more readers, design became more complex. Artists began taking more liberty with page design, breaking away from simple columns of text running around photo boxes and using color.

By 1998, the magazine's nonprofit owners decided to sell *Yoga Journal* to a publishing company, and newly available resources helped the magazine grow. Editors and designers revisited the publication's purpose. In recent years, yoga had become an American lifestyle—more as exercise than spiritual expression.

It made sense, therefore, that *Yoga Journal* should once again focus on the topic that started it all. "We had to make the magazine accessible, editorially and visually, to attract a broader audience," says design director Jonathan Wieder.

The relaunch of *Yoga Journal* in 2000 included a redesign that accentuated yoga. On the covers, graceful yoga positions speak for themselves without backgrounds or novelty fonts. Inside, instructional and inspirational photographs drive the book's simple, natural flow. Pages changed from glossy to matte for a more modern look and to better represent photographs.

The pure, serene covers help *Yoga Journal* stand out against more cluttered faces on the newsstand, which, along with a new direct-mail marketing campaign and the nation's overall obsession with yoga, has driven readership. Subscriptions rose 50 percent between 1999 and 2000.

above Departments and features were still running in black and white in 1990, including the "Asana" section on beginning yoga poses. Pages were generally two- or three-grid layouts with text wrapped around boxed photographs.

left above Designs began to transcend their usual boundaries. For instance, photographs of poses in the "Asana" section moved out of their small boxes to help balance of the department's two pages.

left below A constant throughout *Yoga Journal's* changing history, the "Asana" department came into its own with the redesign. Richly colorful photographs of bending, flowing shapes create effective negative space, which helps balance pages.

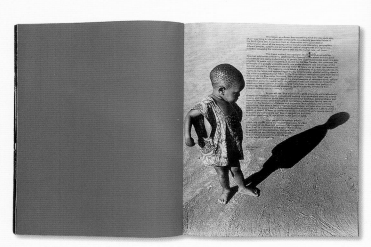

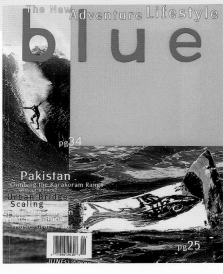

Readers also clamored for larger pictures, so although *Blue* still experiments with cropping and sizing, it allows some gorgeous images to spread their wings across entire pages. This is also noticeable on the covers, which began to feature strong, single images as time passed.

Blue's trademark is its use of boxes to contain text or simply add a mark of color. This is another trait that's matured since the magazine's inception, developing from choppy, awkward squares to natural inserts that facilitate an easy dialog with the reader.

The alterations to *Blue's* design satisfied the demands of readers and attracted new ones. Newsstand sales immediately shot up 10% when the magazine introduced its first cover using the "more commercial approach"—literal adventure subject matter combined with innovative graphics, according to editor in chief Amy Schrier.

Blue

Experimental Puzzle to Adventurous, Attractive Layout

Blue emerged during a monumental era in magazine design—the mid-1990s, which birthed the transcendent pages of such magazines as *Wired* and *Raygun*. The travel magazine's founding art director was David Carson, the famous magazine designer (and *Raygun* art director), known for his experimental use of text.

True to this model, *Blue's* layouts always pushed boundaries. Text boxes shoved and jutted into each other, white type lay against light images, and photos were reduced to tiny slivers. Crazed pages fit with uneven pieces were followed by startlingly lucid layouts. Just like the best adventures, pages always kept readers guessing—even if they were also squinting to read type.

"If you look at the first issues, you will see type that is too small to read and text is running over images, which also challenged readability," says art director Christa Skinner. *Blue* even defied such conventions as folios, so readers had a hard time finding articles from the table of contents.

The magazine won several awards for its groundbreaking design, but some readers complained that it was hard to read. In *Blue's* second issue, Skinner made a few changes, such as incorporating page numbers into the middle of layouts. By the next few issues, care had been taken to make text legible while still allowing it to subvert the norm.

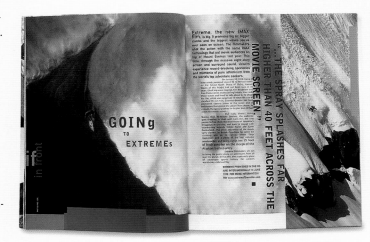

right Single spectacular images found their way onto *Blue's* covers in later issues.

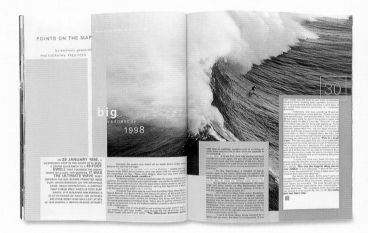

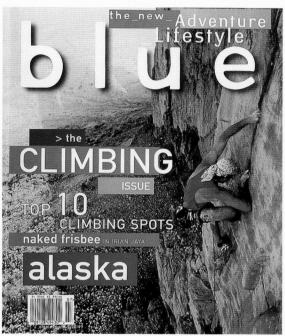

above Early use of boxes was choppy.

right In more recent issues, the boxes have come into their own and are now a modern, elegant feature of the layout.

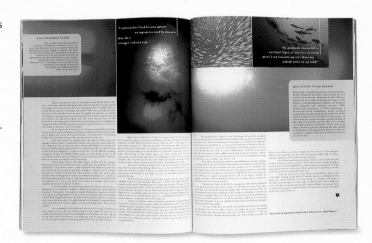

Code

Busy and Bright to Suave and Sophisticated

Code is a good example of how a brand-new magazine finds itself during its first years of publication. Debuting in mid-1999, the magazine was passed among creative directors before finally arriving at its final look—for the time being, at least.

In its first several issues, the magazine alternated between wild breakouts of color and sleek, conservative layouts. The front-of-the-book department, "Decode," was perhaps the most experimental. It used cut-out colored text boxes against images or different colored backgrounds and bright layers of color behind entire pages. Type varied from a smooth sans serif to a serif with extremely tight leading. Pages were busy, bright, and varied.

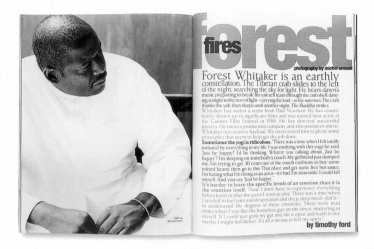

The well stuck to black and white, with two columns of body copy and beautiful full-page fashion shoots. Features experimented with type, to some extent, but usually stayed with a tiny serif face. Back departments also evolved from a simple two-column format to pages surrounded by heavy double black rules.

In the summer of 2000, a new creative director stepped in and altered the magazine's look. Patterned after European style for a hipper, younger look, the new design wiped out the frenetic color in the front of the magazine and replaced it with clean pages, lots of white space, and a chunky all-caps sans-serif typeface. The back of the book shed the smothering black border and used thinner, open-ended rules.

above Early issues of *Code* frequently experimented with type. In this profile of actor Forest Whitaker, font size, color, leading, and style are all over the board throughout the body of the article.

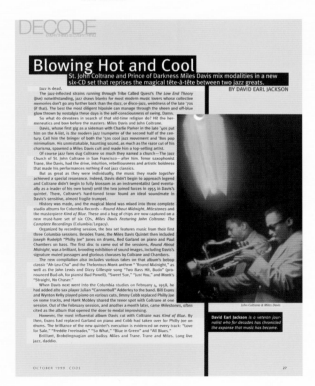

above Tabs of color behind headlines and body copy were characteristic of the department "Decode," the section in the front of the book, in *Code's* first issues.

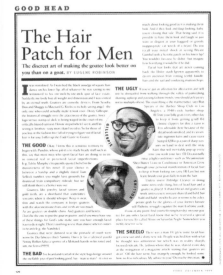

left Designers began sectioning off back-of-the-book departments with heavy double rules along the margins.

Finally, in early fall, creative director Charlie Hess took over and redesigned again, this time for good. "All the sections of the book were kind of getting lost, so they needed to be defined and give a presence," Hess says.

Hess and the design staff boiled down the fonts to a handful of mature but casual and distinctive fonts. The clean, sophisticated look of the previous redesign remained, with a commitment to neat white pages with tasteful touches of color, cool photography, and playful illustrations. The back and front of the book got the most attention. "Decode," the front department, was set apart with a sans-serif typeface, wide margins, and a hip, clubby look. Back departments fell into identical templates, with a heavy side rule distinguishing them from the rest of the book.

The many changes made little difference in the magazine's acceptance by consumers and the publishing industry, though—in summer 2000, in the midst of all the tweaking, *Code* walked away with four Maggie awards, not the least of which was Best Overall Design/Consumer.

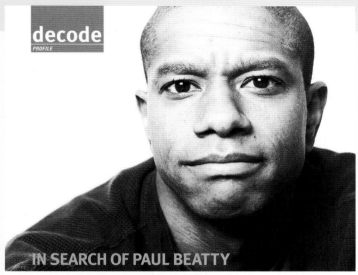

decode PROFILE

IN SEARCH OF PAUL BEATTY

HIS OBSERVATIONS ON RACE IN CONTEMPORARY SOCIETY ARE SO PROFOUND THAT LAKERS COACH PHIL JACKSON PASSES THEM ON TO HIS PLAYERS. WHO IS THE PAUL BEHIND THE PROSE? BY ADELE SLAUGHTER

IT'S ONE O'CLOCK. THE PHONE RINGS IN PAUL BEATTY'S NEW York apartment. He crosses the floor and reaches his long arm for the receiver. "Hello," he murmurs, worried, to the voice of a reporter he has never met. His pad is void of background noise; no television set. The voice asks a brief, polite opening question.

Just short of six feet tall, Beatty pauses, as if rubbing his shaved head. He feels off-kilter talking to reporters. Especially an unseen one, with a disembodied voice. But he has already agreed to this interview. Frequently, brilliant writers are kind of stiff, even though their written language is rich and exuberant. Paul Beatty does not disappoint.

After writing two books of poetry, Beatty emerged onto the literary scene with *The White Boy Shuffle* (Houghton Mifflin Co.) in 1996. It was a well-received first novel, and got reviews in the *New York Times*, the *Los Angeles Times* and the *Nation*.

In May of 2000, his second novel, *Tuff* (Alfred A. Knopf), hit

bookshelves. It's a picaresque work of Twainian wit, whose 320-pound teenage hero roams Spanish Harlem, taking on parenthood, identity politics,

Beatty is a genius. At least that's what writers such as Alan Cheuse, Jessica Hagedorn and E. Ethelbert Miller assert. *He* is far too humble to make such a claim. His work is, however, undeniably funny. His influences seem to come from the likes of Ishmael Reed and Richard Pryor. Beatty's work is like the comics—*Boondocks*, perhaps—or maybe it's like Chris Rock writing a novel.

Asked how he feels about the media today, Beatty pulls no punches. "On the whole, most journalists are lazy. Everything's soup of the day," he says. "Everything's written the same way. You could substitute skateboarding for poetry and it wouldn't make a difference. At the same time, there is a lot of good investigative journalism. Some of these live TV documentary shows are kinda good, I have to say. They're a little less manufactured than the things you get on the news."

The voice clears its throat, perhaps in a spot.

20

CODE JULY 2000

top right In the summer of 2000, "Decode" got a new look, with department heads that changed colors according to the department section.

right A change in art direction prompted a younger look. Type on the July 2000 cover was chunkier and metallic, with playful plus signs and hyphens to spice it up.

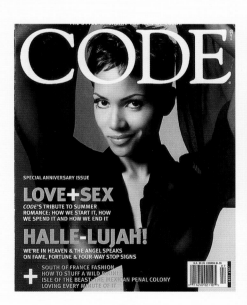

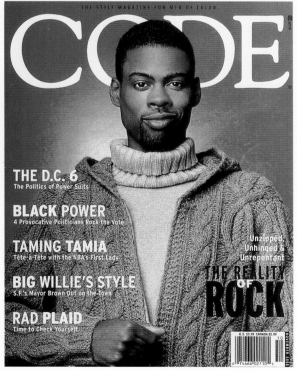

right Finally settling comfortably into its design, *Code* adopted a limited lineup of typefaces, including this sophisticated sans serif used on the November 2000 cover.

A Picturesque Guide to Luxury Travel

When people are young, they dream of the things they'll have when they grow older: a nice house, luxury car, perhaps a boat or farm or other place to escape to when the daily grind overwhelms them. Inevitably, exotic vacations become part of the fantasy. Whether it's an amenities-rich villa in Italy or a tropical beach on an island, many adults save for the day when they can discover the finer things beyond the borders of their own town.

Travel & Leisure fuels this wanderlust. American Express's travel magazine presents travelogs of trips to places that are attainable, yet dreamlike and gorgeous.

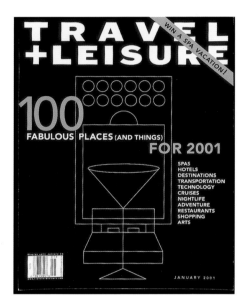

above   Covers usually feature photographs from stories but, for the January 2001 issue, simple line art became a cosmopolitan introduction to *Travel & Leisure's* new millennium. Modern type and illustrations appeal to affluent, image-minded readers.

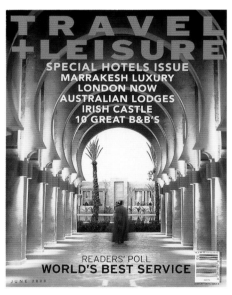

above   Breathtaking scenes and vistas open most issues. Here, the awe-inspiring size and hush of a Marrakesh hall acts as a gateway to the June 2000 issue.

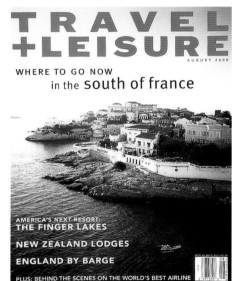

above   In this issue, on the other hand, the photographer draws back for an aerial shot of a seascape in southern France.

WHY IT WORKS:

Spectacular photographic collages tell the intriguing stories and fire readers' imaginations. A simple layout sets a quiet and marked pace that reminds readers it's time to slow down.

Adventure with Luxury

The magazine's audience is educated, affluent, and an average of 45 years old—a crowd that may be adventurous but still appreciates comfort and luxury, says creative director Pamela Berry.

"We pick places that are realistic to go to," she says. "We wouldn't do a profile on a sacred trek through Bhutan." Instead, features are focused on how readers can fill their days and nights during trips to cities and tourist-friendly countryside—Canada's Gulf Islands, the south of France, the small towns of England. Emphasizing self-guided trips rather than bus tours or

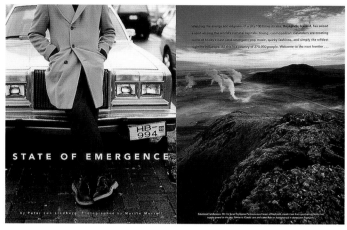

package deals, articles often twist together the author's own experience with the usual information about accommodations and food.

The *Travel & Leisure* crowd is also one that cares a great deal about what's fashionable and stylish. "There's a big style aspect to the magazine," Berry says. Of course, its just as important to impress others with your tales and photos of original vacation spots as it is to enjoy the places while you're there, so places that are luxurious but still off the beaten path are favorites of these readers.

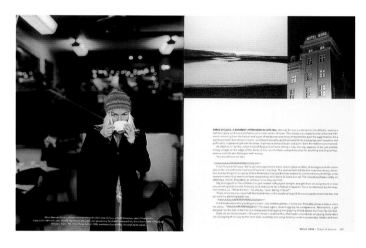

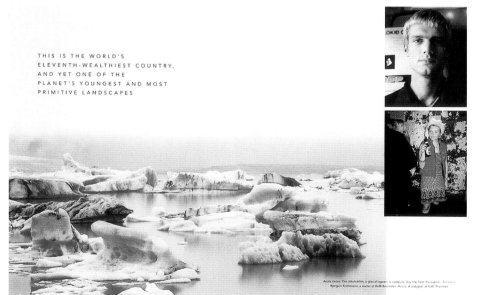

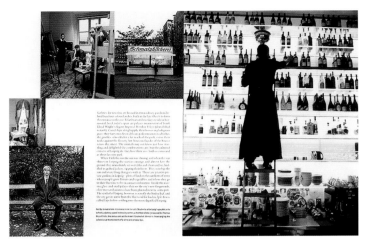

left Varying photographic styles make scenery more interesting. This layout precariously balances black-and-white, colorized black-and-white, and color photographs. On the facing page, a backlit bar is a twist on the views associated with travel features.

Intermingled with these are equally beautiful and interesting perspectives: the fish offered at an outdoor market in Marseilles, a cactus fence in Costa Rica, surfboards stacked against a palm tree in Honolulu.

Photo essays never fail to include people, whether they're models running through fields or swimming in pools or locals posing for the camera. The human factor gives the magazine its personal touch, allowing readers to more readily imagine themselves in similar scenarios.

Building the Dream

The design must therefore be modern and fresh but retain a folksy feeling that suggests a personalized experience. Berry relies heavily on photographs to create this balance—in fact, to dictate most of the magazine's look and feel. "We let the pictures speak for themselves," she says. "I let photographers do most of the work, because this magazine is about the dream of the images."

Travel & Leisure turns to a versatile cadre of photographers to shoot its breathtaking scenes, using travel photographers but also hiring professionals specializing in fashion and other disciplines. This allows the magazine not only to break the mold of traditional travel photography but also to stay in tune with style.

A typical travelog may include remarkable bird's-eye views of a town, a corner of masterful architecture, or a cloudless blue sky behind a mountainous landscape.

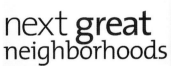

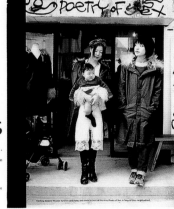

next **great** neighborhoods

It starts with a whisper and crescendoes to a buzz ...

These four up-and-coming districts—in Tokyo, Sydney, Chicago, and London—are suddenly the talk of the town

photographed by Marie Hennechart

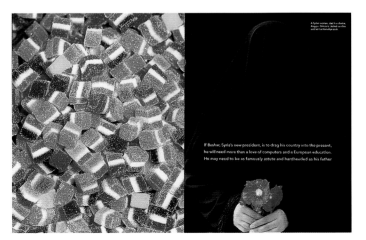

above Because travel involves more than buildings and scenery, features usually include photos of people, which sets the magazine apart. Here, a busy shot of urbanites under a graffiti-like sign sits opposite a perfectly white page.

left In a brilliant example of how designers contrast photos to establish a tone, brightly colored candy faces a portrait of a Muslim woman holding a matching flower in this opening spread for a feature on Syria.

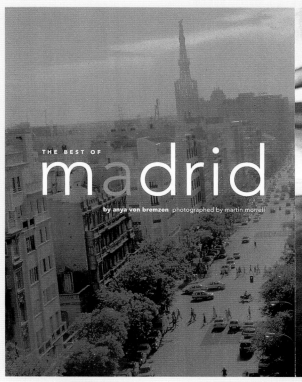

THE BEST OF
madrid

by anya von bremzen   photographed by martin morrell

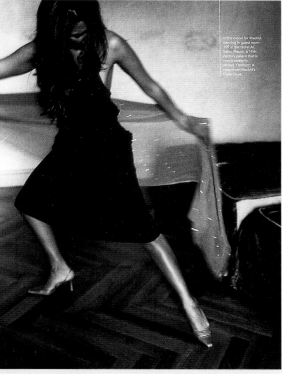

In the mood for Madrid: dancing in guest room 199 at the Hotel AC Santo Mauro, a 19th-century palace that is now a celebrity retreat. Opposite: A view down Madrid's Calle Goya.

left and below Another example of the packaging of features, this article on Madrid dedicates four full pages to photographs, while smaller images dominate the rest of the pages. Body text in these spreads is limited, though feature articles are often longer.

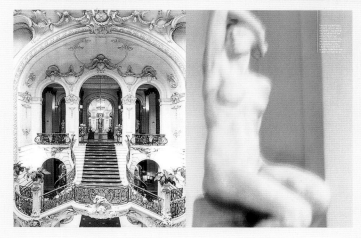

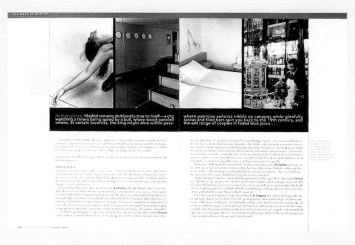

Photographic Emphasis

Luscious, full-page photos often open feature spreads, but within articles and departments, a patchwork of smaller photos marches across pages. The format creates a visual array, but it originated largely for utilitarian reasons.

"Our wonderful photography is great and difficult at the same time," Berry says. "It's so exciting the first time a box of photographs comes in from a photographer. There are so many good shots, you could make a book! It's hard to condense it into a few pictures."

That's why every picture is as captivating as the next. The photographs are festive with color, light, and detail. Light plays off the deep red and pale green of furniture, fruits, and flower arrangements in a collage of photos from Japan; landscapes blur wildly in an article about driving through Costa Rica. Black-and-white shots contrast dramatically from softer color images.

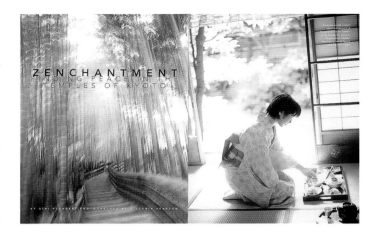

To give photographs the most play, Berry refrains from overdesigning the rest of the magazine. "I try to maintain a consistency in the design," she says. "I don't encourage a different way of seeing things through design but instead let the photographs do the work."

Designers rely on a basic grid and try to keep pages as clean as possible. Berry uses as much white space as possible to achieve this, often surrounding photographs, though her ability to use a great deal of it is limited by the thin paper *Travel & Leisure* is printed on. "We get a lot of see-through," she says.

The magazine doesn't try to add too much color to the already bright photo montages; the occasional subhead, drop cap, or pull quote may contain a touch of color, but that's about as far as it goes. Photographs are often detailed, and the addition of color would put pages at risk of looking too busy, Berry explains.

above An opening spread for a story on Kyoto conveys serenity and painstaking beauty with ethereally lighted photos, slightly out of focus. *Travel & Leisure* recreates the mood of a place through photographic layout.

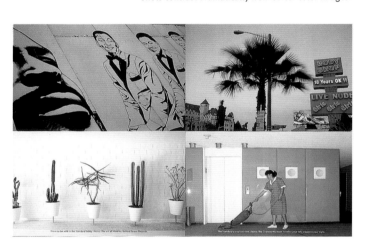

above To recreate a mood, designers stack images from a photographer's shoot on top of and against each other. Here, a mural of the Standard Hotel's history combines with images of its orderly interior, seedy exterior, and daily life.

right Sometimes there are so many great photographs of a subject that designers have a hard time choosing, which is how the checkerboard technique common in *Travel & Leisure* came to be.

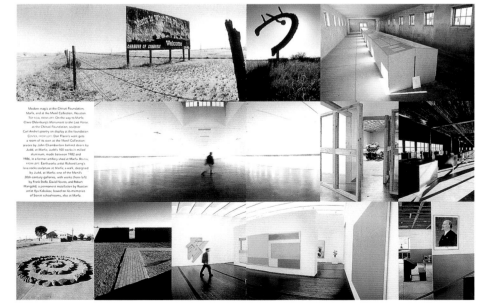

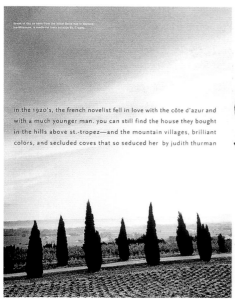

in the 1920's, the french novelist fell in love with the côte d'azur and with a much younger man. you can still find the house they bought in the hills above st.-tropez—and the mountain villages, brilliant colors, and secluded coves that so seduced her by judith thurman

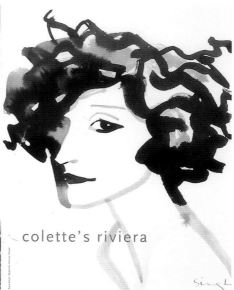

colette's riviera

left A mood of romance and intrigue is set by this opening spread, a barren black-and-white scene set against the generous brushstrokes of a retro-style painting.

Modern Type and Personality

One section is set apart by an innovative use of the black-on-white motif. The middle of the magazine houses the "Update" section, a news analysis of issues surrounding travel or other countries. To give this section a more serious tone and to invoke the look of newsprint, designers surround the articles with black rules of various weights.

"It's the only section in the magazine that isn't about what to buy or where to shop," Berry says. "It's about what's happening in Lebanon, for example. [The black rules are] an attempt to make it more newsy."

The rest of the pages, though, are simple layouts of columns of text on pure white pages. A custom-designed serif face provides a delicate touch to body text. Sans-serif fonts such as Interstate and Meta express the magazine's personality. "We were looking for something fun," Berry says.

Similarly, the magazine's newly redesigned logo helps set *Travel & Leisure's* modern tone. Wide and chunky block letters stretch across the page, with a plus sign

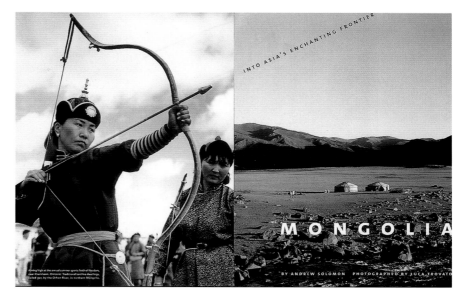

substituted for the old ampersand. Berry notes that the new logo is "a little more modern, and it pops out on the newsstand."

Travel & Leisure caters to a range of travel-happy readers, from dreamers who want to let their imaginations run wild to sophisticated travelers who aren't easily bowled over. The design serves them well with tasteful, modern elements and a photoscape that fulfills their most exquisite travel fantasies.

above Though type and graphics are usually straightforward, occasionally designers become playful. In this opener for an article on Mongolia, the deck on the right-hand page tilts toward the subject's arrow on the left.

Blue

The Adventurer's Travel Magazine

For some people, nothing is daunting. They're the ones you see on TV commercials plowing through rivers of mud on mountain bikes and hanging from the sides of rugged cliffs. *Blue* was created for these adventurers—or those who aspire to be them.

The travel magazine's design never rests, yet, since its birth in 1997, *Blue* has learned to balance its daring design with the need to be legible and accessible to readers. The result is a controlled chaos of sorts, a boundless exploration without getting lost in the forest.

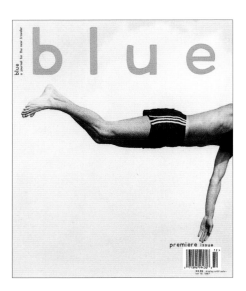

above *Blue's* is about freedom and exploration. The photograph on its first cover suggested readers should dive in without seeing what's ahead—an unconventional approach for a travel magazine. The cover prompted sales 200 percent higher than average launches.

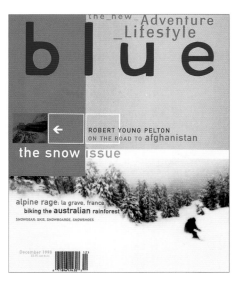

above This cover combined a blurred skiing shot and icy blue boxes. A tiny, dark photograph of trucks would blend into the background if not for the boxed arrow directing attention its way.

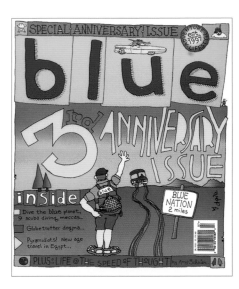

above Hobo artist Dan Price adds a folksy, cartoonish slant with his hand-lettered designs. He designed the cover for the magazine's third anniversary issue.

WHY IT WORKS:

Pages are exhilarating, edgy, and alive with color. Around every corner is an unexpected perspective; every space is assigned an unconventional purpose. Layouts play off images rather than merely incorporating them. Like its readers, *Blue* is constantly pushing the limits.

right There's no dull moments in layouts like this one for a focus on Alaska. Photos run together and overlap, boxes contain bits of text, and empty spaces become cells of color that project the article's mood.

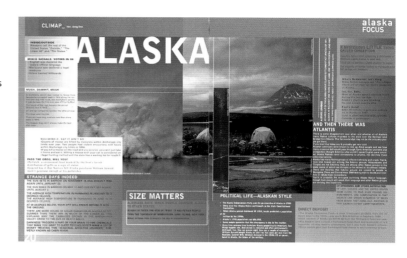

The Adventure Generation

Blue's philosophy is that space, despite what science fiction fans believe, is not necessarily the final frontier—there are plenty of adventures to be had right here on our own planet. A metaphor for "blue sky, blue sea, blue planet," *Blue* aims to inspire its already ambitious readers with tales of thrilling expeditions into barely chartered territories.

The magazine targets 19- to 35-year-old readers who aren't interested in the mainstream options that were available to previous generations. When they travel, they're less likely to choose a French getaway with the finest champagne and the most luxurious hotel, says publisher and editor in chief Amy Schrier.

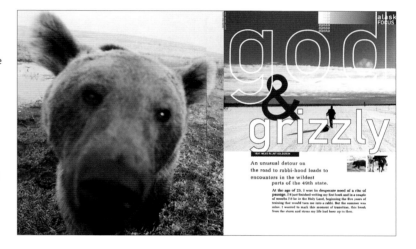

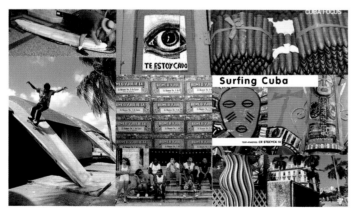

above Assembling photographs of very different subjects and in varying styles builds off-balance, stunning montages, such as in this article on Cuba.

Instead, they're more aware of their access to remote locations and choose to get there in less conventional ways—hiking, biking, kayaking, and camping their way through Malaysia or Peru instead of riding tour buses and staying at inns recommended by the guidebooks.

Design plays a critical role in speaking to these readers. "If you look at other titles in the travel category, you see them in traditional columns of type with rigid photography," says Schrier. Pages are usually white and clean, and photographs depict blue skies, friendly environments, exquisitely prepared feasts, and charming, peaceful settings. This formula has little to do with the way *Blue's* readers view their own adventures.

"We wanted to bring the travel experience to life," Schrier says. "The pages had to recreate the intensity and freedom of traveling."

above Photographs aren't always the distant, technically perfect achievements they are in other magazines. Sometimes out of focus, motion-blurred, grainy, or dark, they portray a realistic, imperfect view of adventure.

Flexible, Frenetic Layout

Transmitting the vicarious thrill of adventure travel through design is a twofold process. "On one hand, we have to convey the frenzy of travel," says Schrier. "On the other, we try to provide a crystal-clear, fresh view, a clean window to the world."

At first glance, the frenetic vision seems to be uppermost. Layouts are packed with stacked photographs, overlapping boxes, changing typefaces, and experimental dingbats. Varying shades of color fill empty areas, eliminating romantic notions of white space. The pages buzz with a nonchalant energy and the awareness that rules, in travel, design, and life, are meant to be broken.

Blue has never used a grid. "Every page is a hand-done page," says Schrier. Design ideas begin at a meeting between Schrier and art director Christa Skinner, who designs about 90 percent of the pages herself. By starting from scratch, Skinner can run with ideas inspired by the stories and artwork. "It slows me down, but also allows for more flexibility and surprises in the layout," she says.

For example, Skinner may pick up a shape in a photograph and repeat it graphically, as in a story on the Egyptian pyramids that overlaps perpendicular triangles and multiple photos of the architectural wonders in the desert. Photographs are repeated, cropped for a different perspective, or sliced into pieces and spread intermittently among other images. A single color in a photograph, such as the green of a surfboard in an otherwise white and brown surfing shot, is picked up and used in boxes and banners throughout the rest of the layout.

At *Blue's* inception, defiance of convention was a bit more extreme. Type was tiny and ran over images, which made it hard to read. Even page numbers were eliminated. The magazine earned a reputation for illegibility. In response to reader feedback, more recent issues are subversive and energetic while still making sense.

"It's a tough problem to solve, keeping it from being too boring," Skinner says. "Everyone is trying to be so simple. I don't think it is *Blue's* place to jump on the simple bandwagon due to its subject matter. *Blue* is about energy, exploration, mystery, and fun."

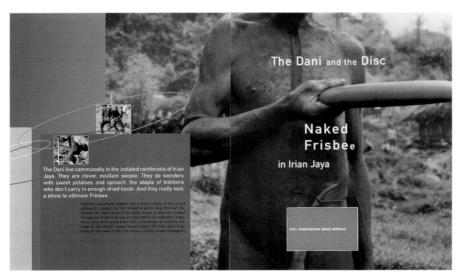

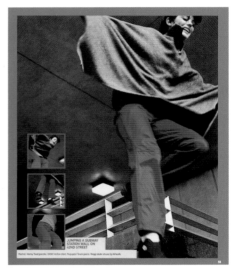

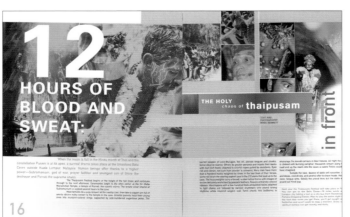

top left Photos also get up close and personal, as in this layout for an article on a rainforest tribe.

top right In an unusual approach to fashion shoots, this layout shows models of sports gear in action.

left Once again, unusually cropped photos are sprinkled across a layout for a constantly changing perspective.

below Without a grid, art director Christa Skinner can surprise herself with sudden ideas. She begins with the photographs and builds layouts around them.

right Another fashion layout shows the clothes in action.

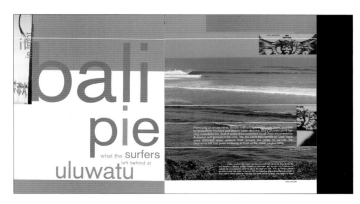

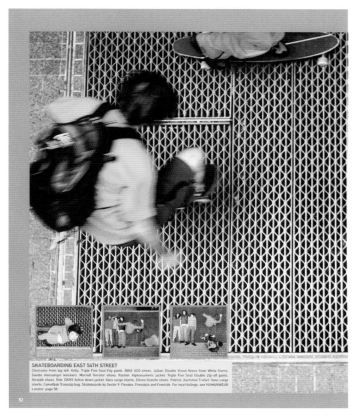

Boxed Text for Legibility

One way *Blue* solves the readability problem is with its habitual use of boxes. Text boxes, often laid over photographs or each other, stack together to make up entire articles. They're useful as captions, as labels for maps, or even as a way to break up paragraphs in stories.

The box technique emerged naturally as a way to communicate to the Internet generation, says Schrier. "We've been compared to a Web site, but we did it instinctively."

"It's a good way to get text and a lot of color on a page," says Skinner. "I began doing it early on and have continued as part of the *Blue* look."

Boxes are stacked with photos of all sizes to create a sort of montage. The magazine doesn't buy into the idyllic idea of letting stunning, blown-up images speak for themselves; there are too many other things to see. A scenic mountaintop view may border a grungy closeup of a mud-splattered mountain bike. When a colorful ocean floor or gorgeous sunset is given prominence on a page, it isn't allowed to steal the spotlight. A series of tiny action shots or whimsical graphic dingbats may be laid over it.

Text frequently is layered over photos too. Pages mix a variety of typefaces and colors; Skinner likes to experiment with many fonts, often within single layouts. Occasionally, headlines, captions, callouts, and even body text is contained in boxes or long strips filled with colors, which suggests the photos have been labeled. Pages hum with activity while emphasizing important text, which keeps the pages readable.

Rugged, Realistic Photography

In the midst of the controlled chaos, *Blue* also tries to provide moments of lucidity. The magazine's window on the world is its photography, from panoramic landscapes to in-the-trenches action shots. Photographs never fail to offer an unusual perspective: the underside of a school of fish or the bottom of a surfer's upturned board, a runner's legs, the shadows of people on the wall of a cave.

Interestingly, while the images are beautiful in their own way, they are rarely the technically perfect photos so prominent in other travel magazines. They're often grainy, sometimes dark and out of focus; occasionally, they're even magnified for intentional blurriness. But they may run alongside crisp and richly colorful photos that more conventional magazines would covet, exhibiting the magazine's wide range.

The technique helps the magazine look gritty and in the moment, a realistic approach to depicting trips that aren't always clean, pleasant, and uneventful. The photography reflects travel that is rugged and high-impact while allowing for moments of deep breaths and exquisite clarity.

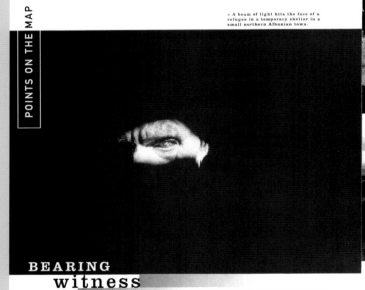

POINTS ON THE MAP

> A beam of light hits the face of a refugee in a temporary shelter in a small northern Albanian town.

BEARING witness

KOSOVO'S SHADES OF GRAY

TEXT + PHOTOGRAPHY: GARY FABIANO

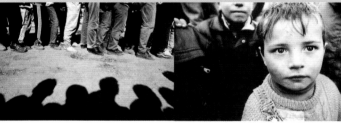

^ Lines of Survival. Refugees spend many hours a day waiting for food, blankets and other supplies.

^ One of the many young faces of war.

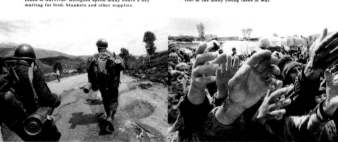

^ Anticipating a Serbian breech of Albania's sovereignty, Albanian soldiers move closer to the border.

The hours of waiting end in chaos. Flailing hands reach for loaves of bread. Where one hand may be reaching to feed a couple of family members, another may have to feed several. How do you feed an entire family on one loaf of bread?

The rules of the world have changed. Aggression has been brought to a new level that, when we look at atrocities committed in recent wars, is almost beyond belief. People talk about a time of innocence. I am not sure when it happened, but innocence was lost—and it wasn't anytime recently.

The world community has a responsibility to prevent "never again" from happening again. Well, in recent years we have not only let it happen again, but again and again. When will it stop?

The world community's inability to step in and help stop past conflicts is what has made the rules of the world change to what sometimes seems a point of no return. A line has to be drawn. A message has to be sent. If you commit these horrible human atrocities, you will be held accountable. Let it be from this day forward that everyone understands that all actions will have a reaction.

I think that all the discussion about the conflict in Kosovo is good. It opens a dialogue that has the potential for resolution. But does what WE say and think really matter? As far as I am concerned, not really. The only opinions that really matter are the ones of those who have to go through this. That's why I take pictures. The newspapers and TV were not good enough for me anymore. I had to see it and find out for myself.

So I spoke to the people. The people who walked nine days in the cold, torrential rain to reach a somewhat safer place. The people who arrived suffering from exhaustion, dehydration and hunger. The people who arrived with their feet open and bleeding from walking so much. The people who sleep on top of a piece of plastic on top of cold, wet mud. The people who fit their whole family on the back of a wagon pulled by a tractor or horse. The people who had to witness a brother or son or father pulled away never to be seen again or executed in front of them.

These are just a few of the hundreds of thousands of examples. As I said before, our opinions really do not matter. I found the people that I spoke with in Kosovo were relieved that NATO exists and has decided to stand up to a despicable human being. I think if misery and destruction were knocking at our door and our families were living through this, we would be wondering who was going to come and help us out.

Our job now is to go from bystander to active bystander and try to help out as much as we can. There are many ways of helping. Find a place to send clothes, money or food. Or go offer your help in person. And while we are at it, we should call the ones we love and tell them how much they mean to us and try and remind ourselves everyday just how great we really have it.

27

above A single eye peers from the shadows in this black-and-white layout for an article on Kosovo.

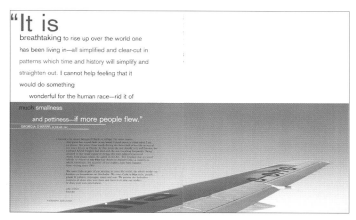

"It is breathtaking to rise up over the world one has been living in—all simplified and clear-cut in patterns which time and history will simplify and straighten out. I cannot help feeling that it would do something wonderful for the human race—rid it of much smallness and pettiness—if more people flew."

GEORGIA O'KEEFFE, in the air, 1941

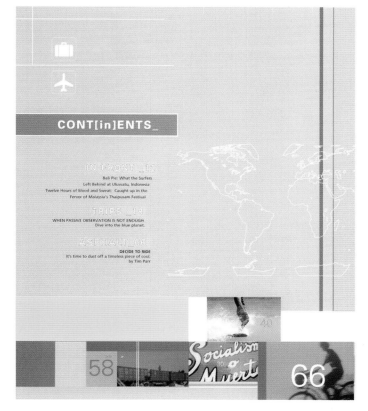

top This letter from the editor illustrates a rare moment of quiet simplicity, yet the curiously cropped airplane wing gives the layout a twist.

right Layered images are plotted over a map of the world in the table of contents.

far right Hand lettering is used to convey a critical tone in this journal-like article on Samoa.

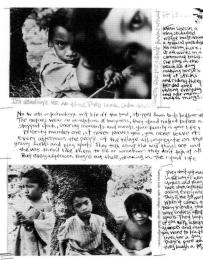

Blue occasionally complements photography with illustrations. Maps are a significant part of the magazine's mission. Readers can step away for a moment from the impact of in-your-face photographs and get a wider, more grounded view of a place from an illustrated map. They play such an integral role in design that maps of the world are always used in the background of the magazine's table of contents.

Other illustrations may encompass entire articles. One regular contributor is Dan Price, a so-called hobo artist who hand-prints the text of articles alongside fanciful sketches as if he's writing in a travel journal. The illustrations add a folksiness to the magazine.

The use of color is another way *Blue* expresses a clear vision. "In many ways, *Blue* is about color," says Schrier. Shades range from nature-inspired tones to magnificent, original blends that Skinner invents herself.

"I don't have a particular palette in place," says Skinner, "But I often use a lot of blues, greens, and yellows, usually many shades of one color throughout an individual article. I usually try to match the majority of the photographs and let that decide."

Color itself is a great communicator. "Color is important because it gives each article an identity of its own," Skinner says. "It gives it a mood, sometimes more energy than the photos provide alone." The result is so stunning, it reminds readers of one of the simple truths of travel: that most things seem more beautiful when viewed from a fresh perspective. In pursuing that truth, *Blue* has designed a magazine that's wide awake, exciting, and true-to-life.

Advertising Age

The most conflicted relationship in magazine publishing is the one between advertising and editorial. Journalism professors and old-school editors preach the separation of church and state, struggling day in and day out to remain objective in the face of financial sponsorship.

Yet it's hard to ignore the fact that magazines depend on advertisers to stay alive. Though subscriptions and newsstand sales remain crucial, staggering circulation costs dilute this income. So unless readers are willing to support the magazine's cause with expensive annual subscriptions (as in the case of *Ms.* and *Adbusters,* socially aware titles that shun advertising's influence), advertising is a necessary ally—or evil, depending on how you look at it.

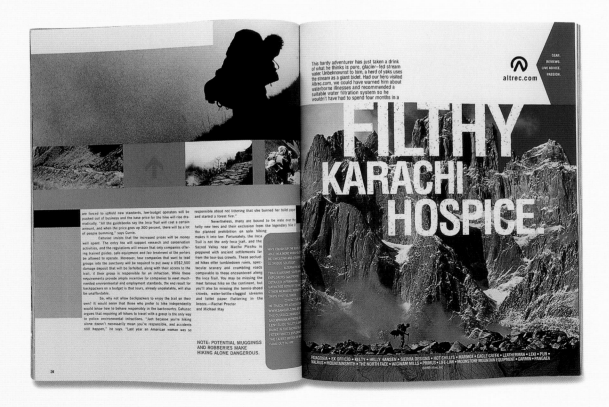

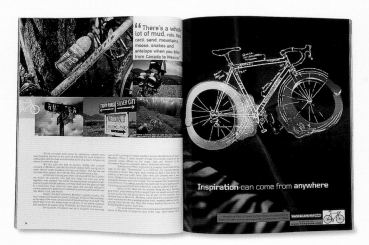

left, below and opposite
Sometimes the reason is intentional maneuvering by the art department, and sometimes advertisers take their cue from *Blue's* design. Whatever the case, ads and layouts have a way of coming together harmoniously.

Advertising's Influence

With ads, magazines constantly have to draw the line in the sand between customer satisfaction and editorial integrity. But without ads, they may be forced to cut back on the resources used to establish that integrity. Look, for instance, at the case of new economy business magazines such as *Red Herring*, which was forced to lay off reporters, designers, and editors when its high-tech advertisers started tightening their purse strings.

One issue rarely addressed in journalism schools is the effect advertising has on a magazine's look and feel. Art directors at trade magazines and smaller journals grapple with this problem often, usually because their

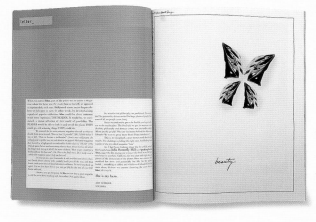

sales teams tend to sell a large number of fractional ads, or ads that take up only a quarter or half of the page, to lower-budget advertisers in order to serve a targeted industry or niche. But even high-powered titles face the concern. What happens when a valued advertiser places an ugly ad? When an ad contrasts sharply with the layout on the facing page?

The designers and art directors interviewed for this book differ in their approach to the advertising-design challenge. Some develop elaborate philosophies about it; others deal with it on the fly. But they are almost all alike in that they rarely leave the result to chance.

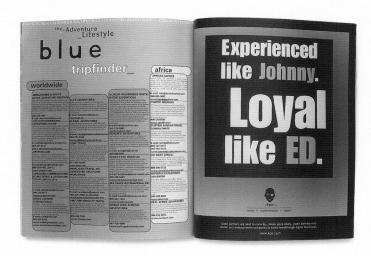

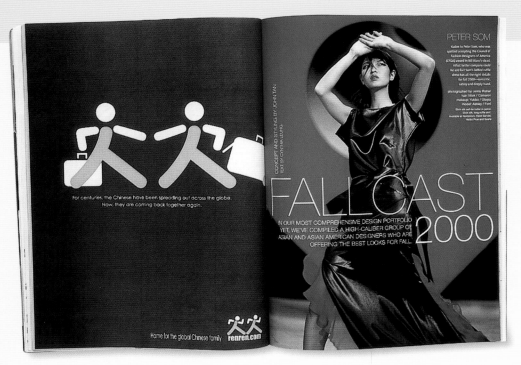

Staying Involved in Ad Placement

Many designers, at the very least, work a glance-over of the magazine into their production process. This involves close cooperation with the ad production department, not only because ads often come in at the last minute and are often placed in layouts last but also because the placement of ads is a sensitive issue.

"We look at the ads and see how they'll look against an article," says Dina Gan, editor in chief of *A*. "Some companies only want to be in the front of the book. Advertisers have their own concerns. Some ads aren't the prettiest in the world, and if they're really bad, we may request a different ad."

Other editors monitor ads closely so they can staunchly defend the magazine's brand. *Surface*, for example, positions itself as a magazine that's so far ahead of the design and fashion curve that it doesn't need to stoop to trendy or novelty concepts. "We need to set a certain tone in order to stay in the black," says

Riley John-donnell, the magazine's co-publisher and co-creative director.

If an advertiser submits an ad that's not in line with this tone, the magazine may turn it away. "We draw the line at anything offensive," says John-donnell. "Those kinds of things are visually not helping the client. Sometimes younger advertisers go for shock value, either visually or contentwise. They're trying to be cutting edge."

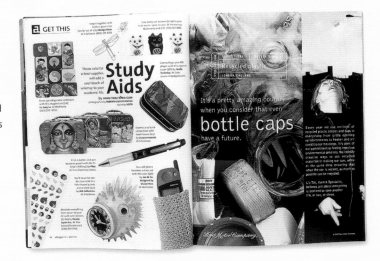

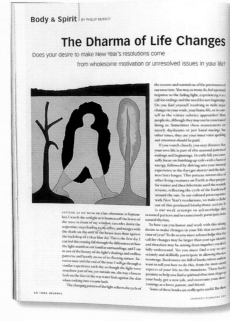

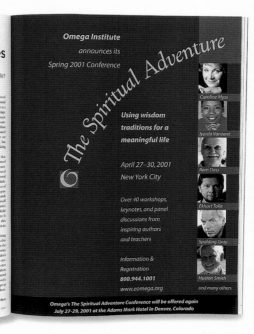

left and below *Yoga Journal* makes an effort to use attractive full-page ads in the front of the book, reserving the back for fractionals.

In the case of *Yoga Journal,* revising the ad layout policy helped the magazine take a big step toward reinventing a visual brand. The 25-year-old magazine had evolved into a new-age journal with dozens of fractionals—many of which were black-and-white ads for environmental products or health foods—scattered throughout the book. As part of the redesign, art director Jonathan Wieder elected to move all fractionals to the back of the book. "This allows us to group the best-looking ads toward the front," he says.

This policy contributed to the magazine's attempt, with its elegant redesign, to develop a broader consumer scope. "It wouldn't do us any good to backslide in terms of design," Wieder says. "A number of advertisers have even created new ads and come up with new ideas based on our new look."

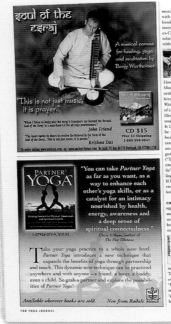

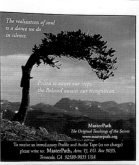

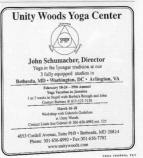

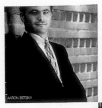
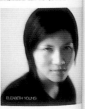
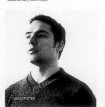
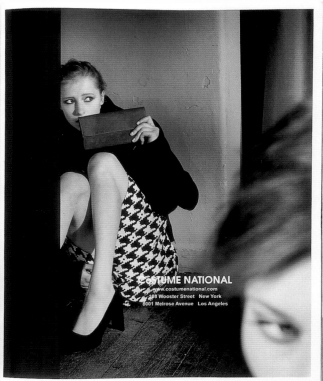

Working in Harmony

Wieder isn't the only designer who sees advertisers changing their strategies based on the magazine's look. "Advertisers imitate us, sometimes," says John-donnell of *Surface*. "They want to turn in something that represents them well in the context of our design."

In truth, the lines between advertising and editorial are increasingly blurred. Greater competition and the struggle to make a profit have brought the camps closer together. The invention of new revenue models on the Web also prompted change. In the race to make money, suddenly the fences didn't matter as much, and online content constantly was being packaged and sold.

This, for example, is why contract magazines—editorially driven publications created to promote international brands—constitute the fastest-growing division of magazine publishing these days. It's also why some designers look to the ads to help establish the overall picture of the magazine.

Blue editor in chief Amy Schrier makes no bones about artists sometimes playing off the ads they run. "We really do think about where they best integrate into

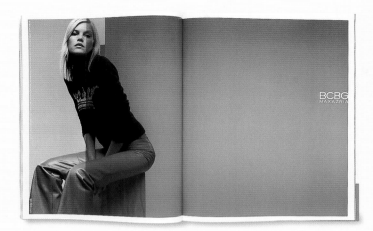

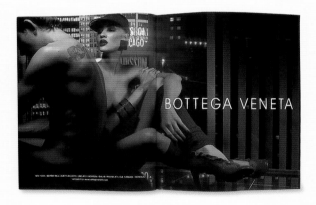

the layout," she says. "For example, we had this ad for a gin company. We put it opposite an article about a notorious alcoholic." Likewise, *Blue* may place ads for climbing shoes next to an article about rock climbing.

Editors and designers are careful not to pander to advertisers unnecessarily; they simply pair concepts to help readers get the most out of the grouping. "It's always clear that the ads and editorial are different," Schrier says. "We make them sufficiently distinct."

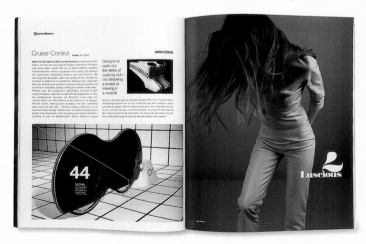

Advertisers' exhilaration at such placement often pays off for *Blue's* editors and artists, who see better synergy with their design in the ads that clients submit. "We promote adventurous graphic design, and that rubs off on the advertiser," Schrier says.

The most important thing to remember when grappling with this problem at your own magazine is to make sure all staff members understand and agree about what it takes to build and maintain a branded design—even if it means turning away an ad that doesn't fit with the look.

Graphic Design Ideas at Work

Trade magazines have always gotten a bad rap in the design department. Though they may easily make as much money as their consumer counterparts, they historically do not place as much emphasis on glamour and style. One reason is that they're more utilitarian—meant to be read and used rather than flipped through passively. Another is that, which the exception of a few, they don't depend as much on the draw of their covers on the newsstand.

But when you're a magazine for the design industry, your pages should look as good as the work you showcase. That was the idea behind *HOW* magazine's redesign in February 2000, which the design ideas magazine rolled out with a chronicle of its redesign process.

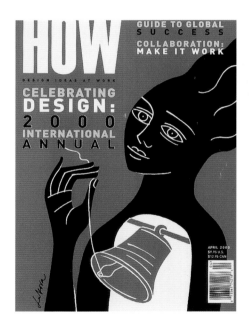

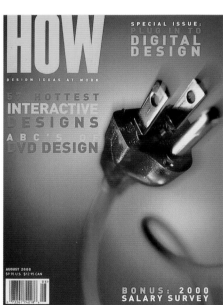

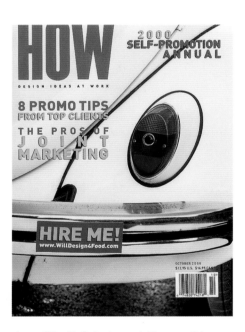

above *HOW*'s cover art always reflects the theme of the issue and recognizes skillful art and design at the same time. Here, the cover introduces a personality—illustrator Luba Lukova, who is profiled in that issue—while incorporating her vision for simple, colorful design patterns.

above Artistic depictions of well-designed objects often whimsically illustrate concepts on the covers. For the digital design theme issue, a simple electrical plug takes on a motion, light, and mood of its own.

above "Hire Me!" pleads a quaint bumper sticker on the bumper of an old car—the lines and shapes of which create an eye-catching cover for *HOW*'s October 2000 issue.

WHY IT WORKS:

The new design combines creative uses of color and type with a simple, organized layout that is pleasant to read and complements the artwork used to tell its stories.

right To introduce a feature on design contest winners, this spread integrates the judges' profiles into the pages' design. Overlapping boxes with rounded edges converge to create a Web-minded layout.

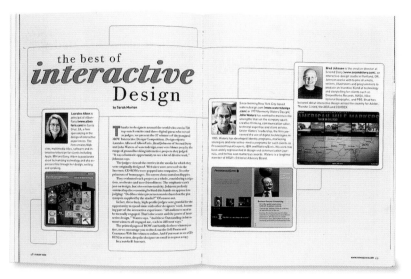

Learning Experience

Actually, *HOW* is a newsstand magazine, though it largely reaches toward a specific audience. Targeted readers are design professionals, from the principals of firms to the creative team members who populate them.

Designers, like all artists, are by nature influenced and inspired by other designers' work, and they learn from each other in every aspect of their business. *HOW* collects the ideas of successful firms and highlights what they're doing correctly so readers can learn from each other. The magazine is as much about the people and business practices of the graphic design world as it is about the work designers do.

Each bimonthly issue has a theme—promotion, creativity, and so on. Like the other titles by publisher F&W Publications—also known for *Writer's Digest* and several artists' magazines—the issues are packed with resources, ideas, and a host of takes surrounding each theme. Articles are meant to get readers thinking, then send them to the drawing board with the proper tools.

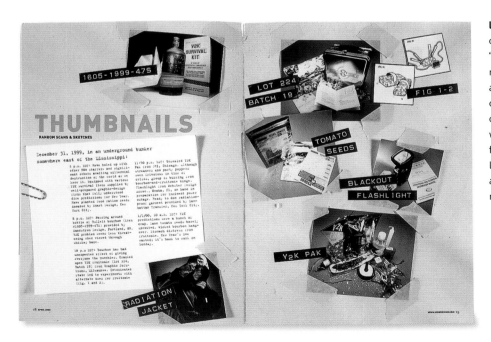

left *HOW* unleashes its own creativity in the "Thumbnails" department, here featuring an apocalyptic journal, crude labels, and photos of survival products invented by graphic design firms. The mixed-media layout experiment takes a humorous dig at paranoid Y2K watchers.

Grid for Structure and Variety

However, with all the tips and resource boxes that went into putting articles together, *HOW's* designers noticed layouts were getting too boxy. During the re-design, headed by outside designer Alexander Isley of Isley Design in Redding, Connecticut, the magazine went back to a smoother look to communicate concepts more completely.

The magazine usually runs articles over six to eight pages in the well, rarely divided by ads. "Nearly all features open on a spread," says editor in chief Bryn Mooth. "Those opening spreads require a big idea, a central concept that's supported by both the opening image and the headline and deck."

The design employs a flexible six-column grid; departments and features alike stick to the grid, but art director Amy Hawk may vary the number of text columns she uses. For instance, departments usually have three columns, but opening pages may include only one column, which may shift location but must still adhere to the grid. "The idea was to create a grid that gives structure but doesn't lock us into a cookie-cutter format," says Mooth.

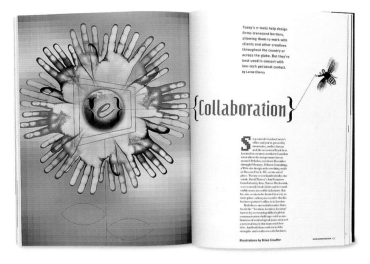

Feature articles are typically long, around 1500 to 2500 words. A single article may include several case studies or nuances related to a given topic. Colored text sub-heads divide articles frequently, every few paragraphs or so. By spreading articles over several pages, Hawk also dodges the danger of their looking too heavy.

As part of the redesign, *HOW* also standardized the types of sidebar it uses throughout the magazine. Lists of tips or other sidebar articles occupy parts of columns and are left open, without borders; instead, they're differentiated by a sans-serif font and a typeface of a different color. A colored "Source Box" typically bleeds off the bottom of a page and contains phone numbers and e-mail addresses for people quoted in an article.

above *HOW's* artist interprets the grid and uses type to create a mood. Here, the pixilated headline font suggests computerization while the illustrations express organic nature—the contrast between technology and human interaction explored in the article itself.

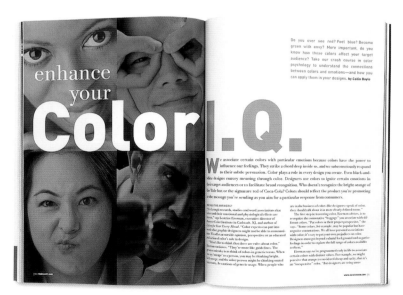

left A checkerboard of duotones—tinted according to the magazine's palette—introduces an article on the effect of color on design.

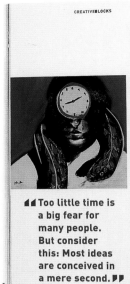

DESIGNERS ARE SCAREDY-CATS

The first question in my investigation—What blocks your creativity, especially when facing a pressing deadline?—elicited universal and deeply emotional responses.

What blocks creativity for most designers? Fear.

Of course, not everyone used the f-word. Fear manifests itself in a variety of forms. But you'd have to be as blind as a vampire bat to miss the message behind the responses. It was definitely clear that, in the words of Franklin D. Roosevelt, "The only thing we have to fear is fear itself."

Time, stress and judgment are the culprits designers identify as their main creativity blocks. "Time" means too little time, too much time or the deadline itself. "Stress" takes the form of worrying, lack of self-confidence or fear of failure. And "judgment" means the evaluation you get from clients, a boss or even yourself.

As president of Before & After in Tiverton, RI, I am a full-time creative-thinking coach who works with thousands of professionals each year. From that perspective, I assure you that—combined or alone—time, stress and judgment equal fear. From my experience, the best way to help people cope with fear is to help them better understand it. For example, when you were a child, if someone had said, "The lump under the rug isn't your dead uncle's body; it's a warped floorboard," your fear would've disappeared. Bingo.

Remember that fear is an integral part of the creative process. If something is truly creative then it isn't proven or known, and we usually fear the unknown. If you have no fear when you design something because you know it will work, it's a sign that your design isn't truly creative. Your design approach has probably been taken before; it's not wrong, it's just not so creative.

Simply knowing that fear is normal in the creative process doesn't make you immune to it, but it may make your fear a little easier to bear. It may help to know that some very accomplished creative people have been victims of the fear beast. You probably think that people such as Mick Jagger and Keith Richards, two of the most successful songwriters in rock music, are exempt from fear. Did you know that the original songs penned for their first albums were recorded under the handle "Nanker Phelge"? Why a pseudonym? Fear.

TIME IS ON YOUR SIDE

Let's break each of the fear factors down, starting with time. Too little time is a big fear for many people. But consider this: Most ideas are conceived in a mere second. Knowing this should take some pressure off you. Even if you have only three hours until deadline, you have more than 10,000 opportunities for inspiration in those three hours—a veritable eternity.

A good way to stretch your effective time on a project is to visit the assignment a few days before you start it. Then you don't have to physically work until the proverbial 11th hour, but your mind will start working on the project immediately. Once you expose yourself to a problem, your subconscious mind races to find solutions. Just make sure you're ready with pencil and paper when inspiration strikes, because it often comes without warning and retreats just as quickly.

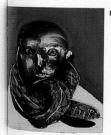

Conversely, some people find that too much time to do an assignment creates pressure. My suggestion is that if you have a lot of time early on, budget an hour or two to do some spade work—digging for ideas. Then walk away from the problem for a week or more. The worst thing that can happen is your mind will keep working on it. And that's not really a bad thing. Just have pencil and paper ready.

Another source of fear is the concept of the deadline. Let's admit it: They could've chosen a better word than "deadline." They wanted it to be less daunting—whoever they are. Maybe we don't need fewer deadlines; maybe we need more. Think about it. The Big Deadline is pretty final. But giving yourself mini-deadlines—like until the end of today to start the project—is way less scary when the ultimate deadline is still a week or so away. Give yourself until the end of tomorrow for one step and to the end of the next day for another task and so on. Ironically, if you take the ultimate deadline pressure off, you'll likely find yourself working ahead of schedule.

DON'T STRESS ABOUT MISTAKES

Studies show that worrying about stress is usually more stressful than the actual cause of the stress. And, yes, most people worry about failure. But did you know that successful people worry more often than unsuccessful people? The University of California at Davis recently conducted a worldwide study of more than 2,000 scientists. The most successful scientists failed much more often than their less successful colleagues.

You may have heard about the failure rate of baseball great Babe Ruth. The Bambino hit more home runs than anyone else in his era, but he also struck out more than anyone else in modern sports. Michael Jordan is a failure of great magnitude. He missed more shots than any other player during each of his last three NBA championship series. In fact,

> **Too little time is a big fear for many people. But consider this: Most ideas are conceived in a mere second.**

> **Studies show that worrying about stress is usually more stressful than the actual cause of the stress.**

CREATIVE SURVIVAL TIPS

What do your peers do to break out of their creative ruts? Creative-thinking coach Tom Monahan polled graphic designers via the HOW Web site about what makes their creative juices flow freely. It may seem obvious but, hey, maybe "taking a nap" is just the advice you need to hear. Here are their suggestions:

Listen to music.
Look at art or photography.
Spend time with children.
Hang out with other designers.
Dream.
Read.
Go for a drive.
Break out of your routine.
Walk away from your work and take a break.
Exercise.
Sleep.
Visit a bookstore.
Encourage others.
Don't work just for money.
Switch to another project.
Work on paper instead of the computer.
Think like a child.
Talk it out; don't let ideas just rumble around in your head.
Enjoy being creative.

left Subheads, information boxes, and pull quotes are helpful in determining the pages' flow. Boxes frequently bleed off the page, as with this sidebar on "Creativity Survival Tips."

right This layout integrates *HOW's* own ideas with other companies' featured designs. A story on building Web sites utilizes Lego blocks surrounded by colorful screen shots. Individual Legos act as keys for information boxes.

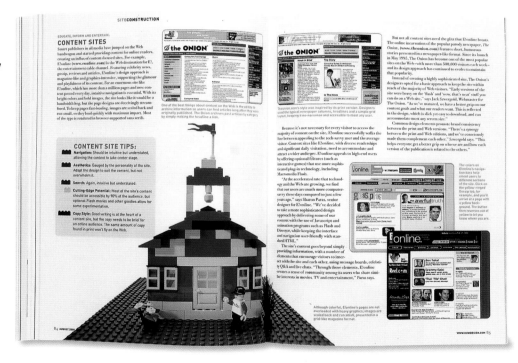

EDUCATE, INFORM AND ENTERTAIN:
CONTENT SITES

Smart publishers in all media have jumped on the Web bandwagon and started providing content for online readers, creating an influx of content-focused sites. For example, E!online (www.eonline.com) is the Web destination for E!, the entertainment cable channel. Featuring celebrity news, gossip, reviews and articles, E!online's design approach is magazine-like and graphics-intensive, supporting the glamour and playfulness of its content. For an enormous site like E!online, which has more than a million pages and new content posted every day, intuitive navigation is essential. With its bright colors and bold images, the site looks like it would be a bandwidth hog, but the page designs are deceivingly streamlined. To keep pages fast-loading, images are scaled back and run small, so they load quickly with maximum impact. Most of the type is rendered in browser-supported sans serifs.

Because it's not necessary for every visitor to access the majority of content on the site, E!online successfully walks the fine between appealing to the tech-savvy user and the average visitor. Content sites like E!online, with diverse readerships and significant daily visitation, need to accommodate and attract a wider audience. E!online appeals to high-end users by offering optional features (such as interactive games) that use more sophisticated plug-in technology, including Macromedia Flash.

"At the accelerated rate that technology and the Web are growing, we find that our users are much more computer-savvy these days compared to just a few years ago," says Sharon Paras, senior designer for E!online. "We've decided to take a more sophisticated design approach by delivering some of our content with the use of Javascript and animation programs such as Flash and Director, while keeping the interface and navigation user-friendly with standard HTML."

The site's content goes beyond simply providing information, with a number of elements that encourage visitors to interact with the site and each other, using message boards, celebrity Q&A and live chats. "Through these elements, E!online creates a sense of community among its users who share similar interests in movies, TV and entertainment," Paras says.

CONTENT SITE TIPS:

Navigation: Should be intuitive but understated, allowing the content to take center stage.

Aesthetics: Gauged by the personality of the site. Adapt the design to suit the content, but not overwhelm it.

Search: Again, intuitive but understated.

Cutting-Edge Potential: Most of the site's content should be accessible by 90% of the audience, but optional Flash movies and other goodies allow for some experimentation.

Copy Style: Good writing is at the heart of a content site, but the copy needs to be brief for an online audience. The same amount of copy found in print won't fly on the Web.

But not all content sites need the glitz that E!online boasts. The online incarnation of the popular parody newspaper, *The Onion*, (www.theonion.com) features short, humorous stories presented in a newspaper-like format. Since its launch in May 1995, The Onion has become one of the most popular sites on the Web—with more than 500,000 visitors each week—and its design approach has continued to evolve to maintain that popularity.

Instead of creating a highly sophisticated site, The Onion's designers opted for a basic approach to keep the site within reach of the majority of Web visitors. "Early versions of the site were heavy on the 'flash' and 'wow, that's neat' stuff you can do on a Web site," says Jack Szwergold, Webmaster for The Onion. "As we've matured, we have a better grip on our content goals and what our readers want. This is reflected in the design, which is slick yet easy to download, and can accommodate most any screen size."

Common design elements promote brand consistency between the print and Web editions. "There's a synergy between the print and Web editions, and we've consciously made them complement each other," Szwergold says. "This helps everyone get a better grip on who we are and how each version of the publication is related to the others."

Theonion.com's style was inspired by its print version. Designers used the typical newspaper columns, headlines and a simple grid layout, keeping it no-nonsense and accessible to most any user.

The colors on E!online's navigation bars help orient users to different sections of the site. Click on the yellow-ringed Gossip tab, for example, and you'll arrive at a page with a yellow background. The button then reserves out of yellow to let you know where you are.

Although colorful, E!online's pages are not overloaded with heavy graphics; images are scaled back and run small, presented in a grid-like magazine format.

157

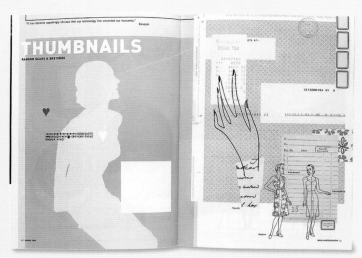

Restrained Design to Showcase Work

HOW's main objective was to avoid overshadowing the work it featured by getting carried away with its own design. Photographs are spread throughout the long features to allow for white space and pay tribute to featured art. "Prior to the redesign, features often were jam-packed," says Mooth.

Photos alternate between scenes of designers in their workspace and the work itself—Web sites, brochures, ads, and multimedia screenshots. The sophisticated, stylish colors of many of the products often reflect those of the walls with which designers surround themselves for inspiration, so photographs naturally tend to sprinkle diverse bits of color throughout the white pages.

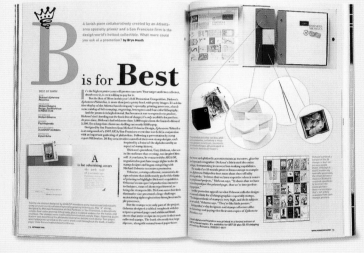

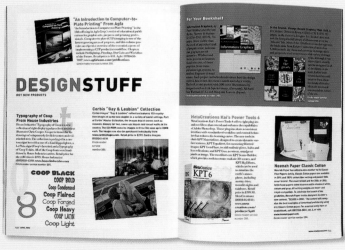

While restraining herself to let these photographs carry much of the show, Hawk does use *HOW's* own palette to add personality and to complement the shades that shine through in photography. Subtle but snazzy red oranges, violet blues, grass greens, and rich golds touch up text, specifically headlines, captions, subheads, and sidebars.

Color in section headers also separates departments from features. Front-of-the-book columns each are assigned their own color, and two-word headers run together, one word in vivid color, the other black. However, colored bars—sometimes with textured backgrounds that reflect the types of paper designers love to use—run across the tops of pages in the feature well.

above Callout circles and small photos dissect a complex design piece that won countless awards. The soft background color, gold type, and crowning graphic touch atop the headline set a refined tone while illuminating the white pages of the featured brochure.

left "Design Stuff," a regular department in the back of the book, is a colorful but simple gathering of short product reviews. Note how the magazine's palette is used to distinguish each short write-up.

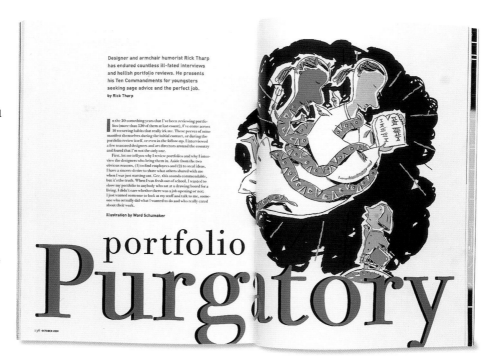

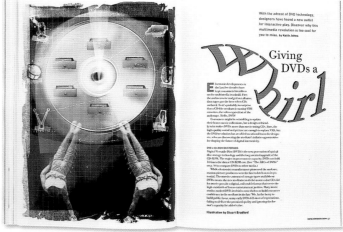

right This richly colorful opening illustration influences the colors used for type and accents throughout the rest of the article.

below The floating letters of this story's headline play off the skewed, scattered type on the facing poster, while the black background offers dramatic contrast to the bright colors and loud patterns of both.

Designer and armchair humorist Rick Tharp has endured countless ill-fated interviews and hellish portfolio reviews. He presents his Ten Commandments for youngsters seeking sage advice and the perfect job.
by Rick Tharp

Illustration by Ward Schumaker

portfolio
Purgatory

With the advent of DVD technology, designers have found a new outlet for interactive play. Discover why this multimedia revolution is too cool for you to miss. by Keith Jones

Giving DVDs a Whirl

Illustration by Stuart Bradford

Unity Through Type

Another way *HOW* makes sure the magazine reflects the design excellence it showcases is through type. During the redesign, the team chose faces that were modern, flexible, and interesting, yet would be consistent and identifiable from issue to issue.

ITC Bodoni serves as *HOW's* no-nonsense body text, while a medium-weight, versatile sans-serif font called DIN stands in as headlines, subheads, and sidebar copy. Hawk takes liberties with the copy, switching

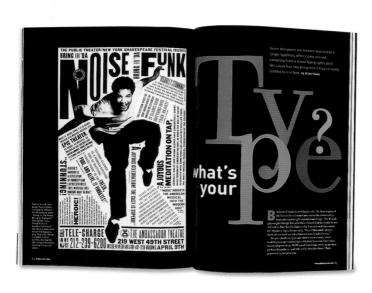

back and forth between all caps and initial caps with the sans serif, for instance, or manipulating the serif face with shadows and outlines for themed headlines.

All in all, experimentation with design is subtle, but *HOW's* touches result in a unified look, from issue to issue, that meets its purpose: to preserve the achievements of the graphic designers the magazine serves.

above The magazine's artist, Amy Hawk, often manipulates headline copy to drive home the theme of the article. In this headline on DVDs, the word whirl gets an added swirl.

159

I.D.

The International Design Magazine

Does design make the world go round? That's debatable, of course, depending on whose world you're talking about—but from the perspective of *I.D.* magazine, design is the core around which an entire universe revolves.

Making the pages of this magazine is a prestigious accomplishment for graphic, furniture, industrial, architectural and digital designers. *I.D.* successfully strives to find the most elegant and innovative ways to display examples of design excellence, building tasteful, smart layouts around simple images of products.

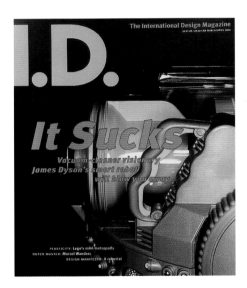

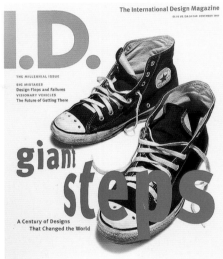

far left Funny and startling, the bright pink cover line for a focus on robotic vacuum cleaners leans toward streaks of light for a flashy product portrait. Color and type create an electric atmosphere that animates products.

left A battered pair of Converse sneakers is a comfortable symbol of influential design. Literally interpreting the theme of the article, cover lines with apparent distance and depth play off the headline "Giant Steps."

WHY IT WORKS:

Brilliantly simple backgrounds, creative photo editing and placement, and electrically charged colors and type team up for a sleek, modern gallery of designers' work.

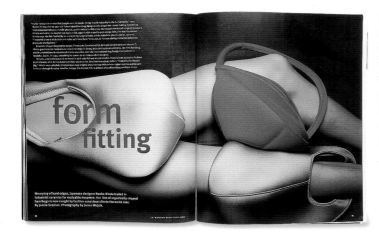

Global Design Focus

Published since 1954 and originally a trade publication focused on industrial design, *I.D.* has evolved to cover the "art, business, and culture of design" around the world. "In its early years, *I.D.* mirrored the excitement of the post-World War II American design scene," says executive editor Jenny Wohlfarth. "Since then, the magazine has blossomed to become more international and eclectic in its scope,"

In 1988, the magazine shed its strictly trade image and revised its tagline to read "International Design Magazine," reflecting both its global reach and its coverage of a wide scope of design topics ranging from architecture, industrial design, and graphics to fashion, interiors, technology, and design culture. As a hybrid trade/general-interest magazine, *I.D.* is as accessible to the design-curious consumer as it is to trained artists.

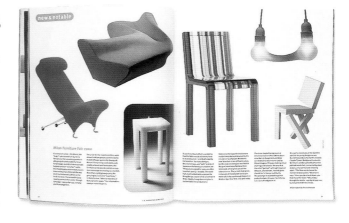

Long based in New York City, the magazine was purchased by F&W Publications in 1999 and moved its editorial headquarters to Cincinnati, Ohio, in 2001. *I.D.* continues to stretch its tentacles around the globe; furniture and gadgets from Milan and Berlin mingle with those from the vibrant Manhattan design community.

"*I.D.* is to the design industry what *Wired* is to technology," Wohlfarth says. "It pushes the proverbial envelope—both in content coverage and design—exploring the most primitive and fascinating kernels of design-related topics while philosophically scrutinizing their significant implications on culture and society. Its greatest strength is its own dichotomy: It's both provocative and simplistic, serious and sassy, focused on details while always revealing the bigger picture."

I.D.'s readers fall into three categories: designers who want information about the art and culture of the design industry; business executives who want to take advantage of the positive impact that innovative design has on their business; and design aficionados—nondesigners who love great design and who understand and appreciate the importance of aesthetics.

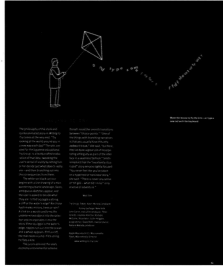

161

Playful Image Placement

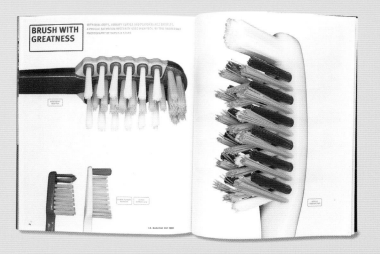

In fact, products or design work often take on lives of their own. Many pages simply feature silhouetted photos on blank white or tinted pages, with small blocks of text placed strategically.

The way *I.D.'s* designers manipulate these images makes them truly effective. For example, designers may blow up an image until it's absurdly out of proportion to its perceived importance—vacuum cleaners, sneakers, and humidifiers all get their day in the sun. Or they may use repetition to parade products across a spread, as they did with an army of toothbrushes magnified beyond life-size proportions. The pages are reminiscent of an old science fiction film or a surrealist painting in which inanimate objects come to life—but the images are frankly, purely true to form.

In other instances, cropping, magnification, or angular approaches accentuate features of objects that may be overlooked when they're shot straight on. Photos home in on the sly curves of a cord on a hanging lamp, the delicate texture of a woven chair, the humble design of a control panel for a common household appliance.

"Images define and drive the design in *I.D.*, reemphasizing the magazine's mission to bring attention to the designs of products being featured and not the design of the magazine itself," Wohlfarth says. "*I.D.'s* design seeks to be noteworthy without being too noticeable."

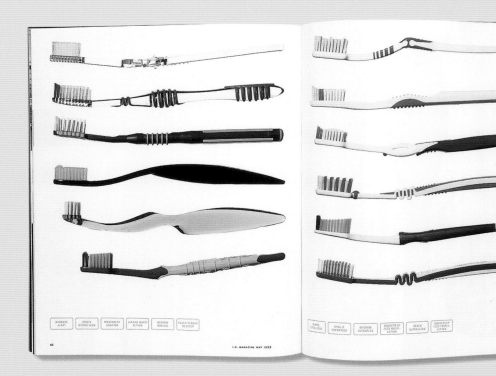

above and left   The intricacy of an everyday product is the theme of this feature on high-tech toothbrushes. The first spread gets in your face with blown-up photos of the contoured bristles and gentle curves, while the second uses even repetition to impress readers with the inventiveness of design.

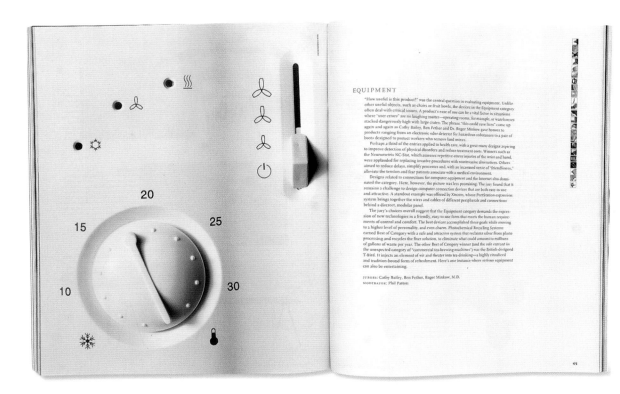

left This climate control unit received a nod for excellent design in *I.D.'s* annual review; a closeup of its sensible white interface also mirrors a white page of text for a minimalist and elegant layout.

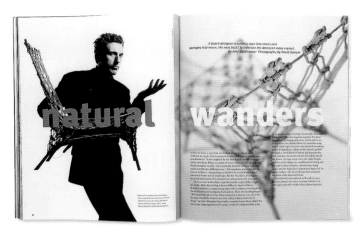

above In the hands of Marcel Wanders, this chair looks like ordinary furniture—but on the opposite page, it's a web hanging behind the text. *I.D.'s* propensity for imaginatively magnifying, cropping, and organizing photos creates unexpected perspectives.

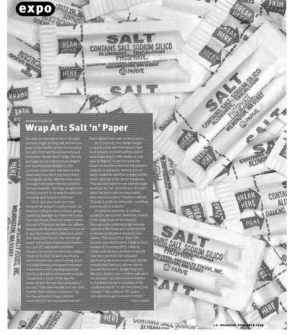

above Andy Warhol would be proud: This layout pays tribute to a packaging concept that's ordinary and rarely recognized. A bright red box with white type reverses the modest red printing on curved salt packets.

163

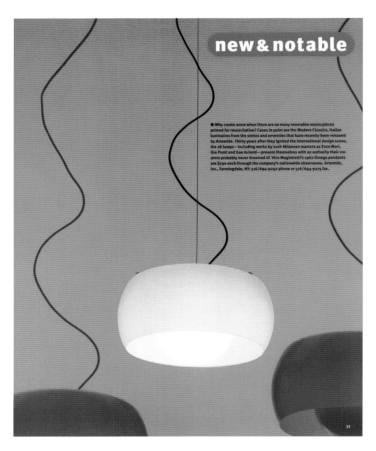

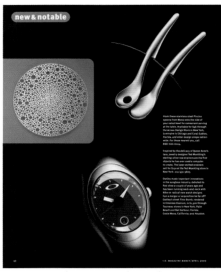

new & notable

far left Bright orange dramatically backlights the snaking cords on these Italian lamps, another example of *I.D.'s* use of contrast.

left Adding black background color to negative space gives these products a space-age look. *I.D.* is especially strong at using negative space to build dramatic contrast.

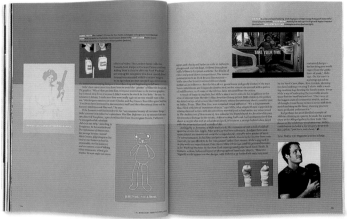

Contrast Through Space

The use of contrast is an important technique for calling attention to the excellent design of featured products. This is accomplished largely through the use of negative space.

The front of the book is more compact than the expansive feature well. "Expo," a roundup of design and technology news, projects, exhibits, and excursions, is compartmentalized using different colored backgrounds to create simple divisions of short articles. Next is "New & Notable," an exquisitely designed exploration of the latest and best-designed products for work, home, and play.

In the feature well, editors keep article length to a minimum, so text never dominates a spread. Short blocks of text swim in a sea of negative space, surrounded by a few large images. Despite the liberal use of negative space, however, pages stick closely to a grid, again keeping in tune with a classic, Swiss design approach. Images take on interesting and diverse relationships with text, but they are always neatly disciplined.

above Plastic-happy colors act as backdrops for an article on designer and filmmaker Mike Mills, who is inspired by American suburbia. The background color adds a campiness that helps readers understand the tone of the article.

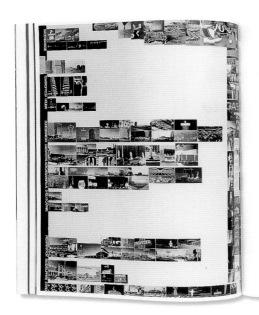

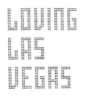

LOVING LAS VEGAS

Digital Color and Typefaces

Contrast is also accomplished through color. *I.D.* has an affinity for the use of straightforward white and black interrupted by sudden outbreaks of digital ecstasy— hot pinks and bright blue-greens, fluorescent greens and oranges. For the most part, though, articles stick to black text on white or pale-colored backgrounds, with frequent reversed white on black pages for variation.

The modernistic and digital feel created in the layout of images is perpetuated in the choice of typefaces. Type usage also continues the magazine's goal of letting the images of products prevail. "*I.D.* is deliberately sparse in its font usage, almost exclusively sticking with the Scala and Meta families throughout each issue," Wohlfarth says. "Diversions are rare, but purposeful. This strict adhesion to two classic font families helps preserve the magazine's overall design mission: to be beautifully unobtrusive."

In this way, *I.D.* achieves what good design is about— putting function before form. The magazine's design establishes a mindset and acts as inspiration while never failing to remember that the featured designer's work is the star of the show.

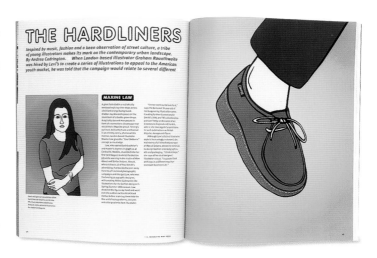

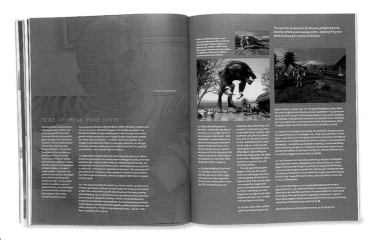

Eleven Steps...

to a Successful Redesign

A redesign can be the best—or worst—thing to happen to your magazine in years. Two design consultants who speak frequently about redesigns at publishing industry events discuss how to navigate the process for the best results.

Periodically evaluate the magazine's design.

Rob Sugar, president of Auras Design in Silver Spring, Maryland, recommends that clients evaluate the design of their publications about every five years. It's time for an overhaul if (1) editorial changes create a new structure for the publication, (2) the publisher wants to reach a different audience, (3) technological or cultural advances alter editorial content, (4) a new business plan repositions the media strategy, (5) new competitors require the magazine to reposition itself in a niche, or (6) the creative team begins experiencing boredom, repetition, or difficulty fitting new ideas into the current format.

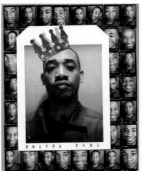

left *GQ*'s redesign allowed designers to refocus emphasis on imagery and make layouts less about the type, which helped reinstate a feeling of consistency.

Evaluate the magazine's mission.

If you don't have a written mission statement for your magazine, develop one that defines content, structure, and plans for growth, says Sugar. Then study the magazine according to the mission, asking how well the current design serves the reader and what needs to be changed to engage the reader better. Also, identify what it is about your publication that sets you apart from your competition. "Editors and designers ought to ask, 'What unique content and structure in features and departments define our vision?'" says Sugar.

Align the editorial, design, and business teams.

A redesign shouldn't cover the magazine's look and feel only. It should reflect a reevaluation of the magazine's editorial content and business plan as well, says John Johanek, coprincipal of Ayers/Johanek Publication Design in Bozeman, Montana. A new palette, grid, and set of typefaces mean little if they don't mirror updates in editorial focus or marketing and demographics. "If you haven't fully analyzed your objectives, you're just putting a new look on old problems," Johanek says. Use the redesign as a way to rethink the magazine as a whole, and hold frequent meetings with editorial and business departments to be sure everybody is headed in the same direction.

Put function before form.

Make all decisions about your design for concrete reasons based on research and knowledge of the magazine's goals. "A clear idea of the publication's function is often the source of inspiration for me," says Sugar. "There is a distinct difference between design as ornamentation and design as structure—just like in architecture—and revealing the structure of a publication is the designer's first duty. A new reader should be able to pick up any copy of the magazine and understand it from a glance through the book, even without looking at the contents page."

Cull inspiration from other sources.

You learn a great deal about the niche you serve by studying your competition during a redesign—but be careful when looking to other magazines for design ideas. "I call it the ugly duckling syndrome," says Johanek. "It's an easy trap to look at other magazines and grab the things you like for your own design. But you end up with a hodgepodge of elements that don't work well out of context." A healthier way to find inspiration, he says, is to look outside publishing for design ideas—to fashion, art, architecture, or advertising, for example.

Consider outside design firms.

If you're like most art departments, you barely have enough time to close your latest issue, let alone plan and implement a full redesign. But time isn't the only reason for bringing in design consultants. "A lot of magazines are strapped with company history and feel limited by what they've never been allowed to do," says Johanek. "Outside companies may feel the freedom to be more experimental." When interviewing outside design firms, Sugar recommends looking closely at their previous work—before and after samples, the questions they consider, and the order the redesign takes. Also ask about their philosophy of redesigns in general and how much they're willing to tackle. "It should be expected that a design firm will be involved with editorial structure, even to the level of suggesting departments and editorial initiatives," Sugar says.

Get your inside designers involved.

Of course, artists who have worked on a magazine for years may feel territorial about letting consultants take the reins. "You're going to run into a problem if the art department isn't made part of the redesign," says Johanek. "Everyone needs to be part of the final product." Hold frequent meetings between in-house artists and contracted designers. Let everybody review each style sheet and mockup as it's finished and allow them to discuss the meaning behind design choices with consultants. Then, when it's time for the art staff to take over the new design for regular implementation, they can interpret the design as it was intended.

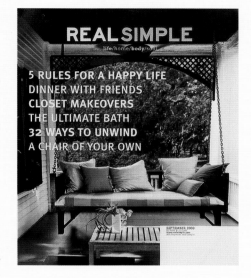

above Design tweaks during *Real Simple*'s first year of publication were responses to comments by readers that the magazine was too simple to apply to readers with chaotic lives. The magazine's designers made efforts to include more personal images and unexpected departures in visuals.

Prepare readers for the redesign.

It's important to let readers know the redesign is coming and why. At the least, an editorial should explain the reasoning and emphasize the positive aspects of the new look. "Remembering that a magazine is an ongoing conversation with its readership, a relaunch ought to invite the readership behind the scenes to encourage their continued participation," says Sugar. Some magazines do teasers, showing half the new logo and half the old one on the cover of the issue previous to the redesign. No matter how you approach the subject, stay positive. "You want to avoid anything that smacks of apologizing," says Johanek.

Market the redesign to your advertisers.

The launch of a redesign is a good opportunity to sell extra ad space. "Sales reps should use the redesign as a tool," says Johanek. "They can promote it as a special issue, talking up the fact that it will have a longer shelf life and a bigger press run. The ideal situation is that you generate enough bonus revenue to offset the cost of the redesign." Also don't forget to communicate the occasion to the rest of the world, Johanek says. Send press releases to *Folio:* and other trade journals or newspapers.

Do your research.

If time and budget allow, you may want to conduct focus groups and surveys with long-time readers, the magazine's staff, and a few people who are unfamiliar with the magazine. "The goals of the survey are to find out how much people remember the structure of the publication and what they found the most—and least—intriguing," says Sugar. One problem with groups is that readers often pinpoint problems without suggesting solutions. Another is that feedback may stray radically from the designers' original intent. "You have to balance the focus groups with good judgment and not be totally swayed by opinions," says Johanek.

Stick with the redesign once it's launched.

Roll out the redesign all at once in a single issue, accepting that you will inevitably hear negative comments from at least a few readers. If you've done your research, the new design should be right on target and only minor changes should be necessary. "Tweaking is an unavoidable part of redesigns," says Sugar. "Some ideas simply don't work when applied to real-world deadlines or budgets." But unless readers lash out violently against the new design, make your adjustments without announcing you're doing it. "Letting the conversation play itself out in a letters department is a good approach to keeping reader input alive but confined and, after a few issues, even that can be dispensed with," Sugar says.

The Best in Entrepreneurial Ideas

"It's more than a magazine—it's a movement."

You'd expect this kind of statement from a grassroots title like *Utne Reader,* but it seems a strange assertion from a business magazine. Yet that's the groundwork on which *Fast Company* is built and, among loyal readers, the six-year-old title is a staple of the changing business culture. From its inception, the design has been integral in the "movement" by screaming for change through bold covers, unconventional images, and a propensity for breaking the rules.

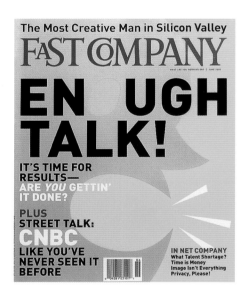

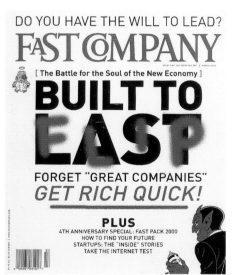

far left   The cover of *Fast Company* is emblazoned with the brilliant ideas and quotes of people profiled inside. Loud colors, humorous graphics, and sensational type reflect the creative energy of these entrepreneurs and experts.

left   When they're not all-text proclamations, covers often feature funny illustrations. Here, the March 2000 cover portrays the "battle for the soul" of the economy, in which the devil has spray painted over the original headline.

WHY IT WORKS:

Fast Company incites readers to embrace new ideas with bold, illustrative type and intrigues them with insightful, entertaining photography. Once covers and opening spreads draw them in, basic layout and a careful use of white space keep them hooked through long articles.

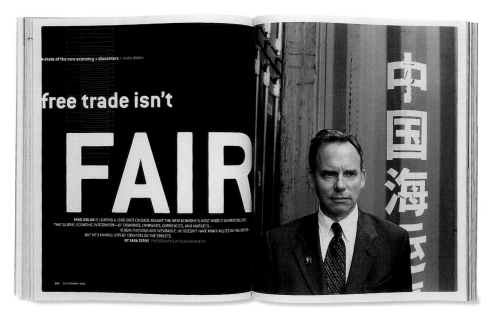

Radical Business Ideas

Fast Company positions itself as the mouthpiece for a radical new breed of businesspeople who invent the rules as they go along. "*Fast Company* was the first business magazine to fully realize that the Internet was about to change everything," says creative director Patrick Mitchell. "For our audience, it changed the way people worked, where they worked, the way they managed people, the way they communicated."

Founded in 1995 by two former editors from *Harvard Business Review,* the magazine has grown to include a well-known Web site, an organization of readers called Community of Friends, and an education program as part of its brand.

The formula has been wildly popular and, amid competition from other new economy titles, it experienced exponential growth. Paid subscriptions soared 500 percent since the magazine's inception, while newsstand sales increased 155 percent.

The magazine targets businesspeople who have big ideas, uninhibited energy, and the strength and positioning to make a difference. Readers tend to be in positions of power at established or startup companies, yet young and open-minded enough to plow through convention. According to the magazine's media kit, "Their goal is to overthrow the status quo."

Fast Company's design reflects this maverick way of doing business. "The goal of the design was to capture the excitement and almost revolutionary undertones of what was happening in business and society," says Mitchell.

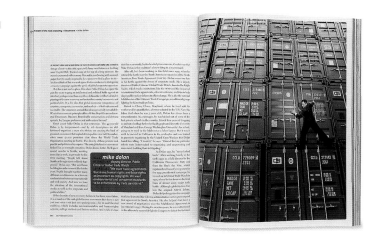

Covers Tell the Story

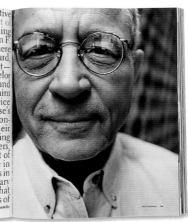

The magazine stirs up enthusiasm for the theme of its latest issue starting with the cover. The bold, text-driven headlines and cover lines that are now familiar to newsstand readers actually derived from *Fast Company's* first issue, where an all-type cover proclaimed the magazine's manifesto for the new rules of business: "Work is personal. Computing is social. Knowledge is power. Break the rules."

After several issues, designers set about to recapture on the cover the same magic and excitement that articles within the magazine conveyed. "Our conclusion that it wasn't the people we wrote about that were interesting, it was the things they were thinking about and the things they were saying that were unique," Mitchell says. "Suddenly, it was clear what should be on the cover. The whole magazine design philosophy is inspired by the brilliant ideas and quotes that are in the articles."

Beyond the text-heavy covers, the same commitment is made throughout the magazine. Occasionally, quotes instead of a static headline will open a feature article. A catchphrase may inspire an issue's theme and pop up in openers throughout the magazine. For example, one issue argued the difference between companies

"built to last" and those "built to flip." A handwriting-like script typeface was assigned to the concept and followed it through several related articles.

Generally, though they call up type to embody the golden nuggets of stories, *Fast Company's* designers stick to two or three typefaces. They use FF Din for a sans serif and Electra as a serif, occasionally employing HTF Knockout for "Net Company," the "magazine within a magazine."

"The limit of fonts is another thing I chalk up to experience," says Mitchell. "Our early issues were all over the map typographically. As I learned that simplicity was the way to go, one of the ways to achieve that was to strip everything down, including the typefaces. [Simplicity] also really united the overall look of the magazine and created its signature style."

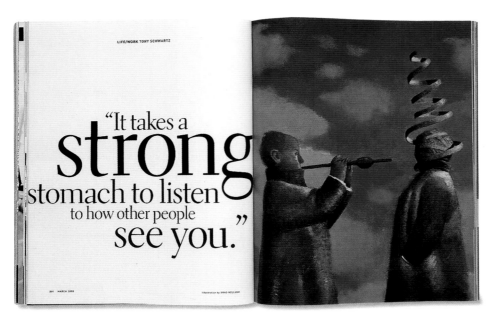

above Designers stick to a few typefaces used in varied ways. A large serif face with little leading introduces this feature, reversing the magazine's commitment, on subsequent pages, to wide spaces between short text blurbs.

left A single quote acts as the headline on a story's opening spread, with only a surreal illustration backing up the strong statement.

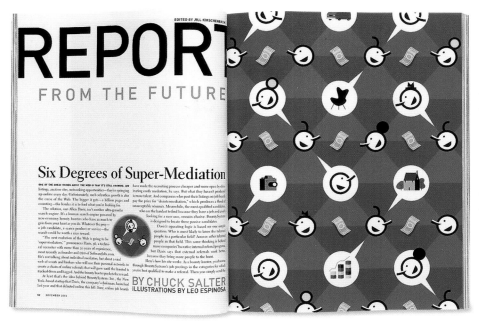

left A pattern of cartoon heads and other icons accompanies an article on the future of recruiting. The left page repeats the motif; text reflects the illustration's colors. Generous space gives the page breathing room.

below A bouncy feature on Web site Weather.com features employees affected by wind, ice, and sudden rain. Note the wide top margin, a technique for creating space and continuity throughout the magazine.

Integrating White Space

The theme of simplicity, in fact, overtook the magazine's entire design two years into publication. While still indulging in a hyperactive use of type and art, designers scaled back the chaos by including more white space, consistent design elements, and relatively clean pages. Now, when a layout steps into the experimental realm, it stands out even more among other low-lying designs.

The revival of simplicity emerged from Mitchell's personal revelation. "The concept of white space was a result of a sudden urge in 1997 to simplify everything—my life, my job, and especially my magazine," he says. "The times just seemed to call for it." Mitchell's own design style, though, did not adapt to the decision easily. "It didn't come naturally to me," he says. "But I knew we needed it, so I just built it into the grid. Then I didn't have to be conscious of leaving room for space—it was just there."

Adding a tall margin to the top of the page was the most significant step. Nicknamed the "attic" by *Fast Company's* art staff, this white space persists throughout the feature well. Designers try to leave it open, though occasionally they'll add pull quotes to the space.

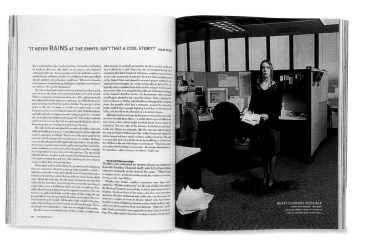

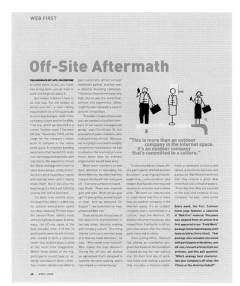

left This quiet department page is a lesson in simplicity. The four-column article with a tiny stick-figure illustration and orange type complementing the pink background tells a compelling story about corporate culture.

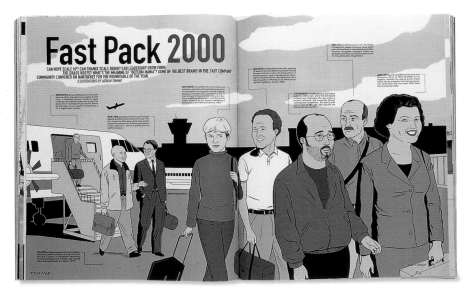

Capturing Personality and Spirit

left *Fast Company's* illustrations are its hallmark. For a story about the magazine's roundtable of experts, cartoon likenesses of each participant arriving at the site of the event are used rather than photos.

Because *Fast Company* is about people and their ideas, the magazine relies heavily on photography. Portraits may be candid—a series of snapped facial expressions, a group photo in which most people are looking away from the camera. They can also be staged for humorous or curious effect. Whatever the scenario, images are meant to provide insight into the subject's character, an approach as effective at telling the story as the article itself.

"One of the first things we decided about *Fast Company* photography is that if the best we can do is get a picture of a guy at his desk, we suck," says Mitchell. "That type of image is contrary to the spirit of *Fast Company* and the business environment today. You may be the CEO of a multimillion dollar corporation, but you're also a mother, wife, sister, gardener, painter, juggler, and a thousand other things. If we simply take your picture at your desk, we ignore all that."

That's a radical approach for a business magazine— but then, business culture has seen unbelievable changes in the past decade. *Fast Company* has not only grown to reflect those changes but also has been instrumental in helping shape them. Design helps each issue shout new rules and ideas across the culture like a town crier, documenting them as they emerge in the context of new outlooks and possibilities.

below Portraits of businesspeople, as in this shot of roundtable participants, are unfashioned and unexpected, meant to capture subjects' complexity. Depicting professionals as regular people is *Fast Company's* commentary on the changing landscape of business.

While artists try to be more restrained, the team is still dedicated to art and color that reflect the accelerated spirits of die-hard readers. Color inside the magazine, for instance, generally is muted, reserved for information boxes and display text, but the cover may scream fluorescent orange, rich sunny yellow, or more subtle blue and beige. The magazine doesn't use a palette, though designers tend to stick to brighter colors as the situation calls for them.

Artwork is another way *Fast Company* steps outside the boundaries of simplicity. As in other business magazines, illustrations take on great importance. Rather than always being the abstract depictions of a complicated concept common in other titles, however, illustrations in *Fast Company* are often more literal, sometimes even replacing photographs with caricatures of profiled people.

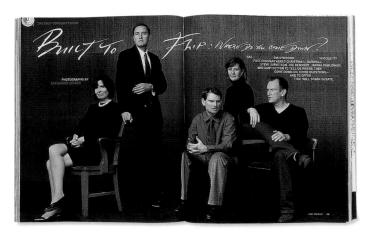

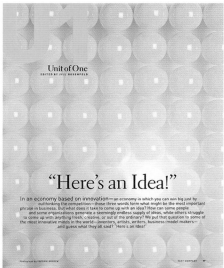

above The hauntingly beautiful monotony of row upon row of light bulbs opens a series of profiles on innovators. The word idea in the headline is placed directly over the one lighted bulb.

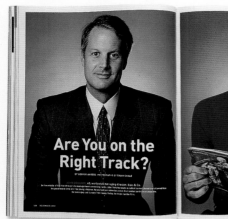
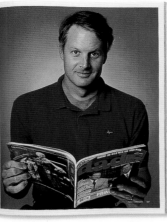

Are You on the Right Track?

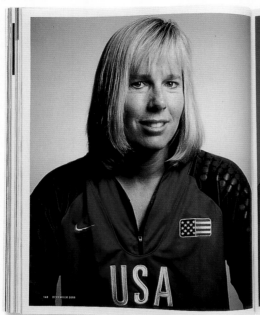
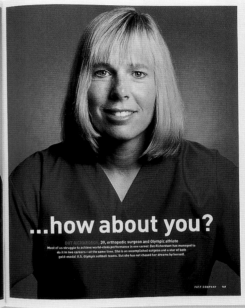

...how about you?

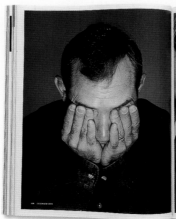
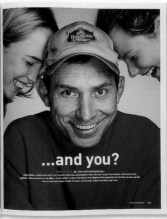

...and you?

above, center, and below
Once again using portraits to explore a subject's many sides, designers delegate space for three opening spreads—with a progressive headline— before getting to the meat of the story.

New Business Rules for a New Economy

The information age has altered the way people read. There's so much information that people, by necessity, have to tune out in order not to be overloaded. They also have come to expect content to be fast, lively, and interactive, even in two-dimensional print media.

Nobody relates to this more than the businessperson, especially the founders and executives of fast-track startups who work 17-hour days and have hundreds of magazines and Web sites clamoring for their attention.

To bring this audience the longer-form analyses and profiles they need to run their business, *Business 2.0* keeps its approach simple. The magazine puts articles center stage and offers visual tools to help readers apply what they learn in an enjoyable, hassle-free way.

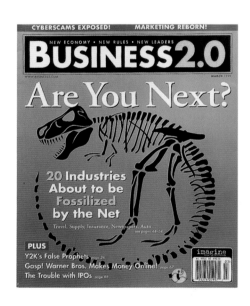

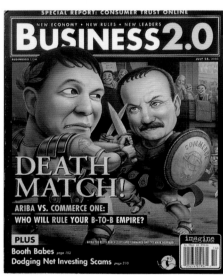

far left   Covers must grab the attention of fast-moving readers, so they're clever without being complex. For the March 1999 issue, a dinosaur skeleton is a humorous poke at the Internet's effect on old-school industries.

left   Illustrator Thomas Reis came up with this parody of business-to-business competitors when the movie *Gladiator* was released. The illustration is an instantly recognizable concept that inspires a laugh and a second look, another newsstand grab for hurried passersby.

WHY IT WORKS:

Business 2.0 is dedicated to making articles as user-friendly as possible. Infographics, callouts, type treatment, and simple layouts work together to build a pleasant, easy, and familiar read.

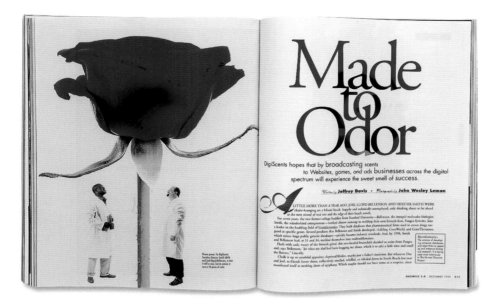

Fun with Business

The business magazine's concept grew out of a social conversation between Chris Anderson, CEO of publishing company Imagine Media, and several friends, including Amazon.com head Jeff Bezos. The title launched as a monthly in late 1997 and hit the newsstands half a year later.

Many new economy business titles also were emerging around that time, so *Business 2.0* had to carve its niche. "We weren't going to be a news magazine," says art director Laura Morris, who helped found the magazine with editor in chief James Daly. "We offered bigger package stories. Instead of making it newsy, we made it a how-to magazine, explaining how to make it in the new economy."

Unlike business magazines of the past, new titles had to be more "mass consumerish," Morris says. Suddenly, everybody wanted a piece of the action. Therefore,

though content was aimed at upper management and CEOs, design had to appeal to a broader audience. "I made it a little more fun and creative than other books, something that a non-businessperson would find dynamic visually," Morris says.

The model was so successful that, in June 2000, *Business 2.0* went biweekly. Currently boasting an all-paid circulation of 350,000, the magazine packs its pages with business tutorials and short pieces on new products and market trends as well as long, thoughtful pieces on the smartest paths to steer.

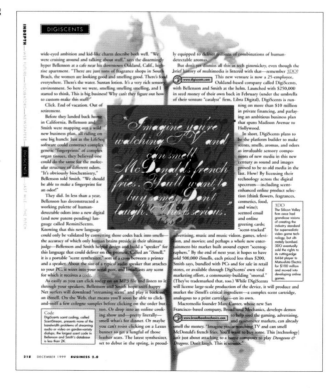

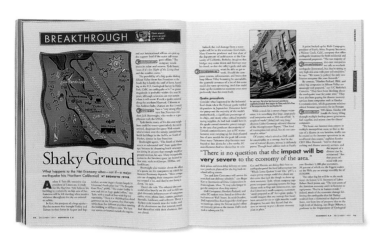

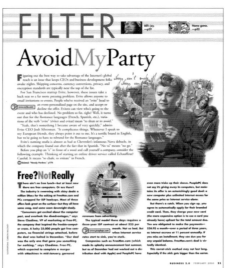

left Color-coded header tags separate departments from features; the front-of-the-book sections are tagged in power-tie red. The words in headlines run together in alternating gray and black.

far left Writing out Web site URLs in body text consumes space and wrecks alignment, so the magazine inserts callout tabs next to Web company references. The tabs borrow the pointy hand icon familiar even to Web amateurs.

Morris admits that while she doesn't necessarily feel she's been influenced by Web design in her creation of the magazine—"It's a totally different thing," she says—she borrowed the color-coding navigation idea from online media.

That's not the only Web element *Business 2.0* uses, in fact. Elements that are immediately recognizable in the Web platform, such as the pointy hand cursor and linked underlined words, take their places in *Business 2.0's* design. Every time an article refers to a Web site, a small gray tab preceded by pointing hand icon juts into the text to call out the related URL. When interesting facts or definitions relate to a term addressed in the paragraph, the term is underlined and colored red, and a nearby box contains the data.

Designers also like to stick information in boxes, especially as sidebars or resource lists, to make it more accessible. "We like to provide as many entry points, as many different places to pull the reader in, as possible," Morris says.

Borrowing from the Web

One reason for *Business 2.0's* success is the simplicity of its presentation. Morris and her team make ease of reading and navigation a top priority. "A businessperson who's very busy doesn't need design that overshadows text," she says. "We needed to design a magazine that wasn't too complex."

Morris points out a prime example of this commitment to navigability: The table of contents resides just inside the magazine's front cover. A gatefold page opens up to a spread ad, but the contents pages are the first readers see—a rarity in magazine publishing, where the contents usually are buried between layers of ads.

To keep readers aware of where they are and what they're looking at while flipping through the magazine, designers color-code sections of the magazine. Red tabs head pages in the front of the book, black ones run across the well of in-depth articles, and blue tabs mark the back of the book.

right The colorful table of contents is always located inside the front cover, with a gatefold ad underneath. This is another technique aimed at helping busy executives easily navigate the magazine.

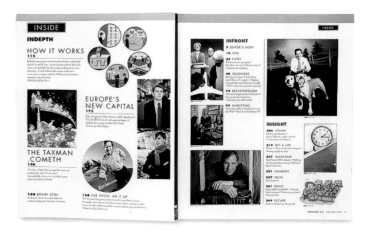

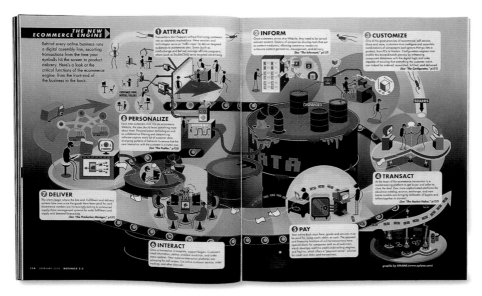

left The magazine first hired Xplane to portray workflows and diagrams, such as this e-commerce engine map. The ant people that characterized Xplane's illustrations eventually became an integral part of *Business 2.0*'s brand.

Simple Touches That Make the Brand

Morris doesn't like to overdesign the magazine; pages are generally white with black type, with colored sub-heads, pull quotes, single images, and the occasional icon or illustration to break up text. Type rarely strays from the classic, matter-of-fact Garamond and Futura families. Pages occasionally dip into a palette of violet, rust brown, pink, and pale green but often stick close to the primary navigational colors for accents. Gray-beige and mustard gold are often used for backgrounds.

One technique *Business 2.0* has employed to enliven its pages, however, has become an important part of its brand. Early on, the magazine hired a company called XPlane to make a diagram of a business concept to il-lustrate a story. What emerged were elaborate info-graphics abuzz with what Morris calls "little ant

people"—stick figures with funny facial expressions racing from one section of the diagram to another.

The infographics help *Business 2.0* explain concepts in an easy-to-use format, but the illustrations have also become a large part of the magazine's personality. The stick people now make cameos on the front cover and in other products, including conference literature and the Web site.

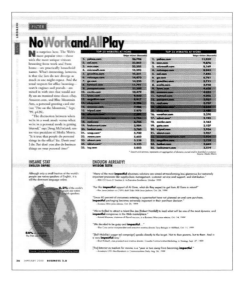

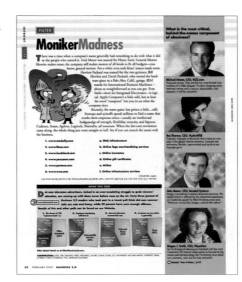

right Horizontal striping is a common motif through-out *Business 2.0*. Note the combination of solemn gray with loud primary and secondary colors and steady portraits with tilted graphs and silly illustrations.

far right Sometimes designers pull out all their am-munition at once—at least in the color department. The magazine's entire palette is represented in this listing of the top 25 Web sites.

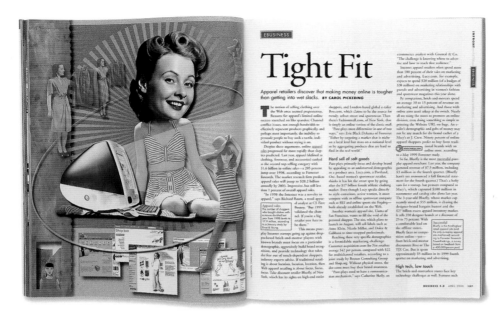

left Upbeat illustrations and collages accompany stories that don't warrant photography. Even in this bad-news feature, retro images of smiling models glow opposite the report that e-tailers are struggling to sell clothing online.

below Illustrations can take a cliché and add a more realistic perspective. Here, Jeff Bezos, the perpetually happy CEO of Amazon.com, appears as a perspiring wretch to illustrate a story about his close call with bankruptcy. Designers reflected the background pattern and colors in the drop cap and headline.

Personality Through Illustration

The XPlane graphics make up only a small part of the illustrations in *Business 2.0*. These people-focused pastels and collages generally add life to layouts without being heavy-handed. They're friendly, vaguely literal depictions of concepts and scenarios.

Covers are a little different in this regard. Though some are all text, they are always bright and demanding. A big part of the readership buys individual issues at airport magazine shops, Morris says, so the front has to scream at hurried consumers racing to catch a flight. So while not complex, covers are, at times, high-concept.

For example, for a cover story called "VC Scorecard," Morris got the idea to put players' faces (in this case, venture capitalists on the move) on baseball cards. On another cover, a dinosaur skeleton served as the perfect icon for a story about industries becoming extinct in the face of e-business.

Designers try to be similarly creative with photography, which is usually reserved for portraits. "These people aren't comfortable in front of the camera," Morris says. "We try to do enjoyable things, get people out of their offices." The point of the pictures is to show how much fun the subjects are having in their jobs, she says. Ironically, photographers often need to separate them from their work in order to depict that.

By establishing a laid-back atmosphere in its design, *Business 2.0* can proceed with establishing an authoritative but casual voice—a tone to which people in today's fast-paced business world are receptive. Design works like a twinkle in the eye, quietly and playfully supporting the magazine's new ideas.

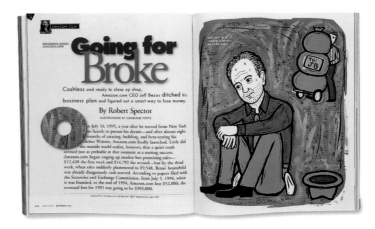

Brochure Design

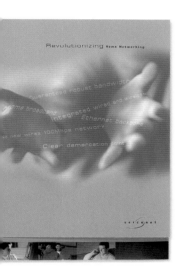

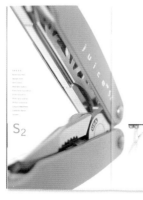

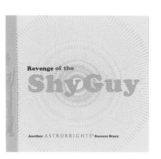

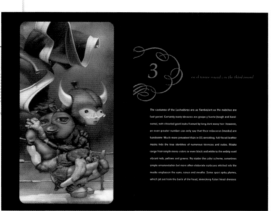

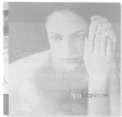

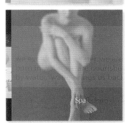

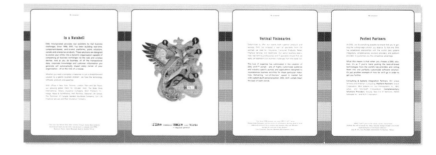

the greater toronto airports authority

CLIENT:
The Greater Toronto Airports Authority (GTAA) is a privately owned company that manages public resources.

FIRM:
Aegis Toronto

CREATIVE DIRECTOR:
Michael Dila

ART DIRECTOR:
Greg Salmela

DESIGNER:
Moses Wong

PHOTOGRAPHER:
Various architectural and stock photography

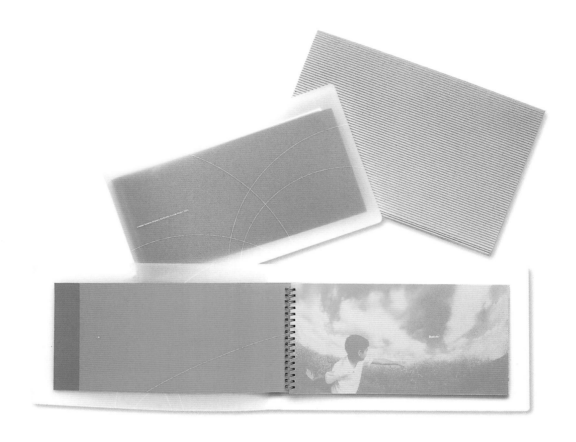

ABOVE: **Each section, alternating from orange to blue, begins with an aeronautical theme, which serves to express parallel meanings. A single key word introduces the theme and is followed by an associated image printed on translucent paper—Neenah UV/Ultra II in radiant white.**

Structure within Structure

The GTAA's long-awaited international airport is already under construction. The challenge for the design team at Aegis Toronto was how to develop an annual report that will instill importance, value, ownership, and pride in what is currently perceived as a massive, multibillion-dollar obstacle. "We didn't want people to focus on the trucks, concrete, and steel girders, but on this great thing that looms in Toronto's near future," says project manager Michael Dila. After visiting the airport and getting a feel for the environment, the design team developed several concepts that were critiqued internally before the final idea was presented to the client. "What is

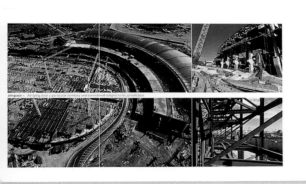

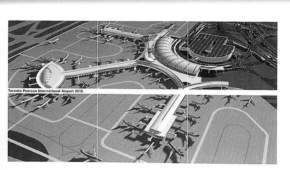

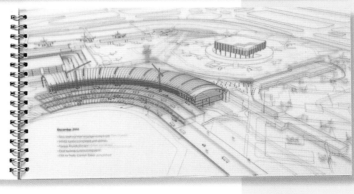

OPPOSITE: The aeronautical theme continues with a series of pictures that helps to visually support the message. The key word *lift* refers to the lifting of a structure from the ground as well as the lifting of a plane. On the opposite page, an orange text block poetically explains the conceptual connection between the key word, images, and message.

TOP AND BOTTOM: To convey the project's metamorphosis over time, translucent overlays, all relating to one an-other, are used to show a quarter-by-quarter view of the construction's progress. Using a CAD system, the artwork is created through collaboration between the design team and the airport's architectural firm.

remarkable about the project is that the new airport was being constructed over the existing airport, which continues to run largely unaffected," comments art director Greg Salmela. "I immediately had a picture in my mind of a translucent structure over a solid structure, which later became the cover. In the interior layout, I wanted to continue the same vision, where the images and the copy had to be less tactical and more emotive."

Even though the design team thought this was a dream project to work on, there were several technical challenges along the way. They struggled with how to support and fasten the paper report within the polyurethane cover so that it laid flat and did not droop. "We went through a whole string of tests to find a way of attaching the cover so it would support its own weight and withstand wear and tear," shares Salmela. "We ended up doubling over 100-lb. Potlatch McCoy matte finish cover stock and fastening it with rivets to the cover." It's critical that the piece remains sound because the physical structure of the report is integral to the overall message. The impressive annual report is printed in eight colors.

What Works

Through its size, shape, structure, and layout, the annual report conveys a sense of scope, scale, wonder, and achievement. The juxtaposition of the architectural linework, imagery, and text propels the narrative from front to back. A project once seen as an obstacle has now become an inspiration for the community, the city, and the country.

herman miller

CLIENT:
Herman Miller, a contract furniture manufacturer, is introducing its latest innovation, the Resolve System.

FIRM:
BBK Studio

CREATIVE DIRECTOR:
Steve Frykholm

DESIGNERS:
Yang Kim and Steve Frykholm

PHOTOGRAPHER:
Herman Miller archives

ILLUSTRATOR:
Jack Unruh

COPYWRITER:
Clark Malcolm

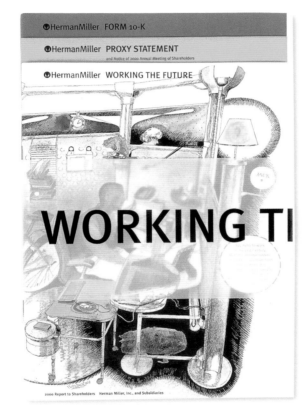

ABOVE: The annual report breaks up into three sections—theme book, proxy statement, and form 10-K. They are wrapped and held together by a bellyband.

Personal and Friendly

"Every year we get together with the client to talk about a theme for the annual report. This year's theme was about the introduction of a new product line called Resolve," says designer Yang Kim. "The product is very unique in that it redefines and transforms the office environment. The whole idea behind the line is that it creates communities and areas of personalization. So, with this annual report, we tried to give the piece a human quality that is friendly and fun." Researching the intricacies of the product line was crucial to ensure that it would be portrayed appropriately. "We took a lot of snapshots, looking at locations and making sure we had the right product mix represented throughout the book," Kim details.

The design team chose illustration as their venue for interpreting the new and innovative line, and the whimsical handwork of illustrator Jack Unruh was the perfect choice to convey the message. Within each illustration, there are sidebars—concepts that Herman Miller wanted to communicate to its audience about how to improve work environments. In the midst of the theme book, a gatefold illustration depicts the Resolve product development team. "They are the main people that helped launch the product," notes Kim. "It's sort of a homage to the team." In addition to the report, BBK Studio developed a booklet of "firsts"—Herman Miller innovations over the past fifty years. The booklet was also used as a stand-alone brochure. "It is a reminder of the great things that Herman Miller has to offer, and it ends with the new Resolve line," offers Kim. The illustrated annual report breaks up into three sections that are wrapped and held together by a bellyband. The annual report also serves as a corporate overview brochure for Herman Miller.

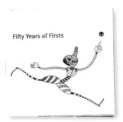

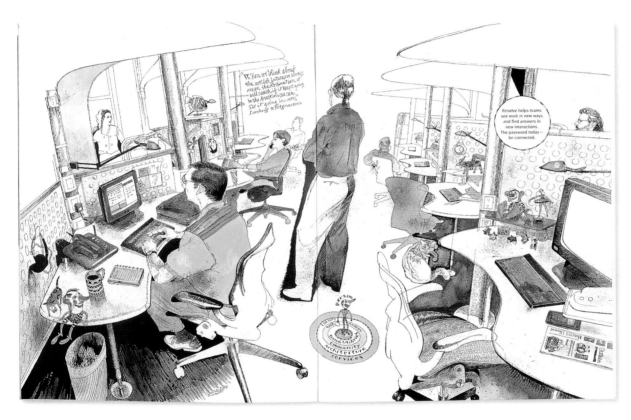

LEFT: **In each spread, the Resolve line is illustrated in a warm, friendly, and inviting manner. In conjunction with the annual report, the "first" booklet highlights fifty years of innovative designs from Herman Miller. The booklet ends with the new Resolve line.**

What Works

Distributed to shareholders and institutional investors, the illustrated annual report communicates the personal side of the high-tech product. "It was a hit with the sales force," notes Kim. "They essentially use it as a kind of capabilities piece with prospective clients."

dwl incorporated

CLIENT:
DWL Incorporated's enterprise
customer management applications
consolidate fragmented customer
relationship management (CRM),
back-office, and e-business systems
into unified industry solutions.

FIRM:
DWL Incorporated
(in-house creative services)

ART DIRECTOR/DESIGNER:
Shawn Murenbeeld

ILLUSTRATOR:
Allen Crawford/Plankton Art
Company

PHOTOGRAPHY:
Hill Peppard

COPYWRITER:
Leslie Ehm

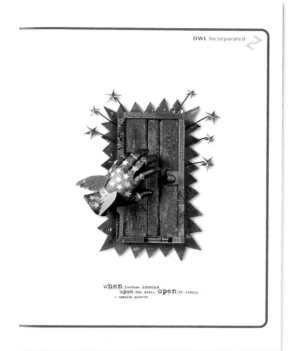

Creating Distinction

Because this was the first corporate brochure for the
company, it was important that it stood out from the
competition. "The main message of this piece was to
convey that DWL is a different kind of company," claims
in-house art director Shawn Murenbeeld. "In order to
create distinction, I went antitechnology while the
competition was going supertechnology." Throughout the
brochure, a handmade quality prevails not only in the
illustrations but also in the type. "That kind of attention
to detail helps to convey that the company cares," adds
Murenbeeld. "It also sets us apart from our competition,
especially when we go to tradeshows."

Originally four ideas were developed, but one stood out
above the rest. Insightful proverbs were used to introduce various key points. "When I get a job, I like to have
a theme to pull everything together, and proverbs
seemed to work," comments Murenbeeld. "The writer
and I went through books and the Internet and got
hundreds of them. We selected the ones that would most
closely relate to what we were talking about in the

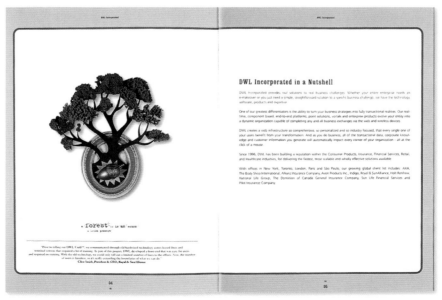

ABOVE LEFT: **DWL is able
to make a mark in the
industry by creating a
corporate brochure that
goes against the norm.**

LEFT: **In this spread, a
nutshell or acorn is
present in the illustra-
tion, headline, and
proverb. They all work
together to get the main
point across. The color
palette was pulled directly
from the illustration and
used as a border accent.**

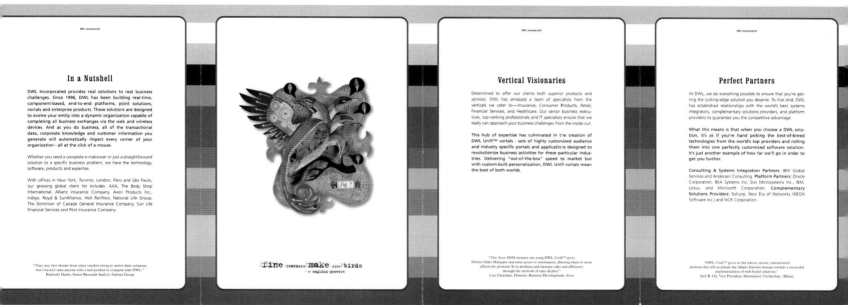

brochure." Once the proverbs were chosen, the art director went in search of the appropriate illustrator. "I went through the *Alternative Pick* because they have the most interesting illustrators out there," says Murenbeeld. After reviewing the work of several artists, three-dimensional illustrator Allen Crawford was chosen to do the job. "I gave him the proverbs and let him go with it. I don't like to art direct that much," claims Murenbeeld. "I like to hire illustrators because they have a certain style, look, or idea that I do not have." Once the art came in, it was photographed. Each spread contains an illustration, a proverb, a headline, and some text that all work together to deliver the message. "Copy and image must work hand-in-hand to be successful," concludes Murenbeeld. "It's only when designers and copywriters work together that effective communication can be produced."

What Works

By moving away from creating a technical brochure—the typical form of communication in the industry—DWL was able to create distinction for their brand. With its illustrative presentation and astute attention to detail, the corporate brochure brings a personal face to a rather high-tech company. Targeted primarily to corporate CEOs, this brochure established DWL as a unique company in the marketplace. It had such positive reviews that the color scheme was later used to accent DWL's various products. "The piece has been very successful for us," shares Murenbeeld. "Overall, everybody liked it, including the salespeople."

ABOVE: **Along with the corporate brochure, a smaller four-paneled tradeshow brochure was printed. It contains several of the major points from the larger 20-page brochure.**

xfera

CLIENT:
Xfera is a mobile communications company that offers a new generation of services and solutions.

FIRM:
Summa

ART DIRECTOR:
Wladimir Marnich

DESIGNER:
Griselda Marti

PHOTOGRAPHER:
Various stock

COPYWRITER:
Conrado Llorens

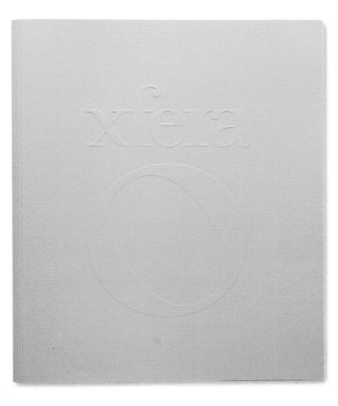

ABOVE: Because Xfera means "sphere," the design firm created a unique mark incorporating the spherical letterform as a play on words. The embossed logo sits predominantly on the vibrant yellow cover. The specially designed font, called Xfera Taz, distinguishes the company's new identity.

A Step Above the Rest

Xfera was in the midst of developing an identity for their company. "This was a brand book created for the official launch of their new mark and name," says art director Wladimir Marnich. Designed as an internal communications device, the brochure was used to inspire and inform employees about Xfera's new identity and key messaging. "We did a lot of research to help understand the market, develop the brand, and position the company," recalls Marnich. "We traveled throughout Europe—looking at the latest in mobile telephones. We realized that there was a lack of real quality amongst their competition." Xfera was a fairly new company entering a very competitive market, so they could not survive or compete on price alone. "Because Xfera was coming out with the latest in technology, we focused on quality, simplicity, and humanizing the whole business instead," adds Marnich.

Inside the brochure, words and images work together to clearly communicate the company's new brand. The images, mostly lifestyle in nature, reinforce the key values and give a human quality to the overall identity. "We spent a lot of time researching photos," notes Marnich. "We not only had to get the concept to go with each one of the values, but we also had to choose images with a similar quality. It was very difficult." Because of budget constraints, the design team had to use stock photography. The brochure concludes with the presentation of the company's new mark and overall visual look.

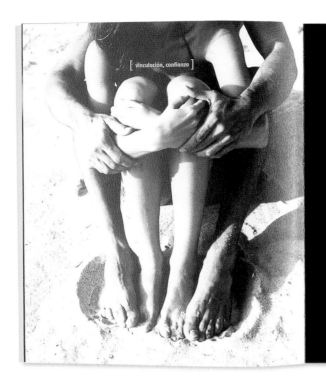

[vinculación, confianza]

01 **Una marca**

Una marca es, fundamentalmente, una promesa de satisfacción de necesidades y un vínculo entre la empresa y sus clientes.

Para que aporte valor, la marca debe nacer de una visión distintiva y relevante en su mercado, y debe comportarse desde el primer día con plena significación, demostrando su particular forma de ser y de pensar en todo aquello que tenga a su alcance: desde la creación y el diseño de los productos o servicios a la propia imagen de los puntos de venta, desde la estética de los canales on-line a la comunicación, y por supuesto, en todas las oportunidades de contacto personal que existan entre la empresa y sus clientes. Hoy, construir una marca ganadora es una necesidad. En mercados competitivos, es decisivo contar con el poder de convicción y seducción de la marca.

Este brand book tiene la intención de describir la esencia de nuestra identidad, de forma que todos los que mantenemos una relación con Xfera, sintonicemos con ella y contribuyamos al fortalecimiento de uno de los principales activos con los que contamos: nuestra marca.

...una promesa

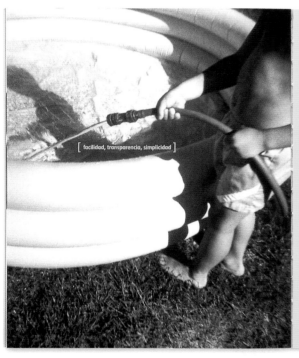

[facilidad, transparencia, simplicidad]

05 **Claridad**

Frente a la complejidad y confusión reinante, Xfera ofrece una respuesta comprensible, práctica y accesible. Si aspiramos a facilitar la vida de las personas, lo primero que tenemos que lograr es que nuestros productos, mensajes y actuaciones sean claros, comprensibles y transparentes para la mayoría de la gente. Queremos hacer sencillo el uso de la tecnología más avanzada, convirtiéndola en un instrumento al servicio de las personas.

LEFT: Throughout the brochure, each spread uses key words and lifestyle imagery to clearly communicate the company's nine core values. The entire brochure plays off the corporate color scheme—yellow, black, and gray. Gloss varnish is applied to the headline type to make it stand out.

What Works

The simplicity in layout and text helped to clearly communicate the company's new brand and identity to Xfera employees. "People were quite pleased and really tuned into what we were trying to say," details Marnich.

giloventures

CLIENT:
GiloVentures is a venture capital
and management company.

FIRM:
Jennifer Sterling Design

ART DIRECTOR/DESIGNER:
Jennifer Sterling

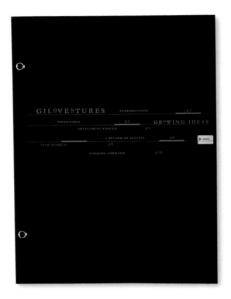

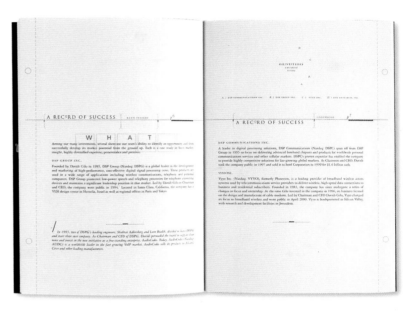

ABOVE AND OPPOSITE: The engraved and
die-cut cover is bound to the inside
pages by rivets, instead of saddle
stitching, to give the appearance of a
museum-quality book. Each inside
spread is accented with blind debossing
and blue engraving to give the piece
a tactile quality.

Simplicity and Sophistication

GiloVentures was looking for a sophisticated yet
understated brochure that would detail their approach
in funding and running a business. Because the
design firm had developed a complete program for the
company, they knew exactly what they needed to say
and do in this piece. The biggest challenge was working
within the client's somewhat restrictive budget. "In
Chinese, *constraint* is the word for disaster, which is
the same as opportunity. Constraints, and changes as
well, force you to solve things in a different way," says
art director and designer Jennifer Sterling. "This particular piece is quite conservative for a venture capital
company. Even though it may look expensive, it is not.
There are a lot of tricks we did to make it more substantial." Each page of Fox River Archiva 70-lb. text has
been Japanese-folded to add bulk and weight to the
simple 16-page book. The cover adds consistency by
folding the stock over and pasting it together, creating a
double-thick front and back for the piece.

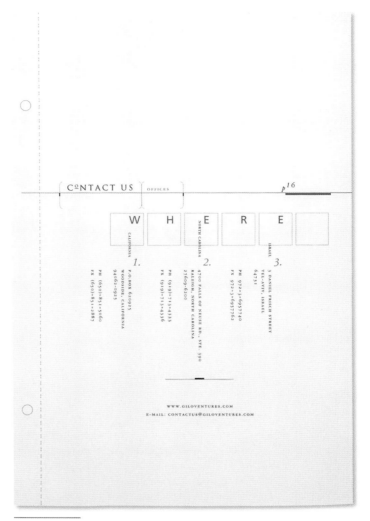

The die-cut cover is engraved with blue on a brown cover stock, Carnival Coco. "The blue engraving and die-cut really help the cover to pop," adds Sterling. "I also like going with a colored sheet rather than a printed one. When you flood the sheet with ink, you get cracks when you fold and score it, showing the white of the sheet." The rivets, used to bind the book, aid in making the piece appear more substantial. Inside the brochure, a consistent circular pattern ties in the rivets with the rest of the piece. The questions who, how, what, and why are framed in a graphic series of boxes to draw attention and carry the viewer through the key elements in the brochure. Because the design firm was very familiar with the identity and brand of the company, they were able to create something that not only described GiloVentures in an interesting and informative way but also suited the company's limited budget.

What Works

With its die-cut and engraved cover, rivet binding, Japanese-folded pages, interior blind debossing, and interesting use of type and white space, the simple but elegant brochure adds personality and distinction to the venture capital and management company.

One Step Beyond

Production Techniques That Communicate

Today, creatives are breaking the norm and seeking outlets outside their industry when it comes to production. Because of technological innovations, designers' options are only limited to their imaginations. "Don't be afraid to explore outside your traditional venues," offers art director Russ Haan. "Investigate custom bookbinders or go to printers and look at their finishing capabilities. Go to a sheet-metal facility or a food-packaging plant. Get catalogs from cosmetic manufactures. There is a lot of great stuff out there." Art director Jennifer Sterling agrees, "For years, the really successful designers have always looked toward fashion, music, film, textiles, and even product design."

The latest trends show an increasing interest in alternative and innovative formats and bindery. To create distinction, designers are exploring everything from tiny, interactive flipbooks to die-cut multipieced assemblages and everything in between. Fasteners vary as designers are exploring products—some even seek out the local hardware or office-supply store. Tactile processes like laser die-cutting, sculpted embossing, and hot foil stamping are being done on a variety of materials—custom papers, leather, linen, plastics, and the like. Inks have also come a long way. Heat-sensitive inks, available in various transitional colors, allow a page to transform. For special effects, traditional inks, printed either on top or underneath the heat-sensitive ink, can also be applied. "As designers, we want to push the envelope," notes art director Eleni Chronopoulos. "Finding new ways to combine different materials can be an interesting approach to any project."

Creatives are also re-embracing some old techniques. "In the last five years, I've seen the resurgence of letterpress and handwork—especially on covers," says Haan. "Closures that require the tying of a cord or a rope are also becoming more a part of the bigger picture."

More important than following trends, designers should always select a material or process that supports the overall message of the assignment. The creative use of production techniques should never come before effective communication. If the two do not work in tandem, then the clever use of techniques only becomes window dressing. "Good design comes out of a strong concept," says Haan. "When a design firm presents a client with something that is conceptually united with the design, they usually slam dunk home the idea. It is a rare day that a client will say no if something matches the concept." When the message drives the design, production techniques can truly enhance the visual experience.

CLIENT:
Reebok's I3 collection is a unique line of apparel designed to reflect the individuality of Allen Iverson, a star player for the Philadelphia 76ers.

FIRM:
Reebok Design Services

ART DIRECTOR:
Eleni Chronopoulos

PHOTOGRAPHERS:
Gary Land and Michelle Joyce

RIGHT: This pocket-size brochure is designed to be versatile and interesting with lots of texture as it reflects the nonconventional persona of Iverson. The blind de-bossed cover, made of domestic full-grain black leather, had to be die-cut and trimmed separately from the interior booklet. Seam-stresses who traditionally work for the sailing industry created the hand-stitched bindery. The graphic color scheme of mostly deep reds and black also reflect the look and feel of the apparel.

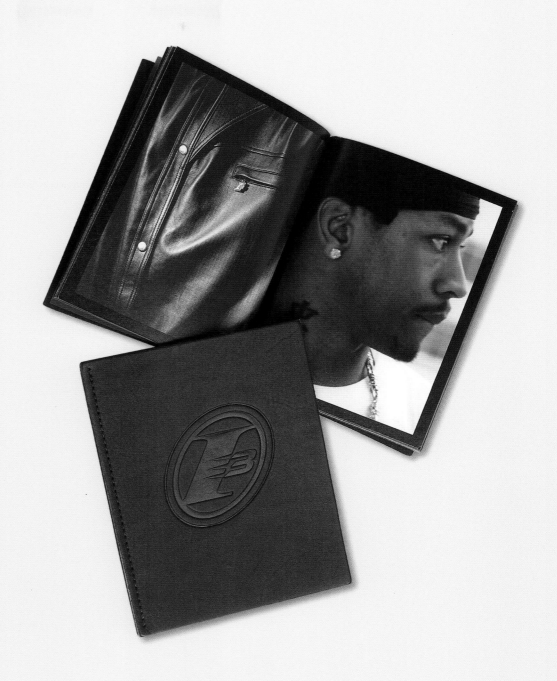

CLIENT:
Fox River Paper Company
introduces a new paper line to
the design community.

FIRM:
Jennifer Sterling Design

ART DIRECTOR/DESIGNER:
Jennifer Sterling

PRODUCTION:
Clare Rhinelander

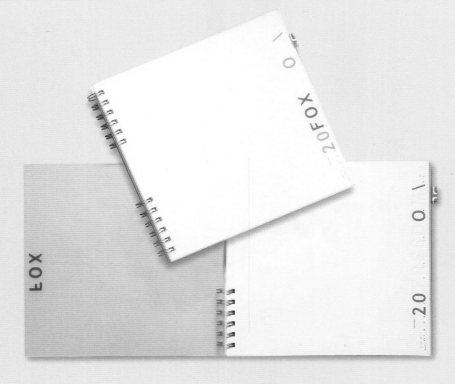

LEFT: A silk-screened polyurethane cover—a big leap for a paper company—works in conjunction with the printed and blind debossed inside cover. Together, they set the tone of the overall concept of freedom. As you look through the brochure, beautiful shades of white paper are microperforated, die-cut, laser-cut, and letterpressed.

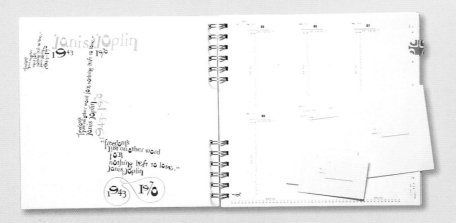

LEFT: This functional piece, created to showcase the myriad uses for Fox River Paper, serves as a 24-hour/7-day timer for busy designers. It is divided into sections by legendary quotes from JFK, Martin Luther King, and Janis Joplin. The inspirational words are hand drawn and letterpressed deeply into each Japanese-folded sheet. Along the outer edges exists a circular laser die-cut to identify each month. Blue and white kiss-cut stickers, printed on Fox River Paper, can be applied as tabs.

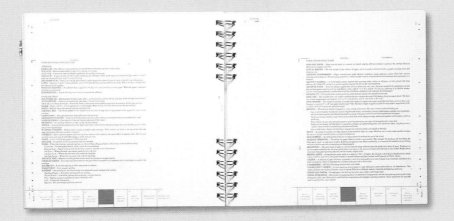

LEFT: Throughout the book there is information about the new Fox line, as well as industry facts about paper that both young and seasoned designers may not know.

CLIENT:
bluespace is a top executive training company that works nonconventionally with multinational companies to rejuvenate intuition and creativity in the corporate environment.

FIRM:
After Hours Creative

ART DIRECTOR:
Russ Haan

RIGHT: This unusual brochure, which cannot be opened without ripping it, serves to promote the radical approach taken by bluespace's staff to retrain executives to look at things in a different way. Always given out in the presence of someone from bluespace, this brochure challenges the recipient and most will not rip it open. A bluespace representative then asks, "What are you so afraid of?" and tears the piece open. The brochure dictates the entire sales process and fits bluespace's business development strategy perfectly.

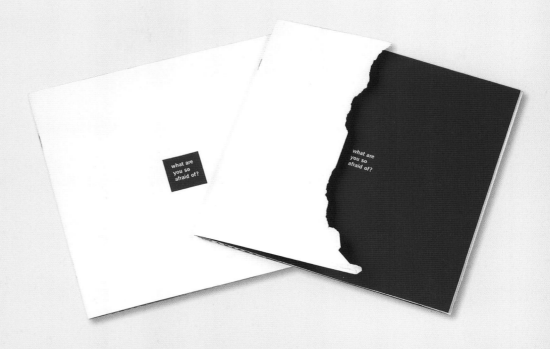

RIGHT: Designing a brochure that cannot be opened is a challenge. The interior of the book has to entice the reader—not so big it shows too much and not small enough to discourage. Yet, it has to be closed securely enough so that it cannot be easily opened. After numerous experiments with closures and mock-ups, a wraparound cover adhered with one-inch (2.5 cm)-wide industrial-strength glue, hidden and flush to the back, worked the best.

leatherman tool group, inc.

CLIENT:
Leatherman Tool Group, Inc., is the originator of the Classic multi-tool, a pocket-size all-purpose hand tool for the do-it-yourselfer.

FIRM:
Hornall Anderson Design Works

ART DIRECTORS:
Lisa Cerveny and Jack Anderson

DESIGNERS:
Andrew Smith, Andrew Wicklund, and Don Stayner

PHOTOGRAPHER:
Jeff Condit, Studio Three

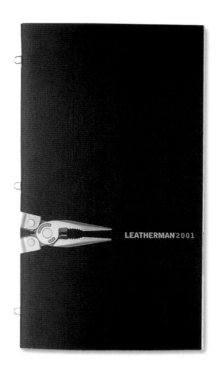

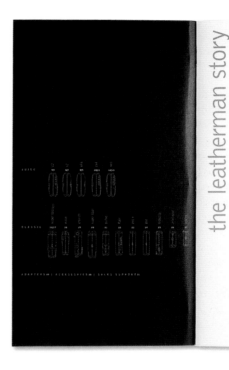

ABOVE: This 6-inch x 11-inch (15 cm x 38 cm) loop-stitched brochure opens by displaying both the Juice and Classic product lines on the inside cover. Directly opposite sits the Leatherman story, a brief history of the company and its founder.

Traditional and Sporty

Leatherman Tool Group, Inc., is expanding its offerings to include an entirely new and more fashionable product line called Juice. This dual-purpose product brochure not only features the Leatherman Classic line but also introduces the innovative Juice series of products to a broader base of customers. "We collaborated with the client, discussing the objectives of the new line. We came back to them and presented three ideas," notes art director Lisa Cerveny. "One of them was pretty interesting, but too much of a leap for Leatherman. It equated the new colorful tools with different beautiful insects. We ended up combining the other two directions to reflect what you see now." The Juice tools, smaller and more colorful, appeal to a more urban customer, while the Classic line tends to appeal to the rugged outdoorsman. The challenge came in combining the Juice products, upbeat and trendy, with the Classic products, traditional and conservative, into a single brochure that reflects a unified company vision. The Juice product spreads are fashionable and dynamic, while the Classic line remains straightforward in presentation. "Captured with a digital camera, each of the Juice product shots uses soft focus photography to capture an interesting depth of field and movement," explains Cerveny. "The fresh and clean use of white space accents the distinct color of each tool." For additional reinforcement, smaller graphics are used to identify each product and to visually display its unique capabilities. Each product spread includes a unique feature shot, an image portraying a particular usage, a full technical rendering, and a closed version of the product followed by a colored sidebar complete with the product name and color. The color-coding system aids in locating any one product, especially for those readers quickly skimming through the brochure. The cover is printed on Graphica Lineal 80-lb. cover stock in cool white and the inside on McCoy 100-lb. text stock in a matte finish. The Bell Gothic family of fonts is used throughout.

What Works

By presenting the new Juice product line in a fashionable and dynamic way, the brochure appealed to a more urban audience. The straightforward presentation of the Classic line, on the other hand, maintained its rugged and outdoorsmen appeal. Targeted towards retailers, the business-to-business product brochure was very successful in marrying the two distinct product lines under one corporate vision. "It is a very effective piece," adds Cerveny. "Leatherman is actually having a hard time fulfilling their orders for Juice."

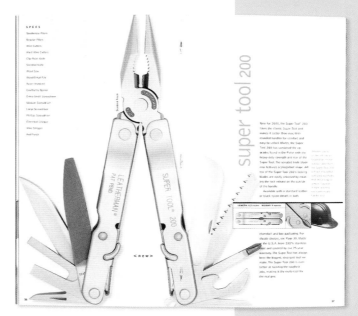

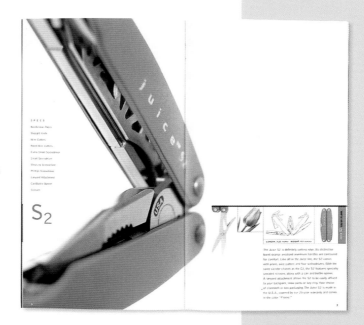

LEFT: As you flip through the brochure, the Juice line, the primary focus, is introduced first and the Classic line follows. Laid out in a clear and concise manner, each spread focuses on the unique attributes of a particular tool.

dwl incorporated

CLIENT:
DWL Incorporated's enterprise customer management applications consolidate fragmented customer relationship management (CRM), back-office, and e-business systems into unified industry solutions.

FIRM:
DWL Incorporated
(in-house creative services)

ART DIRECTOR/DESIGNER:
Shawn Murenbeeld

MANUFACTURER OF HEADS:
Sculpture Connection

ILLUSTRATOR:
Shawn Murenbeeld

PHOTOGRAPHER:
Michael Kohn

COPYWRITER:
Alex Baird

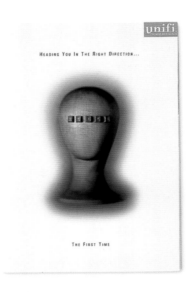

ABOVE: On the cover image, a wooden head was sanded and oiled. Then old computer parts, purchased from a junk store, were attached with reusable adhesive putty called Tac'N Stik. The interior is broken up into six modules, each featuring a key attribute of the product.

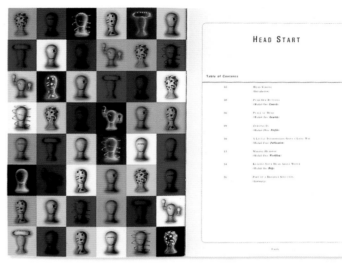

Getting Ahead

DWL was looking for an innovative and interesting piece to explain the benefits and features of their core product offering, an Internet software known as Unifi. "The key objective of this project was to produce a technology brochure that would appeal to top-level business people with little or no technology background," says in-house art director Shawn Murenbeeld. In trying to develop a theme that would tie in all of the product's key attributes and benefits, the idea of using the human head emerged. "As the control center for the body, the human head has many parallels with the Unifi product," explains Murenbeeld. "When I looked it up in the dictionary, there were a lot of different variations I could use, like 'get ahead and stay ahead.' It was very powerful."

The first challenge came in trying to locate a prototype head to work with, but nothing from mannequins to wooden hat forms seemed to fit the bill. "I eventually hired a wood carver and gave him a sketch of what I wanted. He went in with a chainsaw and carved out a

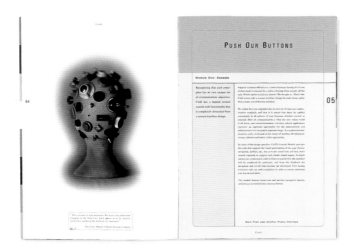

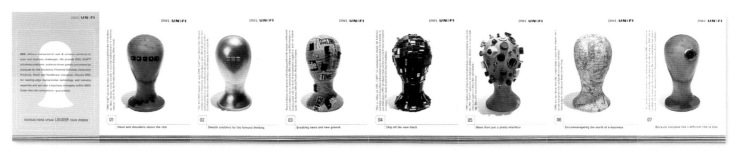

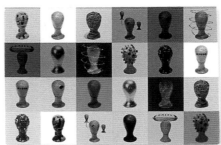

rough shape with no eyes or gender," recalls Murenbeeld. "Once I had the carved heads, I just added stuff to them." Several Styrofoam heads were also carved. Everything from international magazines and newspapers to refrigerator magnets, connectors, and computer parts were used to symbolically convey the message of each key attribute. "For the module on security, I went to a fence place, bought barbed wire, and twisted it into an invisible tornado," details Murenbeeld. "The barbed wire was held in place with this clever device created with washers and bolts." Once the heads were photographed, it was a challenge to get all of the colors to match and the gradations to be consistent. The layout, however, was a breeze. Each spread features the concept illustration, a select quote from a customer, a clever headline, and the appropriate text to explain each featured attribute.

What Works

By symbolically using the human head in various ways, the innovative product brochure was able to clearly explain all of the product's main attributes and benefits in an interesting and captivating way, attracting attention from top-level management. As a result, the brochure has been well received by both prospective clients and business partners alike. "IBM was so impressed that instead of developing materials for us to promote Unifi, they let us design our own material," adds Murenbeeld. Because of the versatility of the head image, it became the standard icon for Unifi.

appleton coated

CLIENT:
Appleton Coated, part of the fine, specialty, and coated papers division of Arjo Wiggins Appleton, is promoting their Utopia line of paper.

FIRM:
SamataMason

CREATIVE DIRECTORS:
Pat Samata and Greg Samata

DESIGNER:
Steve Kull

PHOTOGRAPHER:
Sandro

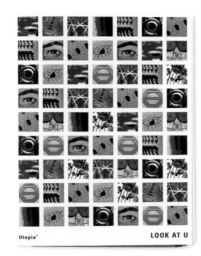

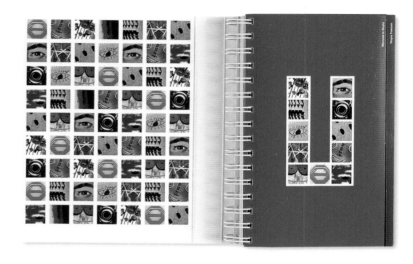

ABOVE: The cover is printed in four-color process with a matte film lamination on Utopia Premium blue white gloss 150-lb. cover stock. The divider pages are printed in four-color plus an overall satin varnish.

Creative Exploration

"We didn't want Appleton Coated to be just another paper company," offers creative director Greg Samata. "The whole idea behind the concept *Look at U* was that we wanted people to look at themselves and think of Utopia as the medium for their creative output. We wanted people to see that they could do just about anything on this paper. We were trying to raise the perception of the brand and the product."

To show the creative potential of this product line, several well-known designers, who also use the product, were asked to create a mask that best communicated their individuality. "We wanted them to create a mask where they look inside themselves and reflect what they are as creative people," adds Samata. "The idea was to get them to explore who they really are." Each designer was photographed in a black suit wearing his or her own mask creation. After the masks were shot, details of each were selected digitally and interestingly recomposed in a gridlike pattern onto the cover and in various other places within the book. "We wanted something that would give us a way to combine all of these thoughts and ideas subconsciously," says Samata. "It served as a thematic tapestry and a background for the messages." The highly textural masks also helped to show the high printing quality of the paper. Throughout the book, several papers under the Utopia line were easily recognizable and accessible through brightly colored dividers. The spiral-bound swatch book was distributed to designers, advertising agencies, printers, and paper merchants along with a poster that utilized the same visuals. The masks were such a hit that they were also used in a national advertising campaign.

What Works

The Utopia brand—seen as smart, witty, and fun—is communicated well in this very imaginative and creative product brochure. By integrating the creativity of designers with the paper product, the design team was able to make a connection between the two. "With all the consolidations and the closings, we are in one of the worst paper markets. Yet, Appleton has been incredibly successful," acknowledges Samata.

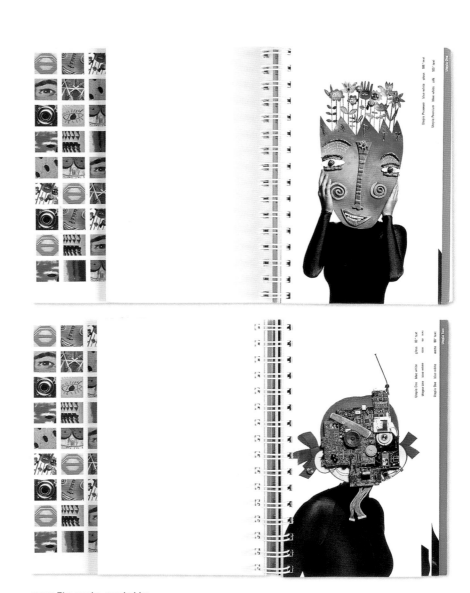

ABOVE: The masks, created by several well-known designers, are used to communicate the creative potential of the product line.

mohawk paper mills, inc.

CLIENT:
Mohawk Paper Mills, Inc. is one of North America's leading producers of premium printing papers.

FIRM:
EAI

CREATIVE DIRECTOR:
David Cannon

DESIGNERS:
Nikki Riekki and Ali Harper

PHOTOGRAPHER:
Catherine Ledner

COPYWRITER:
David Cannon

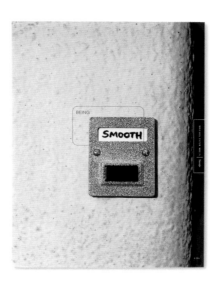 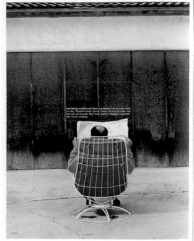 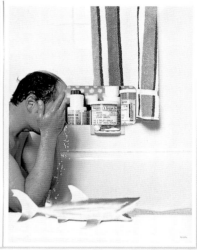

ABOVE AND OPPOSITE: **The cover, featuring a doorbell, is our introduction to Mr. Smooth. The inside pages present a day in the life of the main character, Steve Smooth. The imagery, highly textural and detailed, highlights the Navajo line's main characteristic–smoothness.**

Smooth Interpretation

Mohawk Paper needed a series of brochures for several of their paper lines. EAI was one of five different design firms chosen to produce a brochure in the five-part series. Each design firm was assigned a product line and given a unique attribute that had to be conveyed. "The paper we were given was Navajo, and the attribute that they wanted to highlight was smoothness," shares creative director David Cannon. "The piece had to work on varying levels of expectations. There was the design community that simply wanted something cool and eye-catching. There were paper distributors who wanted to show the versatility of the paper, and printers who were mostly concerned with the paper's performance." The design team had to work within a given size and page count, but the rest was theirs to interpret as they saw fit. "Most paper promotions don't have a true concept," remarks Cannon. "We wanted to make sure that this piece had a lot more storytelling to it. Our main goal was to create a piece that people would keep."

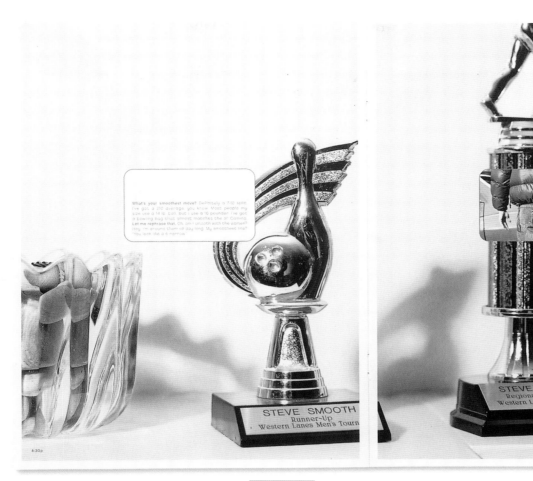

The design team played with several ideas, but one seemed to stand out from the rest. "We liked the idea of taking Mr. Smooth out of the phone book and doing some kind of documentary on him," adds Cannon. "We sat down and brainstormed about all of the different things that could convey Mr. Smooth and his identity, whether it was his mailbox, driver's license, or bowling trophies." To play Mr. Smooth, the photographer proposed several potential prospects. With his receding hairline and crooked teeth, one guy just fit the bill. Given carte blanche, the photographer shot numerous situations for the design team to choose from. Throughout the piece, the pseudo-cool life of Steve Smooth was documented using a variety of interesting textures and situations that highlighted the smoothness of the paper and its ability to capture sharp details.

What Works

The satirical brochure is not only interesting and entertaining but also effective in communicating the smoothness and printing potential of Mohawk's Navajo line. The clever use of storytelling helps to engage the audience while delivering the product line's overall message, a different approach than most paper promotions. "It was very well received from the design community," adds Cannon. "Print reps said it was a very effective sales tool."

polygon group of companies

CLIENT:
Polygon Group of Companies is a homebuilder and Klahaya is one of their upscale developments in West Vancouver, one of Canada's most prestigious neighborhoods.

FIRM:
Thumbnail Creative Group

CREATIVE DIRECTOR:
Rik Klingle

DESIGNERS:
Valerie Turnbull and
Lindsay Rankin

PRODUCTION:
Paul Townson and Judy Austin

PHOTOGRAPHER:
John Sinal

COPYWRITER:
Martha Ophir

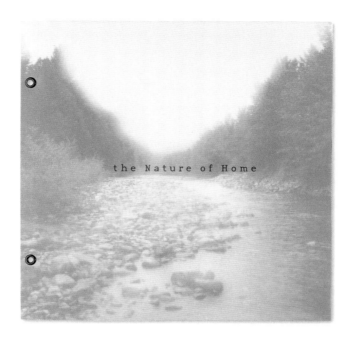

the Nature of Home

ABOVE AND RIGHT: **The vellum cover entices our curiosity, while the textural uncoated stock, French-folded, adds bulk and substance to the overall piece. The 12-inch x 12-inch (30.5 cm x 30.5 cm) book is held together by grommets, and the inside spreads feature an artistic interpretation of the natural elements that surround Klahaya.**

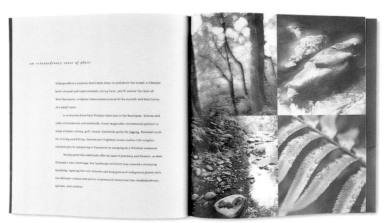

Inspired by Nature

"West Vancouver is a very beautiful area that is full of natural resources," observes creative director Rik Klingle. "In this piece, we wanted to reinforce the pristine nature of the development, so we came up with the theme *The Nature of Home*." Throughout the brochure, nature is depicted in an evocative and inviting way that appeals to the senses. Human elements are absent throughout the piece, allowing viewers to put themselves into the tranquil and soothing environment of Klahaya. "In our initial research, we did a lot of walking through the forest—helping us to develop a clear idea of what we wanted to show in the photography," recalls Klingle. "There is a sensuality that comes when you walk through the forest after it has rained. You can feel the ferns brushing up against your legs, the water droplets on your pants, and you can just smell the freshness." To break away from typical nature shots, Klingle hired photographer John Sinal to create a series of photographs from around the site that not only evoked emotion, integrity, and truth but really explored nature as art.

Because the brochure targeted a very educated and affluent audience, the text was handled in an elegant yet poetic fashion, quoting William Wordsworth along the way. The palette, an array of muted tones, is soft and dramatic. "Our idea with this piece is to create a coffee table book that would continue to inspire people about where they live. We really tried not to make it a typical development brochure. From the ground up, we wanted to do something special," concludes Klingle. "People see with their hands first. I've always believed the architecture of a piece is very important. It sets up an expectation that there is something to be explored."

What Works

The brochure, distributed by hand and mailed to a very targeted audience, generated a great deal of interest and sales for this unique and exclusive development. "The reason this brochure was so successful was because everybody involved—the architects, interior designers, landscaper, and the client—came together at the beginning," explains Klingle. "We talked about the vision and where it could go. Everybody was in sync. It was very much a collaborative process." The brochure was so inspirational that the interior designers used the same color scheme for the exterior trim of the development, and the photography outtakes were used as wall art in the suites themselves.

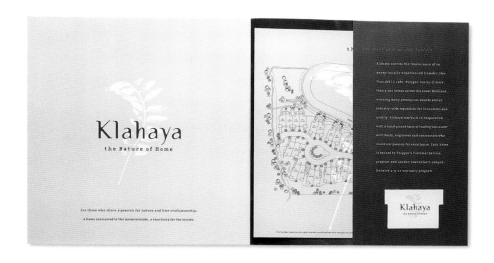

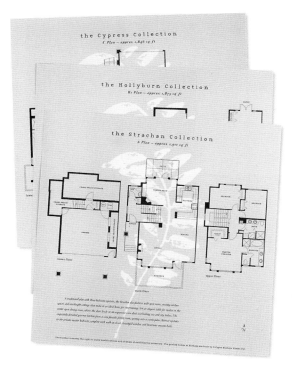

ABOVE AND LEFT: The back pocket holds the functional aspect of the brochure—six inserts detailing the various floor plans, amenities, and the site itself. The Klahaya logo is a fern that was created by hand using a linoblock technique.

yupo corporation america

CLIENT:
Yupo Corporation America is a paper company that makes a variety of synthetic papers.

FIRM:
Renee Rech Design

CREATIVE DIRECTOR/
DESIGNER:
Renee Rech

ILLUSTRATORS:
Keith Graves, Richard Borge, Cathy Gendron, Joe Sorren, Katherine Streeter, Rick Sealock, and Yucel

COPYWRITERS:
David Bell and Renee Rech

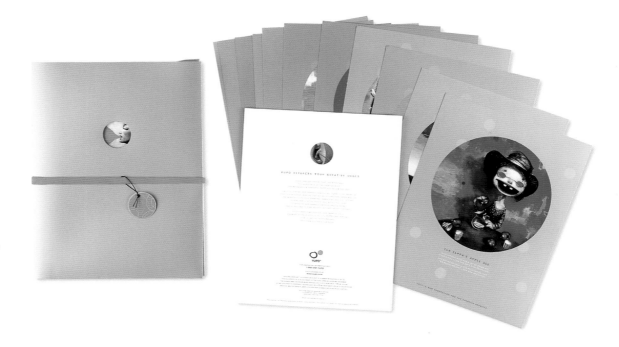

ABOVE: The pocket folder was printed with a UV-curable primer and two hits of metallic silver, a UV match orange, a UV black, and an overall UV satin varnish for durability. The inserts were printed with a match silver using stochastic technology. The thick pocket allows room for the inserts, other paper samples, and swatch books, making it a very versatile piece.

Palindrome Inspired

The year 2002, a perfect palindrome, inspired designer Renee Rech to develop a fun and highly creative promotion for Yupo Corporation America to show off their new line of synthetic cover stock. "They wanted something innovative to launch their new 14-pt. paper out in the marketplace," recalls Rech.

Using the tag line *A New Temptation for the Creative Appetite*, the designer began developing interesting palindromes—12 to be exact—which would serve as the launching pad for the imagination of several illustrators. Each artist was given a different palindrome, a template in which to work, and the creative freedom to do what his or her heart desired. Mostly food related, each wacky and whimsical illustration helped to reinforce the creative possibilities that can happen when using the paper product. The finished illustrations were used to create a calendar of satirical palindromes. "Because it's a synthetic paper, it can magnetically hold onto anything that your creative mind wants to throw at it," adds Rech. With spiral clips and

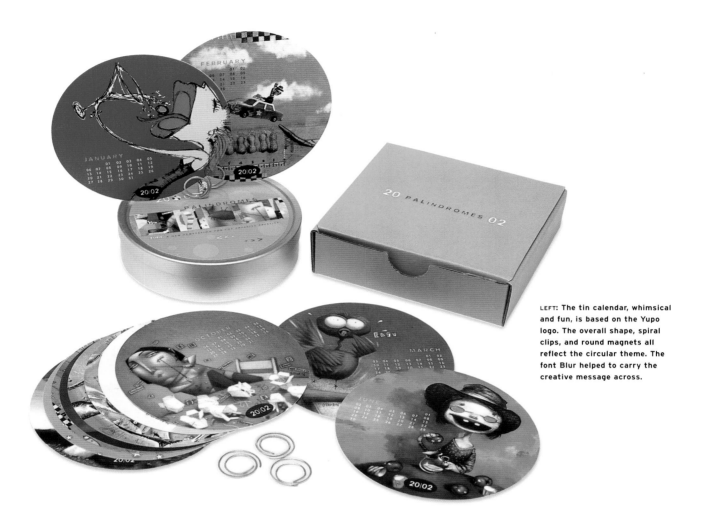

LEFT: The tin calendar, whimsical and fun, is based on the Yupo logo. The overall shape, spiral clips, and round magnets all reflect the circular theme. The font Blur helped to carry the creative message across.

round magnets for a stand, the calendar sits inside a tin container that was hit with a coat of satin varnish to dull the shine. The tin fits nicely into a custom-made box that also acts as a self-mailer.

In addition to the calendar, a matching pocket folder with sample inserts was created. "To keep it flexible, I designed a pocket folder with a Velcro slip in the front that could feature current ads or one of the inserts," says Rech. Each insert, printed on the new 14-pt. paper, visually matches the months of the calendar promotion. "The pocket folder also launched the use of silver with Yupo," notes Rech. "Their corporate colors are orange and black, and we added the silver as another color." A circular and curvilinear theme was carried throughout. "It plays on the Yupo logo," shares Rech. "The shape of the pocket, die-cuts, spiral clips, round magnets, and cover tag all reflect the logo." The overall design is clean and simple while the stories and the illustrations speak for themselves.

What Works

The illustrated promotion gave Yupo a fresh and highly imaginative look and generated interest for the new line of paper in the creative community. The promotion was not only interesting but also functional—something that designers would want to keep and use in their daily lives. "We want designers to sit the calendar on their desk for 12 months. That way, when they have a project, they can remember to use Yupo," reminds Rech.

serconet

CLIENT:
SerCoNet develops a range of products for networking applications that target home and small office networks.

FIRM:
Jason & Jason Visual Communications

CREATIVE DIRECTOR:
Jonathan Jason

ART DIRECTOR:
Tamar Lourie

DESIGNER:
Dalia Inbar

PHOTOGRAPHER:
Yoram Reshef and stock photography

COPYWRITER:
SerCoNet

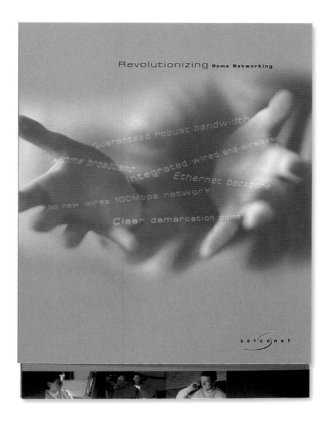

ABOVE: To create distinction for the home networking company, the design team created a unique cover image that sets the tone for the promotional package. The hands symbolize the home, the string symbolizes connectivity, and the typography represents key product attributes.

Home Technology

SerCoNet was just starting up and was looking for a brochure that would position them as a major player in the industry. To portray the company as innovative, the design team developed a very dynamic and eye-catching promotional package filled with die-cuts and interesting angles. "Because they also wanted us to portray them as revolutionizing home networks, we tried to create a balance between technology and home throughout the brochure," says art director Tamar Lourie. "Also, because the product itself is something on the wall with a whole area of technology hiding underneath, we wanted to create a feeling of multiple layers."

Inside the pocket folder is a company overview brochure and several product specification sheets. "The data sheets were more technical, while the pocket folder and overview brochure were more metaphorical," adds Lourie. For the cover of the pocket folder, a custom-designed illustration was created to help portray the company's unique message. "We came up with a metaphor for the cats-in-the-cradle game. The hands symbolize the home, the string symbolizes connectivity, and the typography represents the different applications that they do," notes Lourie. "It was a unique image that really represented the company with both the home and technology parts working together." The entire package was printed in four-color process with the pocket folder laminated for durability. The piece was distributed to vendors and retailers in the communications industry.

What Works

The innovative and dynamic promotional package helped to distinguish the start-up company in the communications industry. "In the days of a turbulent economic environment, it is a must for companies to use a single one-shot image to grab attention and deliver their message," offers SerCoNet COO Yaniv Garty. "Jason & Jason were able to visually capture our messages and turn our vision into a set of collateral that really works."

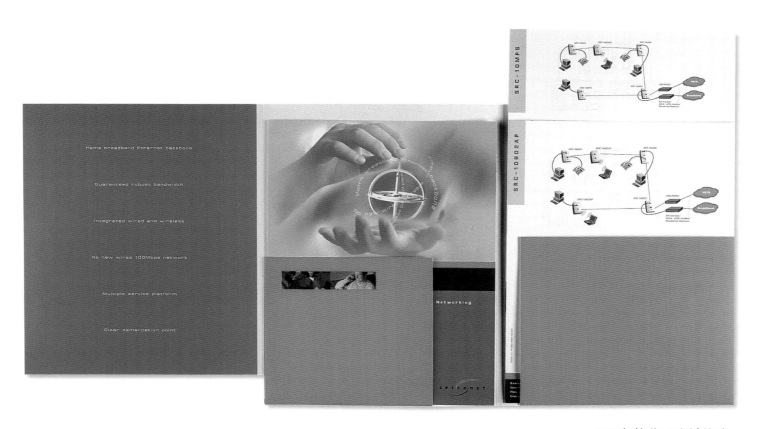

Home broadband Ethernet backbone

Guaranteed robust bandwidth

Integrated wired and wireless

No new wires 100Mbps network

Multiple service platform

Clear demarcation point

SRC-10MPS

SRC-1002AP

Networking

serconet

ABOVE: Inside the pocket folder is a company overview brochure and several product specification sheets. To portray the company as revolutionary, the design team developed a layered package filled with die-cuts and interesting angles—balancing both aspects of technology and home.

creative nail design

CLIENT:
Creative Nail Design, experts in nail care, manufactures a product line called Creative Spa.

FIRM:
Miriello Grafico

CREATIVE DIRECTOR:
Ron Miriello

DESIGNER:
Dennis Garcia

PHOTOGRAPHER:
Alberto Tolot

COPYWRITERS:
Andrea May and Melissa Osborne

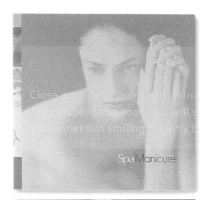

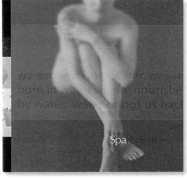

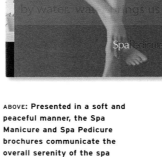

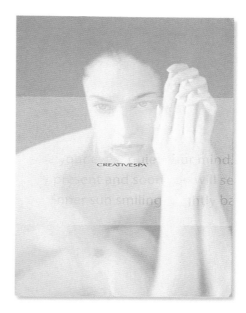

ABOVE: **Presented in a soft and peaceful manner, the Spa Manicure and Spa Pedicure brochures communicate the overall serenity of the spa experience. Both brochures can easily fit into the adjacent pocket folder.**

Experience the Serenity

Creative Nail Design was interested in re-launching its Creative Spa product line for nail care to both customers and trade personnel. "They had introduced this product line a few years earlier and did not have the level of success that they would have hoped," recalls creative director Ron Miriello. "So, they decided to invest in repackaging and presenting it in a way that focused on the overall spa experience rather than so much on the products' chemistry and makeup." Both the Spa Manicure and Spa Pedicure brochures are designed in a highly visual and poetic fashion— playing off the primary ingredients found in each line. "For Spa Manicure, they wanted to include elements and colors that would convey the smell, feeling, and flavor of citrus. In the color scheme, we used bright greens and oranges that are very reminiscent of spring," adds designer Dennis Garcia. "In the Spa Pedicure piece, the ingredients are much coarser, like exfoliatives. They are more reminiscent of things found at the beach."

Prior to conceptualizing the two-part series, the designer went to a salon to get into the mindset and experience the products firsthand. "We were looking to create serenity and inner peace," shares Miriello. "We felt the spa experience was about going inside instead of just looking good on the outside." They also did extensive research, looking through various books on meditation, Zen, and fashion, as well as going online and investigating exclusive spas around the world. The research enabled the design team to pinpoint the type of photography that they wanted to use. "The client was very particular about the models having nails that were in the best shape, and a lot of attention was given to the right age and image type. The models had to be beautiful but not unapproachable," says Miriello. "We also created an entire library of images that the client could use in catalogs, exhibits, advertising, and online."

What Works

Under the redesign and launch, the spa products were now being presented in a highly visual and poetic fashion—appealing more to the end user. By focusing on the serenity and overall sensual experience of a spa manicure and pedicure, the brochure series really helped to position the brand in a more captivating way. "The product line is doing extremely well relative to a flat market, and they have been actually exceeding their sales expectations," notes Miriello.

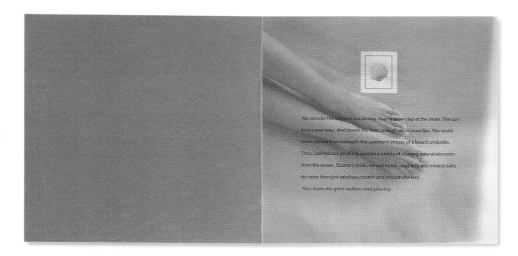

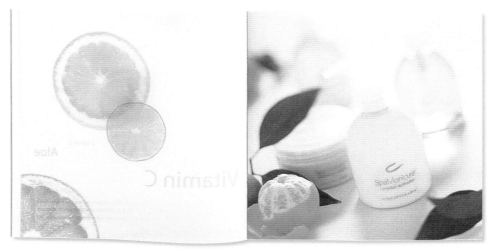

ABOVE: **Translucent vellum sheets overlay soft, dreamlike imagery with type that is poetic and abstract. Each piece is printed in five colors—process plus silver—on Cougar opaque uncoated cover stock 80-lb. throughout.**

just one

CLIENT:
Just One is a company that specializes in club music, clothing, and events.

FIRM:
After Hours Creative

CREATIVE DIRECTOR:
Russ Haan

DESIGNERS:
After Hours Creative

PHOTOGRAPHER:
Tim Lanterman

ILLUSTRATORS:
Rich Borge and
After Hours Creative

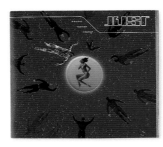
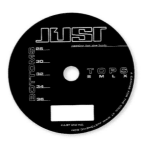
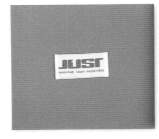
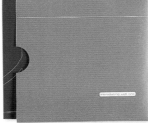

ABOVE: **The cover image, created in layers in Adobe Photoshop, is symbolic of the beginning of life—playing off the egg and sperm during the moment of conception. Inside the brochure, the various product lines are featured.**

Nightlife

Just One is a hip new company that targets the club scene in major cities across the country. "They are an interesting company," says creative director Russ Haan. "They plan events, make club wear, and distribute CDs." Because of the diverse products they provide, Just One needed a brochure that would not only unify them as one company but would also call attention to the various product lines they carry. "They were looking for a brochure to launch their new company and brand," adds Haan. "We also wanted to make it clear that all of what they do is related." To get an understanding of the market, the design team visited various clubs. "We wanted to see what everybody was doing and wearing, and what the overall attitude was," details Haan. "The whole crowd was young, upbeat, and positive—just wanting to have a good time."

After experiencing the mood and flavor of the nightlife scene, the design team developed a cover image for the brochure. An illustration, symbolic of the beginning of life, portrays a woman inside an egglike mass surrounded by various potential male candidates, all dressed in Just One clothing. "When life occurs, only one gets the chance to make it happen. It's really just about two adults getting together," explains Haan. "It's upbeat and fun in an irreverent way." All of the models were shot on white backgrounds and brought into different environments and assembled in Adobe Photoshop. Inside, there are clothing labels, a mini product catalog, and a CD. The mini catalog shows both clothing lines—the JO line, an edgy, grungy, and graffiti-like collection, and the Just One line, a more fashionable alternative. The CD features primarily electronica music. The entire package was mailed to a variety of club owners, potential retailers, and buyers. It was also sent to the media.

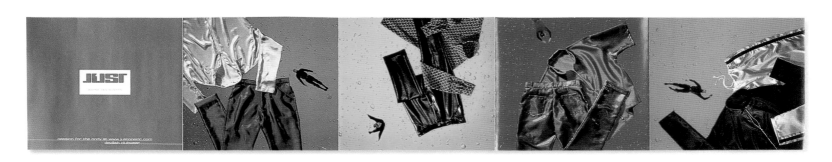

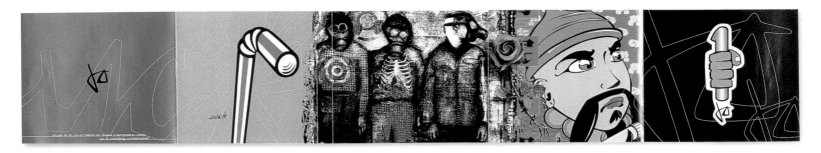

What Works

Because the piece was fun, upbeat, and in tune with the club entertainment scene, it grabbed a lot of attention across all products lines. The visual, tactile, and musical piece works hard at capturing the attention of a youthful and active audience. The overall packaging is not only innovative, but also serves a multitude of purposes, from selling the clothing lines, music, and events to promoting the overall image of the new and happening company. "It went over really well, and they made out great in sales. It was a very positive launch," notes Haan. "They also got a lot of media coverage in the fashion trade magazines and in the music media."

ABOVE: The mini product catalog displays both clothing lines. One side shows off the illustrations present in the streetwise line called JO. The other side premiers a more fashionable club wear line.

One Step Beyond

Visually Speaking

With the proliferation of stock and royalty-free imagery, many designers have forgotten the benefits that original illustration or photography can provide. Although stock may offer a quick and convenient solution, it is not necessarily the best. Working directly with an illustrator or photographer offers many advantages—customized solutions, the creation of work in a series, and the assurance that you are dealing with the person who is most knowledgeable about what you are buying. When it comes to specialty work, such as medical illustration or product photography for instance, corporate stock houses are not always versed in the intricacies and really only sell generic mass-marketable works. For distinction, commissioning original illustration or photography is the best way to go.

With all of the source books, mailers, and websites out there, it is sometimes difficult for a designer to distinguish the reliable talent. "It's not a question of what they have in their portfolio, but what they can produce day to day," adds art director Jennifer Sterling. "You want to find out if they can produce, work under pressure, work within your boundaries or the client's, or make changes and still be fresh." Good resources in which to look for talent are the juried annuals, like the ones produced by the Society of Illustrators or the Art Directors Club. The trade publications like *Communication Arts*, *Print*, *Step-by-Step Graphics*, *How*, and *Applied Arts* all have annuals and are worth looking at.

Commissioning work, for some, also means giving up a certain amount of control over a job. But there are benefits to this process. "I like to collaborate with more than one artist—getting a variety of interpretations," shares art director Mark Murphy. "The artists bring out things that I would not have. They add their perspective—capturing feeling and emotion. Working as a group creates a sense of community that is very inspiring. It is also one of the ways we, as designers, can keep learning and growing." When outsourcing illustration or photography, it is important to be clear about your intent and to provide as much information as possible in the beginning of the assignment. Maintaining an open dialog with the talent throughout the working process is also important. "Give them parameters that are somewhat loose so that they have an opportunity to explore," offers Murphy. "At the same time, you also have to continue your dialog with the client—being passionate about wanting to use illustration or photography to convey their message." With proper organization and collaboration, commissioning creative work can truly enrich any communications brochure with storytelling and imagination.

CLIENT:
Murphy Design Inc. is a marketing and communications company that focuses on creative business strategies.

FIRM:
Murphy Design Inc.

ART DIRECTOR/DESIGNER:
Mark Murphy

ILLUSTRATORS:
Gary Taxali, Jorge R. Gutierrez, Joe Sorren, Rob Clayton, Christian Clayton, Charles Glaubitz, Jonathon Rosen, and Rafael Lopez

PHOTOGRAPHER:
Eric Rippert

COPYWRITER:
Matt Hall

ABOVE RIGHT: **This perfect-bound promotional book called** Guapo Y Fuerte (Tough and Handsome), **an overview of Mexican wrestling, was sent to 5,000 art buyers. The vividly colored book was printed direct-to-plate in four-color process plus one solid hit of gloss varnish on every page.**

BELOW RIGHT: **Each chapter is fully illustrated, detailing both the historical and political aspects of this interesting subculture. "I really wanted to create a book to educate people about something that is very different from our culture," says Murphy. "Mexico is a rich resource for inspiration."**

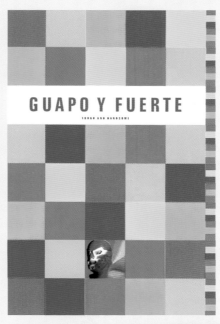

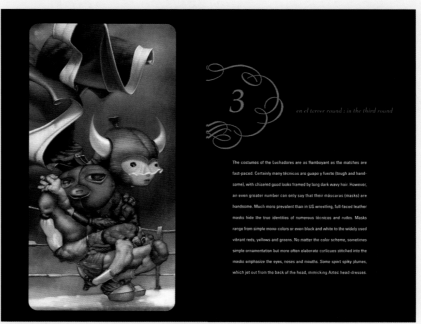

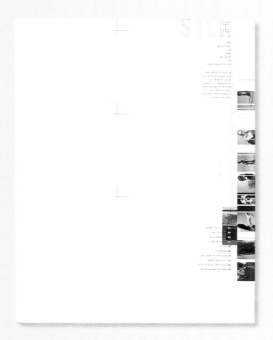

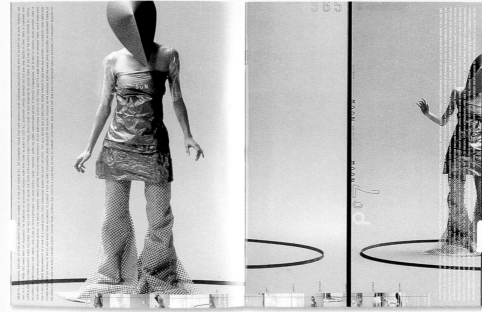

CLIENT:
Consolidated Papers Inc. is promoting its premium printing paper called Reflections Silk.

FIRM:
Jennifer Sterling Design

ART DIRECTOR/DESIGNER:
Jennifer Sterling

TYPE DESIGN:
Jennifer Sterling

PRODUCTION:
Clare Rhinelander

PHOTOGRAPHER:
John Casado

COPYWRITER:
David Ewing Duncan

ABOVE: **Designed to read horizontally like a calendar, this paper promotion is based on the concept of time. Models are conceptually dressed like biblical figures in a variety of materials to convey how various textures and details can be reproduced on a coated sheet.**

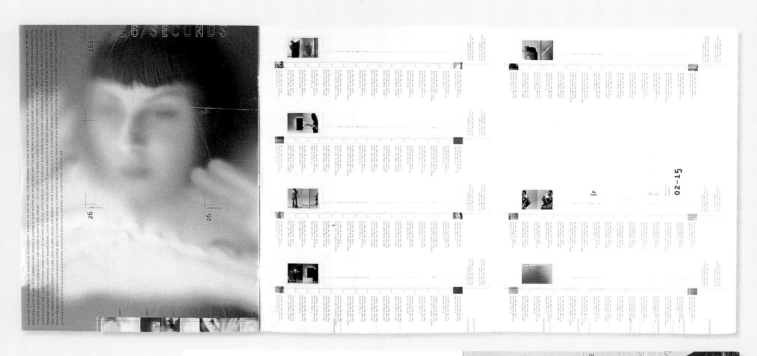

ABOVE AND RIGHT: The back panel flips out to show the production specifications for each spread throughout the calendar. Crop marks, dates, key words, and page numbers are carried throughout to aid in the pacing of the piece.

mulvanny/G2

CLIENT:
Mulvanny/G2 is an architectural design firm.

FIRM:
Hornall Anderson Design Works

ART DIRECTOR:
Katha Dalton

DESIGNERS:
Jana Nishi and Hillary Radbill

PHOTOGRAPHER:
Fred Housel and stock photography

COPYWRITER:
Suky Hutton

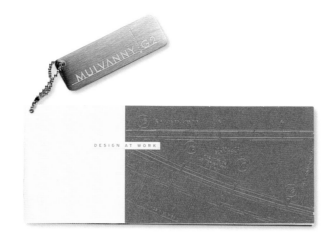

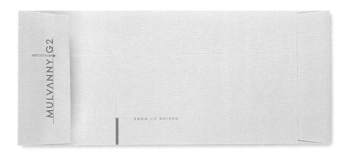

ABOVE: Embossed on the cover is the schematic design of Mulvanny/G2's new corporate headquarters. The attached stainless-steel tag, etched in an acid bath process, boldly portrays their logo.

Architecturally Moving

After 30 years in business and a relocation of their corporate headquarters, Mulvanny/G2 wanted to reposition themselves in the marketplace. To launch their new identity, celebrate their thirtieth anniversary, and show off their newly designed building, Mulvanny/G2 needed a multipurpose brochure with distinction, character, and elegance. "They wanted this piece to be a celebration of their architectural design skills and to raise some eyebrows," notes art director Katha Dalton. "But we really didn't want it to be about what they have built. We wanted it to be a celebration of the aspiration. This brochure had to do lot of things in a really small package."

After a brainstorming session between the design team and copywriter, the concept of moving was born. "Moving can mean a lot of things," adds Dalton. "We decided to play off the idea and show what it meant to be moved emotionally by something as well as what it meant to move something to a new place." With a desire to create an interactive piece, the first round of comps resulted in a pop-up brochure with die-cut windows

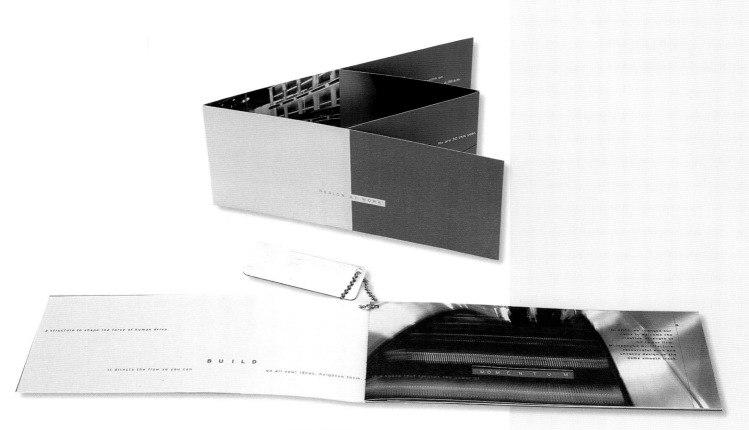

that you could look through and view the new space. The client liked the idea, but not for the brochure. So a special open house invitation was created in addition to the launch brochure. Under the redesign, the brochure maintained the die-cut windows and adopted foldout pages, poetic text, and mostly abstract imagery. "The placement of the die-cuts was a real challenge. It took a lot of back and forth between designer and copywriter to make it work," recalls Dalton. "There was also considerable discussion on how literal the images should be. We really pushed for something more metaphorical." The key line *Design at Work* was used to actively show that architecture puts design to work for people. "It's hardworking and functional," adds Dalton. Broadly targeting current and potential clients, trade people, developers, and property managers, the brochure and invitation were sent in a nicely designed envelope.

What Works

This interactive and tactile brochure created quite a stir in the architectural design arena. The die-cut windows, foldout pages, etched steel tag, poetic text, and metaphorical imagery all worked together to reposition Mulvanny/G2 as a different kind of architectural firm— forward-thinking and innovative. "The response was great, and their perception in the marketplace was uplifted," shares Dalton. "The client is getting a lot of good meetings, and the party that they held to celebrate the new launch and the new building was a mob scene."

ABOVE: On each spread of the brochure, stair-stepped type graphically combined with visuals and various die-cuts work together to get the message across. On the three-dimensional pop-up invitation, you can view the newly designed corporate headquarters in an interesting and interactive way.

precis

ABOVE: **The embossed and foil-accented cover is made of light board and gives a sense of elegance to the piece.**

CLIENT:
Precis measures communications effectiveness for media-based companies.

FIRM:
Lewis Moberly

CREATIVE DIRECTOR:
Mary Lewis

DESIGNERS:
Bryan Clark and David Jones

ILLUSTRATORS:
Bryan Clark and Steven Sayers

COPYWRITER:
Martin Firrel

Graphic Messaging

Because the offerings of Precis were quite complex, the design firm's first task was to get a clear understanding of the company and to simplify the communication into a provocative brochure. "Most of the research was getting into the client's shoes and trying to understand what it is they do and to flush out key headlines," says designer Bryan Clark. "We learned that the service they deal with provides knowledge—informing clients how they are, how they are perceived, and the extent of their media."

Once the design firm had a direction, the challenge became how to conceptually and technically convey their idea. "We decided to develop a series of questions that would illustrate simple graphic stories about uncovering information," recalls Clark. "The before-and-after approach was used as a point of illumination. This created audience participation that endeared the reader to carry on and to look forward to the next point being made." This simple, interactive guide takes the reader, in an interesting and captivating way, through all the key points of the company. Colored film is used throughout to reveal information and change perceptions. "The tradition goes back to children's storybooks where you open the flap and certain things appear and others disappear," observes Clark. "Precis is about uncovering new information and showing people things. The illustrations are a metaphor for discovering something new." The graphic images were initially sketched out on paper and then finalized in Adobe Illustrator. With the addition of an embossed cover, the interior spiral-bound brochure gained a more formal presentation. "We played up areas to make it look more special," notes Clark. "Initially, we looked at different things like varnishes and litho printing, but embossing was more tactile and raised the presence and feel of the brochure. It was the overture to the beginning."

What Works

By using a before-and-after approach, the brochure was able to clearly communicate, in an interactive and captivating way, key points about the company's ability to uncover new information. The engaging brochure helped to define and clarify exactly what Precis can offer their clients and how this service can impact their communications effectiveness.

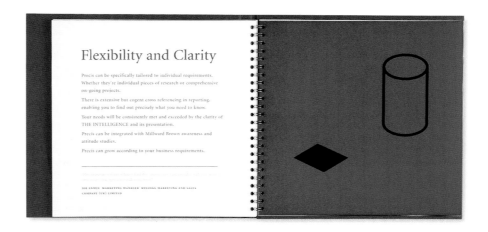

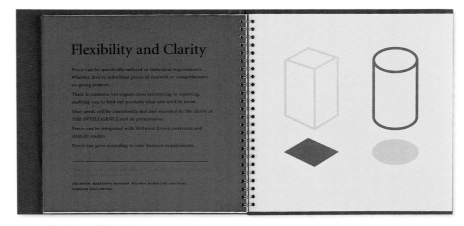

ABOVE: **Each spread illustrates a key point. The colored film allows certain things to appear and to disappear—cleverly delivering the message.**

frank clarkson

CLIENT:
Frank Clarkson is a New England–based photographer who specializes in editorial portraiture.

FIRM:
Plainspoke

ART DIRECTOR/DESIGNER:
Matt Ralph

PHOTOGRAPHER:
Frank Clarkson

COPYWRITER:
Frank Clarkson

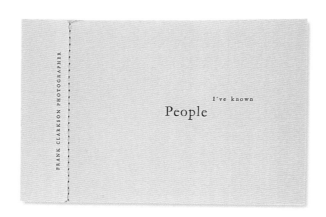

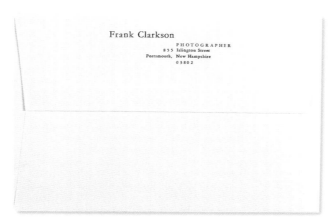

ABOVE: The cover is letterpress printed in two colors on Gilbert Voice 80-lb. cover stock. The entire 32-page booklet is bound with a singer-sewn stitch and mailed in a two-color letterpress-printed envelope.

New England Charm

Photographer Frank Clarkson wanted a promotional piece that would attract attention from art directors by highlighting his ability to capture the unique characteristics of people and their environment on film. "I suggested that we do a little keepsake, a booklet that provides an insightful glimpse into the lives of several unique New Englanders," comments art director Matt Ralph. This 7 1/2-inch x 5-inch (19.3 cm x 12.5 cm) journalistic brochure, entitled *People I've Known*, is a collection of eight portraits and the stories behind them. "I was given several images to work with and narrowed them down," recalls Ralph. "This particular series seemed to work well together in subject matter, style, and sequencing." The handcrafted look and feel of the piece reinforced the unique photographic vision of Frank Clarkson. "I wanted to create something interesting that had a nice textural quality to it," shares Ralph. "I also wanted a bit of a contrast between the brightly colored pictures and the more traditional elements."

Each page of text is letterpress printed in black onto an uncoated and French-folded 75-lb. sheet of Luxana Canaletto. Under each caption lies a distinctive illustration. Taken from various Dover clip art books, the illustrations were scanned into the computer to create plates for the letterpress process. The photographic images, in contrast, are offset printed on an 80-lb. sheet of coated Sappi Strobe. Because this was the first time that the designer had used letterpress printing, he did a lot of preparatory research. "I went to a letterpress shop and spent a good part of the day discussing the job and learning about the process," notes Ralph. "Letterpress allowed me to create something with a real tactile and handcrafted quality."

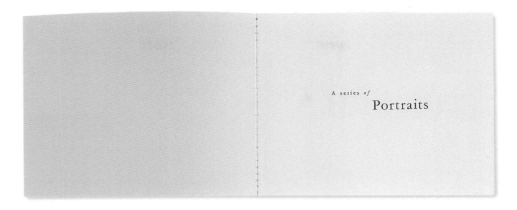

A series *of*

Portraits

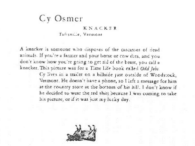

James Bouldin
FARMER
Brunswick, Maine

James sells canned goods from "Hattie's Kitchen"
at the Brunswick Farmer's Market. Hattie is James'
wife, and her kitchen is in Bowdoinham.
James was a Commander in the Navy, and he carries
himself like a military man. What I remember about
James is his gentle voice, and the twinkle in his eye
when he told me about Hattie.

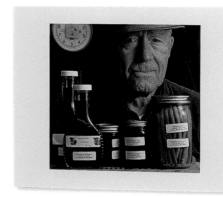

Cy Osmer
KNACKER
Taftsville, Vermont

A knacker is someone who disposes of the carcasses of dead
animals. If you're a farmer and your horse or cow dies, and you
don't know how you're going to get rid of the beast, you call a
knacker. This picture was for a Time Life book called *Odd Jobs*.
Cy lives in a trailer on a hillside just outside of Woodstock,
Vermont. He doesn't have a phone, so I left a message for him
at the country store at the bottom of his hill. I don't know if
he decided to wear the red shirt because I was coming to take
his picture, or if it was just my lucky day.

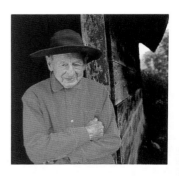

What Works

The handmade look and feel of this journalistic
brochure reinforced the personalized approach that
photographer Frank Clarkson takes in his portraiture
work. The letterpress printing and illustrated accents
makes it worth holding onto. Going after a regional
audience, Clarkson mailed the story-driven brochure to
designers and art directors in the New England area.
"He got a great response and booked several
interviews to show his portfolio," adds Ralph.

carter richer and stark

CLIENT:
Carter Richer and Stark is a group of classically trained craftsmen specializing in stone carving and conservation masonry.

FIRM:
Soapbox Design Communications

ART DIRECTOR:
Gary Beelik

DESIGNER:
Jim Ryce

PHOTOGRAPHER:
Alison Wardman

COPYWRITER:
Brian Richer

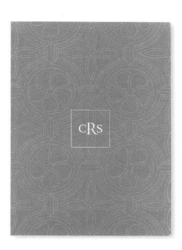

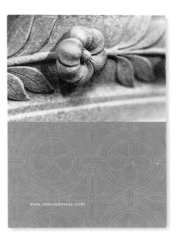

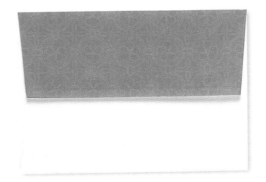

ABOVE: The small-format promotion piece has a sophisticated and worldly quality to it. The front cover and back panel, printed in a soft stone blue, feature a rosette-like pattern found in a book on European stone carvings. The square-flapped envelope repeats the same pattern.

Carving Out an Identity

As a fairly new company, Carter Richer and Stark needed a way to establish themselves in the industry as highly skilled artisans. After researching the client's competition, the design team came across a stream of very slick and glossy brochures. "I really wanted to focus on the craftsmanship of their work and not the commercial aspect," says art director Gary Beelik. "Because it was going to interior designers, architects, and city planners, I wanted the piece to be modern yet traditional."

Wanting to highlight the beautifully detailed work of Carter Richer and Stark, the design team sent in a photographer to capture the carvers actively working in their creative environment. At the time, they had landed a major contract for St. James Cathedral, one of the older and more traditional-style churches in downtown Toronto. "Because they were just finishing off these pinnacles for the cathedral, we decided to feature them in the brochure," notes Beelik. Throughout the accordion-folded piece, cross-section line drawings and schematics of the project were lightly displayed in a blue-gray. "We also took found images and drawings that they had in their studio and scanned them into the computer," Beelik adds. Using Adobe Illustrator, the drawings were cleaned up and carefully placed into the layout that alternated from large to small black-and-white imagery.

CLIENT:
Etheridge is a high-end printer who works primarily with design firms and corporate in-house design and print managers.

FIRM:
BBK Studio

ART DIRECTOR:
Michael Barile

DESIGNERS:
Kelly Schwartz and Michael Barile

ILLUSTRATORS:
Allen McKinney and Michael Barile

PHOTOGRAPHERS:
Susan Carr and Gary Cialdella

COPYWRITER:
Randall Braaksma

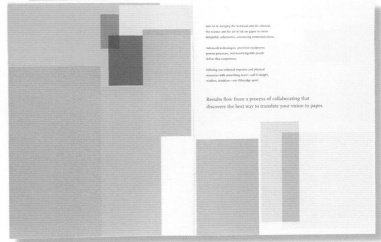

RIGHT: This capabilities brochure is the first in a series that helps to explain, in depth, the printing process to designers. Throughout the brochure, squares of color interact with montage imagery and poetic haiku—adding a flair of artistry to the science of printing. The brochure is printed in eight colors—four-color process plus four PMS match colors on Consolidated Reflections Silk coated text and cover stock. In this particular piece, color is used to show the subtle blending and building of color available with stochastic printing.

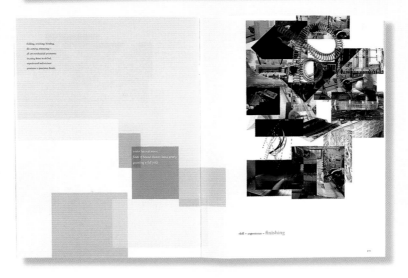

the massachusetts college of art

CLIENT:
The Massachusetts College of Art
is an art institution that offers a
variety of both undergraduate
and graduate programs.

FIRM:
Stoltze Design

ART DIRECTOR:
Clifford Stoltze

DESIGNERS:
Tammy Dotson and Cynthia Patten

PHOTOGRAPHERS:
Ilan Jacobsohn, Michael Mulno,
Susan Byrne, and Heath
Photography

COPYWRITER:
Rebecca Saunders

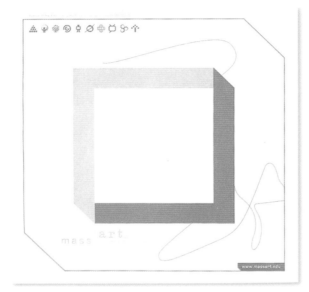

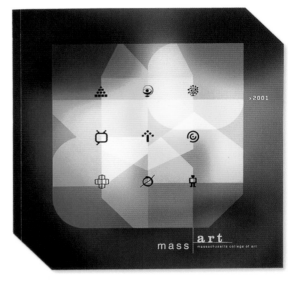

ABOVE: The die-cut cover features
an unfolding box that reveals the
various artistic disciplines. The
view book is sent to prospective
students in a specially designed
envelope that carries both the
organic and geometric elements
that appear throughout the book.

Thinking Outside the Box

For years, the Massachusetts College of Art has produced
a complete and extensive catalog for their institution,
including everything from a background on the school to
course offerings. This year was different. With the
Internet becoming more and more popular, the college
decided to use their website as the primary source for
information. This decision changed the role and scope of
the catalog, making it more of a visual view book, focusing
on the philosophy and artistic diversity of the school.
"One of the things that we did with this project was to
develop an overall concept," says designer Tammy
Dotson. "We thought about the process of learning and
how all of the various disciplines start with the basic
geometry of form and shape." With a spatial approach in
mind, the interior graphics and layout, as well as the corner
die-cuts, all became metaphors for thinking outside of
the box. "The book can be seen as a dimensional object,
and when you open it, different aspects of the school and

the various departments unfold," adds Dotson. The view book breaks up into three major sections—the introduction, the areas of study, and the graduate program.

Within the art college, there are eight disciplines in which to study. Each discipline is introduced with a montage of student artwork, giving the piece tremendous visual impact and personalization. "On each spread, there is a detailed section of a student's work that is used as a large background, and then we repeated the image full frame somewhere else on the page," Dotson explains. Each area of study is coded with a graphic icon that is prominently displayed on the cover and repeated within the specialization. "Representing a different department, each one specifically links up to the website," notes art director Clifford Stoltze. "There is a lot of continuity between the design of the site and the view book."

What Works

Designed to inspire a diverse range of potential students, the brochure creates a nice balance between the structural disciplines and the more expressive ones. Because the book is conceptual in nature, it appealed to the creative and inquisitive mind of an art school student. This highly functional and visually interesting view book was mailed to high school guidance counselors and prospective applicants. "The joint effort between the view book and the website has made a significant increase in the number of applicants," acknowledges Stoltze.

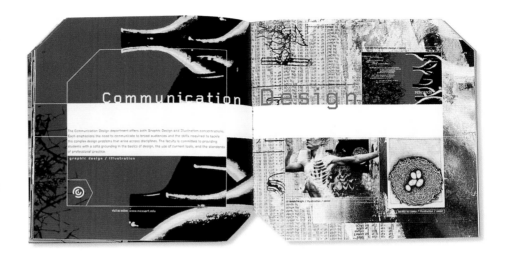

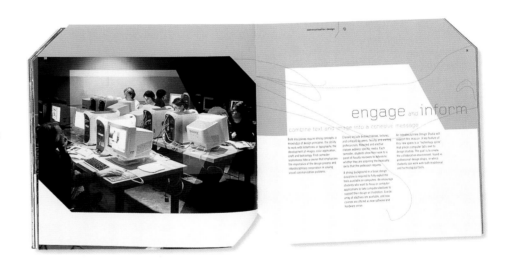

ABOVE: **Each discipline visually opens with a montage of student artwork. The fluid linework adds an organic, handmade quality to the overall graphic and geometric design.**

the university of technology, sydney

CLIENT:
The University of Technology, Sydney is an educational institution in Australia.

FIRM:
Emery Vincent Design

ART DIRECTOR/DESIGNER:
Emery Vincent Design

MANAGING DIRECTOR:
Penny Bowring

PHOTOGRAPHER:
Sandy Nicholson

COPYWRITER:
Supplied by client

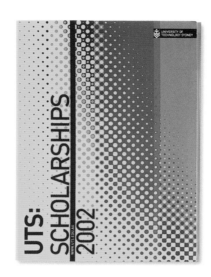

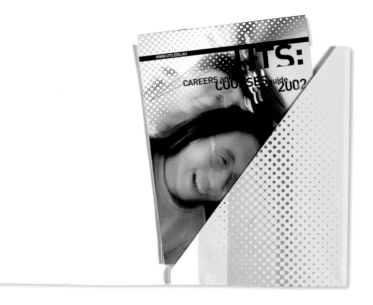

ABOVE: **The catalog and pocket folder graphically work together to capture the attention of a youthful audience.**

Trend Setting

The University of Technology, Sydney (UTS) was looking for a career and course guide that would have a strong visual impact in the education marketplace. Positioning the university as cool, hip, and slightly alternative helped to attract graduating high school students to the not-so-traditional school. "The piece is directed at the youth market and needed to be appealing and effective," notes managing director Penny Bowring. "The imagery has abstract qualities that reference popular culture graphics. The use of unconventional type and the haphazard placement of elements is designed to appeal to the rebellious nature of the target market." In addition to being visually appealing, the piece also had to communicate the university's wide range of studies in a clear and easily accessible manner. "The overall impression is that it is a highly professional organization that also looks cool," says Bowring. "The landscape format and the use of the structured table and grid provides for maximum information in an easy-to-read format."

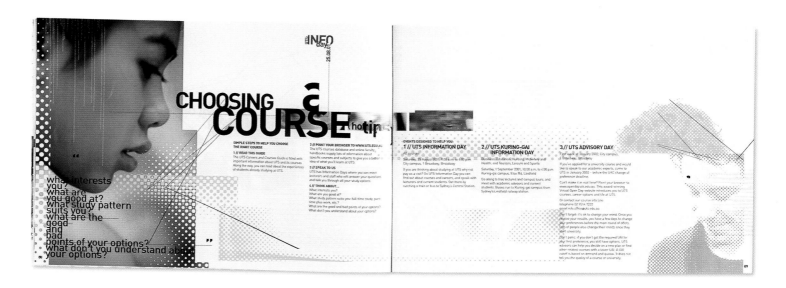

A photographer was commissioned to visit several campuses, shooting a broad range of students from various disciplines. "The goal was to capture the vibrancy of real-life situations at UTS," adds Bowring. Throughout the catalog, intersecting lines, type, and a dot-pattern grid overlap photography in an interesting and dynamic way. "The layering of imagery evokes how students learn and discover throughout the course of their studies," details Bowring. "The screen creates a dynamic counterpoint to the clear, sharp photography, setting up an interesting tension. The intersecting lines represent the potential directions that the students can take in their studies." Distributed to graduating high school students, the catalog fits nicely inside a pocket folder, along with other necessary enrollment information generated by the university.

What Works

By using unconventional type and graphics in an easy-to-read format, the brochure helped to attract the trend-conscious youth market. With its dynamic and appealing design, it has not only significantly increased enrollment, but has also established a trend for more innovative educational catalog design in the Australian market. "It has produced real returns for the university," claims Bowring. "Some rival universities are currently pursuing similar design approaches."

ABOVE: **Intersecting lines, type, and a dot-pattern grid overlap photography to communicate the learning process that exists within a flexible curriculum. The screen effect is also printed as a varnish—adding an interesting surface texture to the already visually exciting page.**

compugen

CLIENT:
Compugen is a pioneer in the field of predictive life science achieved through the convergence of molecular biology and advanced computational technologies.

FIRM:
Jason & Jason Visual Communications

CREATIVE DIRECTOR:
Jonathan Jason

DESIGNER:
Meirav Tal-Arazi

PHOTOGRAPHER:
Yoram Reshef and various stock

COPYWRITER:
Audrey Gerber

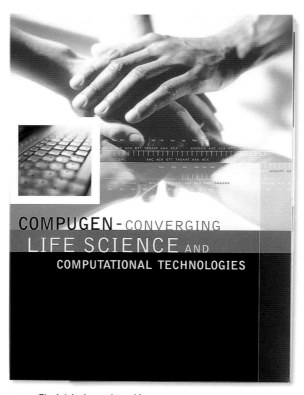

ABOVE: The intriguing and graphic marketing package symbolically combines both the human and mathematical aspects of the company. Throughout the piece, strings of genetic information are seamlessly combined with symbolic lifestyle imagery to convey the overall message.

The Human Touch

Compugen wanted to re-brand and position themselves as a company that merged computational technologies with molecular biology and medicine. "They were well known in the industry for being able to decipher genetic information," notes creative director Jonathan Jason. "But they wanted to be positioned as being more biology focused and less computational, because they felt that it would put them more in touch with their market. In order to position them this way, we had to come up with an image that combined the two."

The biggest challenge for the design team was how to effectively communicate the highly complex company. "We were asked to make their technology easy to understand," recalls Jason. "We spent a lot of time researching—sitting with them for weeks, learning about the biology and the technology aspects. We viewed their labs, interviewed people, and researched all of their competition." Because the company's offerings were more sophisticated, the design team chose to use metaphorical images to describe in a simple way what Compugen's products do. On the cover of the promotional package, various hands were used to show the combining of different disciplines to form a new discipline. "It's an analogy of math and life science that works together to provide solutions," notes Jason. "The hands bring in the human side of what they do." Throughout the piece, strings of genetic information were combined with symbolic lifestyle imagery to convey Compugen's commitment to raising the duration and quality of life by advancing drug discovery and development. The overall marketing package consists of a company profile brochure, two product brochures, three product data sheets, and a corporate annual report.

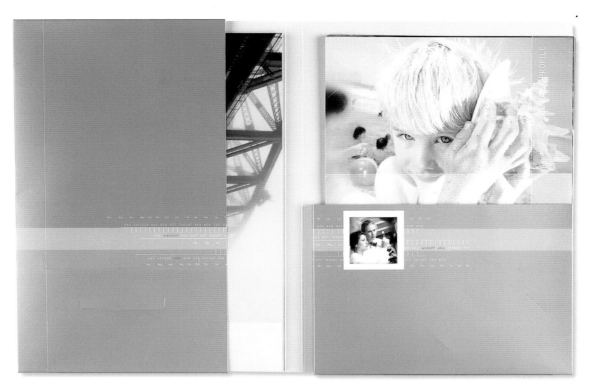

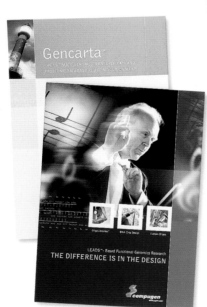

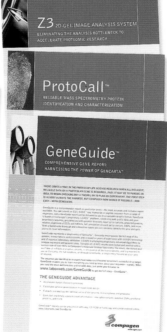

ABOVE AND LEFT: **Inside the pocket folder is a company profile brochure, two product brochures, three product data sheets, and a corporate annual report. The laminated pocket folder is printed in four-color process plus metallic ink. The die-cut slots house both a mini CD-ROM and a standard CD-ROM.**

What Works

By using symbolic imagery and clear text, the design team was able to successfully communicate Compugen's complex story and new corporate image—positioning the company as a leader in the field of predictive life science. "Jason & Jason created a clear and distinctive new look for the company," adds Tsipi Haitovsky of Compugen. "All of the materials were very well received, both within the company and by our target audiences—investors, media, customers, and those in the scientific community."

the abraham lincoln presidential library and museum foundation

CLIENT:
The Abraham Lincoln Presidential Library and Museum Foundation is raising funds to construct a world-class destination for scholars and the public alike.

FIRM:
Stan Gellman Graphic Design, Inc.

CREATIVE DIRECTOR:
Jim Gobberdiel, Jim Gobberdiel Communications

ART DIRECTOR:
Barry Tilson

DESIGNERS:
Barry Tilson and Michael Donovan

ILLUSTRATORS:
BRC Imagination Arts Inc. and Art Associates Inc. (architectural)

FONT DESIGN:
Tom Carnase

COPYWRITER:
John Fundator

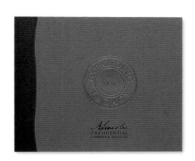

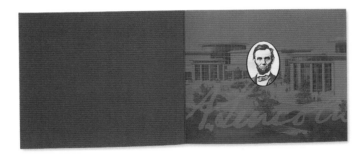

ABOVE: **The small-format brochure is produced with a four-page cover that is doubled over and pasted to give it strength and stability. A title seal is both blind embossed and debossed on Fraser Passport 80-lb. cover stock to add texture and presidential appeal to the piece.**

Promoting a Legacy

The Abraham Lincoln Presidential Library and Museum project was in need of funding. To approach potential donors, a brochure was created to excite and provide information about the new endeavor that was to be erected in downtown Springfield, Illinois. "The total funding needed for the museum and library is $115 million," shares creative director Jim Gobberdiel. "It's an opportunity for corporate sponsors to be connected with a project of this caliber. It will also give everyone an opportunity to have a real look at Lincoln's life and legacy." Because the project was a massive undertaking, it was important that the brochure communicate a sense of confidence that the endeavor would indeed be completed. "The quality and content of the brochure needed to convince people that this is a doable objective," adds Gobberdiel. "The brochure needed to solidify the idea that the project is really going to happen." The distinguished-looking design has several unique touches—a blind embossed and debossed title seal on the cover, a custom-designed font called Illinois Palatino, and various storytelling illustrations.

The historic-looking brochure commences with an overview of the project and the universal appeal of Lincoln. It continues by highlighting the economic benefits such a project would bring to the state of Illinois and the scholarly potential it would offer the world. "There has been no central museum to convey and expand upon the legacy of Abraham Lincoln," notes Gobberdiel. "Within the brochure, we discuss the three major components of the project—the museum, the library, and the tourism center. From there, we talk about all of the facilities and exhibitions and the multitude of programs." The brochure concludes with various funding options. Inserts, located in the back pocket, are used as a cost-effective way to present items that would change over time, like schedules and naming opportunities.

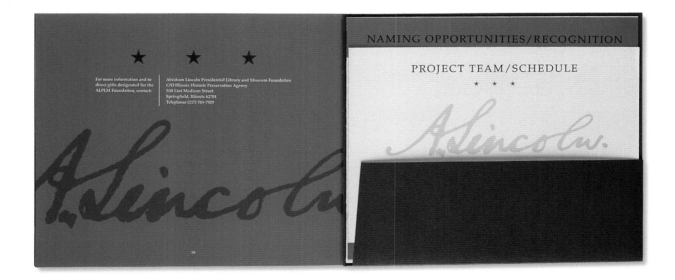

What Works

In addition to capturing the look and feel of the Lincoln era in a clean and sophisticated format, the fundraising brochure was able to communicate the importance of preserving the legacy of the former president. The overall quality and strength of the content helped corporations feel confident about donating money to this new venture in Illinois.

ABOVE: The interior pages discuss the overall theme, *Expanding the Legacy*. To give the piece a historic look, each spread is printed on natural Nekoosa Solutions 100-lb. text stock in four-color process plus two PMS colors. The insert sheets are designed to be separate as a cost-effective way to update information without having to reprint the entire brochure.

brown medical school

CLIENT:
Brown Medical School is part of Brown University in Providence, Rhode Island.

FIRM:
Plainspoke

ART DIRECTOR/DESIGNER:
Matt Ralph

PHOTOGRAPHER:
Len Rubenstein

COPYWRITER:
David Treadwell

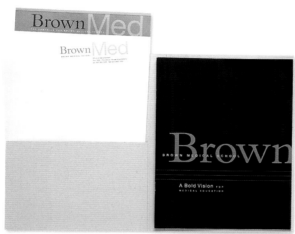

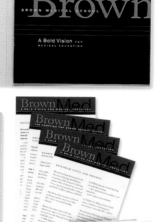

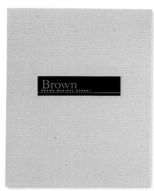

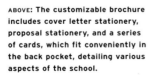

ABOVE: **The customizable brochure includes cover letter stationery, proposal stationery, and a series of cards, which fit conveniently in the back pocket, detailing various aspects of the school.**

Contemporary View on Tradition

With an increase in competition for both students and funding, Brown Medical School was looking for distinction. They wanted a bold, contemporary feel to their promotional material that still respected the traditions of the university. "The real trick was to balance the two sensibilities without going too far either way," recalls art director Matt Ralph. "This piece also had to be flexible. They wanted it to help them with fundraising, but they also wanted it for other things, like student recruitment and public relations."

To begin the project, research was conducted in the form of interviews. "The writer and I spent a day at the school, meeting with administrators, faculty members, and department chairs and sitting in on a couple of classes," says Ralph. After getting a full understanding of the institution and its students, an editorial approach was set in motion. "In our research, Dr. Anthony Caldamone came to our attention. He is a practicing surgeon who had graduated from the school and now teaches there. We wanted to do a feature and created this center gatefold around him." This day-in-the-life profile captures Dr. Caldamone's commitment to his practice and his patients.

To make the brochure interesting, various other visual approaches were explored. "We looked at a lot of different locations—identifying the people, where they were, and what they were all about," notes Ralph. "Rather than being a shoot that was structured and art directed, I really wanted a spontaneous, authentic storytelling feel. Going with a journalistic approach, we could achieve that." Throughout the brochure, quotes and stories capture the reader's interest with bold and compelling imagery. Designed as a complete package, this multipurpose brochure can be customized in various ways to fit any desired purpose.

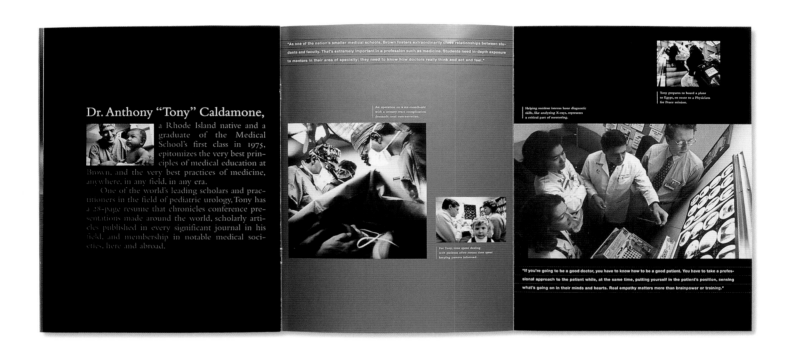

Dr. Anthony "Tony" Caldamone,

a Rhode Island native and a graduate of the Medical School's first class in 1975, epitomizes the very best principles of medical education at Brown, and the very best practices of medicine, anywhere, in any field, in any era.

One of the world's leading scholars and practitioners in the field of pediatric urology, Tony has a 28-page resume that chronicles conference presentations made around the world, scholarly articles published in every significant journal in his field, and membership in notable medical societies, here and abroad.

"As one of the nation's smaller medical schools, Brown fosters extraordinarily close relationships between students and faculty. That's extremely important in a profession such as medicine. Students need in-depth exposure to mentors in their area of specialty; they need to know how doctors really think and act and feel."

An operation on a six-month-old with a urinary tract complication demands total concentration.

For Tony, time spent dealing with patients often means time spent keeping parents informed.

Helping resident interns hone diagnostic skills, like analyzing X-rays, represents a critical part of mentoring.

Tony prepares to board a plane to Egypt, en route to a Physicians for Peace mission.

"If you're going to be a good doctor, you have to know how to be a good patient. You have to take a professional approach to the patient while, at the same time, putting yourself in the patient's position, sensing what's going on in their minds and hearts. Real empathy matters more than brainpower or training."

What Works

This story-driven brochure uses text and image not only to engage the reader but also to highlight the unique characteristics of the school—the distinguished faculty, the liberal medical education, the dynamic research enterprise, and the network of teaching hospitals. "It was successful in that it galvanized their efforts and gave them a tangible piece that they could give to people to tell them about what they were doing," offers Ralph. "In the past, they relied a lot on things they generated themselves. This gave them a professional package that really helped them get people's attention."

ABOVE: In the center gatefold, an inspirational story unfolds. The large photos, printed in a bronze and black duotone, were a challenge. Time had to be built into the project to properly test the sequencing and placement of the ink to get just the right effect. Spot gloss varnish is also used to achieve a nice contrast with the matte finish paper.

One Step Beyond

How Limited Budgets Can Enhance Creativity

Working within a tight budget does not necessarily mean a restriction on creativity. In fact, it can often enhance creative output. Such is the case with Lewis Moberly's annual report for NABS. "We wanted to create something that was interactive, dynamic, and interesting enough that someone in the communications industry would want to read it," details designer Paul Cilia La Corte. "Because the audience was so visual, the piece needed to be something that was unexpected, where the viewer was never quite sure what the next bit was going to do." The bold use of black and white helped to clearly communicate the organization's integrity, while the vibrant burnt orange displayed warmth and energy. The economical color scheme not only kept printing costs to a minimum, but it also allowed for flexibility. "With this annual report, everything had to work very hard. If something went into the piece, it did so with good reason," says Cilia La Corte. "Working with a tight budget, in a way, helped, because it forced us to do things that we may not have otherwise tried. With limitations comes creativity. The more focused you are, the stronger the idea and the communications will be." In a powerful and cost-effective manner, the interactive communications piece took the traditional components of an annual report and reinvented them for the highly visual audience of NABS.

Limitations in budget do not always result in the economic use of production and printing techniques. Sometimes, the project or client can be interesting enough that it attracts attention from vendors and other creatives who are eager to participate pro bono. For instance, PEN Canada, a charitable organization that champions the rights of writers, is a good example of a client that is not only intriguing but also open and respectful of personal vision and interpretation. PEN Canada's annual report, an interesting assignment with full creative freedom, sparked interest from a variety of talent and resources. "As soon as I knew that we were going to be working on their annual report, I started talking to people—warming them up to the idea and what PEN Canada was all about," recalls art director Gary Beelik of Soapbox Design Communications. "I made a lot of personal calls, relying heavily on my relationships with vendors." A full-color comp was produced to show off the concept and entice participation. Because of the strength of the idea, all illustration, photography, and paper were donated, and the printing was done at cost. For a mere $2,000 (Canadian), 25,000 pieces were produced. "It takes a lot of work and a lot of dedicated people to get the project done right," says Beelik. "We all pitched in to get a piece that we were really happy with." When an interesting project comes along, it provides an opportunity to work collaboratively with others to create something outstanding, even when the budget is restrictive. In addition to highlighting the work and talent of all involved, it stimulates creative energy, growth, and renewal. "It's an opportunity to do something inspirational and fun," concludes Beelik. "At the end of the day, that is what is all about anyway."

CLIENT:
PEN Canada is a nonprofit organization that works on behalf of imprisoned poets, essayists, and novelists to secure their freedom.

FIRM:
Soapbox Design Communications

ART DIRECTOR/DESIGNER:
Gary Beelik

ILLUSTRATOR:
Paul Dallas

PHOTOGRAPHER:
James Reid

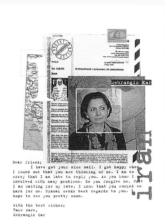

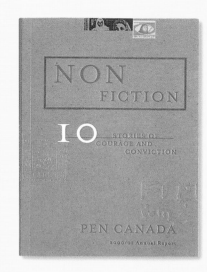

ABOVE: This editorial-style annual report is designed like an old world novel, featuring 10 true-life stories written by members, imprisoned writers, and prominent Canadian authors, like Margaret Atwood. Each handpicked story offers insight and a unique perspective. The cover, printed in full color with an overall matte varnish, was made from a scanned piece of chipboard. To give the piece a worldly quality, elements were debossed and embossed into the cover. A deboss was also applied to the type, creating a letterpress look. The faux stamp, reproduced in four-color, gives the appearance of a hand-applied sticker.

RIGHT: The designer worked closely with the printer to determine the size and maximum number of pages. Because the book was to be perfect-bound, they were not obligated to imposition the pages in any specific order. To get the feel of a full-color report on a mostly two-color job, the printer ran three forms—two of them in black plus one PMS color and the third in four-color. The process color sheets were then dispersed throughout the report to give it visual depth and interest.

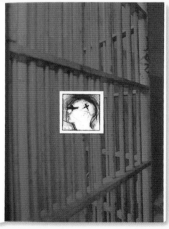

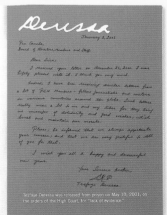

CLIENT:
NABS is a charitable organization that provides a wide range of services for people in the communications industry at every stage of their working life and into retirement.

FIRM:
Lewis Moberly

ART DIRECTOR:
Mary Lewis

DESIGNER:
Paul Cilia La Corte

COPYWRITERS:
Paul Cilia La Corte and Janet Hull

RIGHT AND BELOW: **The introduction piece, vibrantly printed in burnt orange, unfolds the numerous resources and programs that NASBS has to offer someone throughout their career in the communications industry. Each section is housed inside an easily removable folder.**

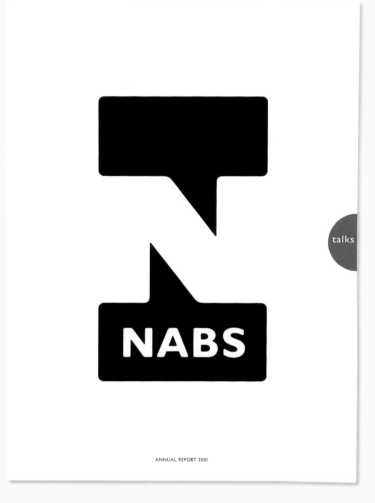

ANNUAL REPORT 2001

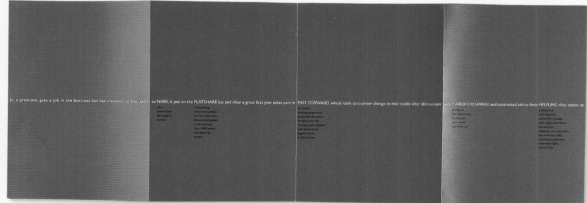

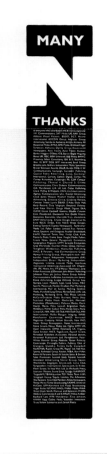

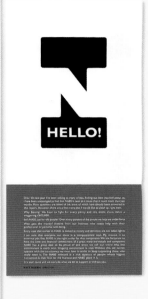

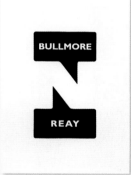

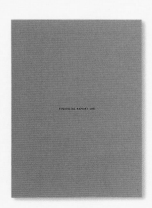

FINANCIAL REPORT 2001

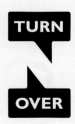

ABOVE AND LEFT: Various sections, printed economically in black, dynamically outline the benefits of being a member or supporter of NABS. *Hello!* details a message from the director. *Bullmore and Reay* continue the conversation, and lastly, *Many Thanks* shows all the people who have contributed throughout the year. Each interactive section, appropriate for a visually literate audience, either flips up, down, or over or unfolds to reveal its message. The package concludes with the financial report.

plainspoke

CLIENT:
Plainspoke is a graphic design
firm that specializes in educational
and cultural work.

FIRM:
Plainspoke

ART DIRECTOR/DESIGNER:
Matt Ralph

PHOTOGRAPHER:
Brian Wilder

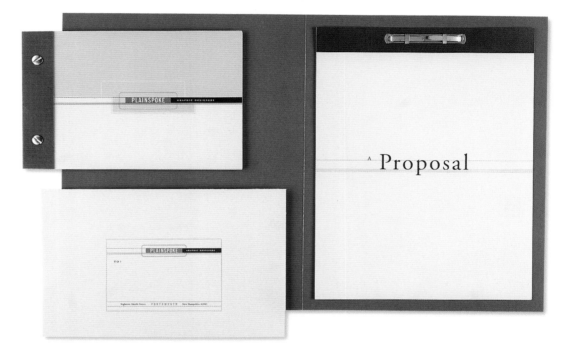

ABOVE: The piece is fashioned to
have the feeling of an old ledger.
The semiwraparound cover not
only conveniently hides the spine,
but also adds to the overall
dimensional quality of the piece.
It is sent out in a matching
envelope, along with a proposal
folder, when necessary.

Thinking about Flexibility

This flexible and easy-to-update promotional brochure
gives prospective clients a glimpse into the strategic
thinking behind the design work of Plainspoke. "I wanted
to have a little compact portfolio presentation that we
could send out to clients," art director Matt Ralph
remarks. "We had been sending samples out, but it got
to be cumbersome. It just made sense to try and corral
some of our best work together in one piece."

The most challenging aspect of the brochure was
developing the descriptive text for each project. "To
distill our creative thinking behind a project into a little
paragraph was difficult but important for the client to
see," notes Ralph. "We always try to really think about
each project and what it communicates. I wanted people
to have background knowledge about the work we do,
rather than just showing a bunch of pictures." The art
director also worked very closely with the photographer
to make sure that the composition on each shot was just

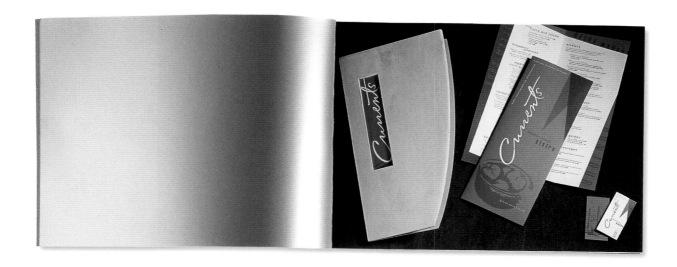

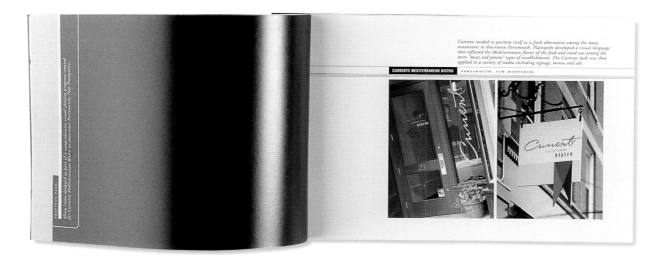

right—varying the images from full bleed shots to more traditionally cropped views. "In the pacing, I wanted to break up the sequencing a bit," explains Ralph. "It was just too repetitive to have everything looking all the same." The text also alternates in placement from front to back.

Two sets of inserts were printed, drilled, trimmed, and stored in sections. Because the pages are loose and not permanently bound, the design firm can customize a brochure to fit any prospective target audience. "We can skew it more towards identity or publication projects. It gives us a lot of freedom and flexibility," adds Ralph. The handy and compact brochure can be easily taken apart by disassembling the Chicago screws, which are usually used on horse bridals. Silver is used as an accent color throughout, tying the screws into the overall color scheme.

What Works

By providing prospective clients with a glimpse into the strategic thinking behind each project, the design team was able to highlight their ability to effectively communicate ideas in a visual way—making the brochure much more than a mere portfolio presentation. Designing the pages to be interchangeable made the promotional brochure extremely useful in the firm's marketing efforts. According to Ralph, "It has generated many more projects for us."

ABOVE: **Each presentation page is printed in six colors—four-color process, silver, and light gray. Spot varnish is also used on Potlatch McCoy matte finish 65-lb. cover stock.**

joel nakamura paintings & illustrations

CLIENT:
Joel Nakamura is an illustrator and fine artist working in Santa Fe, New Mexico.

FIRM:
Joel Nakamura
Paintings & Illustrations

ART DIRECTOR:
Joel Nakamura

DESIGNER:
Greg Hally, Hally O'Toole Design

ILLUSTRATOR:
Joel Nakamura

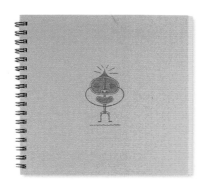

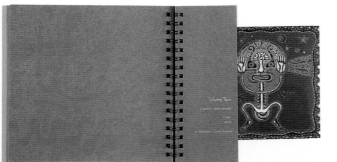

ABOVE: The handsome brochure contains Nakamura's well-known mythological and spiritual illustrations. Each piece is subtly identified on a small sheet, which can be flipped back and forth on the spiral binding. The highly textural cover features the artist's logo, and the solid pages highlight the images and show off the patterns that appear within Nakamura's work.

Spiritual Icons

Illustrator Joel Nakamura needed a way to introduce a new style to his repertoire of work while still maintaining the promotion of his signature style that he had become well-known for doing. "I wanted a promotion that showed different projects and would function in two ways—one, as a vehicle for prospecting illustration clients; and two, as catalog for collectors who buy paintings," shares Nakamura. The biggest challenge for the artist was trying to edit his vast collection of work into a cohesive yet diverse sampling. "Making the right selections was important," notes Nakamura. "I wanted to show work that would be interesting to a variety of clients, from record companies and corporations to galleries. I also wanted to show my ability to think and solve problems."

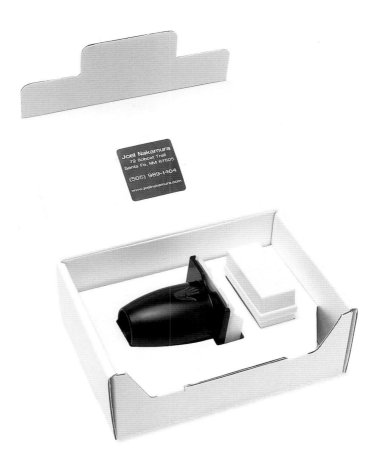

To capture a new and unexplored audience, Nakamura created an interesting package that highlighted his new creative endeavors. "It is what I call my primitive work. It's about line, color, and pattern—more distilled down than my illustration work. A lot of people respond to it, and it has allowed me to venture into different areas," says Nakamura. "Because it's interactive, it was a great way to debut a different wrinkle to what I do." The slide promotion, although complex, was quite easy for Nakamura to produce. "I went to an ad specialty company. They printed the viewer, duped the slides, printed the stickers, and put everything together in a box," he shares. The artist finds that advertising specialty catalogs are a great way to get ideas for interesting promotions, especially ones not typically seen in the illustration or fine arts industries. "It's the kind of promotion that someone is going to get curious about sooner or later, and they are not going to throw it away," Nakamura adds. To maintain market presence in his signature style, a brochure was also created to beautifully display Nakamura's mythological and spiritual illustrations.

What Works

The promotional duo not only helped the artist to maintain his current market presence but also opened doors for a new body of work to flourish. Because the slide viewer was such a novel item, it captured the attention of buyers, who held onto the promotional piece for just the right assignment. "So many illustration promotions go into the round file, the trash can. I feel pretty good that about 95% of the time, people have kept these promotions and shared them with other designers," says Nakamura. "Both the catalog and slide box have brought in a lot of work for me." The promotion ended up in the hands of the Olympic Organizing Committee—landing work for the artist with the 2002 Winter Games in Salt Lake City. "If you can put good things out there, they will always pay off down the road," he concludes.

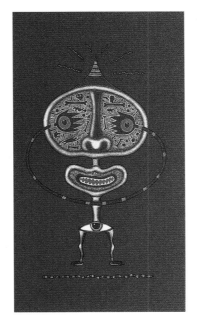

ABOVE AND LEFT: The customized promotional package contains a viewer, slides of the artist's new primitive work, and a business card. It is flexible enough to be sent as a self-mailer or as part of another promotion.

skidmore inc.

CLIENT:
Skidmore Inc. is a full-service design and commercial art studio.

FIRM:
Skidmore Inc.

ART DIRECTORS:
Julie Pincus, Mae Skidmore, and Sue Levytsky

DESIGNERS:
Julie Pincus, John Latin, Robert Nixon, and Laura Lybeer-Hilpert

ILLUSTRATORS:
Gary Cooley, Bob Nixon, Steve Magsig, Ann Redner, Scott Olds, Dave O'Connell, Rob Burman, Toni Button, Jeff Rauf, Larry Dodge, Chuck Gillies, Rudy Laslo, Bob Andrews, John Ball, Wayne Appleton, George Burgos, Carrie Russell, and Ron Alexander

PHOTOGRAPHERS:
Rocki Pedersen and Jeff Hargis

COPYWRITERS:
Mae Skidmore and Sue Levytsky

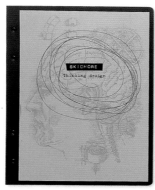

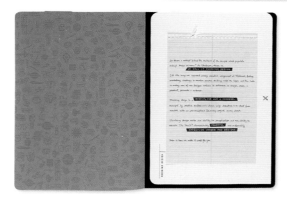

ABOVE: **Created to have an old-fashioned notebook-like feel, the promotional brochure is bound with cloth tape and rivets and accented with a punched label. Focusing on the design process and the various offerings of Skidmore, the piece was distributed in a specially designed envelope that features various little doodles about thinking.**

Changing Perceptions

Because Skidmore began as a commercial art studio in Detroit doing mostly automotive illustration and design, they have been pigeonholed into that market. Since their beginnings in 1959, they have expanded into other areas and needed to communicate that to a more diverse audience. "Because we have been in business for so long, there is a stigma. The great thing is that people look to you for stability. What is not so great is that you don't necessarily get a lot of breaks for being cutting edge," remarks art director Mae Skidmore. "With this brochure, we were trying to counteract some of the impressions that clients had about us." In addition to their design and illustration work, Skidmore also offers web development, retouching and imaging, and marketing services.

Wanting to break into the corporate market, the design team realized that its biggest challenge was determining their strategic plan of attack. "Traditionally, we only called upon advertising agencies. But in the last five years, we have been making a real push to deal directly with Fortune 500 companies," adds Skidmore. "Because we were going after a new area, we really had to spend a lot of time thinking about who we were, what we did, and how we could leverage that to a corporate market. Putting the brochure together was easy once we figured all that stuff out." The design team came up with a promotional brochure that highlighted all of the firm's creative and marketing services in an interesting and captivating way. "We didn't want to do a brochure that said the same thing as everyone else," recalls Skidmore. "We really wanted to get out of that rhetoric and really express the personality of the company."

RIGHT: The brochure is broken down into four major sections that detail the creative process and highlight the firm's offerings.

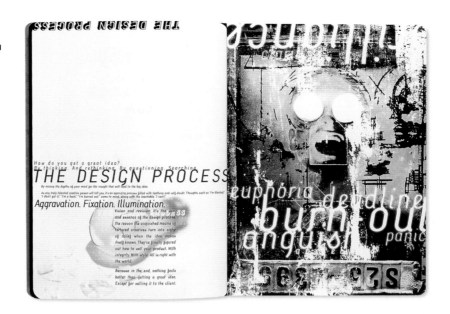

RIGHT: An envelope in the back of the brochure houses several portfolio samples.

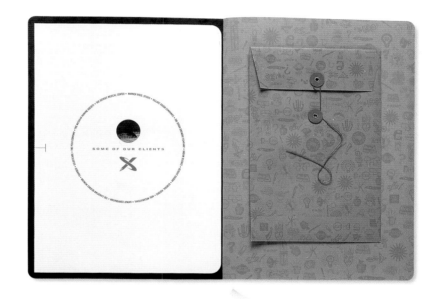

What Works

With their brochure's interesting use of production techniques, illustration, photography, and type, Skidmore Inc. was able to break away from their traditionally accepted role and appear much more cutting edge. By highlighting the design firm's creative abilities and full-service approach, the brochure was able to attract attention from corporate clients outside the automotive industry. "With this piece, we got work almost immediately. Everyone we gave it to was so impressed," shares Skidmore. "The brochure was not only creatively rewarding but also great for image building and increasing company revenues."

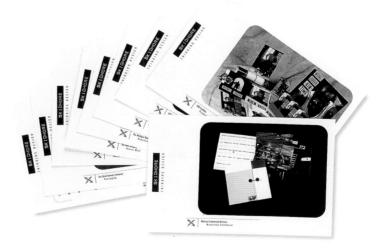

redpath

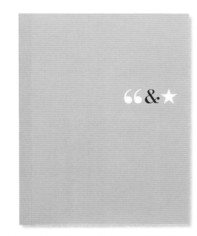

CLIENT:
Redpath is a graphic design company that employs both designers and writers.

FIRM:
Redpath

CREATIVE DIRECTOR:
Iain Lauder

DESIGNERS:
Jason Little and Iain Lauder

PHOTOGRAPHER:
The Picture House

COPYWRITERS:
Richard Irvine and Gerry O'Regan

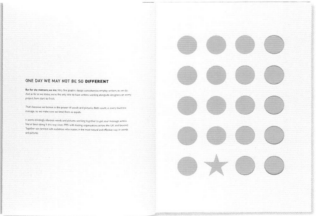

ABOVE: **The front cover hosts the firm's new identity icon, a graphic interpretation of words and pictures. Each page, including the cover, is French-folded with die-cutting and blind embossing as accents to create variety and interest. The entire piece is bound using two staples. The back cover overlaps and folds under onto the front, covering the staples.**

Words and Pictures

Redpath has something unique to offer clients that their competition does not. Unlike most design firms in the United Kingdom, Redpath employs both designers and writers to solve their clients' communication problems. "What sets us apart is the way we approach our projects," says creative director Iain Lauder. "Because everything we do is in words and pictures, we are different, and that is something we wanted to communicate in the brochure." Right from the cover design, the idea of combining words with pictures is conveyed. The fluorescent orange, a corporate color, draws your eye in, and the new identity icon intrigues you to read on. "We wanted this brochure to really jump out at you and not get lost on someone's desk," shares Lauder. "When you look inside, it is quite simple and clearly explains the company and how we view ourselves." The brochure begins by detailing the firm's unique approach to communications and finishes by presenting various client projects, each covering a variety of industries. To capture attention and create interest, various production techniques were brought in. "When doing your own brochure, you always try to push the boundaries," offers Lauder. "We experimented with different printing techniques a bit—doing things that we do not always get to do. The techniques allowed us to explain our whole process in an entertaining way."

The biggest hurdle for the design firm was just getting the job done. "We spent quite a bit of time internally—working on the project until we felt that we had something that worked," recalls Lauder. "Because we were pushing the writing side, it was important that the words were absolutely right." The entire piece took about six months to complete, taking on many shapes and directions along the way.

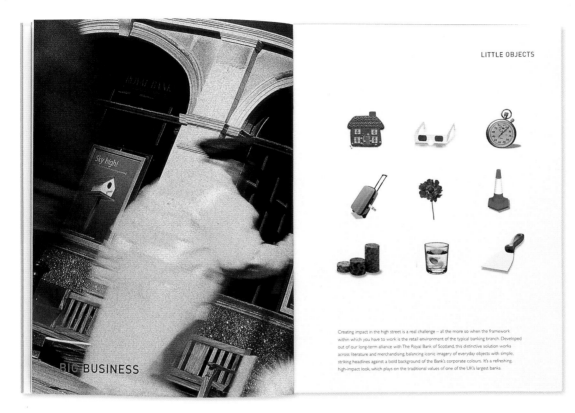

LITTLE OBJECTS

Creating impact in the high street is a real challenge – all the more so when the framework within which you have to work is the retail environment of the typical banking branch. Developed out of our long-term alliance with The Royal Bank of Scotland, this distinctive solution works across literature and merchandising, balancing iconic imagery of everyday objects with simple, striking headlines against a bold background of the Bank's corporate colours. It's a refreshing, high-impact look, which plays on the traditional values of one of the UK's largest banks.

What Works

The rich balance of words and pictures helped to communicate Redpath as unique among its competitors. The brilliant colors, interesting use of production techniques, and imagery made the brochure eye-catching, while the clarity of the copy made it memorable. "It has been very successful," says Lauder. "We have recently had a number of leads with several major clients responding to the piece. They like that we offer them more than other design companies."

michael osborne design, one heart press, anne telford, and cathie bleck

CLIENT:
Michael Osborne, a graphic designer and owner of One Heart Press, **Anne Telford**, a writer, and **Cathie Bleck**, an illustrator, all worked collaboratively on a self-promotion piece.

FIRM:
Michael Osborne Design, One Heart Press, Anne Telford, and Cathie Bleck

ART DIRECTOR/DESIGNER:
Michael Osborne

ILLUSTRATOR:
Cathie Bleck

COPYWRITER:
Anne Telford

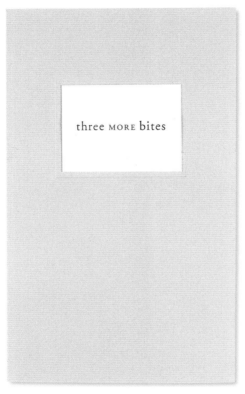

three MORE bites

ABOVE: The accordion-folded book was printed on Somerset White. The self-wrapping cover, with its hand-applied label, was produced using BFK Reeves paper.

From the Heart

It all started with the AIGA "Y" conference in San Diego entitled *Connectivity*. "At the conference, many people focused their presentations on collaboration and connecting with other people," recalls illustrator Cathie Bleck. "It was a real energizing experience." After leaving the conference, all three collaborators were quite inspired and decided to get together for lunch to discuss a possible joint endeavor. "I thought we could do something that I would design and print, Cathie would illustrate, and Anne would write—something that displayed all of our individual talents in one piece," says designer Michael Osborne. Bleck adds, "At lunch, we talked a lot about what the piece would be about. As we were looking at the dessert menu, we noticed that one of the desserts was called Three More Bites. It was a revelation! Our book would include three poems, three pieces of art, and we would call it *Three More Bites*."

The project started with writer Anne Telford. "We asked her to lead the way," notes Osborne. "She sent over several short poems, and we narrowed it down to three." Both the illustrator and writer worked together to select just the right ones for the small, yet intimate book. "I have a large body of poetry to draw from and was very open to having Cathie choose what she related to," says Telford. "In her illustrations, Cathie really got to the heart and soul of what I was writing about." Portraying three central female figures, the illustrations add richness to each page. "It was in the spirit of working with Cathie and the inspiration we drew from the women in our lives," shares Telford.

The type, subtly displayed in warm gray, is both eloquent and graceful. "It is real easy on your eye, and the writing and illustration still remain the heroes," adds Osborne. Once complete, the entire edition was sent to the illustrator and writer to hand-sign.

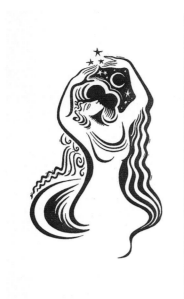

night[time]

Open to the sky,

a field of lights at my shoulder,

I stare at the night,

and will it to be longer.

What Works

Because of the quality and attention to detail, the collaborative promotional piece drew attention from everyone who received it. All of the special touches and care that were put into the piece made it something worth holding on to. "I have gotten so many e-mails, and a lot of them were similar in tone," remarks Osborne. "The responses, much like the piece itself, were warm and heartfelt." The handcrafted piece really celebrates illustration, design, and writing and inspires others to do the same.

three MORE bites

One Step Beyond

The Graphic Use of Typography

In design, type can be more than mere words on a page. Used properly, it can be an effective tool to enhance a communications message. When designer Matt Ralph envisioned an educational brochure for Antioch College, he wanted to use type as a way to reinforce the feeling of experiencing the college and its students firsthand. "The college is an interesting place. They have different kinds of programs and courses that support the students' interest and commitment to social and environmental issues," says Ralph. "Rather than design a book that is organized by departments, I decided to design it as a random walk-through. I wanted the type to reinforce that by changing quite a bit as you go through the book. In some places the type would be simple and quiet and a little more reflective, while in other places it would become a more playful and exuberant, and in others it would get big, bold, and loud." Ralph chose to use type as a way to bring out the variety and diversity of the small town college. As you look at each spread, you are introduced to a new aspect of the school and its unique student body.

Type can also be an expressive, almost pictorial, element used to give visual impact to a page. In a promotional brochure for illustrator Rick Sealock, designer Ken Bessie used type in a highly visual way. "I thought a lot about how I wanted the reader to perceive the type," recalls Bessie. "I went with an asymmetrical type layout because Rick's illustrations are so colorful and aggressive." Bessie's painterly use of type brought variety and spontaneity to each spread. "I wanted to do something a little bit different on every page. I'd put a lowercase letter in a full cap word, change the color for one letter, jump the baseline, and use different point sizes and leading in the same text block," details Bessie. "When words repeated or when punctuation was used, I really wanted the reader to get a sense of the emphasis on these words. I wanted the piece to be typographically fun to read." Through his inventive and playful use of type, Bessie was able to tell a visual story while also highlighting the illustrator's whimsical work.

By far, the most important aspect of type is that it be legible to ensure that the communications is clearly disseminated. "You have to think about your audience," concludes Ralph. "Once the information is readable and understandable, you can go off and be more expressive and playful. I like work that blends the two."

CLIENT:
Rick Sealock is a whimsical illustrator working in Alberta, Canada.

FIRM:
Blackletter Design

ART DIRECTOR:
Rick Sealock

DESIGNER:
Ken Bessie

ILLUSTRATOR/COPYWRITER:
Rick Sealock

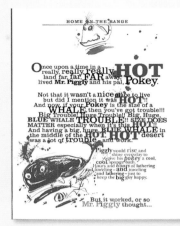
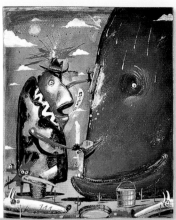

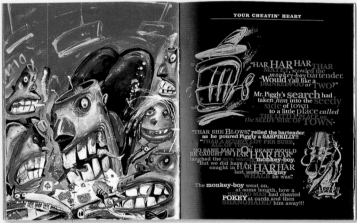

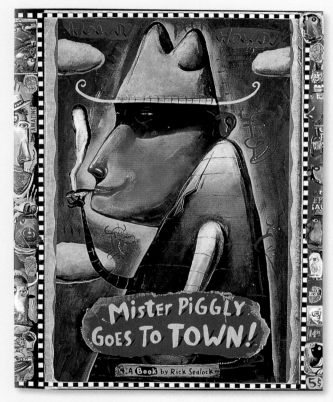

ABOVE: Taking a children's story-book approach, the 14-page promotional piece was created to attract the attention of a variety of clients—editorial, publishing, and advertising. The asymmetrical layout and whimsical use of type reflects the story and the imagery—colorful, energetic, and fun.

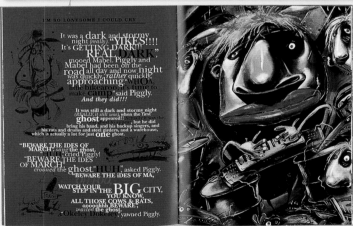

ABOVE: Two typefaces, Clarendon and ITC New Baskerville, are used throughout the illustrative promotional book.

CLIENT:
Antioch College is a liberal arts college in Ohio where individuality and independence are nurtured.

FIRM:
Plainspoke

ART DIRECTOR:
Matt Ralph

DESIGNERS:
Matt Ralph and Stephanie Brazeal

PHOTOGRAPHERS:
Brian Wilder and Dennie Eagleson

COPYWRITER:
David Treadwell

RIGHT: The educational brochure is designed to convey the feeling of walking through the Antioch College campus—experiencing the culture, people, and unique programs. The brochure was mailed to prospective students in a custom-designed envelope.

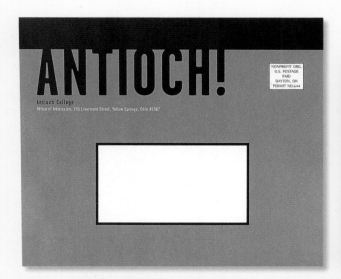

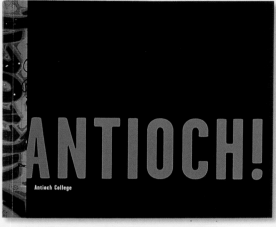

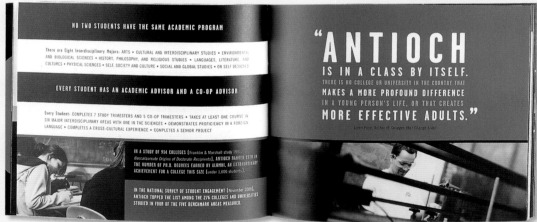

ABOVE AND CENTER RIGHT: The profile pages help to reinforce the cultural diversity and interests of the student body. By varying the posture, height, and weight and repositioning the kerning, leading, and column structure, Ralph was able to portray Antioch College with clarity and impact. The typefaces vary from Garage Gothic to Trade Gothic with Mrs. Eaves as an accent.

BELOW RIGHT: Within the brochure, actual postcards are reproduced to highlight the study abroad program in a fun and personal way.

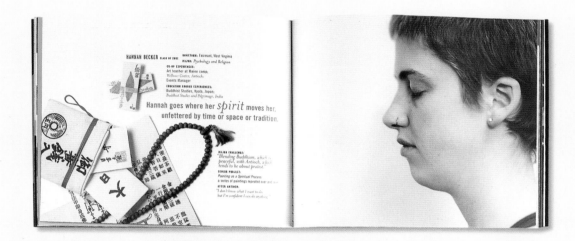

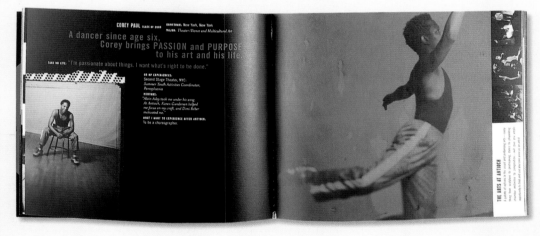

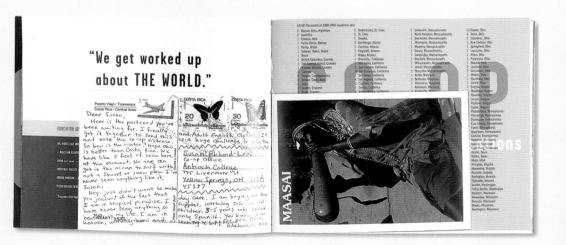

casa da música

CLIENT:
Casa da Música is an opera house.

FIRM:
R2 Design

ART DIRECTORS/DESIGNERS:
Lizá Defossez Ramalho,
Artur Rebelo

PHOTOGRAPHERS:
Pedro Magalhães and
Henrique Delgado

COPYWRITERS:
António Jorge Pacheco,
Luís Madureira, Nuno Carrinhas,
Cristina Fernandes, Ricardo Pais,
Brad Cohen, and Adrian Mourby

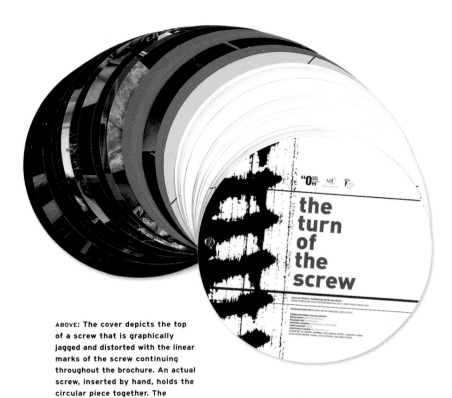

ABOVE: The cover depicts the top of a screw that is graphically jagged and distorted with the linear marks of the screw continuing throughout the brochure. An actual screw, inserted by hand, holds the circular piece together. The uniquely round brochure can be opened either by fanning or flipping. It is up to the viewer to decide.

Good vs. Evil

Casa da Música was looking for a single brochure to depict two different opera performances by the group Estúdio de Ópera do Porto. *The Turn of the Screw* and *L'Amore Industrioso* were to exist in the same brochure but function independently. "Opera brochures, at least in Portugal, are very traditional and a bit classical," acknowledges art director Lizá Defossez Ramalho. "With this piece, the client wanted something different, something that would reach people, and he gave us the freedom to add our own interpretation." To solve the functional aspect of the brochure, the design team chose to run the operas back-to-back. *The Turn of the Screw* is on one side and *L'Amore Industrioso* is on the reverse.

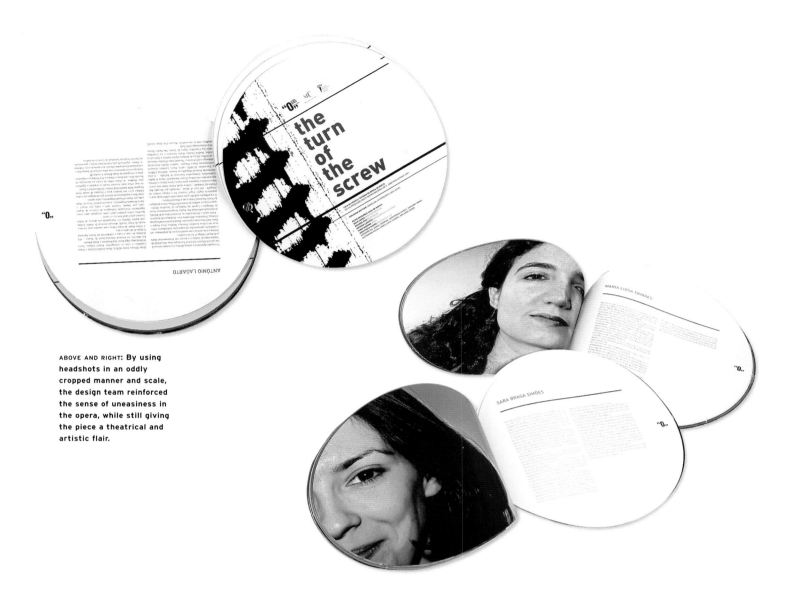

ABOVE AND RIGHT: By using headshots in an oddly cropped manner and scale, the design team reinforced the sense of uneasiness in the opera, while still giving the piece a theatrical and artistic flair.

Because the text and graphics already existed for *L'Amore Industrioso,* the design team focused their efforts on *Turn of the Screw,* a gothic horror story about the strange things that happen to a governess and the two orphan children in her care. "There are ghosts, and they come to play with the children and, in a sense, abuse them," recalls Ramalho. "There are two opposing feelings. There are these awful things that happen in the story, but with that, there are a few moments of joy. When you turn the pages you get different feelings." As you move throughout the brochure, solemnly colored pages gradually begin to brighten. The juxtaposition of color helps to balance the moments of joy with those of sorrow. "It was a

challenge to create a brochure for an opera that we couldn't see," comments Ramalho. "Instead, we read the text, met with the director and music coordinator, and went to the theater to see drawings of the clothes and the backgrounds." With no performance photos to work with, the design team chose to focus on the performers. "We wanted the portraits to be a bit suffocated in the confines of the brochure," notes Ramalho. "To establish intimacy, we wanted to get a close proximity in scale between the people who are reading the brochure and the portraits." The aggressive use of portrait photography helped to portray the pressure that the children were feeling throughout the opera.

What Works

Distributed at the end of each opera, this nontraditional brochure captivated its audience much like the opera itself. "We attended the opera and saw the people getting the brochures, and they were very excited because it was so different—round and colorful," offers Ramalho. "The client also saw the people wanting to grab the brochure. All of the actors and the people who worked on the opera were also very pleased."

the national illustration conference

CLIENT:
The National Illustration Conference is a nonprofit organization whose purpose is to provide a platform for illustrators to address issues facing the industry.

FIRM:
Murphy Design Inc.

ART DIRECTOR/DESIGNER:
Mark Murphy

ILLUSTRATORS:
Joel Nakamura, Amy Guipp, Gary Taxali, Cathie Bleck, Vivienne Flesher, Gerard DuBois, Christian Northeast, and Mick Wiggins

COPYWRITER:
Anne Telford

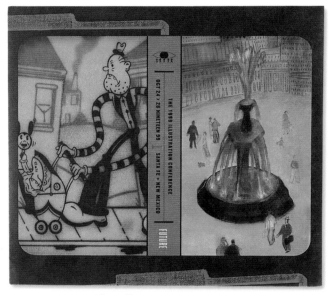

ABOVE AND TOP RIGHT: **The motivational brochure features the work of various illustrators and styles to generate a broad range of interest in the conference. The focus is on empowerment and reinvention.**

Power in Unity

At the first National Illustration Conference, many illustrators emerged from their studios to unite. It was a crisis meeting to address industry-related concerns and discuss potential solutions. This grassroots effort began a movement of unity and empowerment that has since gained momentum. "The whole idea behind the conference was to bring illustrators together to talk about serious issues facing the industry—fees, stock, and copyright issues," reflects art director Mark Murphy. "We were trying to generate interest and get across the concept that the future starts with you."

This illustrated six-paneled self-mailer, designed to maximize the press sheet and to minimize postage costs, engages the reader with a variety of visually rich content. "My idea was to take different styles of illustration, people that were prominent in the business, and blend them together in one piece. I chose Cathie Bleck, whose work is feminine and sensitive, and juxtaposed her with Gary Taxali, who is a little more irreverent. I had to find a balance in styles because illustration is such a subjective art form," remarks Murphy. "It also helped to attract a variety of illustrators to the conference." The interesting texture that accents the brochure throughout was created with a Xerox machine. "I scanned in the texture as a black-and-white TIFF file and kept the resolution high so that it could be made larger or smaller," details Murphy. "I then added color at will and layered it in Quark." The designer has, over the years, built an extensive collection of textures that he utilizes in various assignments.

As the outside excites, the inside spread outlines the two-day conference agenda—motivating people to register. The mailer is part of a series. Several postcards were also created to spread the word and generate interest for the conference. All of the artwork, design, paper, and printing were donated.

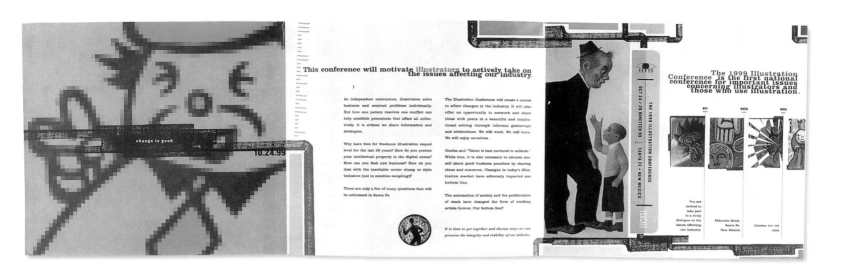

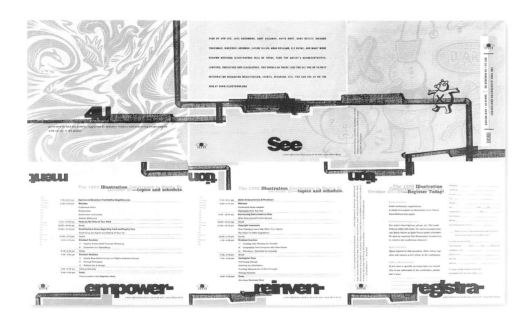

What Works

"Because the brochure had a community feel and did not center on any one illustrator or style, but on many making up one industry, it excited a lot of people to connect," says Murphy. "There was room for 500 people at the conference, and they sold out."

ABOVE: The inside six-panel spread houses the schedule of events and registration form.

the seattle supersonics

CLIENT:
The Seattle Supersonics are a professional basketball team.

FIRM:
Hornall Anderson Design Works

CREATIVE DIRECTOR:
Jack Anderson

ART DIRECTORS/DESIGNERS:
Mark Popich and
Andrew Wicklund

PHOTOGRAPHERS:
Alex Hayden, Jeff Reinking/NBA
Photos, and various stock

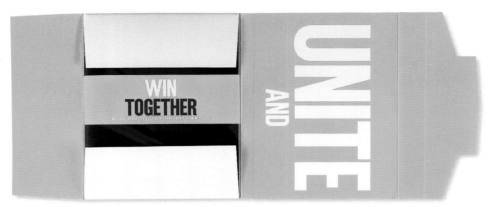

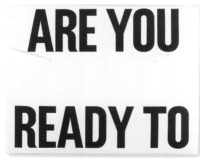

ABOVE: The pocket folder, with its bold messaging, entices the reader to open it. Inside sits the renewal brochure wrapped by a bellyband.

Classic Basketball

The Sonics had come under new ownership that was interested in rebranding the team. The new owners' vision was to bring the fans back into the game. By showing inspirational imagery and sincere text, the brochure identifies and connects with the fan base. The bold use of type and image makes the piece easy to read and the communications clear. "We knew right away that this piece had to be open and honest. It couldn't be full of tricks and gimmicks," details creative director Jack Anderson. "It had to be genuine in its touch and message where each page talks about renewing passion, responsibility, commitment, and respect." As part of the new brand, the team's logo, uniforms, tickets, and overall color scheme were all changed. "We basically went back to the colors that they used to have—green and yellow. We also brought back the arch,"

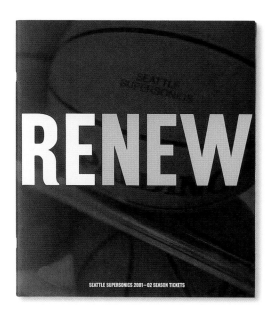

RENEW

SEATTLE SUPERSONICS 2001–02 SEASON TICKETS

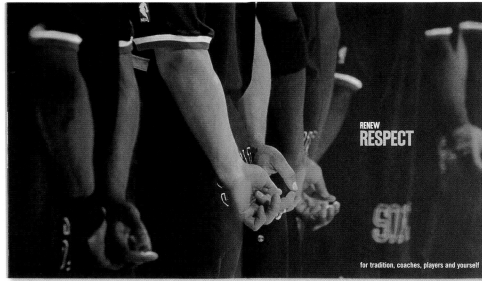

RENEW
RESPECT

for tradition, coaches, players and yourself

recalls Anderson. "Years ago, there was honesty about the team. It was a rich heritage that we wanted to bring back."

Throughout the renewal brochure, four-color photos are interesting intermixed with an array of monochromatic imagery—giving it that classic look. The simple, genuine, and heartfelt brochure was sent to season-ticket holders to renew their subscription. "The Sonics had come off a bad season. There was a new ownership and talk of significant trades," recalls Anderson. "At the time, people were wondering if they could justify buying season tickets again." Because a huge part of the team's income stream comes from season-ticket sales, this communications devise was very important not only to the new management but to the future of the team.

What Works

The integrity and honesty of the piece helped to inspire fans to recommit to their beloved team for another season. "The fan base had some drift and continued fall off in the past," claims Anderson. "This piece helped to stop the flow on that. The whole program has become a model for other teams to follow."

ABOVE: Beginning with a renewal theme, the cover is bold and simple with the background acting as a textural support. Each spread communicates a different aspect of the overall message. The brochure is printed in four-color process plus two PMS colors for the team's new colors—green and yellow.

the council of europe

CLIENT:
The Council of Europe is an intergovernmental organization that aims to protect human rights, promote awareness of and encourage cultural diversity, seek solutions to problems facing the European society, and help consolidate democratic stability.

FIRM:
Summa

ART DIRECTOR:
Wladmir Marnich

DESIGNERS:
Eduardo Cortada and
Griselda Marti

PHOTOGRAPHERS:
Josep Maria Bas, Eduardo Cortada, and Stone Photo Library

COPYWRITERS:
Norbert Paul Engel and
Renee Gautron

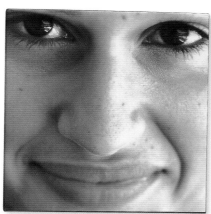

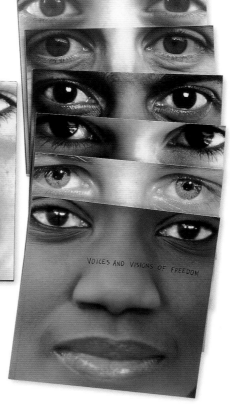

ABOVE: **A series of six books, each entitled *The Voices and Visions of Freedom,* is written in various languages—English, French, Spanish, German, Italian, and Russian. Each laminated book is color-coded on the spine to match the color of the text inside. Collectively they fit together in a specially designed, laminated box.**

Multicultural Approach

The Council of Europe needed a piece to distribute at the celebration of the fiftieth anniversary of the Human Rights Convention. In 1950, an agreement was reached, culminating the signing of the convention for the protection of human rights and fundamental freedoms—a major milestone in European history. For the first time, citizens could claim rights under international law against states, including their own.

To better understand what the Human Rights Convention was all about, the art director went to Strasbourg, France, to visit the Council of Europe. "They explained to me how things worked and how human rights issues are treated within the council," notes art director Wladmir Marnich. "I also interviewed the author who wrote the book, a specialist in human rights issues." Upon his return, a design direction was established. Using mostly conceptual imagery, the initial design attempted to communicate the various articles and rights put out by the council. "In the

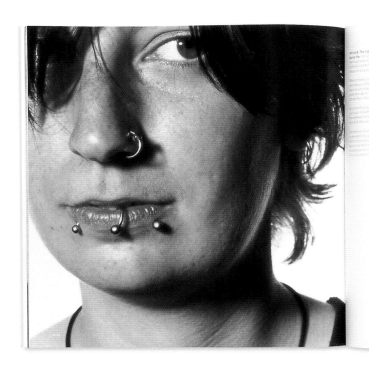

PURSUIT OF HAPPINESS
THROUGH PRIVACY

beginning, we had presented a more abstract design, and it was approved," recalls Marnich. "When we went to work on the cover of the book, I saw an image of a face. I thought it would be great, but it had nothing to do with the inside. So, at the very last minute, I decided to change the whole book." Taking on a more multicultural approach, the design team reorganized the book and the design to incorporate a series of faces—diverse in ethnic background, gender, and age. Because of restrictions in budget and time, the design team solicited friends, family, and acquaintances to be photographed for the book. "We wanted to use everyday faces, not actors or models. I didn't want any decoration or distractions in the book," says Marnich. "We also wanted each person to send a message to the parliamentarians in his or her own handwriting. It was a small detail, but truthful to the idea." Tightly cropped portraits are accented with handwritten messages that act as headers to each section.

What Works

Because the piece took on a multicultural and multilingual approach, it appealed to a variety of people equally. The sensitivity to the issues and the personal touches that exist throughout made it heartfelt and enriching. "At the celebration, each person would take the brochure with the language they knew. The box set was a special gift for presidents, vice presidents, and people in high positions within the Council of Europe," shares Marnich. "The client was pleased, and everyone was happy about the end result."

ABOVE: **Each section is dedicated to one particular issue and features a portrait, a personal message, and some explanatory body copy. To give movement and pacing throughout the piece, each portrait is shot at a slightly different angle.**

the sahara center

CLIENT:
The Sahara Center is a family shopping and entertainment center located in Sharjah in the United Arab Emirates.

FIRM:
Thumbnail Creative Group

CREATIVE DIRECTOR:
Rik Klingle

DESIGNERS:
Valerie Turnbull and Lindsay Rankin

COPYWRITER:
Rik Klingle

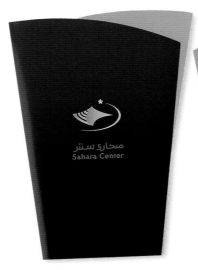

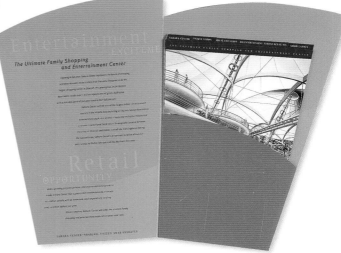

ABOVE: The embossed cover is printed in a gradation of midnight blue and accented by the brilliance of the logo. The overall pocket folder is designed with interesting angles and curvilinear die-cuts—alluding to the dramatic architecture of the Sahara Center. In the arched pocket fits several inserts as well as a CD-ROM and business card.

Arabian Flair

"Our concept for this leasing folder, with its elegant proprietary shape and rich, stunning color, was to position the center as a prestigious and multifaceted jewel in the crown of Al Nahda," comments creative director Rik Klingle. "The Sahara Center, with its unique approach to shopping, represents the new direction in retail and leisure malls of the future."

Inspired by the romance of the Sahara, the gradated midnight blue cover, symbolic of the cool of night, opens up to a rich orange inspired by the warmth of the desert sun. "We felt that it was appropriate to allude to both night and day, because the Sahara Center can offer retail and entertainment experiences virtually 24 hours a day," adds Klingle. The overall dramatic shape and curvilinear die-cuts play nicely off the center's unique architectural design. The insert

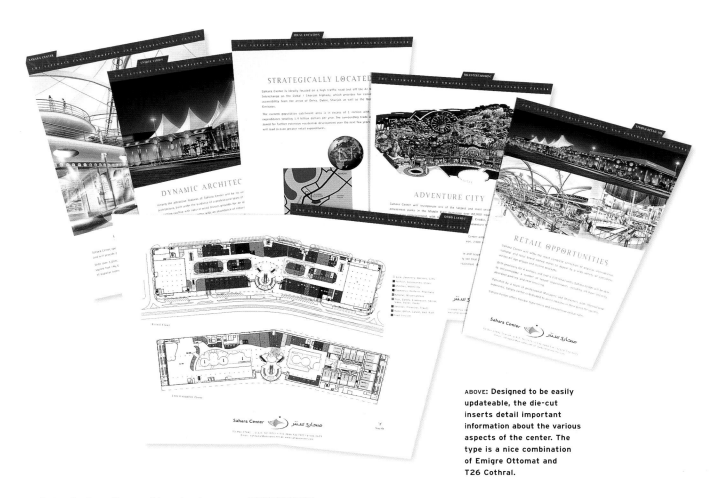

ABOVE: **Designed to be easily updateable, the die-cut inserts detail important information about the various aspects of the center. The type is a nice combination of Emigre Ottomat and T26 Cothral.**

pages, designed to be easily accessible and update-able, fit nicely inside an arched pocket, which also houses a CD-ROM and business card. "One of the reasons why the pages were individual and not bound in was because things had not been totally solidified at the time," explains Klingle. "We went with a pocket folder because the information was changing as we were designing it. It is easier and more cost-effective to revise and reprint an insert sheet, at a later date, than it is to redo the entire folder." The complete package was created to attract North American retailers to the new and exciting family shopping and entertainment center.

What Works

With its interesting angles, curvilinear die-cuts, and vibrant color scheme, the dramatic and energetic leasing brochure excited many North American retailers—attracting enough of them to completely fill the vast space. Because of the success of the brochure, the design team was also asked to create a website and provide the creative for the center's grand-opening campaign.

golden books

CLIENT:
Golden Books is a publisher of children's books and entertainment.

FIRM:
SJI Associates Inc.

ART DIRECTOR:
Jill Vinitsky

DESIGNER:
Alex Rekasi

ILLUSTRATIONS:
Nickelodeon

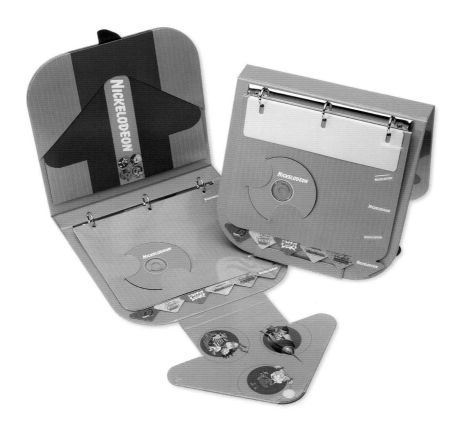

ABOVE: **The fun and inviting promotional kit folds back on itself to become a self-standing presentation binder.**

Presenting Entertainment

Golden Books needed an interesting and captivating way to announce to prospective buyers their acquisition of the rights to use Nickelodeon characters in their books. "They were really excited about it, and they wanted their sales staff to be really excited about it," recalls SJI Associates president, Suzy Jurist. "So, they hired us to come up with a sales kit that would give Nickelodeon its own presence. We really tried to talk to the brand of Nickelodeon while letting the inside pages speak to the individual properties of Nickelodeon."

Because the promotional piece had to be functional as well as visually appealing, the design team came up with a binder design that wraps backwards around itself and becomes a self-standing sales tool. The custom binder houses several divider pages, information about the books, and a CD-ROM. "It needed to be in a presentation format so that the salespeople didn't have to hold it," adds Jurist. "It

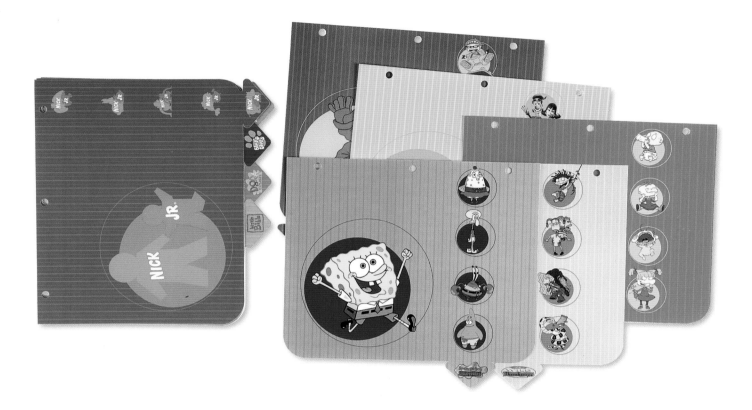

also made it easier to flip through the different sections." To come up with just the right structure, the project designer did extensive research—analyzing the design of other sales kits and their approach to children's graphics. "The main thing was to communicate a very friendly and open feeling, being careful not to be too strict or stuffy," says designer Alex Rekasi. "Both the fonts and the graphics needed to be light-hearted and communicate easily." Using arrows and stripes, the playful and friendly promotional kit draws the reader's attention into the content. "It's an intriguing piece that makes you want to open it," notes Jurist. "Once you are in it, it is very well organized." All of the logos, artwork, and color schemes were provided by Nickelodeon. The binder, wrapped with a 70-lb. litho sheet, was printed in four-color process with a gloss film lamination on top. The interior divider pages were also printed in process with a gloss film lamination on both sides. Only 100 were produced.

What Works

The childlike shape and vibrant color scheme helped to attract attention to the Nickelodeon brand. The eye-catching promotional package, functioning not only as a brochure but also as a presentation binder, made it easy for the sales staff to introduce and promote the new line of books to prospective customers. "It was received incredibly well not only by the sales staff but also by the people they were selling to," offers Jurist.

ABOVE: **The interior dividers help to organize the sales information on various books based on Nickelodeon's line of characters.**

One Step Beyond

Using Grids and Templates

Grids and templates provide a way to organize information and to create balance, unity, and visual rhythm throughout any communications piece. Whether the usage is subtle or quite apparent, an underlying grid can be useful in keeping the reader focused and the communications clear and consistent. "Throughout any piece there has to be something that reoccurs for the reader. Things can vary as long as they are in a common place where they can be found," shares creative director David Cannon. "I think it is important to have a grid system in place to anchor hierarchies of information."

Using a grid system does not mean sacrificing creativity or expression. Like music, variety must occur within the overall structure to maintain interest. By slightly varying the elements within a grid, the page or spread will come alive, creating movement and pacing from one page to the next. Establishing relationships amongst the elements within a layout is also important. By flushing elements to the same grid line helps to establish order. Repeating or echoing similar shapes or textures creates an overall rhythm in a piece. There is also a connection between the outside shape and the interior space of a layout. When choosing an exterior format, keep in mind how it will effect what is going on inside. Varying either one will greatly change the flow, continuity, and organization of a piece. It's best to experiment to find just the right combination to most effectively communicate the client's overall message.

With the convenience and speed of the computer, grids and templates are easier than ever to set up and use. "With the advent of computers, the design grid has been brought to the masses. Now, setting up a grid is as simple as a few clicks of a mouse," offers art director Shawn Murenbeeld. "Knowing what to do once the grid is established is another matter entirely." With this technological advance, a certain level of artistic sensitivity has been compromised, and many designers have lost touch with the craft of constructing a page. The best way to counteract such a loss is to examine the work of the old masters, the great designers of the past. They used and experimented with all kinds of grid systems to produce their work. "Some examples of the earliest and best uses of grids were created by designers in movements like Constructivism, Bauhaus, De Stijl, and later in the Swiss or International Style," adds Murenbeeld. "When you look at the works of Laszlo Moholy-Nagy, El Lissitzky, Jan Tschichold, and Josef Muller-Brockmann, to name a few, you'll see that as well as being practitioners of the grid, they were also pioneers of modern typography." Going back to the basics not only can enrich your understanding of what is possible but can also act as a springboard for your own creative exploration.

CLIENT:
DWL Incorporated's enterprise customer management applications consolidate fragmented customer relationship management (CRM), back-office, and e-business systems into unified industry solutions.

FIRM:
DWL Incorporated
(in-house creative services)

ART DIRECTOR/DESIGNER:
Shawn Murenbeeld

ILLUSTRATOR:
Shawn Murenbeeld

PHOTOGRAPHER:
Hill Peppard

COPYWRITER:
Leslie Ehm

RIGHT: On all of the main divider pages, the header type and the various icon designs are positioned in a consistent arrangement. While maintaining a similar overall shape, angle, and flow, the position of the other elements varies slightly within the horizontal format.

BELOW: Inspired by the look of an old 1940s trade catalog, the modular brochure consists of geometric shapes with rounded corners, which flow from page to page. Each product section has a unique four-column grid that varies. The spreads are slightly different, but maintain their cohesiveness. Having a larger grid system in place provides great flexibility and the opportunity to move and alter elements within the space.

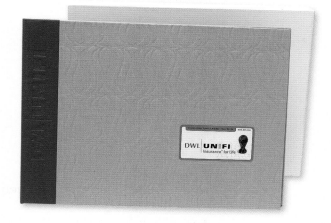

LEFT: The customized three-ring binder is adorned with cloth and book tape and is debossed with an overall pattern that is reminiscent of the corporate head icon. The cover, simple and subtle, is quite flexible. Several color-coded stickers have been designed to label the brochure to meet the needs of the sales staff. To ensure proper positioning, an area has been debossed for the appropriate sticker. Inside, the end papers have been letterpress-printed with a variation of the same icon pattern. The brochure is housed inside a white paper box.

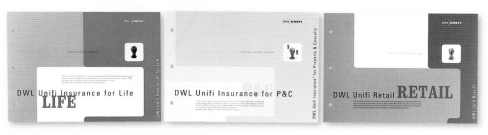

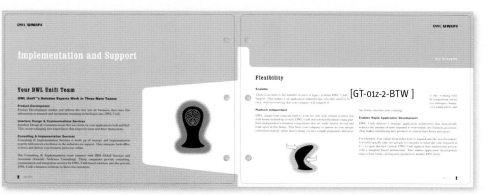

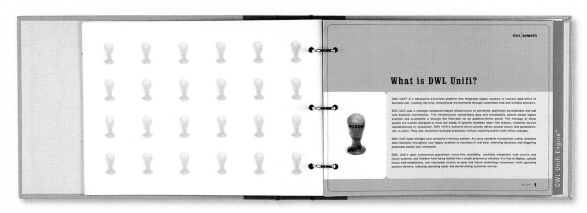

CLIENT:
The Turner Foundation is committed to the preservation of the water, air, and land.

FIRM:
EAI

CREATIVE DIRECTOR:
David Cannon

DESIGNER:
Courtney Garvin

ILLUSTRATOR:
Courtney Garvin

COPYWRITER:
Bruce Barcott

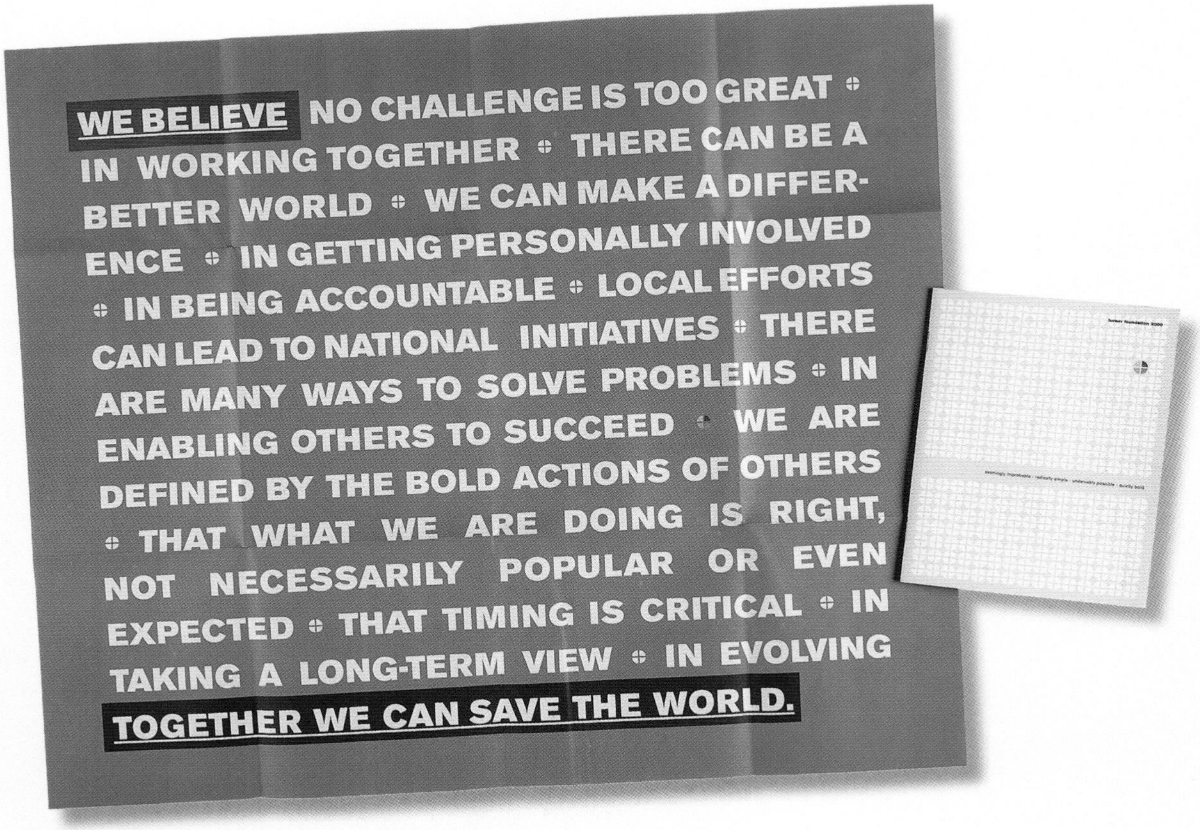

WE BELIEVE NO CHALLENGE IS TOO GREAT ⊕ IN WORKING TOGETHER ⊕ THERE CAN BE A BETTER WORLD ⊕ WE CAN MAKE A DIFFERENCE ⊕ IN GETTING PERSONALLY INVOLVED ⊕ IN BEING ACCOUNTABLE ⊕ LOCAL EFFORTS CAN LEAD TO NATIONAL INITIATIVES ⊕ THERE ARE MANY WAYS TO SOLVE PROBLEMS ⊕ IN ENABLING OTHERS TO SUCCEED ⊕ WE ARE DEFINED BY THE BOLD ACTIONS OF OTHERS ⊕ THAT WHAT WE ARE DOING IS RIGHT, NOT NECESSARILY POPULAR OR EVEN EXPECTED ⊕ THAT TIMING IS CRITICAL ⊕ IN TAKING A LONG-TERM VIEW ⊕ IN EVOLVING TOGETHER WE CAN SAVE THE WORLD.

ABOVE: On the cover of the annual report, a pie icon is used to convey the four key messages—*seemingly improbable, radically simple, undeniably possible,* and *quietly bold.* The wraparound jacket also serves as a poster, stating the beliefs of the foundation. On the back of the poster is a full listing of all of the grantees.

One Step Beyond

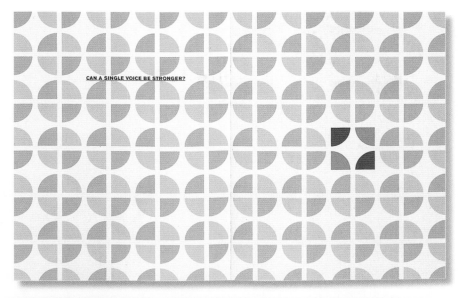

CAN A SINGLE VOICE BE STRONGER?

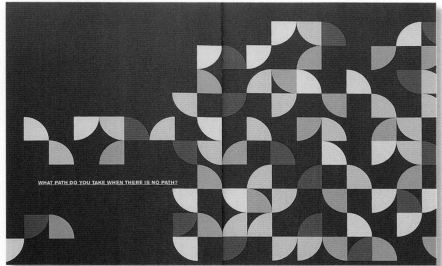

WHAT PATH DO YOU TAKE WHEN THERE IS NO PATH?

LEFT: Throughout the annual report, the pie icon is reconfigured to tell the story of the foundation and to relay each key message. The report is printed with earth-tone colors on tree-free paper made of hemp and sugar cane. The pie acts as a template, which is enlarged, reduced, and repeated to create harmony and continuity throughout.

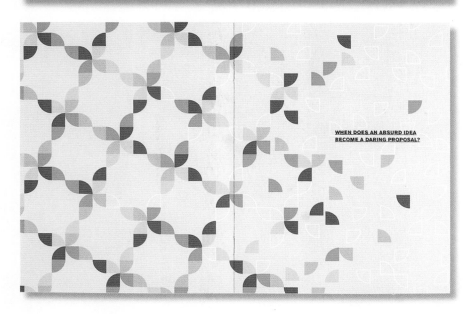

WHEN DOES AN ABSURD IDEA BECOME A DARING PROPOSAL?

Promotion Design

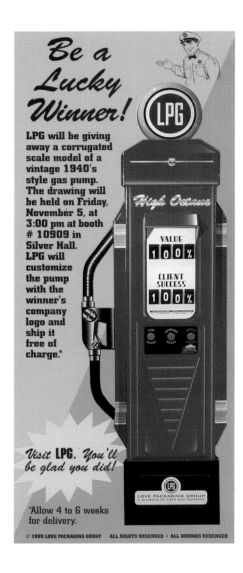

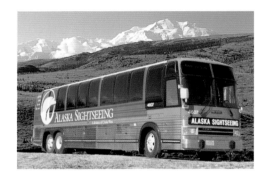

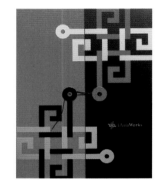

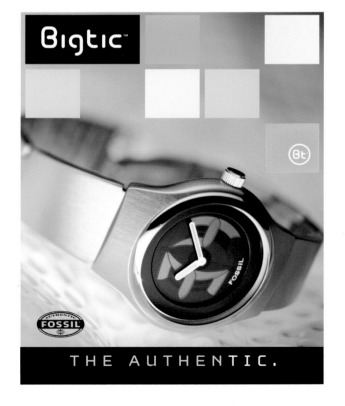

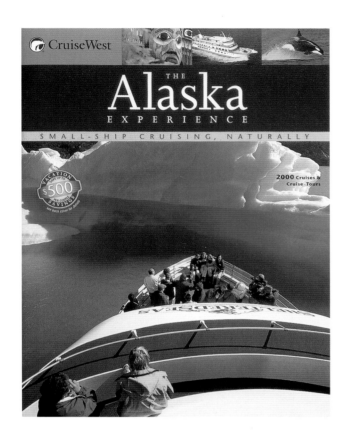

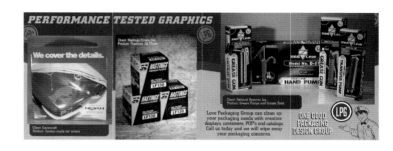

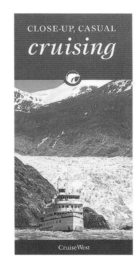 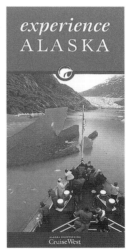

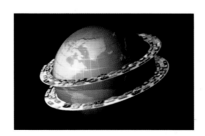 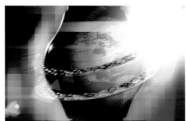 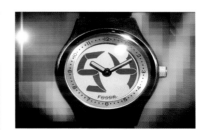

SELF-PROMOTION FUELS TRADE SHOW EVENT

The Client

"We needed something fun," remembers Chris West, art director on LPG Design's Performance Tested Graphics campaign that spotlighted the firm's creative capabilities to the automotive aftermarket industry, which is widely recognized as a lucrative market, albeit one that is also static and stale when it comes to graphic presentations. "We wanted something fun that would promote our point of view about design. It's a very dry market. You're selling hubcaps and transmissions. So, we were interested in ratcheting the excitement level up a little bit."

CLIENT:
LPG Design
(formerly Love Packaging Group)

DESIGN FIRM:
LPG Design

ART DIRECTOR:
Chris West

DESIGNERS:
Dustin Commer, Rick Gimlin, Lorna West

STRUCTURAL DESIGNER:
Mitch McCullough

PHOTOGRAPHER:
Jack Jacobs Photography

CAMPAIGN RUN:
October 1999 through March 2000

TARGET MARKET:
Automotive aftermarket business owners and/or marketing directors

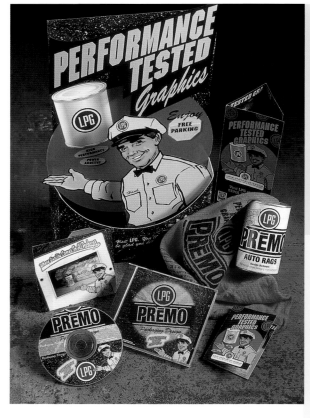

ABOVE: A CD-ROM that played continuously in the booth during the show was also given away to interested parties wanting to learn more about the firm.

The Brief

A division of the Love Box Company, Wichita, Kansas–based LPG Design, formerly known as the Love Packaging Group, wanted to build on Love Box's reputation in the automotive aftermarket, where the corrugated manufacturer had made a name for itself. The SEMA (Specialty Equipment Market Association) trade show provided just the right opportunity to make a statement. Because of its relationship with the Love Box Company, LPG Design had plenty of experience designing corrugated packaging for the automotive market; now, its goal was to tap into that expertise and pursue the industry in its own right.

"Corrugated was our entrée into this market; it's huge and it needs improvement," explains West. However, complicating their message was that few prospects recognized that LPG Design did more than package design, it was also a full-service studio (which is one reason the firm subsequently changed its name officially from Love Packaging Group to LPG Design in October 1999). So, while their trade show message had to emphasize packaging, they also wanted to promote their capabilities with other collateral materials and advertising.

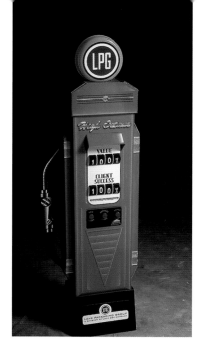

LEFT: Designers created and produced a full-size, 70 inch-tall x 22-inch-wide x 13-inch-deep (178 cm x 56 cm x 33 cm), 1940s-style gas pump constructed of corrugated substrate. Graphics came off a Displaymaker printer in four-color process before it was gloss laminated. Both the structural and graphic design of the piece included plug-in side panels, gas nozzle, laminated Mylar number wheels, plastic knobs, and mechanical workings, topped off with a 9 1/2-inch (24 cm)-diameter plastic globe displaying the LPG logo.

Setting the Scene

The design team opted to pursue a multipart trade show campaign based on a retro, postwar service station theme. Designer/illustrator Rick Gimlin came up with the idea of creating a vintage gas pump of corrugated, and with that as the centerpiece item, designers quickly generated dozens of spin-off ideas.

Foremost, the team decided they needed a character to communicate their message and Gimlin created Hank, "your friendly service station attendant." Because the postwar-era gas station attendant is recognized as an American pop culture icon for incomparable quality, it was the perfect symbol for the campaign. "Remember the days when we had full-service gas attendants? That's what he represents," explains Jolynn Berk, account executive. The concept of full-service easily communicated LPG Design's core message, "meaning that we're reliable; we can provide all of your marketing needs. We're full service," she adds.

As the focal point of the campaign, Hank reinforced the slogan, "Performance Tested Graphics," which linked the automotive aftermarket with LPG's design capabilities in the minds of prospective clients. Designer Dustin Commer added the tagline—*Premo,* which he adapted from a 1920s advertisement he had seen. The word fit the theme perfectly, while communicating premium to its audience.

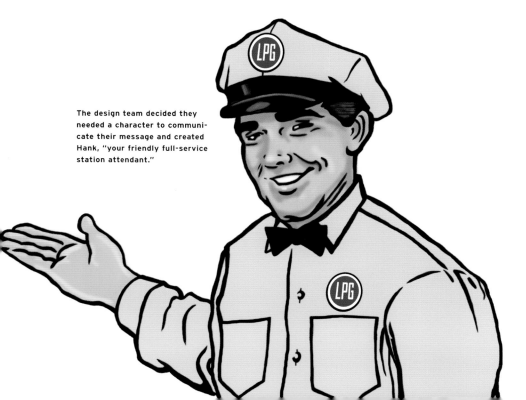

The design team decided they needed a character to communicate their message and created Hank, "your friendly full-service station attendant."

Working with a Minimal Budget

While the campaign was a resounding success, it came with its share of challenges. LPG created this entire campaign in-house with the exception of screening the shop rag, purchasing the tin oil cans, and offset printing three brochures in four-color process—all of which were outsourced. Everything else was manufactured in-house, which allowed designers to produce a campaign with maximum impact with a minimal budget of $5000. Naturally, this covered only outside costs. All design work was completed during off-peak or downtime hours, while the box manufacturing capabilities were also absorbed in-house.

Unusual Materials

The gas pump was among the trickiest pieces to produce, primarily due to its size. Commer's computer sketches went to the firm's structural division group on the Love Box side of the business, where it went through a few variations before it was finalized. From there, the design was sent via computer to a huge vacuum cutting table where the corrugated material was held in place while an automatic knife cut out the pieces like a jigsaw puzzle. "We have all of our pieces precisely die-cut on the cutting table, which is a competitive advantage we offer clients. If they have a prototype and they want to see something that is an idea or a concept, we can make their samples," says West.

In the meantime, the artwork was downloaded to a large format printer and was laminated to the corrugated. "When you deal with corrugated that is 70 inches (178 cm) tall and it's a three-dimensional subject, it is huge when you have it flat. So it was rather difficult to get it figured out, put together, and then get a print on it, laminate it, and get it assembled. But we were stretching the capabilities and that is what we have to show. We stretch the perimeters so that the client can see what we can do for them," adds West.

The Creative Process

The biggest design challenge, according to West, was coming up with the whole marketing scheme in the first place and ensuring that all the elements that worked within the framework of LPG's communication goals while being fun and practical. "I think we did a good job integrating all the pieces," suggests Berk. "Everything is very well thought out as to what the purpose was for each piece."

So how did LPG integrate all these elements into one cohesive campaign? "We have a free flow of ideas and we work from a creative center. We start with our creativity and then we take the elements that need to be addressed within the scope of the project…and keep building on the theme. We had a specific agenda of elements that needed to be included in the whole scope of the project," says West. "We limited our designs to something we could afford and decided to be as creative as we could within that context."

"Everything we designed is producible," adds Commer. "Nothing is too far-fetched."

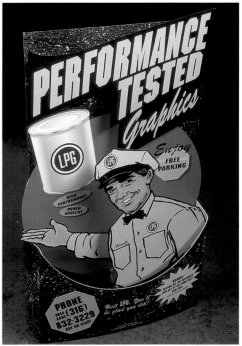

The Build-Up

The campaign began with a teaser black-and-white, 1/8-page advertisement that ran in *SEMA News.* The preshow version with the headline, Performance Tested Graphics, listed LPG Design's booth number and appeared in the October and November 1999 issues; a second version, minus the booth information, appeared in the December 1999 as well as the January, February, and March 2000 issues.

Overlapping the advertising run, was a preshow mailer/teaser that repeated the Performance Tested Graphics headline on a trifold brochure/invitation inviting show attendees to LPG Design's booth to take part in a customized giveaway offer: Visit the booth and register to win a miniature corrugated scale model of a vintage 1940s-style gas pump.

At the Show

The theme was carried out further at LPG's booth. The show displays included numerous items primarily constructed of folding carton, a printable, white heavy-weight card stock that is typically used for doughnut boxes, and corrugated, which is recognized by a sheet of fluting that is sandwiched between paper liners.

In the booth, Hank greeted visitors from a prominent 17-1/2" x 9-1/2" (44 cm x 24 cm) motion-activated display with vintage-inspired graphics using 22-point Carolina Board and a 3/16–inch (4.5 mm) foam core backing. A light-sensing device allowed Hank to wave Hi at passersby. The vintage signage again repeated the Performance Tested Graphics headline.

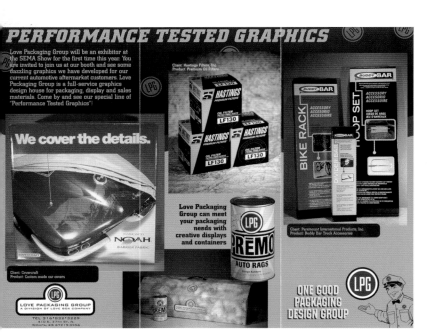

ABOVE: LPG Design created a preshow mailer that directed SEMA attendees directly to the firm's booth.

RIGHT: Hank, "your friendly full-service attendant," added personality to the campaign. Here, thanks to a light-sensor-activated motor, Hank's uniformed image waves at booth visitors from a 17-1/2" x 9-1/2" (44 cm x 24 cm) motion activated display with vintage-inspired graphics using 22-point Carolina Board and a 3/16-inch (4.5 mm) multiple plug-ins (graphic layers) gave the piece dimensionality for a total depth of 3 inches (8 cm).

RIGHT: Tucked inside the giveaway oil cans was a miniature pamphlet showcasing LPG's work along with an authentic shop cloth that was screened with the LPG logo.

FAR RIGHT: The oil cans were showcased in a corrugated replica of a steel, point-of-sale display found in service stations.

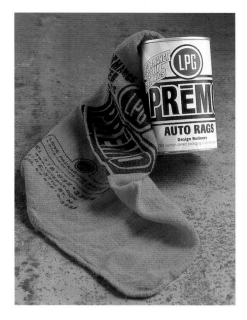

Getting the Message Out

Nearby, LPG Premo brand oil cans were showcased in a replica of the steel, point-of-sale displays found in service stations. The display appears to be made of aluminum tread plate, but is actually made of corrugated that designers laminated with a silver foil. "We can't make a tread plate display, so we made it out of corrugated. That is what is so unique about it," says West. "We make corrugated look like aluminum or enameled metal or brushed aluminum. We try and push the envelope as to what corrugated can look like."

RIGHT: The oil cans were distributed throughout the show in a brushed-aluminum toolbox also made of corrugated.

BELOW RIGHT: LPG's gas can carryall was given to booth visitors to tote around the materials they collected during the show and was later used as a sales kit.

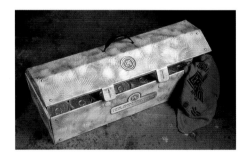

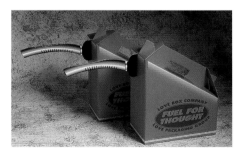

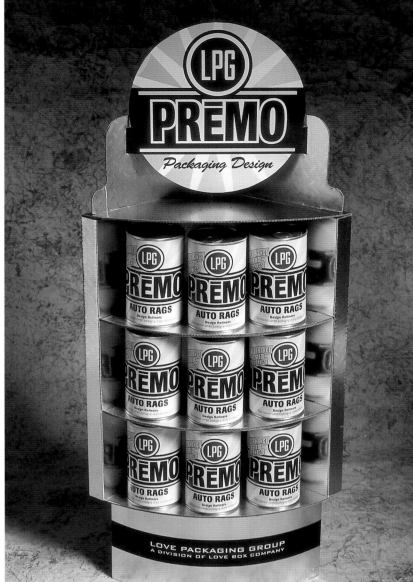

The cans were no ordinary oil cans, either. Open their pop-top and inside is a miniature pamphlet showcasing LPG's work in the aftermarket industry along with an authentic shop cloth that was screened with the LPG logo. The giveaway cans were distributed throughout the show—as an incentive to visit the booth—in a brushed-aluminum toolbox also made of corrugated and laminated with a brushed silver foil. The toolbox held about twenty-four cans.

Another show-stopping piece was LPG's gas can. Designers could have slapped their logo onto a plastic shopping bag, which is commonly seen at such trade shows for exhibitors to tote around all the literature and freebies they pick-up, but they weren't about to do anything so ordinary. They wanted to carry the gas station theme through everything—including the giveaway carryall, which they created to resemble a gas can, complete with a nozzle, using folding carton and corrugated. "We wanted something that could be used as a sales kit because that's another one of our direct-marketing tools that we have a lot of expertise in," says West. "We wanted to express our creativity in this arena so we took the whole idea one step further and created a device for collecting and carrying materials around. And, this one has a spout on it. How much more fun can you have with a sales kit?"

Of course, the centerpiece of the booth was the full-size, 1940s-style gas pump that inspired the entire campaign. Constructed predominantly of corrugated material, it stood 70 inches (178 cm) high and was topped with a round, plastic globe emblazoned with the LPG logo. The artwork for the pump was printed in four-color process on a large-format printer and laminated to the corrugated surface. Both the structural and graphic design of the piece included plug-in side panels, gas nozzle, and mechanical workings, topped off with the lighted globe that was perfectly accented by LPG's logo, which is also circular and sports a vintage styling.

An exact duplicate of the full-size gas pump was produced as a 40 percent scale model, measuring 30 inches (76 cm) high, 9 inches (23 cm) wide, and 5 1/4 inches (13.5 cm) deep. It was made of lighter gauge corrugated, but in all other details was an exact replica of the large version. After the show, LPG Design pulled a name from more than four hundred entrants who registered in the booth for the prize and designers then created and customized a tabletop version of the pump with the winner's name and logo, and then shipped the prize free of charge to their business.

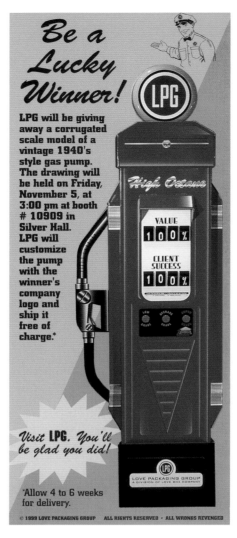

Taking LPG Home

In total, the show displays and giveaways proved to be ample demonstrations of LPG's capabilities. "These are all golden opportunities for a lot of direct-mail devices. It's a fun approach to showing what we can do with corrugated rather than just a box," says West. While all the fun twists on corrugated intrigued visitors, LPG Design did not want to ignore all of its noncarton and corrugated work done outside of the automotive industry and to reinforce its diverse capabilities, they produced a CD-ROM that played continually in the booth and was given away to interested parties wanted to learn more about the firm's creative efforts.

The Finishing Touch

Capping off the campaign was a follow-up thank you that was hand delivered. From start to finish, the design portion of the campaign took approximately fifteen weeks.

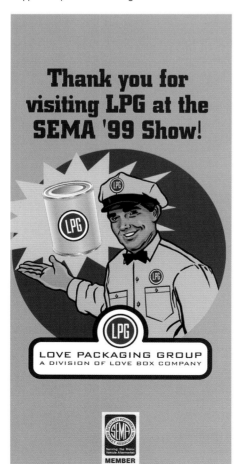

ABOVE: LPG Design created a preshow mailer that directed SEMA attendees directly to the firm's booth.

LEFT: A follow-up thank you brochure was hand delivered after the show.

The results

When the trade show ended, use of these promotional items continued as the campaign continued to gain new admirers. The six ad insertions resulted in forty-two qualified leads. More than 400 leads were generated from the gas pump giveaway registration. Qualified leads from booth attendance totaled 125. Moreover, seven new client contacts established at the event lead to further client meetings and work currently in progress.

 "We even had people who wanted to buy the gas pump and put their own logo on it," says West, citing the fact that they received similar requests from the aftermarket for the toolbox. "In addition, we've been recognized nationally in graphic award publications, so from a designer's point-of-view, that's a measure of success. But from a strictly a bottom line point of view, it has generated a lot of interest in the corrugated end of our business with Love Box Company. It has also increased the awareness of what LPG Design and Love Box can do for a client in that particular market. So in our view, that is a level of success and if you look at our outlay costs, it was worth the investment"

What Worked

So why does this promotion work so well? "I think all the pieces have to integrate well together and work well together in order to focus the theme throughout the entire campaign. And, of course, a very important element to the success of the campaign is follow-up. You can have a very successfully designed and implemented campaign, but if follow-up doesn't happen, the campaign won't be as successful as it could be," says Berk.

"It has an element of fun," cites West, as another reason for the promotion's success. What's his secret to a successful campaign? Simple—a clever use of graphics, concept, and design.

Tips from the experts Integrated Pieces . . . Focused Theme . . . Follow-Up

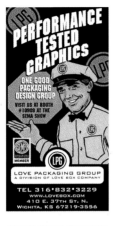 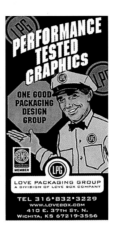 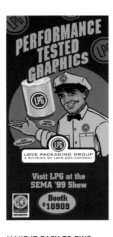 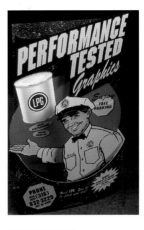

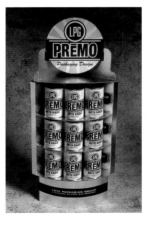

GET THE WORD OUT EARLY

Prior to the SEMA trade show, LPG Design ran a preshow black-and-white 1/8-page advertisement in the *SEMA News;* later, a second version without the booth information appeared in the publication.

MAKE IT EASY TO FIND YOU, AND GIVE THEM INCENTIVE TO DO IT

LPG Design created a preshow mailer that directed SEMA attendees to the firm's booth. Inside the mailer they not only took the opportunity to showcase their work, but they gave attendees a reason to visit them by offering a customized giveaway.

CATCH THEIR EYE

Hank, "your friendly full-service attendant," added personality to the campaign. Here, Hank's uniformed image waves at booth visitors from a 24" x 20" (61 cm x 51 cm) motion-activated display created of folding carton and corrugated, dressed-up with vintage-inspired graphics.

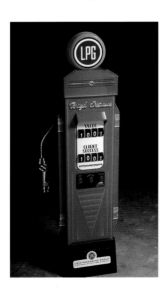

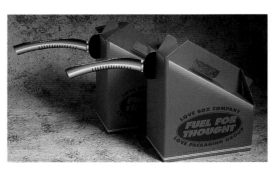

PULL OUT ALL THE STOPS AND SHOW THEM WHAT YOU'RE CAPABLE OF

Designers created and produced a full-size, 1940s-style gas pump constructed of corrugated and laminated with graphics printed in four-color process. The pump included plug-in side panels, gas nozzle, and mechanical workings, topped off with a lighted globe displaying the LPG logo.

GIVE THEM SOMETHING THEY WON'T WANT TO THROW AWAY

Designers wanted to carry the gas station theme through everything—including the giveaway carryall—which they created to resemble a gas can, complete with a nozzle, sporting the catch phrase Fuel for Thought.

TAKE EVERY OPPORTUNITY TO DISPLAY YOUR CAPABILITIES

A replica of a steel, point-of-purchase display holds the Premo oil cans at the booth. While the display appears to be made of aluminum tread plate, it is actually constructed of corrugated that has been laminated with a silver foil.

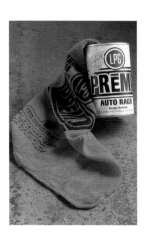

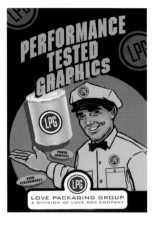

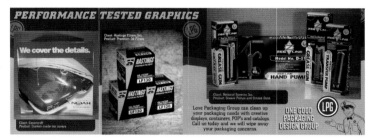

MAKE THEM INTERACT TO KEEP THEIR ATTENTION

Among the popular giveaways was a pop-top oil can that when opened revealed a minibrochure and an authentic shop cloth screened with the LPG logo.

KEEP IT FUN, BUT DON'T FORGET YOUR MARKET

Tucked into the oil can was a minibrochure showcasing LPG's work in the automotive aftermarket.

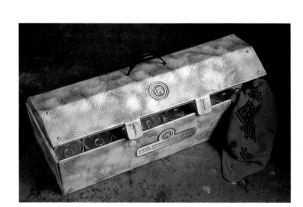

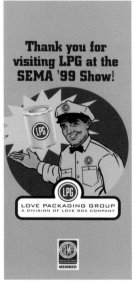

MOBILIZE YOUR MESSAGE AND PULL THEM IN

To distribute the cans as giveaways throughout the show—as an incentive to visit the booth—designers created a brushed-aluminum toolbox of corrugated that were laminated with silver foil and held about twenty-four cans.

SHOW THEM YOU WANT THEIR BUSINESS

After the show, LPG followed up with prospective clients by hand delivering a thank you brochure.

VOLKSWAGEN'S BEETLE GETS EVEN SMALLER AND WINS BIG AUDIENCES

(a bug's life)

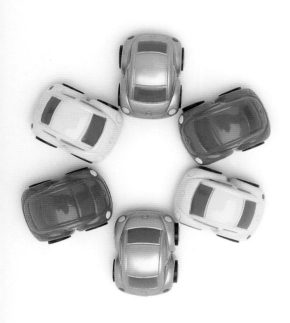

Volkswagen's Pull and Go New Beetle has seized the market's attention and isn't about to let go anytime soon. What began as a simple promotion for the launch of the redesigned Beetle has grown into a marketing gimmick of Rolls Royce proportions.

The idea for a pull-and-go toy was born in Germany amid the Beetle's car designers, who tossed around ideas for a fun promotion that would add a dash of pizzazz to their highly anticipated launch. Their idea for a toy car made its way to Hartmut Warkuss, director of Design Center of Excellence, Volkswagen Design Studio in Braunschweig, Germany, who so loved the idea that he approved it for production on the spot. As a result, moving the car from concept to reality was unusually fast—not at all the norm for typical promotions, but this car was far from typical. "The head of design wanted it done so it was a very speedy decision," says Karla Waterhouse, public relations specialist in Volkswagen's Detroit office.

Volkswagen's designers, accustomed to creating performance automobiles, fashioned the look of the toy car in-house and sent it to various toy manufacturers around the world for production. When the day came to launch the new Volkswagen Bug, the toy cars were featured giveaways in dealerships and were given free to members of the press, drawing nearly as much attention as their full-size counterparts.

Unique to this bug's story is that its life didn't end after the launch. Volkswagen continues to use the toy as giveaways for other promotions, distributing them primarily as media gifts—they recently included the toys in Easter baskets prepared as promotional gifts for the press.

Fortunately, you don't have to possess a press badge to get your hands on this appealing promotion. The palm-sized car, available in six colors—yellow, black, blue, red, silver, and metallic green—are sold for $5 in dealerships as well as through *Driver Gear* magazine, a publication for Volkswagen owners. The car manufacturer has also sold the toys at its booth during Detroit's annual auto show, donating all the proceeds to Detroit's Children's Hospital.

"Executives love them," says Waterhouse of the toy's appeal. "They keep them on their desk and drive them around during lulls in meetings."

Did this promotion work? "Yes," says Waterhouse without hesitation. "It was a success and still is a success. The cars are still being produced. It's a low-cost item that appeals to a lot of people," she adds, noting that the cars are intended as an adult toy and are not suitable for children under the age of three.

CLIENT:
Volkswagen

DESIGN FIRM:
Volkswagen Design Studio

DESIGNER:
Hartmut Warkuss

CAMPAIGN RUN:
Ongoing

TARGET MARKET:
Media, Volkswagen enthusiasts

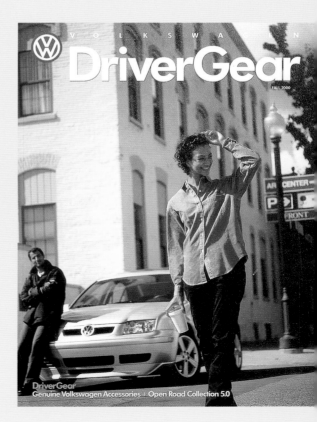

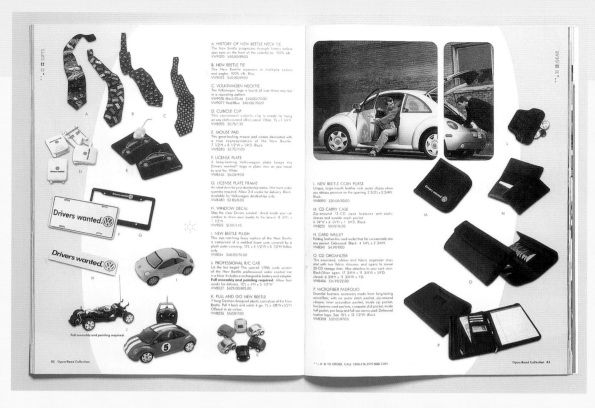

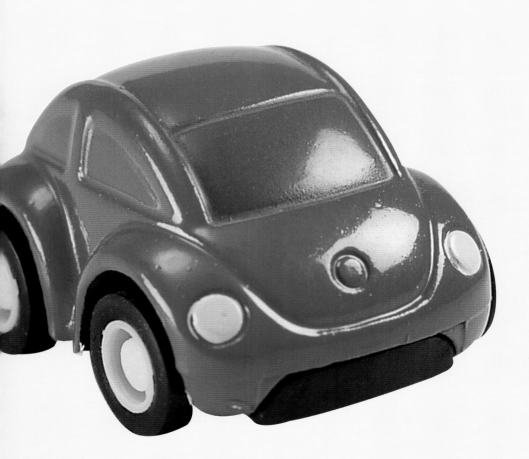

INTERNATIONAL POP CAMPAIGN LAUNCHES FOSSIL'S BIGTIC™

The Client

Some Fossil executives doubted it would sell, but nevertheless, they put money behind a new watch called the Bigtic™. Why Bigtic? Because it was among the first watches with large, digital ticking seconds and analog hands. "We felt the product had a futuristic feel and was very different from any other watch made by our competitors or us," says Stephen Zhang, art director on the project. Skepticism reigned as to whether or not this new product would succeed, but the one thing everyone agreed upon was that they needed a winning point-of-purchase campaign to increase the odds of its success. The responsibility for creating and executing such a persuasive promotion fell upon the shoulders of Zhang and designer John Vineyard, both of whom agreed to make the watch's unique face the focus of the campaign.

CLIENT:
Fossil

DESIGN FIRM:
Fossil in-house design studio

CREATIVE DIRECTOR:
Tim Hale

ART DIRECTOR:
Stephen Zhang

DESIGNER:
John Vineyard

FOSSIL INTERNATIONAL DESIGNERS:
Gabriella Fortunato (Italy), Stefan Muller (Germany)

ANIMATION:
Reel FX

PHOTOGRAPHERS:
David McCormick, Russ Aman

CAMPAIGN RUN:
January 2000 through December 31, 2000

TARGET MARKET:
Consumers 16 to 24 years old

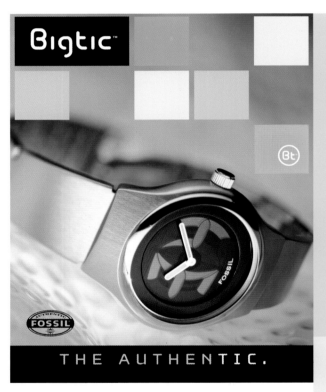

THE AUTHENTIC.

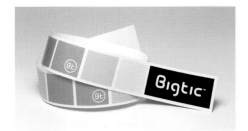

The Brief

Three factors stood out as Zhang and designer John Vineyard assessed the task assigned to Fossil's in-house design team. First, they needed to skew the watch to a younger audience than is typical for most Fossil products and target teenagers and twentysome-things. Second was the uniqueness of the watch. "This watch was an experiment. You see the tick, but don't hear the tick," says Zhang, citing the watch's primary feature that bewildered so many. Fossil developed the all-new technology where seconds are visually count-ed off with big ticks. Aside from offering innovation that differs from other digital technology, the watch didn't provide any new functions; yet it was undisput-edly unique and kids would want it, which led to the third and final consideration. Could they use to their advantage the futuristic, techno look of the watch to play to the current trends in technology so irresistible to today's younger consumers?

Vineyard conducted his own research to find a color or colors that graphically expressed the trend toward youth-oriented, high-tech, futuristic gadgetry. At the time, Fossil had four or five product lines already in existence, each targeting a different market segment and differentiated with its own color scheme, so some colors were already taken. Vineyard's search for a shade that visually shouted "techno" yielded a recom-mendation, but surprisingly, it was not the steely gray, silver, or metallic blue hues that are commonly associ-ated with state-of-the-art technology. Vineyard's color of choice—green—a shade readily associated with conservation, ecology, health, and wholesomeness but rarely, if ever, seen as being cutting edge.

ABOVE: A point-of-purchase poster kicked off the campaign and other elements were added from there.

LEFT, TOP AND BOTTOM: In-case cards and small and caseline static stickers.

RIGHT: **A comprehensive kit was provided to department stores including a poster display.**

BELOW, TOP AND MIDDLE: **Bigtic top-of-counter and watch cuff standees.**

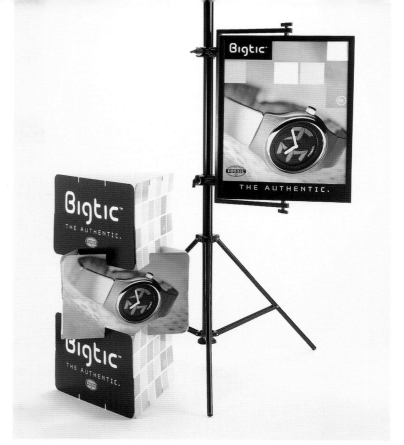

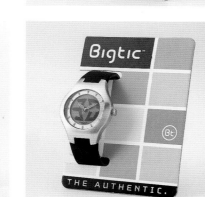

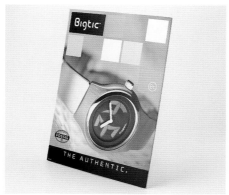

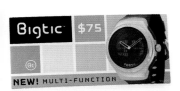

ABOVE, TOP AND BOTTOM: **In-case cards and small and caseline static stickers.**

RIGHT: **A ledgetop display.**

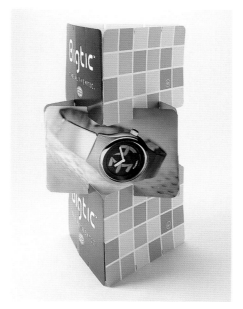

Pulling Everything Together

Initially, Fossil ran few magazine advertisements for the Bigtic before a logo and color scheme were developed. Later, a marketing kit with more in-depth photography and graphics were added to the mix. A point-of-purchase poster kicked off the campaign and other elements were added from there.

Before long, there was a comprehensive kit that was provided to department stores including a poster display along with Bigtic top-of-counter and watch cuff standees, a ledgetop display, in-case cards, and small and caseline static stickers.

These singular items were combined with the product displays to create a cohesive presentation at point of sale.

"[The promotion has] a different look than anything else we'd really done and the look of the posters and the look of the campaign was really different from the look of our stores," says Vineyard, pointing to the retro packaging and merchandising that Fossil has used in the past with considerable success. In fact, the company has built so much equity in the retro look that the move to a futuristic image spurred more skepticism and called for considerable convincing on the part of the design team. "The watch had a digital techno look that was different from anything else that we had done and so called for a campaign that was different from what Fossil has done previously."

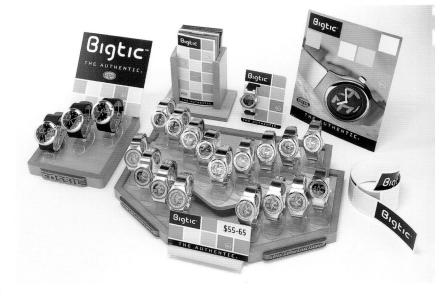

The Sales Pitch

Despite the eye-catching appeal of the sales package, the primary challenge remained gaining acceptance for the product. Selling it internally was hard enough, but the sell-in proved equally difficult as department store buyers expressed their doubts. "'What is it for? What does it do?' Nothing," says Zhang, remembering how they had to field this question from insiders as well as department-store buyers over and over again. "So it wasn't easy to get it launched." To soften the sell, designers created a twisty puzzle (reminiscent of a Rubik's Cube) that echoed the repeating square pattern of the promotional collateral as a gift for department-store buyers.

"The challenge for John was to present this product, which is rather ambiguous...and hard to explain to people," adds Zhang. "The challenge was to visually make it connect to those people, distinguish the watch visually, attract attention, and get consumers to see the watch. Rather than promoting the product from a function standpoint, John created a campaign from a lifestyle, aesthetic, and fashion point-of-view. That's why...the translucent green was really hot. You could see it everywhere in New York, particularly, the small, trendy shops in Soho."

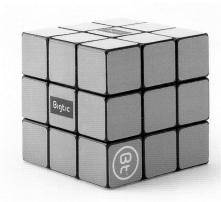

ABOVE: Individual items were combined with the product displays to create a cohesive presentation at point of sale.

LEFT: To soften the sell, designers created a twisty puzzle (reminiscent of a Rubik's Cube) that echoed the repeating square pattern of the promotional collateral as a gift for department-store buyers.

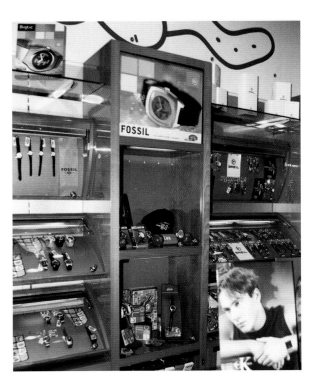

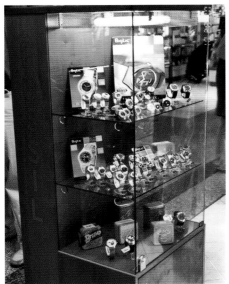

ABOVE AND LEFT: In-store displays from Italy's Coin department store.

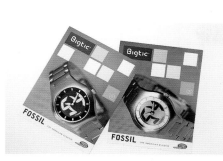

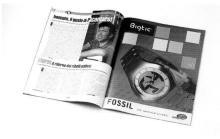

The Creative Process

Vineyard decided to focus on unique look of watch through mood photography to lure consumers into the promotion. "We thought the watch was so interesting and looked so interesting, we really wanted to focus on its uniqueness in the photography and everything we did had to build around that. The watch in the case almost sells itself. So, we didn't want to do anything with the graphics that would take away from that," says Vineyard.

"The watch is so strange and so new, we wanted the watch to speak through the photography," explains Zhang, adding that in addition to the photography, the basic elements of the design include the logo, color palette, and the graphic squares that "abstractly represent the digital, techno style of the watch."

The Photo Shoot

While the futuristic/techno look was considered the campaign's key ingredient, achieving this look through photography presented its own set of challenges. Vineyard spent a great deal of time experimenting with different lights, techniques, and backgrounds before finalizing the lighting setup. Ultimately, he decided to light the background from underneath the watch as well as from other angles, place green gels on specific lights, and remove the crystal from the watch to avoid reflection from the unusual lighting set up. To add a subtle texture and extra depth to the photo, he draped a shower curtain with a bubble wrap–like texture over a sheet of transparent green Plexiglas.

"We had to really work to angle the watch and the camera in a position where we could achieve the selective focus we wanted so that the bubbles in the shower curtain wouldn't reflect off of the watch's black face," remembers Vineyard.

"The strength of the photography in addition to the simple, yet effective, square pattern created the atmosphere we were trying to achieve in this campaign," says Zhang. "The fact that we were able to use the squares on pieces that were too small to use photography effectively helped maintain consistency and interest throughout the campaign."

A Global Effort

Zhang and Vineyard, located in Fossil's Texas headquarters, set the standards for the international advertising and promotion and annually publish a *Standards Guide*. In this case, they provided files and transparencies to other Fossil design departments around the world to replicate as needed. Simplifying matters is that collateral material is always designed to a common size so that posters, countertop displays, and so forth, have the same dimensions regardless of the product line. In some cases, foreign design offices are allowed to use their own discretion in executing the materials so they can be adapted to individual environments, while maintaining consistency with the established design. So uniform is the collateral from country to country that it is hard to distinguish where various materials come from as evidenced by the top-of-counter standee from Japan, flyer and magazine advertisement from Italy, in-store displays from Italy's Coin department store, and Bigtic international brochure that was used in several countries outside of the U.S.

Fossil is acutely aware that to succeed, a global presentation must transcend language barriers, especially when selling across borders and when so much of the company's collateral material is shared. A case in point is a television commercial created by Fossil's U.S. design team for placement on German and Italian television and as advertising in cinemas there prior to showing the feature film. As in all the collateral, the primary message of the television spot was Bigtic's futuristic/techno appeal.

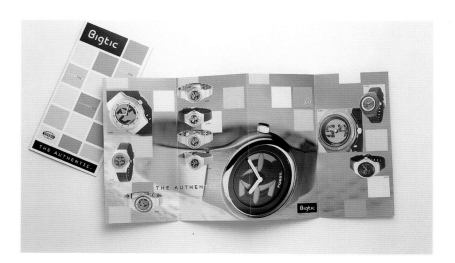

Screen grabs from a television commercial created by Fossil's U.S. design team for placement on German and Italian television and as advertising in cinemas there prior to showing the feature film.

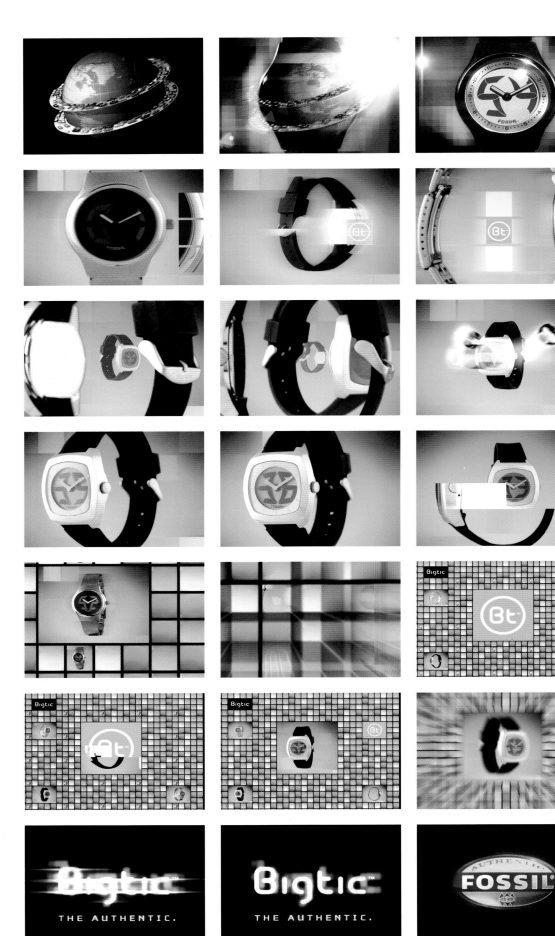

The results

The Bigtic watch is one of Fossil's biggest success stories. "Once launched, it sold easily. It sold out quickly," remembers Zhang. Consequently, the Bigtic has become one of the company's most popular watches worldwide and has been imitated by several of Fossil's competitors. Fossil isn't disclosing any figures, but simply says "sales were phenomenal." While the watch appealed to a young generation, it is clear that the point-of-sale graphics attracted buyers from all age groups.

What Worked

"In malls or department stores, there is so much going on…so much clutter, we had to really do something to stand out. We felt like the watch would sell itself, but we needed something that would grab attention so that you would see the watch and it would stand out from all the other products and all the other brands," adds Vineyard. "I feel like this campaign did that."

"In essence, John's design is a campaign, but it is also an identity for this line. The watch sells itself because people see other people wearing it and if they like it, they will go look for it," Zhang adds. "But I think because the design is distinctive as well as the layout, color, and the execution is very consistent, you can go in and easily spot Bigtic and go to the right place. As an identity, I think it is very successful especially in the international sales environment, where watches are sold primarily in smaller jewelry stores—people usually spot a product on the street through windows."

Tips from the experts Innovate...shun the skeptics...integrate

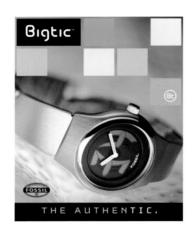

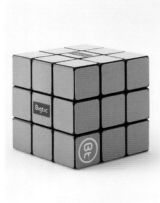

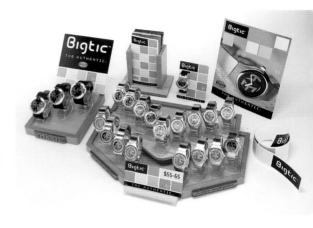

BE CREATIVE WITH PHOTO PROPS

To achieve they look they were after, designers lit the background from underneath the watch as well as from other angles, placed green gels on specific lights, and added a subtle texture and extra depth to the photo by draping a shower curtain with a bubble wrap-like texture over a sheet of transparent, green Plexiglas.

SOFTEN THE SELL

Designers gave department store buyers a twisty puzzle as a promotional gift.

BEWARE THE SKEPTICS

Even Fossil executives doubted the ability of the Bigtic to sell, but it ended up being one of Fossil's biggest success stories.

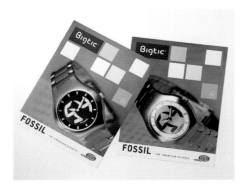

GIVE FOREIGN DESIGN OFFICES LEEWAY

Fossil allowed its foreign design offices to use their own discretion in executing the materials in order to adapt promotions to their market while maintaining consistency with the established design.

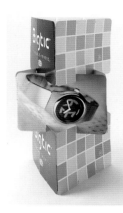

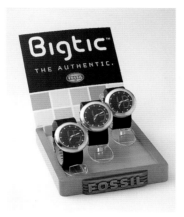

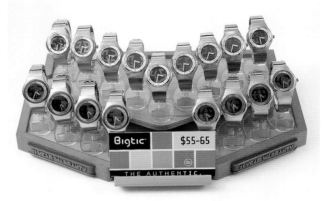

CONSIDER A NONTRADITIONAL COLOR PALETTE

Fossil shunned traditional color palettes of steel gray, silver or metallic blue hues that are commonly associated with state-of-the-art technology and opted instead for green, a shade readily associated with conservation, ecology, health, and wholesomeness but rarely, if ever, seen as being cutting edge.

BUILD ON THE PRESENTATION

Fossil took singular items and combined them with product displays to create a cohesive presentation at point of sale.

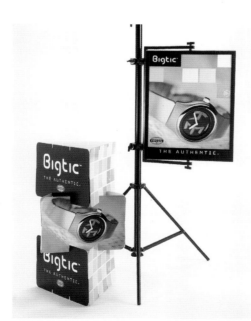

START SMALL AND GROW FROM THERE

The Bigtic campaign started with a poster and grew from there, until Fossil had a comprehensive kit to provide to department stores.

INTERNET SERVER LAUNCH (ancient asian graphics)
COMBINES HIGH-TECH WITH ANCIENT ASIAN SYMBOLOGY

The Client

iAsiaWorks, a leading Internet data center and hosting services provider across the Asia-Pacific region, came to Gee + Chung Design in search of an identity and a name. They also needed help positioning the start-up company as setting the standard for Internet data centers and hosting services providers across the Asia-Pacific region, while supporting their tagline of Global Technology. Asian Focus.

The Gee + Chung design team had a special interest in this prospect because AUNET, as iAsiaWorks was then known, had an Asian background. Gee + Chung Design was well skilled in high-tech clients from its work with IBM, Oracle, and Apple but rarely had the opportunity to do much work that utilized the firm's own Asian roots. Here was the opportunity they were looking for, but there was one hitch. The work had to be done quickly—which posed little problem for this firm, which thrives on tight deadlines.

CLIENT:
iAsiaWorks, Inc.

DESIGN FIRM:
Gee + Chung Design

ART DIRECTOR:
Earl Gee

DESIGNERS:
Earl Gee, Kay Wu, Qui Tong

PHOTOGRAPHERS:
Kevin Ng, Kirk Amyz

PRINT AND WEB PRODUCTION:
Adrian Fernandez

COPYWRITER:
iAsiaWorks, Inc.

CAMPAIGN RUN:
January 1, 2000 through Present

TARGET MARKET:
Multinational corporations, Asian businesses, and leading Internet companies

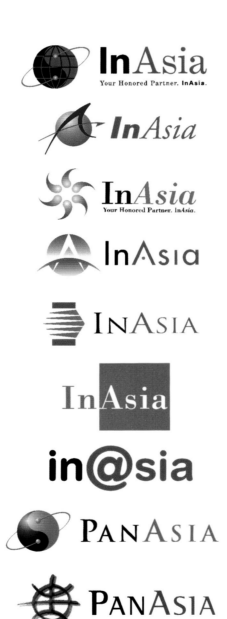

The Brief

The foremost objective was to develop a name and identity. Designers didn't waste any time getting to work on name suggestions and placing them into logo form. InAsia was a top choice as was PanAsia. The client researched the availability of URLs for each name in all the countries they wanted to target while Gee + Chung Design visually interpreted the name as possible logos. Treatments ran the gamut from those that used various interpretations of the Chinese yin yang symbol to graphics of a Pacific wave, rising sun, Chinese lantern, the Chinese symbol for man, and even a collage of interlocking letterforms. Unfortunately, AUNET couldn't secure a URL in all their target countries for either name, but it was only then that they discovered the possibilities of the name iAsiaWorks, which worked as well if not better than the previous names.

As designers settled in to develop the logo for the chosen name, they reviewed the original motifs and decided to borrow an earlier design with interlocking letterforms—stylized capital P's-initially prepared for PanAsia—worked equally well with iAsiaWorks. It was a classic motif and aptly communicated connectivity and high-tech circuitry.

LEFT AND BOTTOM OF OPPOSITE PAGE: Gee + Chung visually interpreted the possible names InAsia and PanAsia as possible logos. Treatments ran the gamut from those that used various interpretations of the Chinese yin yang symbol to graphics of a Pacific wave, rising sun, Chinese lantern, the Chinese symbol for man, and even a collage of interlocking letterforms. When AUNET couldn't secure a URL in all their target countries for either name, they opted for the name iAsiaWorks.

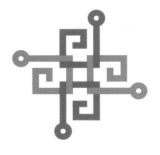

iAsiaWorks

Global Technology. Asian Focus.

ABOVE: The iAsiaWorks logo and variations of it were carried through each element of the campaign to create a visual that when combined with an integrated circuitry pattern functions as a visual metaphor for linking Asian cultures through technology.

RIGHT: The iAsiaWorks stationery system utilizes an outline pattern of the logo simulating gold embroidery on red silk and a dot pattern derived from the logo and representing an ancient Chinese door.

Creating a Visual Metaphor

Because the design objective included communicating the Global Technology. Asian Focus message in the logo as well as each succeeding campaign component, designers decided to include Asian-inspired images as visual metaphors that when combined, compared, and contrasted with high technology images, created unusual and unexpected juxtapositions of graphics. Gee + Chung created several of these design elements that were used consistently throughout the entire campaign.

One such element is the use of a universally accepted Asian color palette of red, gold, and black, which is prevalent throughout many Asian cultures and connotes such positive characteristics as good luck, good fortune, prosperity, and longevity. The word iAsia was set in red type because it complemented the word *Works* in black and the color break played to the logo's advantage. A modified extension of the logo form— an outline—was replicated as a gold outline on a red field, simulating gold embroidery on red silk, and was established for secondary uses. The secondary system also employed a pattern of reversed out, embossed circles—representing the pattern on an ancient Asian doorway and symbolic of a gateway to Asia—which gave the presentation folder a dynamic tactile aspect.

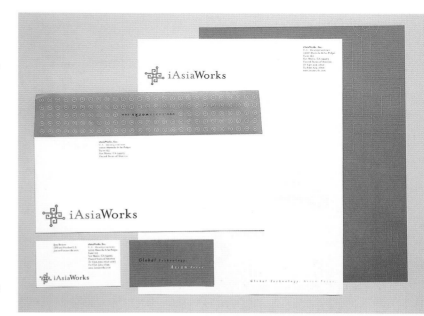

Tying the Imagery to the Message

The iAsiaWorks logo, its outlined version, and other Asian-inspired graphics were carried through each element of the campaign to create imagery that when combined with an integrated circuitry pattern, functions as a visual metaphor for linking Asian cultures through technology. For example, the iAsiaWorks stationery system utilizes both the standard logo as well as the outlined version simulating gold embroidery on red silk and a dot pattern derived from the logo, representing an ancient Chinese door. The presentation folder uses the logo to form a string tie clasp, transforming the folder into a special gift for potential clients. The inside pockets have embossed dots simulating the rivets on an Asian door, and the curved flaps convey a Chinese moongate motif.

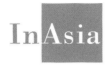
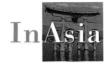

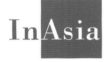

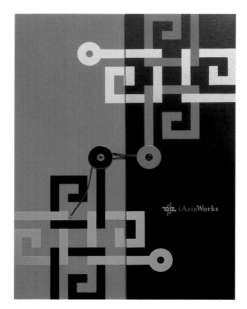

LEFT AND BELOW: **iAsiaWorks'** presentation folder uses the logo to form a string tie clasp, transforming the folder into a special gift for potential clients. The inside pockets have embossed dots simulating the rivets on an Asian door, and the curved flaps convey a Chinese moongate motif.

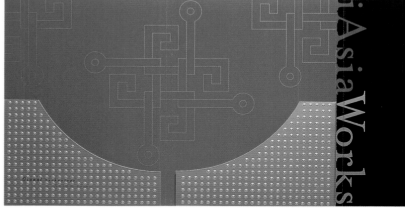

BELOW: **Product data sheets juxtapose similar graphic elements. Where one photographically compares and contrasts the spherical shape of a Chinese fan to the globe, another compares and contrasts Chinese firecrackers to a fiber optic cable.**

BOTTOM RIGHT: **With a limited budget, Gee + Chung Design put their creative minds to work and developed iAsia's party invitation in the form of a large drink coaster. They used letterpress printing on thick blotter paper, creating the effect of a Chinese seal on parchment.**

The trade show promotion uses an accordion-fold format to define who and what iAsiaWorks is—placing its mission statement on one side, while the reverse is a handy reference guide for business travelers in Asia, detailing the language, climate, currency, and business protocol in the twelve regions in which iAsiaWorks has facilities. Originally, this piece was intended to be as a 24" x 36" (61 cm x 91 cm) mission statement poster for hanging on office walls. When Gee + Chung presented the design, they did so at half size, like they do many of their comps. The CEO took hold of the miniature mock-up, which was still readable at its reduced size, and thought it was a nice size to keep handy in one's pocket, luggage, or on a desktop. The obvious question arose: What if we were to build in some utility and function to this piece? As a result, the idea of a poster was discarded in favor of the palm-sized piece. This

piece, too, perpetuates the Asian influence and reads front to back as well as back to front. Because it has a lot of folds, designers developed a handsome sleeve that provides a tidy and compact way to hold it together securely and compactly.

Product data sheets use an interesting juxtaposition of two similar graphic elements—which vary from one data sheet to the next. Where one photographically compares and contrasts the spherical shape of a Chinese fan to the globe, another compares and contrasts Chinese firecrackers to a fiber optic cable.

The Web site, www.iasiaworks.com, incorporates a vertical navigation menu on the right side of the page, reflecting how Asian cultures read from right to left. Conceptual headers combine Eastern and Western visuals through the site. As the viewer clicks on map locations, news about iAsiaWorks in each region pops up.

iAsiaWork's party invitation provided entrée to a must-attend event at ISPCON, a major industry trade show. The budget was limited so Gee + Chung Design put their creative minds to work and developed an invitation in the form of a large drink coaster. They used letterpress printing on thick blotter paper, creating the effect of a Chinese seal on parchment. The low-tech, tactile, craft-oriented appeal of the letterpress printing was a dramatic departure for the high-tech Internet industry, making the invitation a big hit and drawing twice as many attendees as expected while generating plenty of talk about the company.

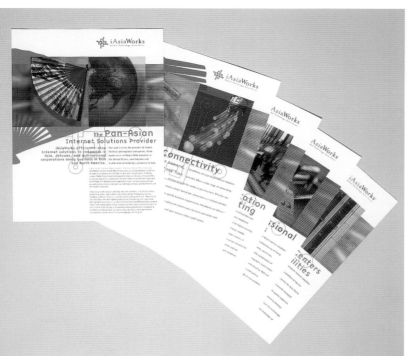

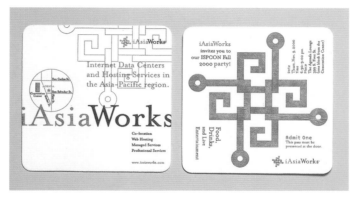

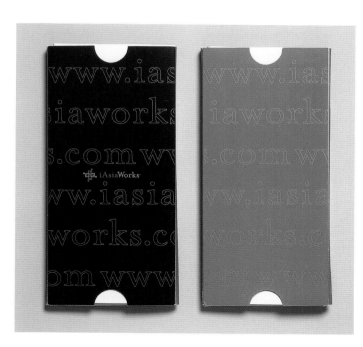

Integrating all these pieces wasn't as tough as one might think; designers treated each piece as a separate project versus a component of a campaign. They did this to avoid using the same elements over and over again, which can lull designers into treating designs as applications versus standalone items. "Keeping things fresh requires looking at each piece individually even if it is part of the graphic vocabulary," says Earl Gee, art director on the project.

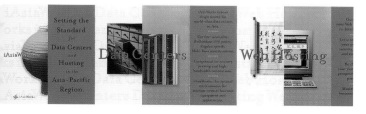

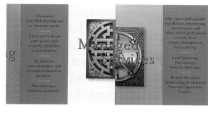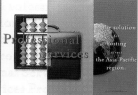

ABOVE, RIGHT, AND TOP OF PAGE: The trade show promotion uses an accordion-fold format to define who iAsiaWorks is on one side, while the reverse works as a handy reference for business travelers throughout the twelve regions where iAsiaWorks has facilities, detailing the language, climate, currency, and business protocol. Because the brochure has a lot of folds, a sleeve provides it a tidy way to hold it together securely and compactly.

Two Messages—One Campaign

"Our biggest problem was the challenge of communicating the dual messages of Global Technology. Asian Focus. We needed to create solutions that were not specifically Chinese, Japanese, or Korean, but concepts that would resonate with and be embraced by as many Asian cultures as possible," says Gee. "We solved the challenge of Pan-Asian communications by determining that China was, by far, the market with the largest potential for our client, and a majority of Asian cultures share elements of the Chinese culture. Consequently, designs with Chinese derivations could work effectively across a number of Asian cultures." Gee specifically points to the photographic elements on the data sheets as a prime example of mixing the high-tech aspects of the project, such as a fiber optic cable, with the Asian focus, graphically communicated by a Chinese firecracker. As the program continues and is extended in other venues and collateral materials, Gee doesn't worry about running about of material. "There are an infinite number of ways to compare and contrast the two messages," he says.

Location, Location, Location

A related obstacle was geography. While iAsiaWorks has an office in San Mateo, California, not far from Gee + Chung's San Francisco office, the company's chairman and CEO, JoAnn Patrick-Ezzell, is based in Hong Kong, a full sixteen hours ahead of Pacific Standard Time in San Francisco. "Our development time frames were severely truncated as iAsiaWorks was a startup in the emerging space of Internet data centers and Web hosting with a very small window of opportunity to make their mark," says Gee. "Five P.M. conference calls became the norm to keep client feedback and approvals on schedule. Our previous experience with the accelerated timeframes of dot-com startups enabled us to work efficiently and quickly to deliver the corporate identity in two weeks (with three name changes along the way), the stationery system in three days, and the presentation folder in a day."

The Budget

As for the budget, Gee + Chung, having worked with a number of Internet start-up launches, found it to be reasonable. But more importantly, particularly in light of the timeframe, the client was efficient with feedback and approvals. Still, the designers were always seeking ways to maximize the budget, primarily by gang printing data sheets and other items whenever possible to economize printing costs.

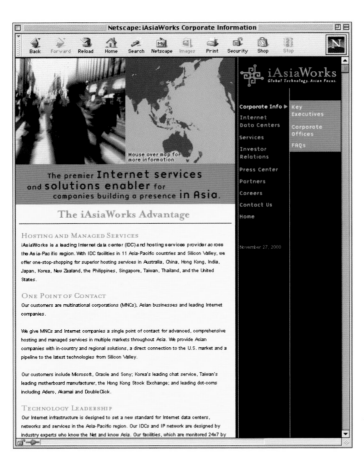

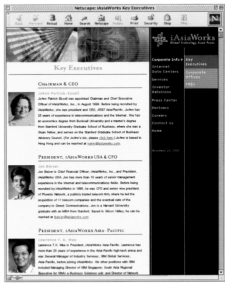

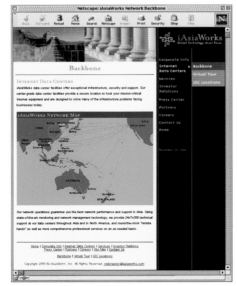

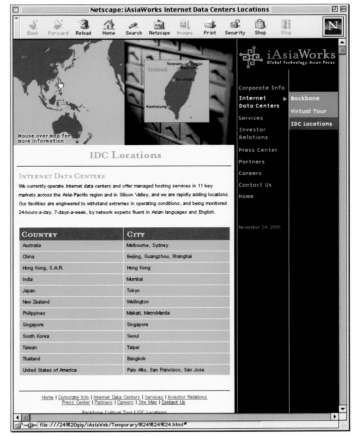

THIS PAGE: **The Web site, www.iasia-works.com, incorporates a vertical navigation on the right side of the page, reflecting how Asian cultures read from right to left. Conceptual headers combine Eastern and Western visuals through the site. As the viewer clicks on map locations, news about iAsiaWorks in each region pops up.**

The results

Gee + Chung's materials for iAsiaWorks have impacted the industry from the moment they hit the street. "Our client has been able to launch a successful IPO while expanding operations from three countries to fifteen countries throughout Asia in only a nine-month span. They have also grown from twenty employees to 250 in the U.S. and Asia," says Gee.

What Worked

"Chairman and CEO JoAnn Patrick-Ezzell credits our unified graphic team as being 'instrumental in iAsiaWorks' expansion and acceptance across Asia, creating communications that convey the company's mission, while resonating with their Asian audiences,'" says Gee. "Patrick-Ezzell was very pleased that after one press conference, a reporter interviewing her commented, 'That is really a nice logo.'"

TIPS FROM THE EXPERTS Experiment...be flexible...build in practicality

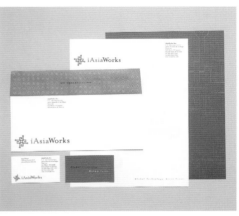

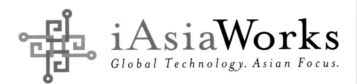

CREATE VISUAL METAPHORS

iAsiaWorks' logo and variations of it created a visual metaphor that link Asian cultures and technology.

KEEP LOGOS FLEXIBLE

Designers created an outline version of the iAsiaWorks logo as part of a secondary system that dresses up the letter-head system and presentation folder.

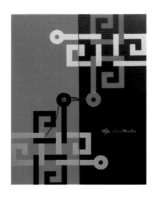

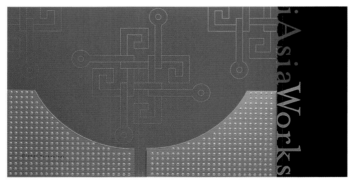

MAKE BROCHURES HARD TO DISCARD

iAsiaWorks' presentation folder incorporates a string tie clasp, embossed pockets, and special die-cutting that transforms an ordinary presentation folder into a special gift that prospective clients will be hesitant to throw away.

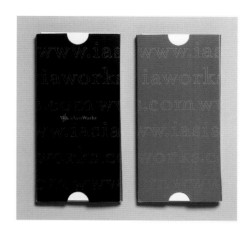

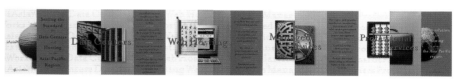

PRACTICAL ITEMS HAVE STAYING POWER

iAsiaWorks' trade show promotion defines who iAsiaWorks is on one side, while the reverse works as a handy reference for business travelers throughout the twelve regions where iAsiaWorks has facilities, detailing the language, climate, currency, and business protocol.

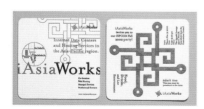

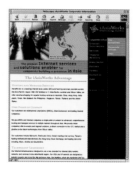
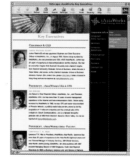
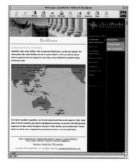
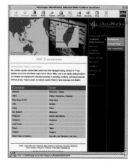

HAVE FUN WITH PARTY INVITATIONS

iAsiaWork's party invitation provided entrée to a must-attend event and developed an invitation in the form of a large drink coaster, which was effective despite the low budget.

BREAK THE RULES

The Web site, www.iasiaworks.com, incorporates a vertical navigation on the right side of the page, reflecting how Asian cultures read from right to left—in stark contrast to typical Web page formatting.

AWARENESS CAMPAIGN SELLS BERTHS ON CRUISE WEST ALASKA

(up-close and casual graphics)

The Client

Cruise West ships are unlike the mega cruise ships popularized on television shows and by celebrities in glitzy advertising campaigns. Cruise West doesn't offer the traditional luxury amenities one so often associates with cruise ships. There are no spas, pools, Broadway theaters, midnight chocolate buffets, pizza bars, or gambling casinos, yet the cost per passenger is much higher than a cruise on a mega ship. Sound like a marketing dilemma? Perhaps. But Cruise West does offer advantages that the mega ships don't—an intimate traveling experience only possible on a small ship. So, when Cruise West challenged Belyea with selling as many berths as possible on its Cruise West ships for the Alaska 2000 season, the Seattle-based design firm took the job and got up-close and personal.

CLIENT:
Cruise West

DESIGN FIRM:
Belyea

CREATIVE DIRECTOR:
Patricia Belyea

DESIGNERS:
Ron Lars Hansen, Naomi Murphy,
Anne Dougherty, Kelli Lewis

COPYWRITERS:
Floyd Fickle, Liz Holland

CAMPAIGN RUN:
August 1999 through July 2000

TARGET MARKET:
Travel agents and sophisticated,
affluent consumers over 55
years old

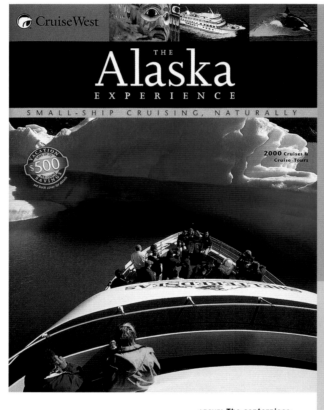

ABOVE: The centerpiece of the campaign, this sixty-page brochure sells small ship cruising and the up-front, casual atmosphere of Cruise West trips through its easygoing writing style and imagery that shows guests and crew gathering together for photos on its cover.

The Brief

In startling contrast to mega cruise ships that routinely carry anywhere from 1500 to 2500 passengers in a floating city, Cruise West is part of a niche category within the small-ship cruising industry, carrying ninety to 100 passengers with minimal luxury amenities. The appeal of the small ship comes from the intimate and low-key nature of the experience that promotes interaction with nature and wildlife along with education on the cultural surroundings. Instead of gambling in the evening, passengers listen to experts talk about the region; instead of being fourteen stories up when a whale breaches beside the ship, prompting passengers to run for their binoculars, they can view the whale up-close from a 4' x 5' (1.2 m x 1.5 m) picture window in their stateroom while writing a postcard home.

"You get more and more involved with your surroundings," says Patricia Belyea, creative director, of the time passengers spend onboard. As a result, passengers "gain so much on this cruise because they learn so much." If wildlife comes near the ship, the captain will stop the engine so everyone can enjoy the scene. If the ship went by too fast to catch a wildlife show, the captain will turn the vessel around and go back for another look. If something happens outside during dinner, everyone goes on deck—including the staff. "The whole world stops for a wildlife experience. People get such a kick out of it. It is what makes their trip...these events just burn into their memories. It is really very, very different from the big cruise ships."

Given these strengths, it is little wonder that Belyea promotes the Cruise West experience with two simple messages—up-close and casual. These messages are evident throughout the Alaska 2000 campaign's collateral material, which while very simply produced, is totally unlike any other travel brochures.

TOP AND BOTTOM RIGHT: The Ice Box bulk mailing, sent to large travel agencies, contained three sets of seven brochures with three "Win a dream cruise" postcards. Agents participating in the contest had to include their preference for itinerary, sailing date, and ship so that they really had to give the Alaska trip some consideration. This mailing, like the rest of the collateral pieces, promotes the up-close and casual theme—to the point of showing a photo of a woman touching a glacier from the bow of a Cruise West ship.

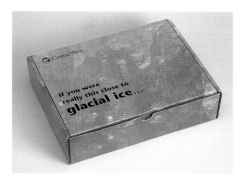

BELOW: Belyea developed a national advertising campaign for national magazines, local newspapers, as well as AAA publications, emphasizing the up-close aspects of small-ship cruising with Cruise West.

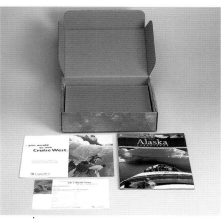

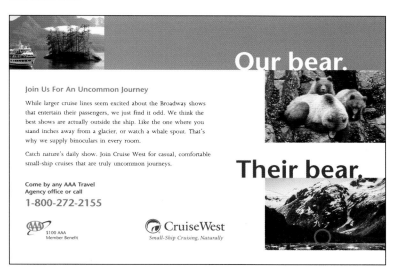

The Strategy

There is a multitude of items in the Alaska 2000 campaign, the centerpiece of which is the Alaska 2000 brochure. The up-close and casual messages are evident immediately in this campaign component. "There's nothing stuffy about the cover—that's the crew and passengers," says Belyea. Within this piece, and everything else that follows, Belyea uses a casual, friendly, and inviting approach. Everything from the photos and the tone of the copy to the layout reinforce that this cruise line is up-close, casual, and offers a unique experience. In all, the packaged campaign underscores the relaxed nature of the travel product and the company's family values, while appealing to the trend toward younger people taking cruises. "You can see the age dropping on who we are trying to appeal to. It used to be [people] over seventy, then it was over sixty, and then it was over fifty. Now, we can actually say we're working on the over-forty group. We've seen a huge change in the demographics. Now, we have this opportunity to talk to people who have never even gone on a cruise...and the only thing they will probably touch or feel before they go on the cruise is this brochure."

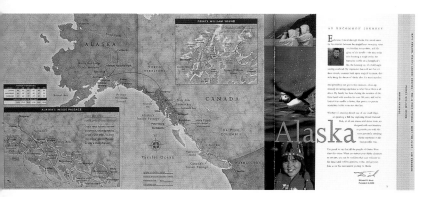

LEFT: Vivid colors and lots of white space with a larger than typical typestyle combine to invite the reader in; the staggered informational pages make it easy for the inquisitive prospect to navigate the details.

RIGHT: Two versions of this Alaska Fall Colors mailing were posted in spring 2000 to give consumers and travel agents a couple of months to respond.

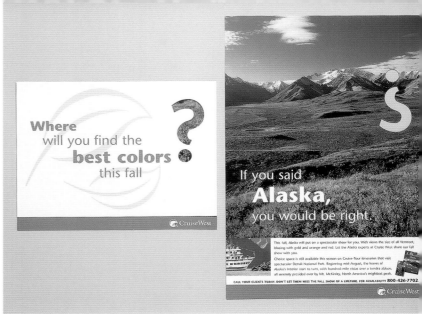

RIGHT: This Alaska video was distributed to consumers through ads and business reply cards; it was also sent to travel agents where it was shrinkwrapped with microwave popcorn. The package insert included a response card for requesting information on other Cruise West destinations as well as information for a friend.

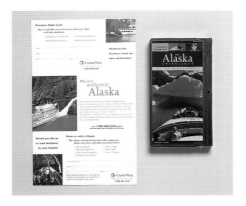

Involving the Audience

Designers crafted each component of the campaign to maximize its selling potential. This was done through design, the message, and a strong understanding of the target audience. For instance, travel agents were sent a simple contest with their Alaska 2000 brochure. To win a free Cruise West Alaska cruise, agents were asked to choose their own trip and provide their preferred itinerary, sailing date, and ship of choice. This meant that the agents needed to get fully involved in the process of choosing a vacation through the brochure—something that their clients do," Belyea explains. "The response rate for this contest was 25 percent. More importantly, it meant that 25 percent of the recipients had actually read through the brochure and become familiar with the Alaska product."

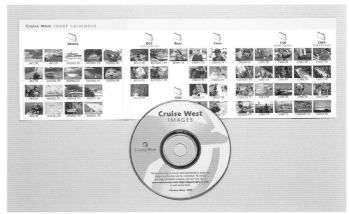

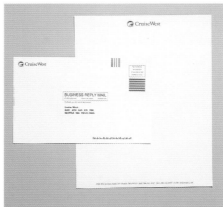

ABOVE: All travel agents were given a package of support materials to promote Cruise West's Alaska 2000 products including ad slicks, a logo sheet, and a CD-ROM loaded with low-resolution color images for the agents to review. If high-resolution images were needed, agents could download them from the Cruise West Web site.

LEFT: To inspire travel agents to actually read the Cruise West Alaska 2000 brochure, agents were encouraged to pick their favorite photo and win a cruise. The catch was they didn't just win any cruise, but one of their choice—compelling them to pick their itinerary, sailing date, and ship of their choice—hence, they had to do more than scan the brochure. Of 15,000 entries mailed, 3700 responses (a 25 percent return rate) were recorded.

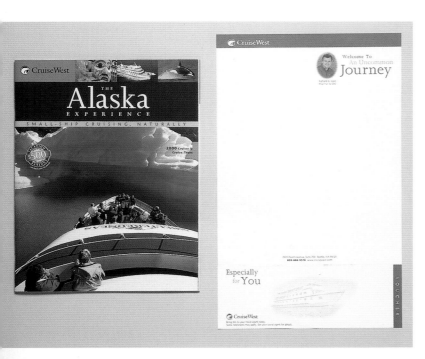

LEFT: Consumers requesting information received their Alaska 2000 brochure as a personalized package, including an envelope custom made for this mailing. A front window allows the mailing address to show through, while the back of the envelope has a large-view window to show the entire catalog cover. A personalized letter accompanied the catalog with a voucher that gave the recipient a time-dated offer that they could give to their travel agent.

Choosing the Imagery

Since the collateral's job is to sell prospective customers through their visual imagery, the choice, quality, and color reproduction of the photography can make or break a campaign. Some photos are client-supplied, while others are purchased through photo houses where images cost an average of $1500 each. The job of overseeing photography is so enormous and detail oriented, it requires a full-time person to head up the effort, make purchases, and ensure that stock images, if used previously, are paid for again. Photo requests are typically handled on the Internet, but Belyea doesn't risk finalizing its choices from the Web. The firm insists on reviewing all transparencies first before finalizing the sale. "We may sound low-tech, but once before transparencies received were not the quality needed. We don't have the time to waste with bad film," says Belyea. "Ensuring images are correct is part of our job."

Proofing the Color

With so much attention devoted to choosing the right image, equal priority is given to ensuring that the color in the photos is as gorgeous as it should be. Belyea works closely with a printer on color issues. Pick-up and new transparencies undergo the same thorough process. When scans are returned from the color house, two designers will examine the color and mark up the artwork before showing the adjustments to the client. Once they have client approval, Belyea will send the images back to color house and await a corrected set of proofs. Proofs will be corrected until they are perfect. "If the color isn't right, it won't be as inviting," says Belyea. "It's a part of the project we make sure is absolutely right." All this attention to detail pays off in Cruise West ships that are whiter, Alaskan skies that are bluer, and water that is not murky but refreshing shades of teal.

Simplifying the Process

Information about the final product offering came late to Belyea and was continually modified. Working with thirty-six itineraries, maps, schedules, and price charts that kept changing required highly detailed production management. Belyea side-steps a potential proofing nightmare by creating a three-person proofing team to check and recheck all documents. They also created all maps in-house to accommodate frequent changes to itineraries.

Throughout the production process—a year-long task—it was Belyea's job to oversee that each piece integrated with the other campaign components and recognize when things needed to be better coordinated. Designers received the campaign project by project and worked on everything over the course of a year, which could make for a scheduling headache and rushed deadlines. Fortunately, Belyea, long accustomed to travel work, had learned that organization and advance planning is key. "When we start in the spring, we know what needs to be done by fall," she says.

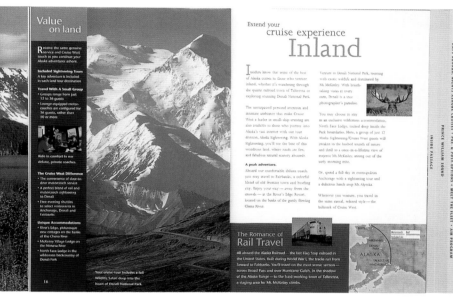

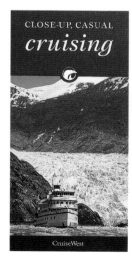

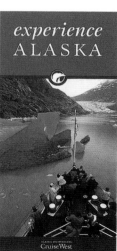

ABOVE: The small photo in the far-left margin was client supplied, while the image of a yellow school bus making its way toward Mount McKinley was a stock image where special care was paid to ensure the sky was as blue as possible and that the snow was a dazzling shade of white.

RIGHT: Travel agents promoted the Alaska 2000 cruise with these ticket stuffers, inserted into airline ticket packages and other documents.

RIGHT: **The Cruise West Alaska Web site offers comprehensive information for consumers, including itineraries, ship layouts, and travel tips; while a password-protected section for travel agents includes PDF files of collateral, a media center, and other updated information on rates, group policies, and more.**

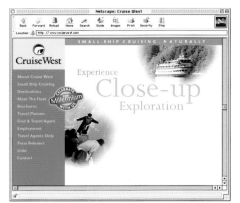

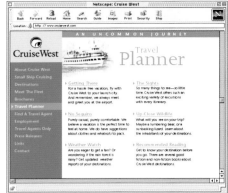

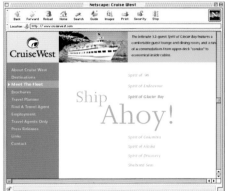

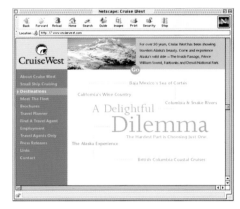

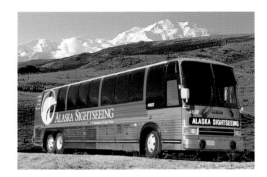

ABOVE AND RIGHT: **Belyea worked with Cruise West to redesign the graphics on their tour buses, where the land arm of their businesses is called Alaska Sightseeing. Designers integrated the polar bear logo with new type that emulated the Cruise West logo, making these buses the most colorful vehicles on Alaska's highways.**

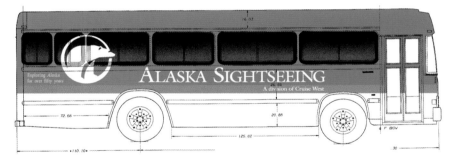

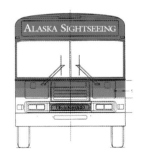

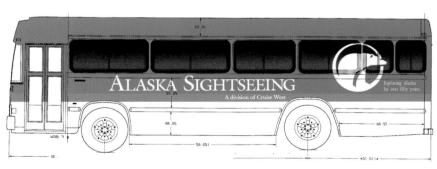

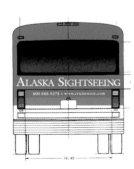

The results

When the Alaska 2000 ship set sail, all indicators pointed to a successful campaign. The travel-agent photo contest generated 3700 responses from a mailing of 15,000, where agents were asked to select their favorite photo for a chance to win an Alaska cruise of their choice, and was among the individual winning elements of the campaign. However, no one doubted that the most important element of this campaign was creating awareness in the Alaska products that translated directly to increased sales.

When all the tallies were in, the campaign delivered on its promise to sell as many berths as possible on the Alaska sailings. In 1999, Cruise West bookings were 79 percent of capacity. At the end of the Alaska 2000 season, bookings had risen to a phenomenal 95.4 percent of capacity. "The 2000 season was successful due to focus-targeted communications to the appropriate audiences in a timely manner. The training programs, collateral, and advertising were consistent to the brand image and supported by strong creative and training of our reservations department," says Mary Novak-Beatty, vice president of sales and marketing, Cruise West.

Also indicative of a healthy promotion is that Cruise West just bought a new ship and is planning on buying another ship in the near future.

What Worked

"It captured the readers' hearts and minds," says Belyea. "I think they could truly begin to visualize what this whole experience could be about and choose to buy it because it would match who they are as people. Not everyone wants to go on this cruise ship because it costs more and [they're asking] 'Hey, where's the spa?' For those people, it's not the right match. But for people looking for an experience that's a cut above, we did a good job helping them choose the right product."

Tips from the experts
Get close...get involved...make it easy

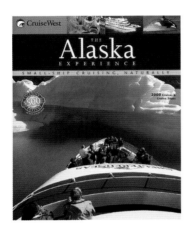

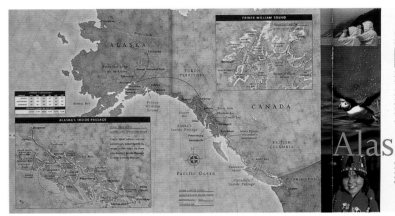

GET UP-CLOSE AND PERSONAL

Don't hesitate to bring photography up close if the application calls for it. Close-ups can bring the prospect into the experience.

MAKE DETAILED COPY EASY TO READ

Use lots of white space and stagger paragraphs to make copy-heavy pages less intimidating and easy to read and navigate.

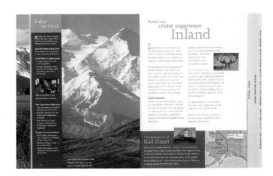

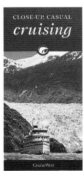

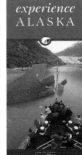

COLOR-PROOF PHOTOS

If your photo looks lackluster, so will your product. Be sure colors are as sharp and vivid as they should be.

MAKE IT EASY FOR AGENTS OR DISTRIBUTORS TO SELL YOUR PRODUCT

Travel agents were supplied with ticket stuffers so they could promote the Alaska 2000 cruises to their clients by stuffing them into airline ticket packages and other documents.

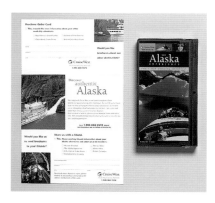

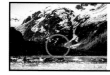

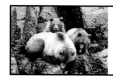

SELLING IS SERIOUS BUSINESS, BUT KEEP IT FUN

Cruise West distributed its Alaska video to consumers through ads and business reply cards; it was also sent to travel agents where it was shrinkwrapped with microwave popcorn.

ENCOURAGE WORD-OF-MOUTH BUSINESS

Cruise alumni can sign up for membership in the Quyana Club (Q-Club) while they are on their cruise. The newsletter comes out biannually and is designed to encourage word-of-mouth business. Members who refer other guests can win a free cruise.

USE EVERY OPPORTUNITY FOR CONTACT

Cruise West delivered holiday greetings to travel agents and business associates.

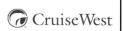

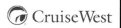

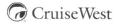

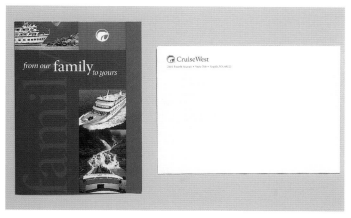

MAKE IT EASY TO BUY

Belyea placed this Web banner—three variations of which promote the up-close message—on *Alaska* magazine's Alaska Directory index page. When readers clicked on the banner, they were instantly linked with the Cruise West Web site.

Identity Design

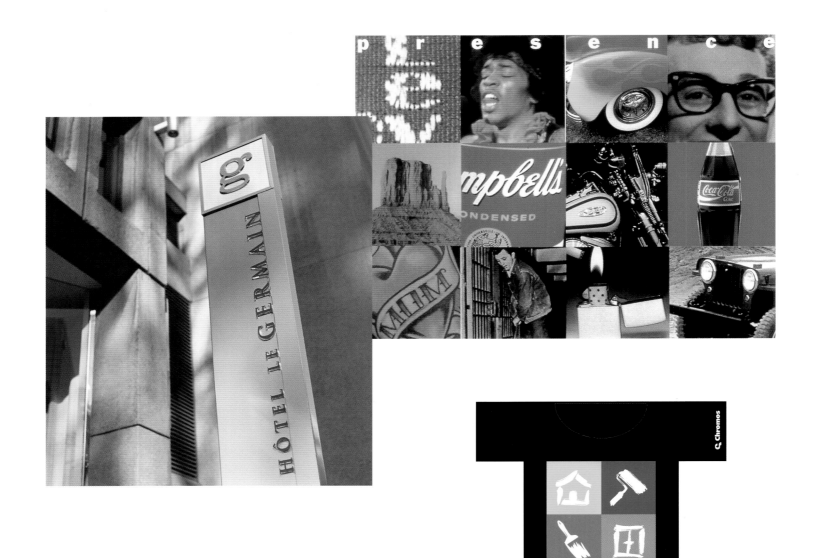

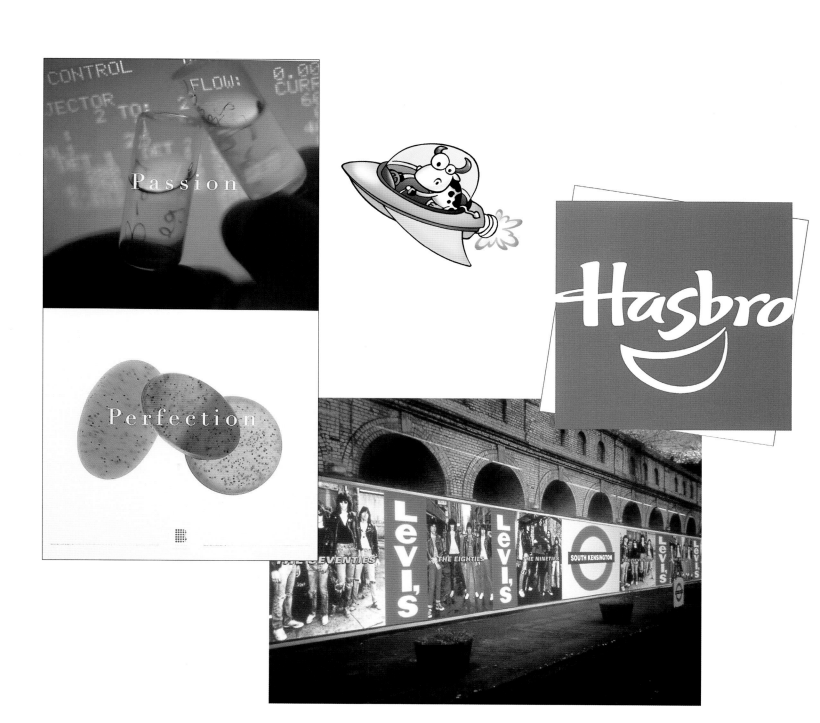

Bradford Soap Works:
An Identity That Comes Clean

DESIGN FIRM:
Weymouth Design

ART DIRECTOR:
Tom Laidlaw

DESIGNERS:
Brad Lewthwait

WEB SITE DESIGNER:
Chris Geiser

PHOTOGRAPHER:
Michael Weymouth

CLIENT:
Bradford Soap
Works, Inc.

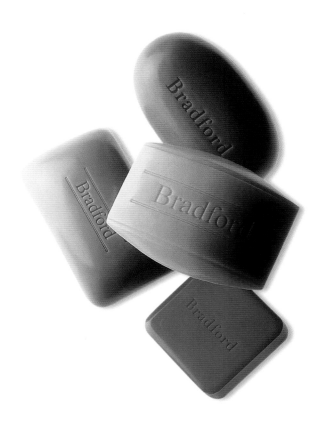

The Process

The Bradford Soap Works, Inc. headquartered in Providence, Rhode Island, and in Chester, England, approached Boston's Weymouth Design for a new look. Its identity was suffering from a dismal lack of distinction. Marketing materials proclaimed that the original Bradford Soap Works provided "excellence in soapmaking since 1876," but the look that message was getting drowned out by an old, musty image.

"The old identity was dated and didn't appeal to the upscale audience that makes up Bradford's market," says Tom Laidlaw, art director, citing his client's original logo that featured a capital *B* in a stylized circle alongside the company name, Bradford, which was also reproduced in capital letters. "We needed to appeal to a more fashion-savvy audience [accustomed] to the Body Shop and other designer label distributors."

Bradford Soap Works is a specialty soapmaker that manufactures soaps for retail stores to sell. Consequently, it needed an identity that would not only win over consumers, but retailers who are very discriminating about sacrificing their precious shelf and floor space. With that in mind, Weymouth Design set about the job of updating Bradford's logo. The capital *B* was prominent in the original logo, so they retained that concept, but gave it a complete overhaul by filling the letter *B* with orange dots, not unlike the shape of Bradford's many soaps, for an abstract effect. It is coupled with the company name, which was reset in a more contemporary typeface.

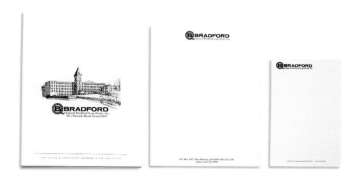

LEFT: The original folder featured the Bradford logo below a pen-and-ink illustration of its Rhode Island headquarters, a look that definitely dated the materials, making the company look stodgy and behind the times instead of the quality soapmaker that it was.

In retrospect, designers say that this logo is the single most important element in the identity as they used it as a major design element on a number of pieces that they created. For instance, when designers tackled the company's information folder, gone was the pen-and-ink illustration of Bradford's Rhode Island headquarters from the old identity. This was replaced with the new logo. The same approach was taken with the business card. Interestingly, designers set the B apart from contact information on the letterhead, mailing label, and large and small envelopes, which gives the icon even more impact and stand-alone strength.

Next, Weymouth translated the identity to the company's product—engraving the name Bradford on its soaps using the new type style. Designers suggested that Bradford send out sample packages of soaps and designed a black mailing carton for the job and wrapped in soap in specially designed tissue paper.

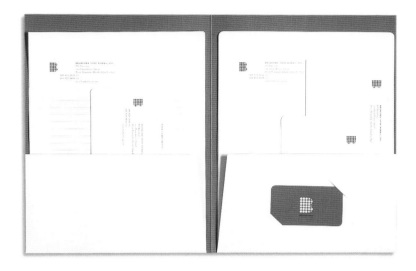

ABOVE: The single most important element of the redesign, according to designers, was the new logo—which is a capital B, in keeping with the old identity, but this time, it is contemporary and abstract, filled with orange dots that mirror the shape of Bradford's product.

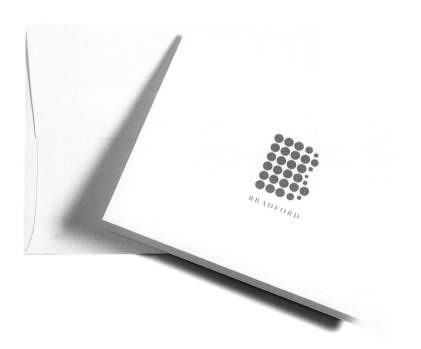

ABOVE: This invitation to a New York trade show invited prospects to see what's new at the Bradford Soap Works.

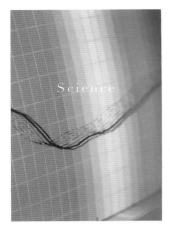

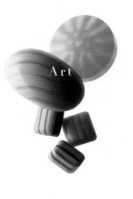

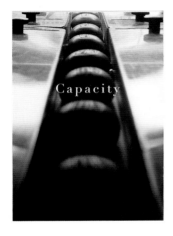

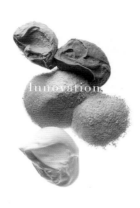

Designers also updated the company's brochure, creating a very clean cover using a photo of four different Bradford soaps against a clean, white background. Interior spreads are vibrant and show off what the company does best—provide excellence in soapmaking. The copy discussed how the science of soapmaking translates to art, passion, and perfection—the perfect message for an upscale retail audience who isn't interested so much in buying the soaps to get clean as they are for their beauty and fragrance.

Anticipating plenty of retail sales, Weymouth also created point-of-purchase materials including a bag with coordinating tissue, which repeats the dot pattern of the logo along with a series of posters that replay the theme of "science equals art, passion, and perfection."

Rounding out the identity makeover was a new Web site, www.bradfordsoap.com, advertisements, direct mail, a video, and a press campaign. Regardless of the application, the graphics associated with the identity are all in line with the upscale feeling of the logo.

"The clean and simple graphics stand out in a world of clutter and uninspired imagery," says Laidlaw. "The company's market is high-end cosmetic manufacturers. The identity needed to be high end as well."

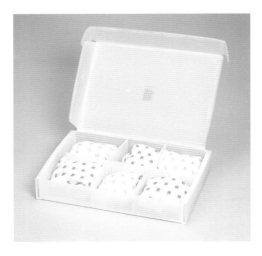

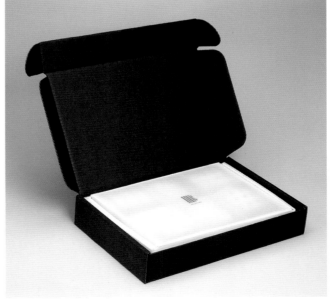

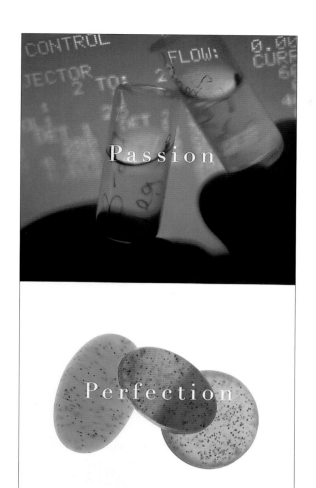

Passion

Perfection

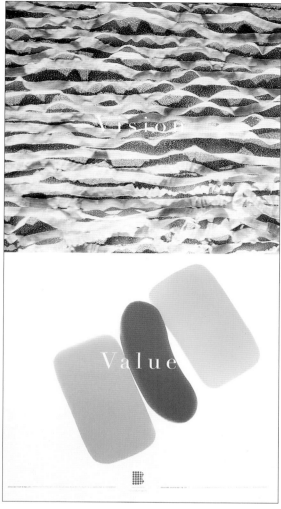

Vision

Value

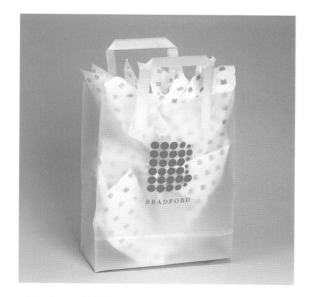

ABOVE: Weymouth Design also created retail materials including custom bags and tissue that replicate the dot pattern found in Bradford's logo.

What Works

The new identity was unveiled at a trade show in New York City in June of 2001. Within six months, there were feature articles in four of the major trade magazines, including *Women's Wear Daily*.

"It's fresh, new and bold in comparison to Bradford's competitors," says Laidlaw. Moreover, it is versatile, he says. "It applies easily to ads, packaging, posters, signage, etc. The new identity is successful because of its strict adherence to usage guidelines and myriad applications have gotten the branding message out, loud and clear."

Chromos:
Painting an Identity

DESIGN FIRM:
Likovni Studio D.O.O.

ART DIRECTOR:
Tomislav Mrcic

DESIGNER:
Mladen Balog

ILLUSTRATOR:
Danko Jaksic

CLIENT:
Chromos

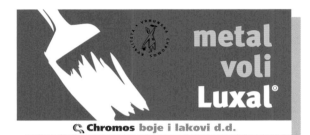

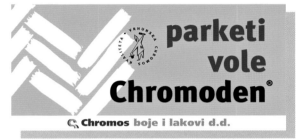

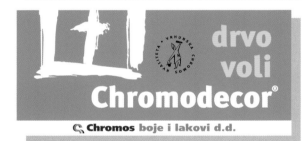

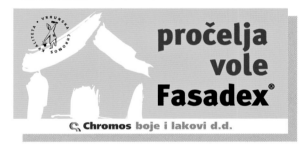

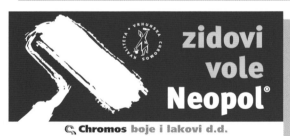

ABOVE AND OPPOSITE TOP:
**Billboard and transit
advertising is colorful, in
keeping with the product
line, and simple since it
uses basic elements, such
as paint tools and brushes
—as identifying icons.**

The Process

Chromos was been the leading manufacturer of paints and varnishes in the former Yugoslav market since the 1930s. However, due to the war, economic transition, and the disappearance of the Common Eastern European market, it has lost its position; when it approached Likovni Studio to help reinvigorate its sales position, Chromos sold product just in the Croatian, Slovenian, and partially Bosnian market, which represents only about 40 percent of the prewar Yugoslav market. This drastic loss of market share demanded swift attention, and the time was right for a new corporate identity and package redesign.

Likovni Studio was asked to remake the company's logo, which had been redesigned just a few years prior by another design firm. Chromos also had a mascot that had been in use since the late 1950s; it was well known and communicated tradition, but neither the previous logo nor the mascot was to be referenced in the new design. Instead, Likovni Studio was chartered with communicating Chromos' high-quality products by introducing new elements that would refresh the long existing brands and unite them in a corporate style.

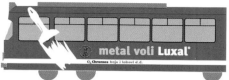

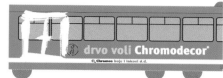

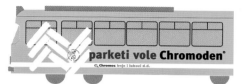

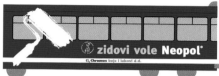

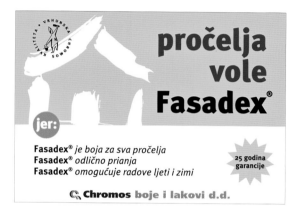

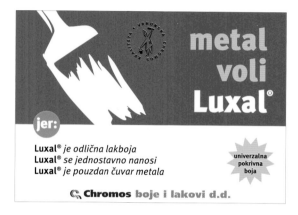

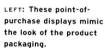

LEFT: These point-of-purchase displays mimic the look of the product packaging.

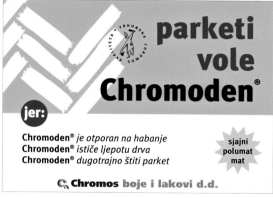

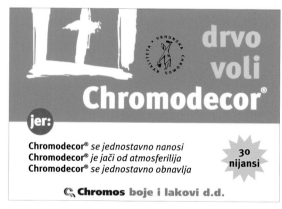

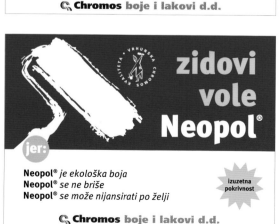

For years, the company had marketed solely to large corporations, including shipyards and big industry, so packaging and design weren't necessarily a priority. "The last redesign was done twenty years go and it was done in a uniform way—all containers were designed to look the same, just wearing different brand names, which was appropriate to the current strategy," says Tomislav Mrcic, art director on the project.

Now, however, designers had to create an identity that not only reflected the company's move to attracting the young, do-it-yourself consumer market, but they couldn't risk alienating the professionals.

RIGHT: Designers created art
for 180 items and introduced
pictographic images showing
paint, tools, and objects.
The number of registered
trademarks was reduced to
four; these were then pushed
as leading brands, according
to the basic paint types—
paints for metal, wood,
interiors, and exteriors.

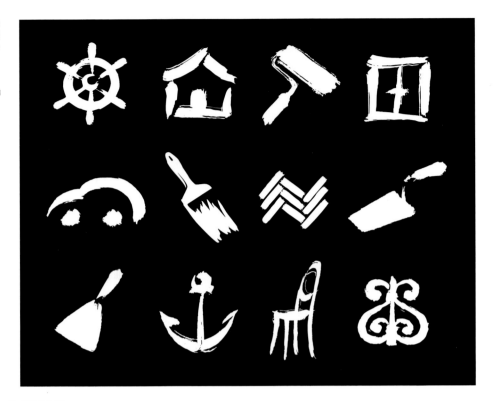

"Following the objectives, we kept the serious, legible, and quite classical layout and typography [of the previous identity and] combined [it] with powerful calligraphic styled graphics and bright colors. Simplicity makes it successful. Like one design critic has said about our work—'eloquent minimalism,'" Mrcic explains. "We based the new identity primarily on a strong graphic for it communicates faster and without words."

"The new corporate identity is based upon a radical packaging redesign totaling about 180 items and introduced pictographic images showing paint, tools, and objects," says Mrcic. "The vast number of registered trademarks was reduced to a few dozen and four of them were pushed as leading brands, according to the basic paint types—paints for metal, wood, interiors, and exteriors."

In keeping with Chromos's product line, all the basic colors were used and, despite the fact that a brush is the basic painting tool, a calligraphic approach was taken with the design. "To strengthen the impact of the brands on the shelves, we standardized typography for all brands by using Meta type family in all cuts including the Cyrillic alphabet for the Macedonia and Yugoslav markets," Mrcic says. "While more or less all of the paint manufacturers are using paradigmatic tools and objects, their packaging design is not so consistent through all the product lines and, of course, is weaker in building the institutional identity."

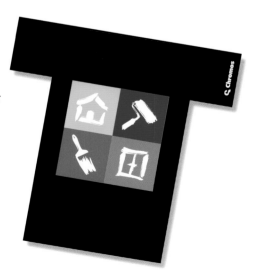

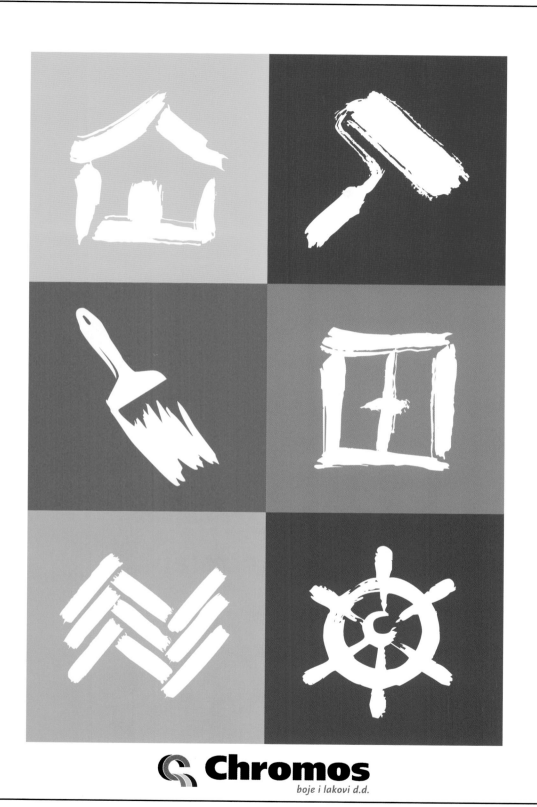

RIGHT AND OPPOSITE: For the first time in its history, Chromos was marketing to the young, do-it-yourself consumer instead of focusing solely on large corporations such as shipyards and industry. The design had to appeal to consumers without alienating its professional customer base. Design was more important than ever, as was packaging, so designers created notepads, shopping bags, and T-shirts that would appeal to consumers and professionals alike.

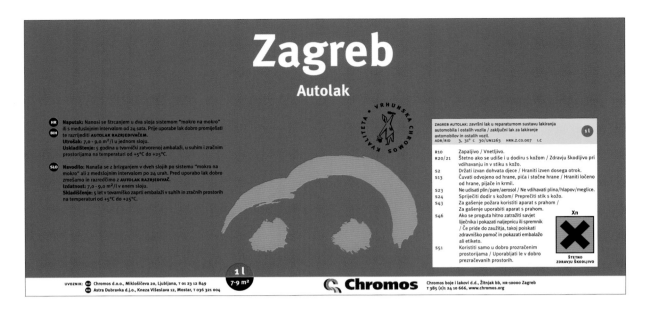

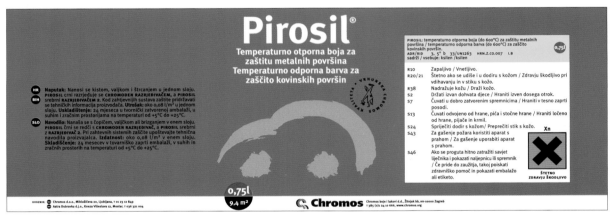

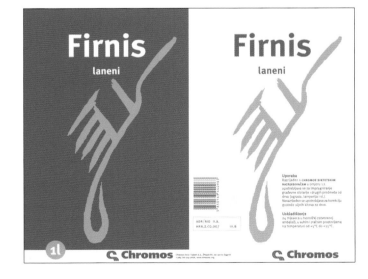

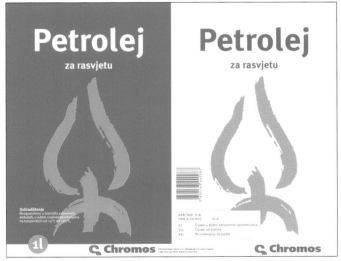

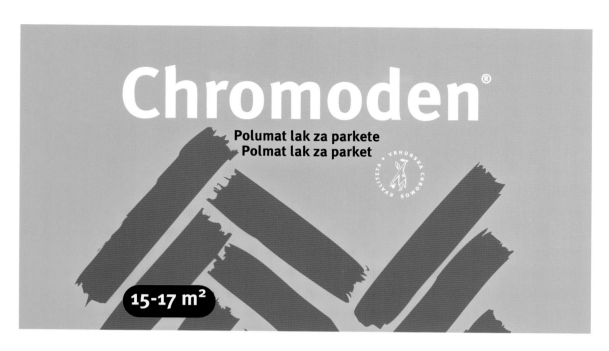

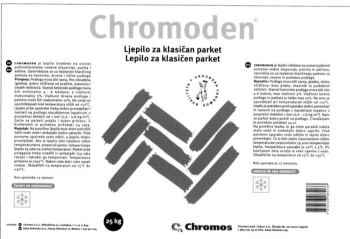

THIS PAGE: Product packaging takes on an array of looks and colors—while maintaining the overall identity—depending on the product and its usage.

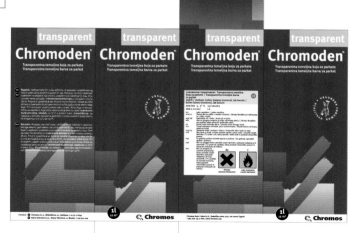

What Works

"In this era of high technology, a high-tech approach is something that undoubtedly and unpretendingly attracts the target group, especially hobbyists who, at first glance, recognize their life philosophy, but at the same time, not pushing professionals aside," says Mrcic. "Painting is high touch by default."

Designers say that while it is still too early to measure the results, first reports from the market show that sales of Chromos products have increased about 30 percent since the redesign debuted.

LEVI'S 501 JEANS:
The Biggest Little Number in Clothing

DESIGN FIRM:
Mike Salisbury
Communications, L.L.C.

CLIENT:
Levi Strauss & Co.

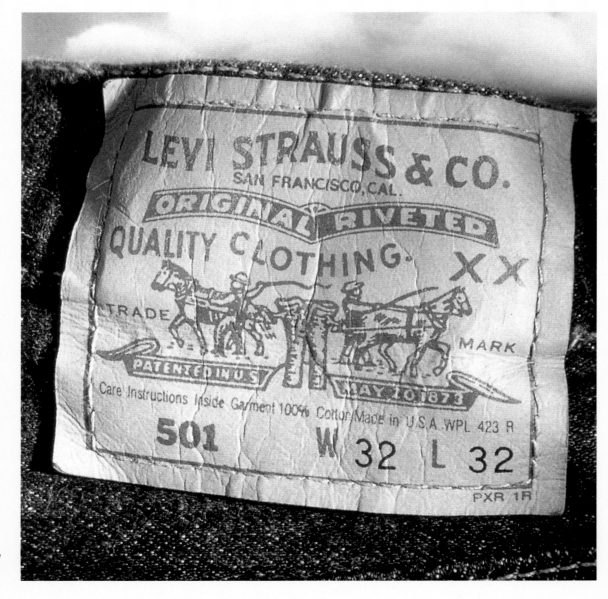

RIGHT: **The original source
of the 501 brand—the
product stock number.**

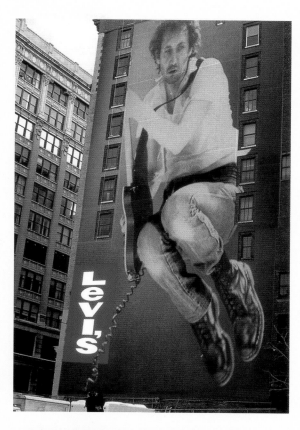

The Process

How did Levi's 501 jeans get their name? One might just as well ask, "Why is the sky blue?" because, like the sky, Levi's 501 jeans are something taken for granted. To that question the average jeans-buying consumer might respond, "What? Weren't they always called Levi's 501 jeans?" The answer is 'no.' In fact, Levi's 501 have become such an all-American icon, it seems as if that name has been around for ages, so it is surprising to note that it is a relatively new development.

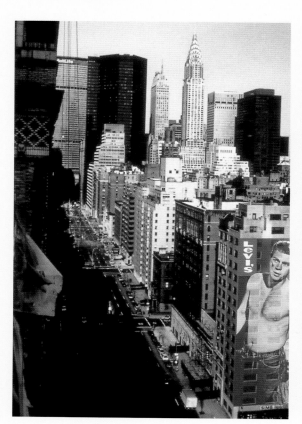

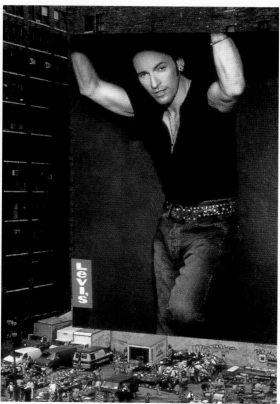

A Look Back

RIGHT: Salisbury's ad explaining the 501 concept "and the inspiration for me to name the product because it was impossible to keep calling the garment the 'Shrink-to-Fit Blue Jeans,'" says Salisbury. "Just call them 501. The rest is branding history. Every maker of denim product has a numbered jeans product."

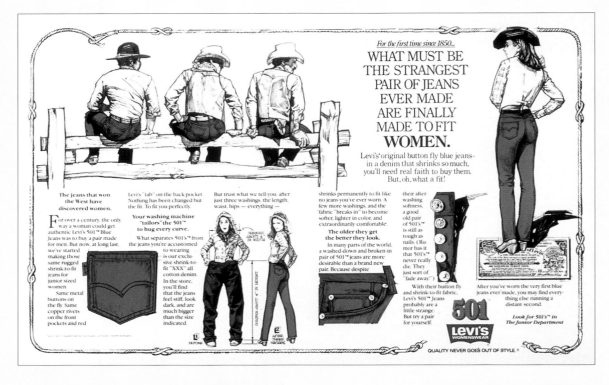

The name actually arose from a suggestion Mike Salisbury of Salisbury Communications L.L.C. made while working on the branding for a Levi's jean product for women. As Salisbury tells the story, for years, women in California had been remaking Levi's jeans for men by soaking them in bathtubs filled with warm water to shrink them to fit their bodies. While this habit wasn't well known in the rest of the country, Levi Strauss & Company realized what they were doing and saw an opportunity. The company developed Levi's Shrink-to-Fit Button Fly Jeans For Women. Salisbury was hired to create an advertising campaign to introduce this new, yet old, product.

"Research said that what was taken for granted in California—that you had to buy Levi's oversized and shrink them to fit—was largely unknown outside the West. My concept to present this new version of an American classic was to create a new symbol of communication to simply explain that what fits men now fits women," says Salisbury.

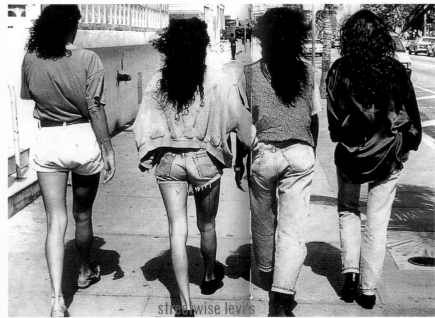

ABOVE: A quiz on who's who from *The Outsiders*—features the members of the group all dressed in Levi's.

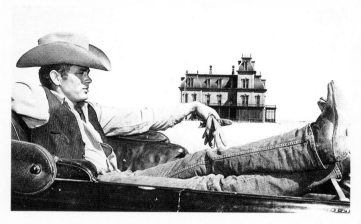

Salisbury draws a lot of his inspiration from pop culture, particularly Hollywood films, so that's where he turned for his idea. "I put a female in a well-known male situation: a situation in which jeans were an organic part of that situation," he explains. "The ultimate symbol to me was James Dean putting his feet up on the back of that car seat, leaning back in the rear seat, slumped down with his hat pulled over his eyes in the film *Giant*. My James Dean was a lady." Salisbury combined these two "easily understood and known symbols" and by doing so, created a visual metaphor for Levi's new product.

The visual metaphor said what no words would explain in billboard advertising and venues where long explanatory copy was prohibitive. However, clients like to talk about their product, so long copy print ads with well-defined illustrations outlining the whole shrink system were created to explain how these Levi's fit women—especially their behinds.

THIS PAGE: Salisbury's idea to sell the concept of Levi's 501 Shrink-to-Fit jeans for women was to create a visual metaphor starting with the image of a famous male icon in jeans—James Dean, as shown in the film, *Giant*, and replacing him with a woman.

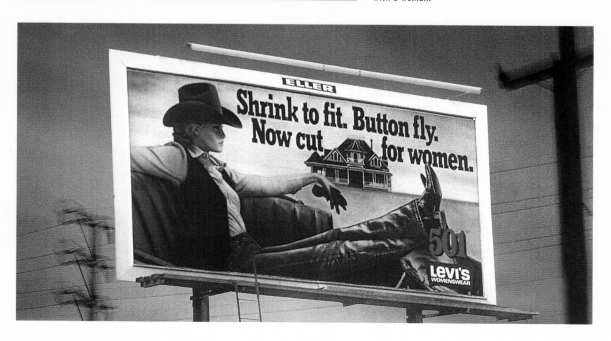

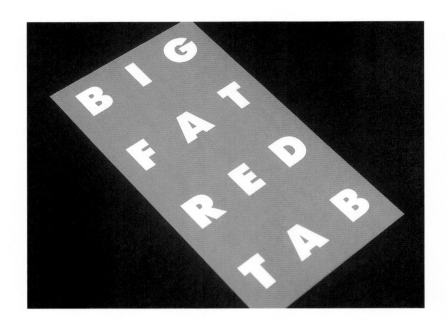

BELOW: This bus poster for a Levi's product is graffiti proof.

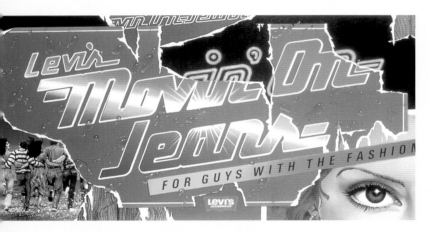

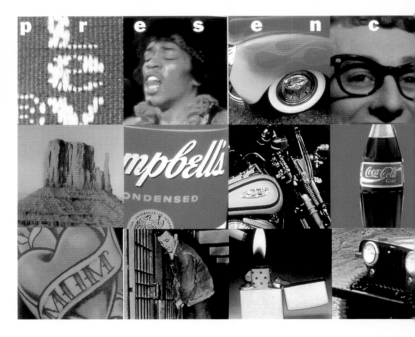

"Originally the tagline to accompany the ad was 'Levi's Shrink-to-Fit-Button-Fly-Jeans-Now-Cut-For-Women.' That's kind of a lot of words for the teeny little space left over on a billboard, print ad, or TV screen," says Salisbury. "Who needs words? The client needs words...that's who. It's their product. But we needed a catch— no one would remember to say all of that when they went into ask for some jeans. We needed a brand.

"Just call the damn things what we call all of them—501s and trademark it!" Salisbury remembers telling the client, referring to Levi's internal stocking number. "That's how Levi's 501 came to be the most well-known brand of clothing in history. It was a combination of everything—simplifying a wordy tagline to a number and reinforcing it with a cohesive, strategic ad campaign. Thus the most famous clothing brand in the world was given to the public to use 100 years after its invention: Levi's 501 jeans—the biggest little number in clothing."

ABOVE: This magazine was given away free at retail to resell the Levi's core brand values to the jeans-buying public.

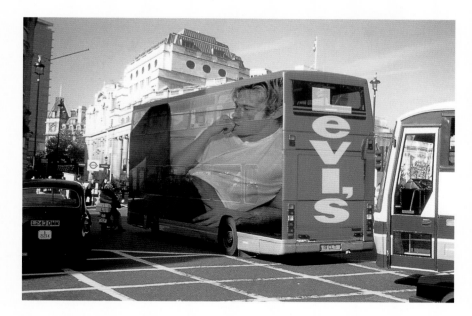

LEFT: **Salisbury Communications, L.L.C. created this campaign for the ad firm Foote Cone Belding when Geoff Thompson was president. "My concept was to bring back to Levi's their brand identity—the world's pants. No fads. No age date."**

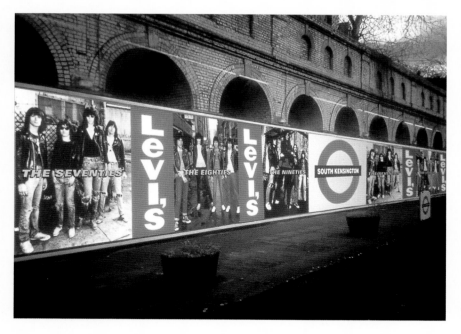

ABOVE: **The goal of this campaign was to show the timelessness of Levi's jeans, so Salisbury crafted this ad to picture the group, the Ramones, at every stage of their career while wearing the same jeans.**

What Works

Today, it's that three-digit number—5-0-1— and the little red tag that consumers readily identify with Levi Strauss & Company. They don't need to know more. That number and the sight of a red tag on the jeans pocket readily identifies them as Levi's products. In fact, if Levi's wanted to, they could probably do without their name on the red tag, the product is that recognized.

So, how did a solution so simple, become an American product icon? Happenstance? Coincidence? A meeting of the minds? Perhaps all of these things. But Salisbury has his own take on how promoting a line of women's jeans revolutionized product branding at the retail level.

"Usually it's the obvious that escapes people, like the world's most famous jeans not even having a brand name, or the fact that Joe Camel was already on the packet."

KNHS:
Unifying Seventeen Groups as One

DESIGN FIRM:
Ping Pong Design

**ART DIRECTOR/
DESIGNER:**
Ping Pong Design

PHOTOGRAPHER:
A. Arnd

CLIENT:
KNHS Royal Dutch
Equestrian Association

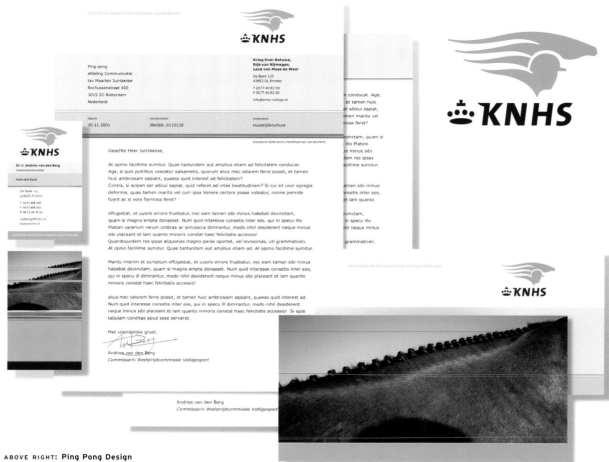

ABOVE RIGHT: **Ping Pong Design created the logo for KNHS, the Royal Dutch Equestrian Association to represent the unification of seventeen separate organizations. The design is subject to interpretation, according to designers. "Some see a horse and rider," says Mirjam Citroen, of Ping Pong Design. "Others see only a dynamic, forward-moving form. The visual interpretation is, therefore, highly personal; and the more personal something is, the more memorable it becomes. In such a situation, ready acceptance is a given."**

The Process

Until recently, seventeen independent organizations represented equestrian sports in the Netherlands, where equestrian events and activities are big business on a local, national, and international level. Each organization operated with its own mission, statue, agenda, and public, until each realized it could better serve the sport and its constituencies if they merged into a single association mandated to represent Dutch equestrians across the board: top-class competition, and recreational riders, and the people and facilities that support equestrian activities.

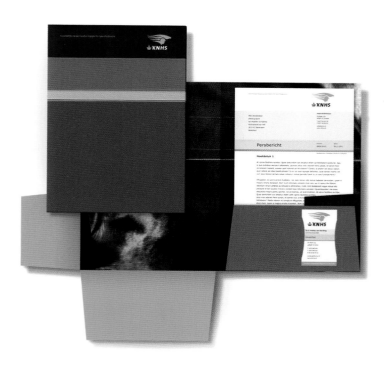

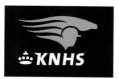

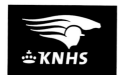

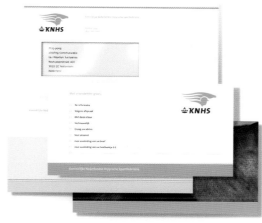

To introduce the newly merged organization to its audiences, KNHS, The Royal Dutch Equestrian Association, as it was named, retained the firm of Nijkamp and Nijboer to develop an introductory strategy, which was formulated by Gert Koostra, and Ping Pong Design to execute the identity and collateral. The entire creative process was allocated a mere six weeks—thirty working days to conceptualize and produce a trademark, letterhead package, clothing, and the overall design program. "This tight deadline intensified the collaborative process," remembers Mirjam Citroen, of Ping Pong Design. "Strategist, designer, and client worked closely and intensively to forge an identity that united the previously independent equestrian organizations visually and emotionally."

Work began immediately on the logo. Designers took stock of the various mindsets represented by the different associations who were banding together to form a single unit and translated these into a form that amply—and jointly—represents their individual needs and concerns.

"Some see a horse and rider," says Citroen. "Others see only a dynamic, forward-moving form. The visual interpretation is, therefore, highly personal; and the more personal something is, the more memorable it becomes. In such a situation, ready acceptance is a given."

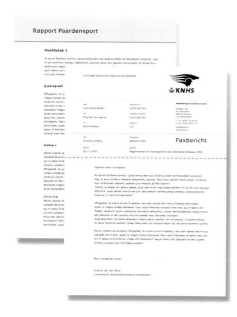

THIS PAGE: The KNHS logo was designed to be flexible enough to work on any number of applications, whether from a stand-alone mark on a coffee cup or reduced in size for use as an insignia on clothing or engraved on a trophy. Designers adapted the logo to a variety of elements in a comprehensive stationery package.

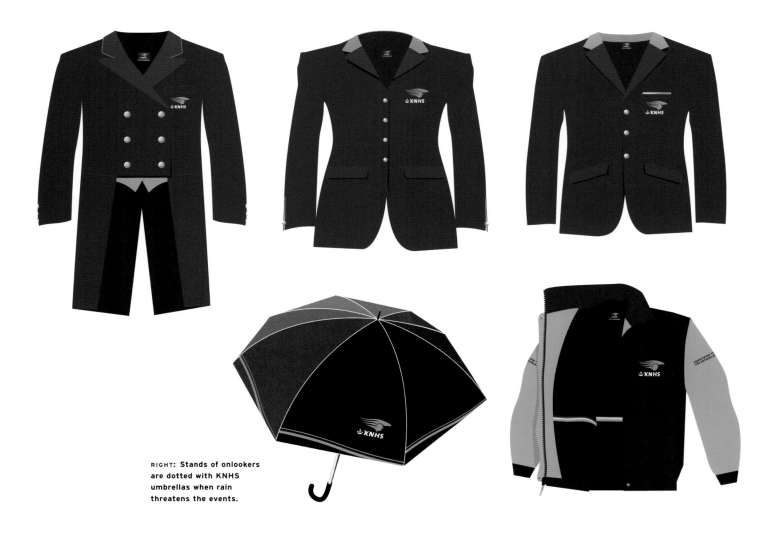

The graphics work within a variety of color combinations, giving it plenty of flexibility so that it can be applied to any number of applications, from the letterhead package and clothing items, such as blazers, to promotional items including blankets, coffee cups, and horse trailers. It also works digitally on a Web site and is equally as effective when reduced in size for use as an insignia or engraved on a trophy.

Designers aren't saying how easy it was to get approval on the design from a unified group of seventeen, but now that KNHS speaks with a single voice, its opinion is overwhelmingly positive. "The graphics present a unified presence among the seventeen previously independent equestrian associations without limiting or infringing on the necessary autonomy still exercised by the different groups," says Citroen.

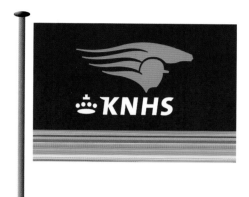

THIS PAGE: Flags are part of the outdoor signage program where each flag carries the logo, designed differently to represent the various categories of competition.

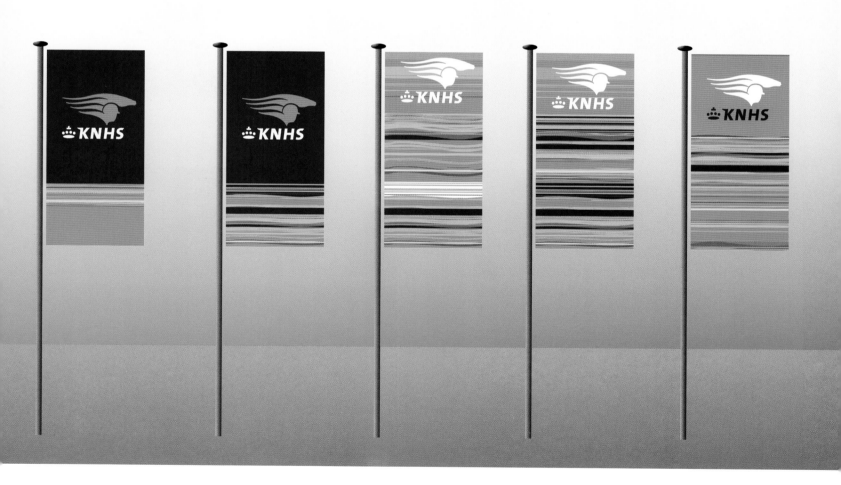

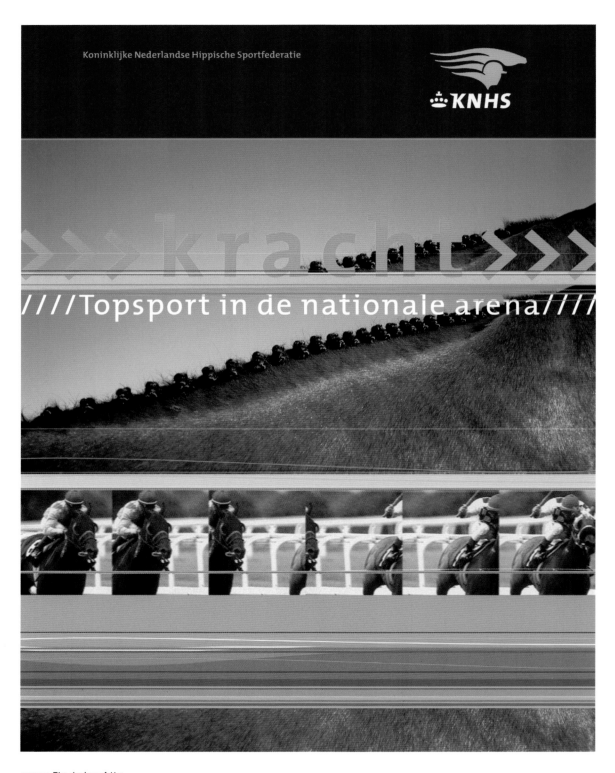

Koninklijke Nederlandse Hippische Sportfederatie

KNHS

Topsport in de nationale arena

ABOVE: The design of the introductory brochure features a horizontal graphic pattern of photographic images that appear to move across the cover like a filmstrip, giving the feeling of speed.

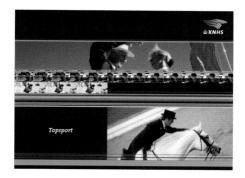 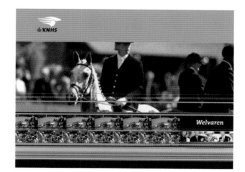 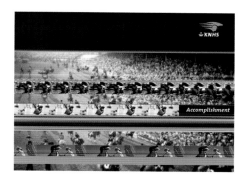

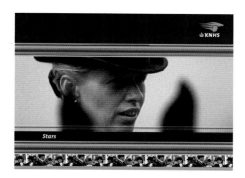 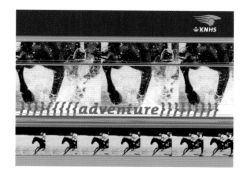 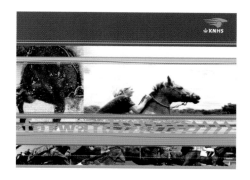

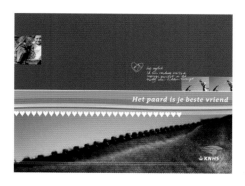 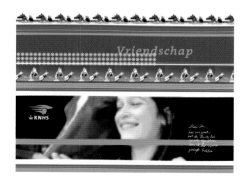 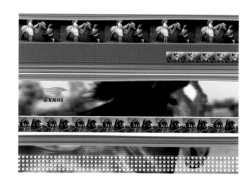

What Works

"The fact that it incorporates the needs, vision, and ambitions of seventeen previously independent equestrian associations helped make it successful, but also the possibility and range of the logo form itself," says Citroen on why the logo works so well. "It is serious enough to depict the focus and discipline inherent in world-class equestrian sport, and it is congenial enough to depict the devotion and affection implicit in young riders and hobbyists.

"The result was that within a remarkably short period of time, we developed a unified style and brand identity that met the needs and fulfilled the expectations of all seventeen associations—no small feat! Our activities proved to be the binding factor that has since allowed the organization to move ahead as a singular organization representing Dutch equestrians at home and abroad."

Galáctea 7:
Space-Age Graphics, Superhero Fun

DESIGN FIRM:
TD2, S.C. Identity and
Strategic Design Consultants

ART DIRECTORS:
Rafael Trevino Monteagudo,
Rafael Rodrigo Cordova Ortiz

DESIGNERS:
Rafael Trevino Monteagudo,
Rafael Rodrigo Cordova Ortiz,
Erica Bravo, Hernandez,
Edgar Medina Graciano,
Brenda Camacho Saenz,
Alejandra Urbina Nunez

ILLUSTRATORS:
Adalberto Arenas Castillo,
Sergio Enriquez Davila

CLIENT:
Helados Nestlé México

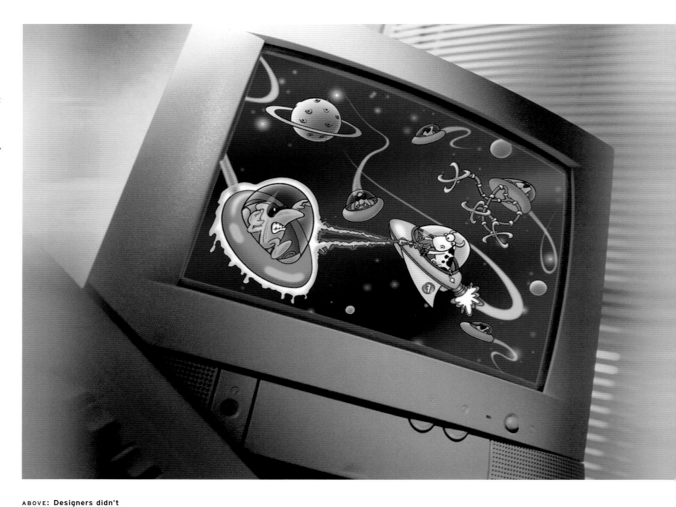

ABOVE: Designers didn't
miss any opportunity to
bring these characters into
kids' daily lives—including
creating a screen saver that
keeps the Galáctea 7 brand
front and center.

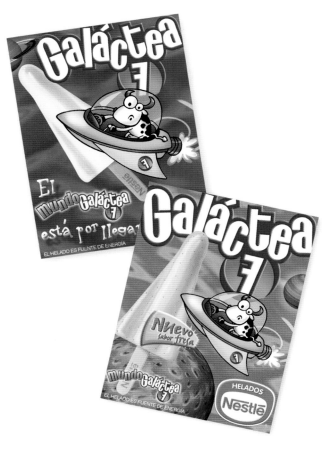

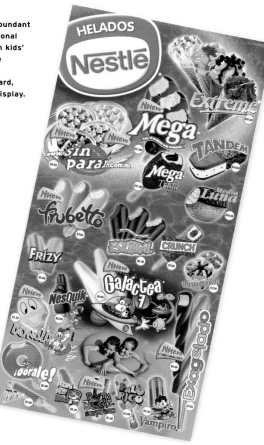

The Process

When Helados Nestlé México retained TD2, S.C. Identity and Strategic Design Consultants to launch its newest ice cream product targeted to eight-to-twelve-year-old kids, three primary objectives were clear. The identity had to innovative, relevant to the preteen market, and, most important, fun.

The dessert was already a known brand—La Lechera—being marketed to adults in a promotion that talked to its older market. This time, the product was being aimed at kids, so Helados Nestlé needed a new marketing approach.

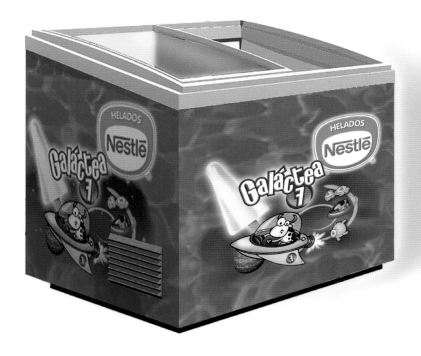

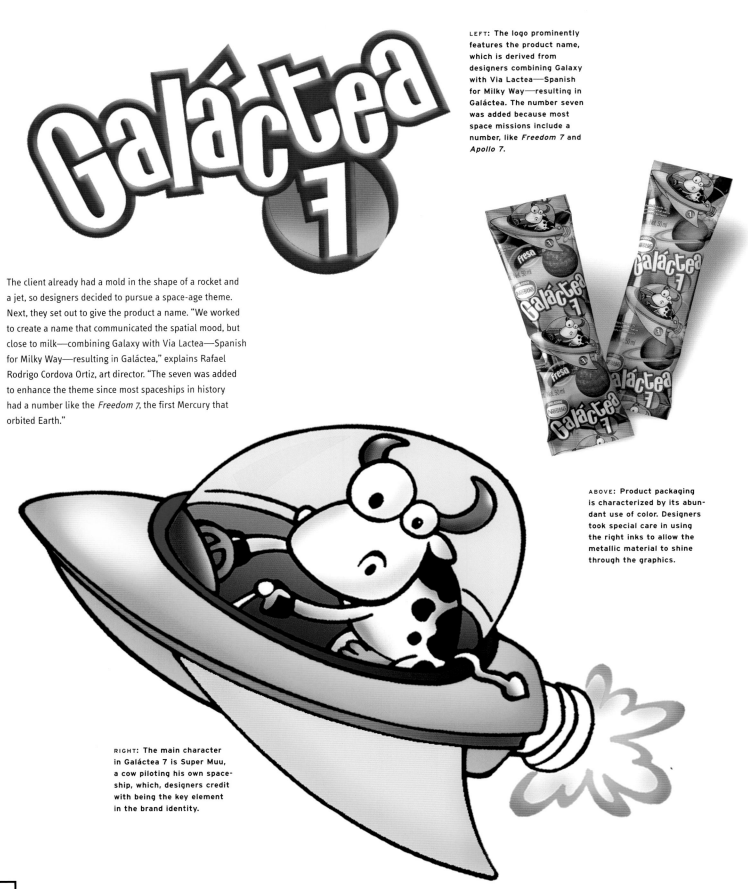

The client already had a mold in the shape of a rocket and a jet, so designers decided to pursue a space-age theme. Next, they set out to give the product a name. "We worked to create a name that communicated the spatial mood, but close to milk—combining Galaxy with Via Lactea—Spanish for Milky Way—resulting in Galáctea," explains Rafael Rodrigo Cordova Ortiz, art director. "The seven was added to enhance the theme since most spaceships in history had a number like the *Freedom 7*, the first Mercury that orbited Earth."

ABOVE: Product packaging is characterized by its abundant use of color. Designers took special care in using the right inks to allow the metallic material to shine through the graphics.

RIGHT: The main character in Galáctea 7 is Super Muu, a cow piloting his own spaceship, which, designers credit with being the key element in the brand identity.

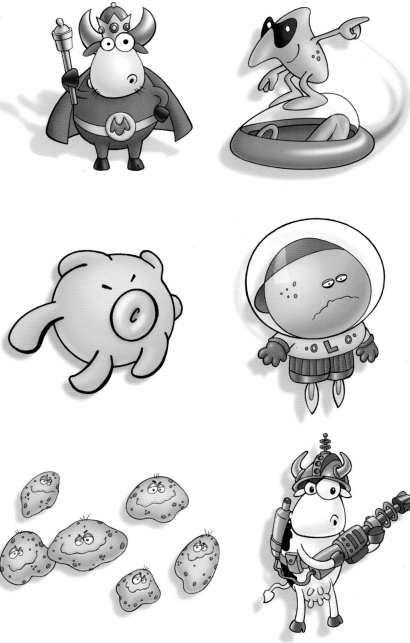

Adding personality and kid appeal to the spaceship is a superhero in the form of a cow—Super Muu, which became the single most important element of the branding, according to designers. "Through the use of humor and a very distinctive use of illustration, we came up with a very successful character," adds Ortiz. Designers went on to develop a family of characters with whimsical names— ReyMuu, Astroratero, Comeleche, LaloLelo, Virulelas, and Vaca Solado—who tell the story of Galáctea 7. Kids wanting to learn more about these characters can read up on their adventures from collectible cards included in the packaging.

ABOVE: The main character, Super Muu, is not alone in space. He has plenty of friends including ReyMuu, Astroratero, Comeleche, LaloLelo, Virulelas, and Vaca Solado—who tell the story of Galáctea 7.

BELOW: Collectible cards, included with the product, tell the individual stories of Galáctea 7's cast of characters.

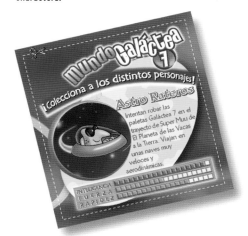

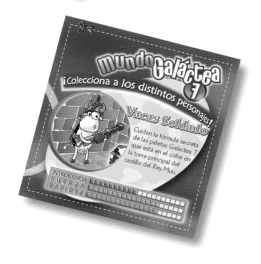

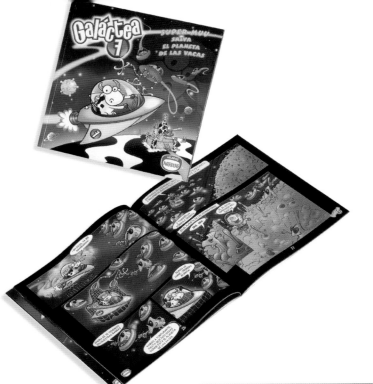

A cast of such colorful characters in space set the stage for action adventures, so designers created an accompanying comic book. Distinguishing all of the promotional elements is color—abundant color, sure to catch the eye of any kid wandering the refrigerated section of the grocery store. The vibrant use of color was no accident but part of the strategic design plan. "To achieve packaging with plenty of impact, we were very careful about using inks with or without a white base to allow the metallic material to live through the graphics," says Ortiz.

Delineating the do's and don'ts of the identity system is an equally colorful brand book. No staid standards manual will do for this product; its manual is as colorful as the packaging.

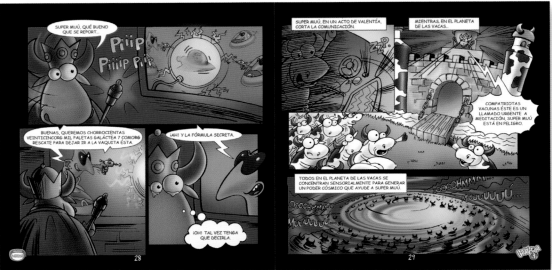

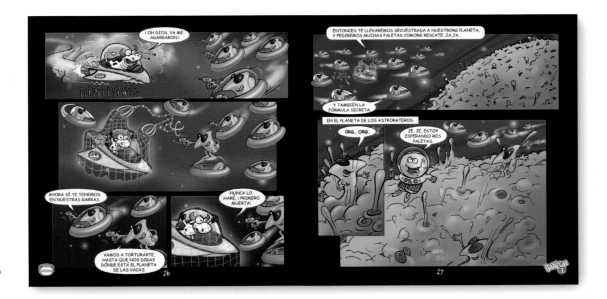

THIS PAGE: A comic book brings the cast of characters to life within an action adventure in space.

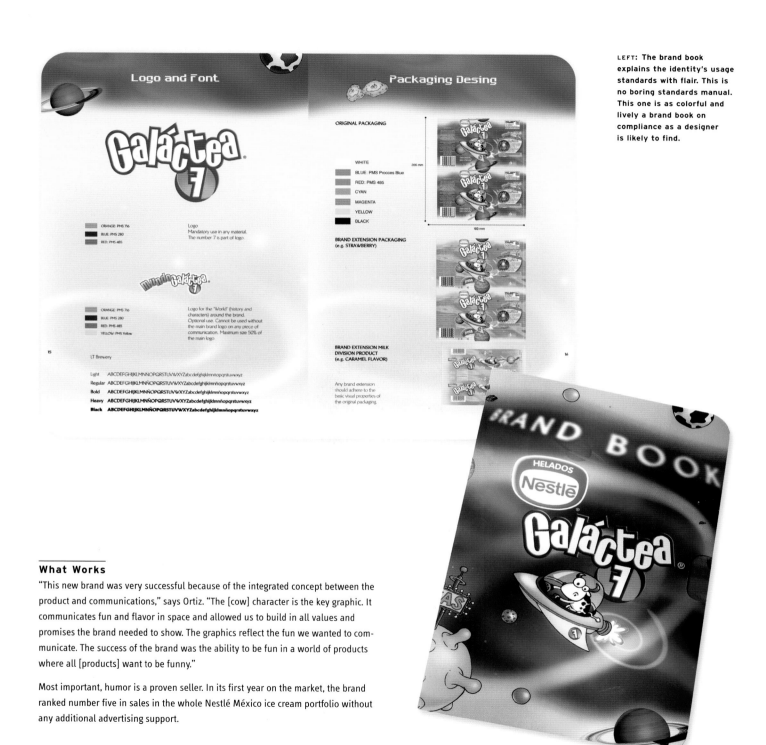

LEFT: The brand book explains the identity's usage standards with flair. This is no boring standards manual. This one is as colorful and lively a brand book on compliance as a designer is likely to find.

What Works

"This new brand was very successful because of the integrated concept between the product and communications," says Ortiz. "The [cow] character is the key graphic. It communicates fun and flavor in space and allowed us to build in all values and promises the brand needed to show. The graphics reflect the fun we wanted to communicate. The success of the brand was the ability to be fun in a world of products where all [products] want to be funny."

Most important, humor is a proven seller. In its first year on the market, the brand ranked number five in sales in the whole Nestlé México ice cream portfolio without any additional advertising support.

HASBRO: Achieving the Logo They Were Always Meant to Have

DESIGN FIRM:
Salisbury
Communications, L.L.C.

CLIENT:
Hasbro

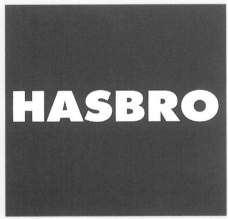

THIS PAGE: **The old logo, above, became a true reflection of the company with it's new logo's smile, right.**

Hasbro, maker of such timeless toys as G.I. Joe, Candy Land, and Monopoly, was looking dated and needed a lift —an image that spoke to kids and to the joy they feel when they play with a new toy.

Salisbury Communications, L.L.C. came on board to help. Designers studied the original logo and decided it was way too serious for a fun-loving toy company.

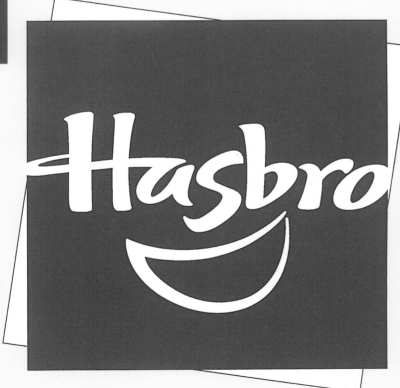

Finally!
The logo we were
always meant to have.

After all, when it comes to fun,
we've got the monopoly...

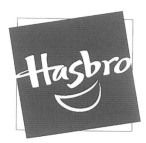

...and G.I Joe, Mr. Potato Head, Candy Land,
Star Wars, Tonka Trucks and Nerf. And we
don't really care what our lawyers say. The world
is welcome to share it.

Many toy companies
consider changing logos.

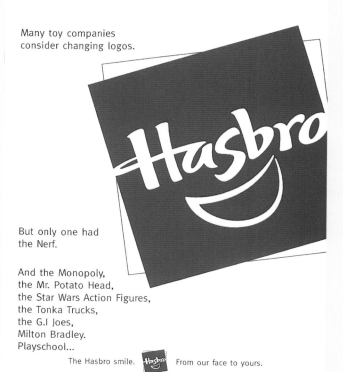

But only one had
the Nerf.

And the Monopoly,
the Mr. Potato Head,
the Star Wars Action Figures,
the Tonka Trucks,
the G.I Joes,
Milton Bradley.
Playschool...

The Hasbro smile.   From our face to yours.

They kept the color palette, but enlivened the mark with
a lighter, more carefree typeface coupled with a smile
"to brand them before McDonald's did with the same
rationale as the hamburger used later," says Mike
Salisbury. "A smile is the most universal facial expression
in the world. Hasbro makes toys. Toys make people smile."

Not everyone involved with the toy industry is as receptive
to change as kids are to trying a new toy. To convince
the board of the need for a brand mark that had impact
—that was a memorable visual for the company—we
created ads to announce the new logo—for *The Wall
Street Journal*, because that is where Hasbro, with its
multitude of brands, needed identifying—with investors,"
says Salisbury.

Hôtel St. Germain:
G is for Graphic Monograms

DESIGN FIRM:
Paprika Communications

ART DIRECTOR:
Louis Gagnon

DESIGNERS:
Louis Gagnon,
Francis Turgeon,
Annabelle Racine

PHOTOGRAPHER:
Michel Touchette

CLIENT:
Groupe Germain

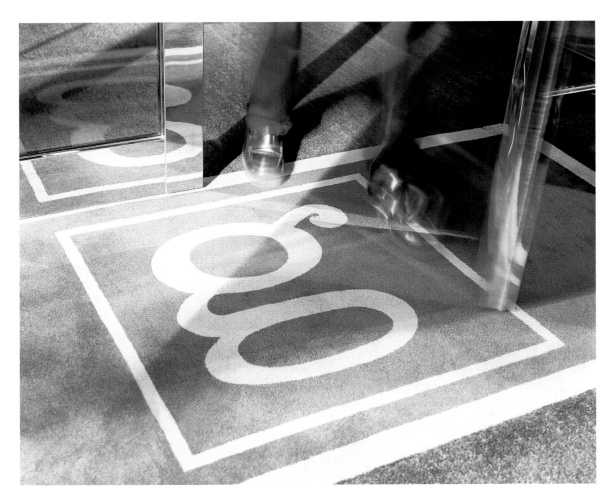

The Process

What started as a simple identity project turned into a comprehensive branding program when Paprika Communications was retained to develop the identity for a new Montreal hotel. The hotel was part of a small chain of boutique hotels, but since it was the first one called Le Germain, designers didn't have to conform to any preexisting graphics standards in place for the two sister hotels. When Germain-des-Prés Developments decided to convert a 1970s office tower in downtown Montreal into the 150-suite Hôtel Le Germain, they needed that special something —that intangible feeling of status and elegance that can be communicated by a well-defined, creative, graphics-based branding program.

ABOVE: Designers opted for a neutral color palette of taupe and cream in keeping with the renovation's architectural and interior design details. Here, the logo and its colors make a statement when guests enter the hotel and step onto its carpet.

HÔTEL LE GERMAIN

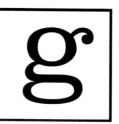

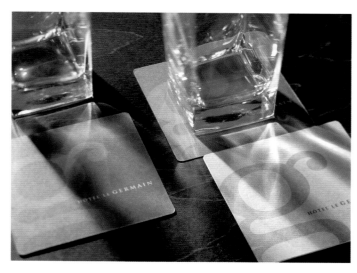

Paprika Communications was awarded the project of developing the new look and corporate identity while the building was being renovated. "The building wasn't particularly bad, but it didn't have all that much character," says Joanne Lefebvre, who cofounded Paprika in 1991 with Louis Gagnon and is now the president. "It was a rectangular structure with large windows and pure, sober lines. You could have given it any personality, really."

The owner wanted a "boutique hotel" that would appeal to sophisticated business customers but also attract upscale tourists; Hôtel Le Germain was to be the best of its kind in Montreal. "We had a very clear idea of what we wanted to accomplish," says Lefebvre. "It had to be considered as one of the best hotels in its category, not only in Montreal, but in North America—New York, Boston, and San Francisco. The most important thing about a boutique hotel is the fact that refinement is… everything. You have to select everything you offer your clients very carefully."

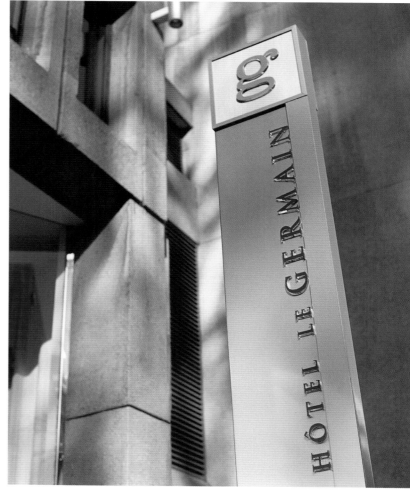

RIGHT: The designers collaborated with the architects during the renovation to make sure that the graphics would complement the new building, which was being transformed from a non-descript office building to a boutique hotel.

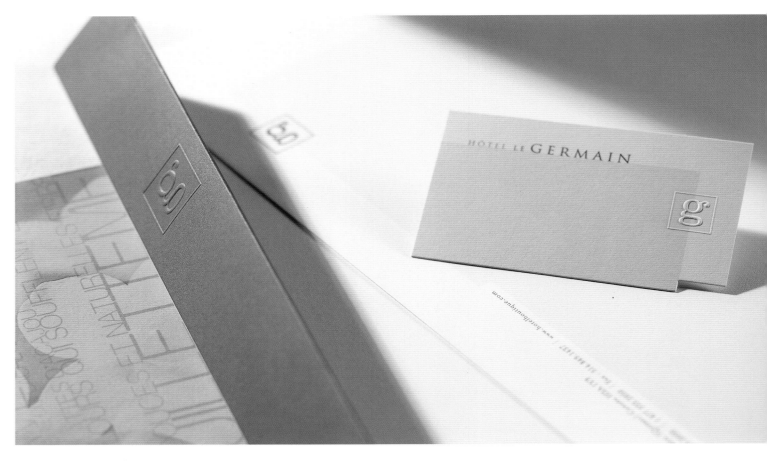

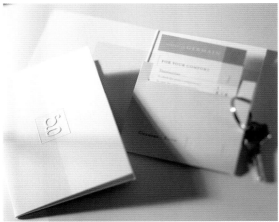

ABOVE: Designers thought the project was just an identity program when they created the hotel's stationery system, but it turned into much, much more.

ABOVE: The key wallet is embossed with the hotel's logo.

That was the reasoning behind designers choosing to use a monogram as the logo. "The *g* would be our quality signature," explains Lefebvre. "We would use it to communicate the fact that we had selected this product or this service to make sure your experience of staying at Le Germain would be the best it can be." Designers also liked the idea of a monogram because it meant they wouldn't have to spell out the full name. "That became increasingly important as the program grew to include more and more items." They set the lowercase *g* in Clarendon, a nineteenth-century typeface. "We wanted something pretty, but also timeless—a mixture of something hip with something very classical."

Designers worked on basic elements of the branding such as the letterhead system and collaborated with architects and interior designers to ensure that the new interior and exterior graphics complemented the work being done as part of the renovation. Designers went for a classical appearance, avoiding anything trendy, and chose a neutral color palette of taupe and cream that would work in tandem with the building's architecture and interiors.

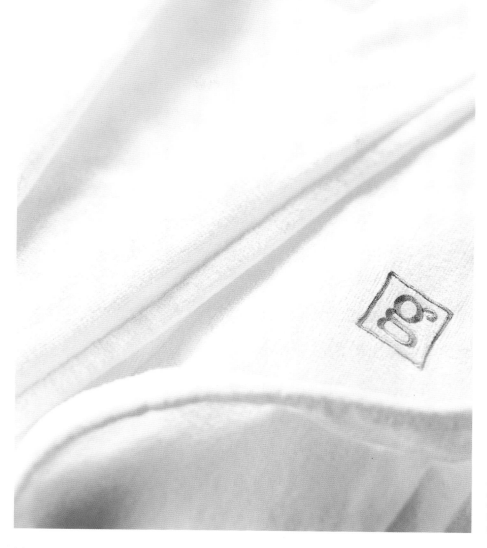

"The creative line was 'hotel of the senses.' We wanted everything to be perfect," says Lefebvre.

Everything is very near perfect, too. The deceptively simple monogram can be seen everywhere. The client liked it so much that they asked designers to incorporate the logo throughout the hotel—effectively branding the building and all of its contents. It shows up where one might expect to see a monogram—embroidered on a hotel robe, as well as in unlikely places, such as on the porcelain faucet inserts in the guest bathrooms and on the carpets. Such attention to detail is abundant in this identity where no opportunity is overlooked to remind travelers of the brand. "It started out as a corporate identity but turned into a branding program," says Lefebvre.

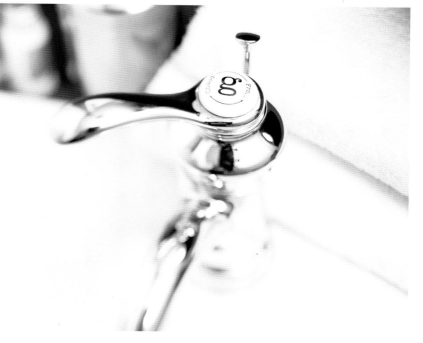

RIGHT: Matchbooks are also high end, with the logo printed on the box tray that holds the matches, while the name of the hotel runs atop the sleeve. The ashtrays also sport the distinct *g* monogram.

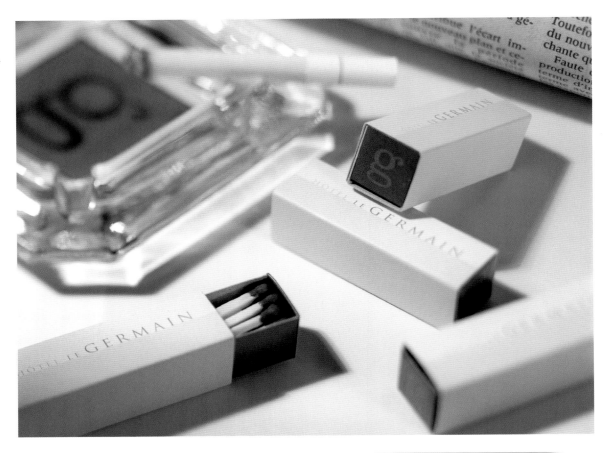

RIGHT: Designers created the packaging for the body care products found in guest rooms and have just completed a promotional brochure that is linked to the hotel's Web site, which allows guests to buy about everything they saw in their room, from its sheets and pillows to its furniture and glasses.

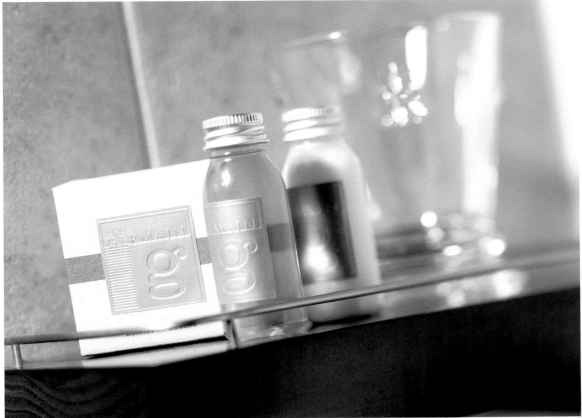

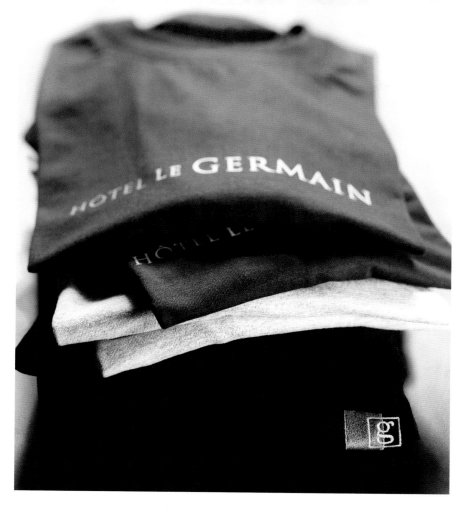

"We must say it was very successful," says Lefebvre. "Not only because of the branding program, of course. But it was the whole operation that turned out to be a very big success."

The project took about one year, but the relationship didn't end when the project did. Paprika Communications continues to create and develop new applications for the logo at the St. Germain. The work is getting plenty of attention, too. The media coverage has been phenomenal and, according to Lefebvre, specialized tourist guides have given the hotel very high marks. Christiane Germain, the president of the establishment, has made appearances on television shows and and has received numerous awards for her work by the tourist industry. The branding program and its components were recognized in major graphic design contests like Communication Arts, Applied Arts, Art Directors Club, Graphis, Grafika, Montreal Design Institute, and Creativity. Most important, the hotel and its ambiance attracted a lot of attention in Montreal and worldwide.

What Works

The logo works. The *g* has become such a strong logo in the tourist industry that the client decided to keep the brand for another new hotel in Toronto rather than risking developing something totally new.

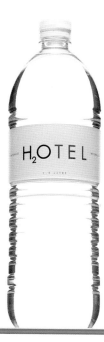

Directory

Action Figure
109 East 10th
Austin, TX 78701
phone: 512.480.5900
fax: 512.480.9860

Aegis Toronto
672 Dupont Street, Suite 402
Toronto, ON M6G 1Z6
Canada
phone: 416.364.2144
fax: 416.364.8841
www.ideaschangereality.com
gsalmela@ideaschange
        reality.com

After Hours Creative
5444 East Washington Street,
    Suite 3
Phoenix, AZ 85034
phone: 602.275.5200
fax: 602.275.5700

Anne Telford
3661 Folsom Street
San Francisco, CA 94110
phone: 650.815.4222
fax: 650.326.1648
annet@commarts.com

BBK Studio
648 Monroe Avenue NW,
    Suite 212
Grand Rapids, MI 49503
phone: 616.459.4444
fax: 616.459.4477
www.bbkstudio.com
yang@bbkstudio.com

BC Design
157 Yesler Way, #316
Seattle, WA 98104
phone: 206.652.2494
fax: 206.749.5015

Belyea
1809 7th Avenue, Suite 1250
Seattle, WA 98101
www.belyea.com

Blackletter Design
606 Meredith Road, NE #4
Calgary, AB T2E 5A8
Canada
phone: 403.209.6112
fax: 403.209.6113
bessiek@cadvision.com

Blue
611 Broadway, Suite 405
New York, NY 10012
phone: 212.77.0024
www.blueadventure.com

Business 2.0
Imagine Media Inc.
150 North Hill Drive
Brisbane, CA 94005
phone: 415.468.4684
www.business2.com

Cathie Bleck
2270 Chatfield Drive
Cleveland Heights, OH 44106
phone: 216.932.4910
fax: 216.932.4616
www.cathiebleck.com
cb@cathiebleck.com

Code
8484 Wilshire Boulevard,
    Suite 900
Beverly Hills, CA 90211
phone: 323.651.5400
www.codemagazine.com
Images courtesy of *Code*
    magazine

DWL Incorporated
230 Richmond Street East,
    Level 2
Toronto, ON M5A 1P4
Canada
phone: 416.364.2045
fax: 416.364.2422
www.dwl.com
smurenbeeld@dwl.com

EAI
887 West Marietta Street,
    Suite J-101
Atlanta, GA 30318
phone: 404.875.8225
fax: 404.875.4402
www.eai-atl.com
d_gahan@eai-atl.com

Eleven Inc.
445 Bush Street
San Francisco, CA 94108
phone: 415.291.1770
fax: 415. 296.1714
www.eleveninc.com

Emery Vincent Design
Level 1, 15 Foster Street
Surry Hills, NSW 2010
Australia
phone: 61.2.9280.4233
fax: 61.2.9280.4266
www.emeryvincentdesign.com
info@emeryvincentdesign.com

Enterprise IG
570 Lexington Avenue
New York, NY 10022
phone: 212.755.4200
fax: 212.755.9474
www.enterpriseig.com

Epoxy
506 Rue McGill
Montreal, Quebec
Canada
phone: 514.866.6900
fax: 514.866.6300
www.epoxy.ca

**Extraprise/Tsuchiya Sloneker
Communications**
140 Geary Street, #500
San Francisco, CA 94108
phone: 415.268.4500
fax: 415.268.9501
www.tscom.com

Fast Company
77 N. Washington Street
Boston, MA 02114
phone: 617.973.0300
www.fastcompany.com

Felix Sockwell Creative
24 West 87th Street, Suite 3B
New York, NY 10024
phone: 212.579.5617
www.felixsockwell.com

Flux Labs
627 St. George's Road
Philadelphia, PA 19119
phone: 215.248.0166
fax: 215.248.0167
www.fluxlabs.com

Fossil
2280 N. Greenville
Richardson, TX 75082
www.fossil.com

Gee + Chung Design
38 Bryant Street, Suite 100
San Francisco, CA 94105
www.geechungdesign.com

General and Specific
285 West Broadway,
Suite 300
New York, NY 10013
phone: 212.219.9919
fax: 212.219.9989
www.generalandspecific.com

GMO/Hill, Holliday
600 Battery Street
San Francisco, CA 94111
phone: 415.617.5100
fax: 415.677.9385
www.gmosf.com

GQ
4 Times Square
New York, NY 10036
phone: 212.286.2860
www.gq.com
Design Director: Arem K.
    Duplessis
Director of Photography:
    Jennifer Crandall

page 90, left
Art Director: Paul Martinez
Designers: Arem K. Duplessis, Paul Martinez
Photo Editor: Jennifer Crandall
Photographer: Michael Thompson

page 90, right
Design Director: Arem K. Duplessis
Art Director: Paul Martinez
Designer: Paul Martinez
Photographer: Robert Erdmann

page 91, top
Art Director: George Moschalades
Designer: Arem K. Duplessis
Photo Editor: Karen Frank
Photographer: Michael O'Neill

page 91, middle
Art Director: George Moschalades
Designer: Arem K. Duplessis
Photo Editor: Karen Frank
Photographer: Art Strieber

page 91, bottom
Art Director: Paul Martinez
Designer: Arem K. Duplessis
Photo Editor: Jennifer Crandall

page 92, top
Art Director: Paul Martinez
Designer: Paul Martinez
Photo Editors: Jennifer Crandall,
    Catherine Talese
Photographer: Tom Tavee

page 92, middle
Art Director: Paul Martinez
Designer: Paul Martinez
Photo Editors: Jennifer Crandall,
    Kristen Schaefer
Photographer: Markus Klinko and Indrani

page 92, bottom
Art Director: Paul Martinez
Designer: Paul Martinez
Illustrator: Kristian Russell

page 93, top
Art Director: Paul Martinez
Designer: Arem K. Duplessis
Photo Editor: Jennifer Crandall
Photographer: Steven Sebring

page 93, middle
Art Director: Paul Martinez
Designer: Arem K. Duplessis
Photo Editor: Jennifer Crandall
Photographer: Michael Thompson

page 93, botton
Art Director: Paul Martinez
Designer: Arem K. Duplessis
Photo Editors: Jennifer Crandall,
    Kristen Schaefer
Photographer: Ben Watts

page 94, top
Art Director: Paul Martinez
Designer: Arem K. Duplessis
Photo Editor: Jennifer Crandall
Photographer: Michael Thompson

page 94, middle
Art Director: George Moschalades
Designer: Arem K. Duplessis
Photo Editor: Jennifer Crandall
Photographer: Norman Jean Roy

page 94, bottom
Art Director: George Moschalades
Designer: Arem K. Duplessis
Photo Editor: Jennifer Crandall
Photographer: Norman Jean Roy

page 95, top
Art Director: Paul Martinez
Designer: Matthew Lenning
Photo Editor: Jennifer Crandall
Photographer: Stewart Shinning

page 95, middle
Art Director: Paul Martinez
Designer: Arem K. Duplessis

page 95, bottom
Art Director: Paul Martinez
Designer: Arem K. Duplessis
Photo Editor: Jennifer Crandall
Photographer: Anita Calero

Hornall Anderson Design Works, Inc.
1008 Western Avenue, Suite 600
Seattle, WA 98104
phone: 206.467.5800
fax: 206.467.6411
www.hadw.com

HOW
F&W Publications
1507 Dana Avenue
Cincinnati, OH 45207
phone: 513.531.2690
www.howdesign.com
Images ©1999 *HOW* magazine

Howalt Design
527 West Scott Avenue
Gilbert, AZ 85233
phone: 480.558.0390
fax: 480.558.0391

I.D.
F&W Publications
1507 Dana Avenue
Cincinnati, OH 45207
phone: 513.531.2690
www.idonline.com
Images courtesy of *I.D.* magazine

i.e. design, inc.
150 West 25th Street, #404
New York, NY 10001
phone: 212.255.1515
fax: 212.255.3102
www.ie-design.com

Jason & Jason Visual Comm.
11B Box 2432
Raanana, 43663
Israel
phone: 972.9.7444282
fax: 972.9.7444292
www.jandj.co.il
tamar@jandj.co.il

Jennifer Sterling Design
P.O. Box 475428
San Francisco, CA 94147-5428
phone: 415.621.3481
www.sterlingdesign.com
marketing@jsterlingdesign.com

Joel Nakamura Paintings & Illustrations
72 Bobcat Trail
Santa Fe, NM 87505
phone: 505.989.1404
fax: 505.989.7448
www.joelnakamura.com
joel@joelnakamura.com

John Borruso Graphic Design & Collage
1243 Union Street
San Francisco, CA 94109
phone: 415.775.9977
fax: 415.775.7977

Kevin Hall Design
87 Kenwood Road
Milford, CT 06460
phone: 203.878.0346
fax: 203.878.2112

Lecours Design, Inc.
3713 Highland Avenue, #4A
Manhattan Beach, CA 90266
phone: 310.546.2206
fax: 310.546.2826
www.lecoursdesign.com

Lewis Moberly
33 Gresse Street
London, WIT IQU
UK
phone: 44.20.7580.9252
fax: 44.20.7255.1671
www.lewismoberly.com
hello@lewismoberly.com

Likovni Studio D.O.O.
Dekanici 42, Kerestinec
HR-10431 Sveta Nedelja
Croatia
list@list.hr

LPG Design
410 E. 27th Street North
Wichita, KS 67219-3556
www.lpgdesign.com

marchFIRST
410 Townsend Street
San Francisco, CA 94107
phone: 415.284.7070
www.marchfirst.com

Matthews/Mark
1111 Sixth Avenue
San Diego, CA
phone: 619.238.8500
fax: 619.238.8505
www.matthewsmark.com

Mauk Design
39 Stillman Street
San Francisco, CA 94107
phone: 415.243.9277
fax: 415.243.9273
www.maukdesign.com

Memo Productions
611 Broadway, #811
New York, NY 10012
phone: 212.388.9758
fax: 212.388.1750

Merge
884 Monroe Drive
Atlanta, GA 30308
phone: 404.724.4942
fax: 404.724.0141
www.mergedesign.com

MetaDesign
350 Pacific Avenue, 3rd Floor
San Francisco, CA 94111
phone: 415.627.0790
www.metadesign.com

Michael Osborne Design
444 De Haro Street, Suite 207
San Francisco, CA 94107
phone: 415.255.0125
fax: 415.255.1312
www.modsf.com
mo@modsf.com

Mike Salisbury Communications, L.L.C.
P.O. Box 2309
Venice, CA 90291
phone: 310.392.8779

Miriello Grafico
419 West G Street
San Diego, CA 92101
phone: 619.234.1124
fax: 619.234.1960
www.miriellografico.com
pronto@miriellografico.com

Buddy Morel
3855 Inglewood Boulevard, #204
Los Angeles, CA 90066-7907
phone: 310.313.6888
fax: 310.313.6889

Mortensen Design
416 Bush Street
Mountain View, CA 94041
phone: 650.988.0946
fax: 650.988.0926
www.mortdes.com

Murphy Design Inc.
1240 Golden Gate Drive
San Diego, CA 92116
phone: 800.486.6275
www.murphydesign.com
murphy@murphydesign.com

Oh Boy, A Design Company
49 Geary Street, Suite 530
San Francisco, CA 94108
phone: 415.834.9063
fax: 415.84.9396
www.ohboyco.com

Paprika Communications
400, Laurier Street West, #610
Montreal, PQ H2V 2K7
Canada
www.paprika.com

Pentagram Design, Inc.
387 Tehama Street
San Francisco, CA 94103
phone: 415.896.0499
fax: 415.896.0555
www.pentagram.com

Ping Pong Design
Rochussenstraat 400
3015ZC Rotterdam
Netherlands
www.pinpongdesign.com

pk(des)gn
78 Orchard Street, #3B
New York, NY 10002
phone: 212.387.9615
fax: 212.210.7474

Plainspoke
18 Sheafe Street
Portsmouth, NH 03801
phone: 603.433.5969
fax: 603.433.1587
www.plainspoke.com
matt@plainspoke.com

Planet Design Company
605 Williamson Street
Madison, WI 53703
phone: 608.256.0000
fax: 608.256.1975
www.planetdesign.com

R2 Design
Praceta D Nuno Alvares
4450 Matosinhos
Pereira 20 5 FQ
Portugal
phone: 351.22.938.68.65
fax: 351.22.938.94.82
liza@rdois.com
www.rdois.com

Real Simple
Time Inc.
1271 Avenue of the Americas
New York, NY 10020
phone: 212.522.1212
www.realsimple.com

Redpath
5 Gayfield Square
Edinburgh EH1 3NW
UK
phone: 44.131.556.9115
fax: 44.131.556.9116
www.redpath.co.uk
redpath@redpath.co.uk

Reebok
1895 J.W. Foster Boulevard
Canton, MA 02021
phone: 781.401.5000
fax: 781.401.4077
www.reebok.com
eleni.chronopoulos@reebok.com

Renee Rech Graphic Design
230 West Tazewell Street, Suite 309
Norfolk, VA 23510
phone: 757.622.3334
fax: 757.622.2274
renee@reneerechdesign.com
www.reneerechdesign.com

Reservoir
141 Beaver Street
San Francisco, CA 94114
phone: 415.558.9605
fax: 415.558.8248
www.reservoir-sf.com
postmaster@reservoir-sf.com

SamataMason Inc.
101 South First Street
Des Plaines, IL 60016
phone: 847.428.8600
fax: 847.428.5664
www.samatamason.com
susan@samatamason.com

Segura Inc.
1110 North Milwaukee Avenue
Chicago, IL 60622
phone: 773.862.5667
fax: 773.862.1214
www.segura-inc.com

SJI Associates Inc.
1001 6th Avenue, 23rd floor
New York, NY 10018
phone: 212.391.7770
fax: 212.391.1717
www.sjiassociates.com
suzy@sjiassoaciates.com

Skidmore Inc.
29580 Northwestern Highway
Southfield, MI 48034-1031
phone: 248.353.7722
fax: 248.353.1199
www.skidart.com
julie@skidart.com

Soapbox Design Communications
1055 Yonge Street, #209
Toronto, Ontario M4W 2L2
Canada
phone: 416.920.2099
fax: 416.920.8178
www.soapboxdesign.com

Stan Gellman Graphic Design, Inc.
4509 Laclede Avenue
St. Louis, MI 63108
phone: 314.361.7676
fax: 314.361.8645
www.sggdesign.com
barry@sggdesign.com

Stoltze Design
49 Melcher Street, 4th Floor
Boston, MA 02210
phone: 617.350.7109
fax: 617.482.1171
www.stoltzedesign.com
christine@stoltzedesign.com

Summa
Roger de Lluria 124
Planta 8
08037 Barcelona
Spain
phone: 34.93.208.1090
fax: 34.93.459.1816
www.summa.es
wmarnich@summa.es

SVP Partners
15 Cannon Road
Wilton, CT 06897
phone: 203.761.0397
fax: 203.761.0482
www.svppartners.com
rls@svppartners.com

t-squared design
10809 108th Avenue NE
Kirkland, WA 98033
phone: 425.822.7524
fax: 425.822.4904

TD2, S.C. Identity and Strategic Design Consultants
Ibsen 43, 8th Floor
Col. Polanco C.P.
11560 Mexico D.F.
r.cordova@td2.com.mx

Templin Brink Design
720 Tehama Street
San Francisco, CA 94103
phone: 415.255.9295
fax: 415.255.9296
www.templinbrinkdesign.com

The Leonhardt Group
1218 Third Avenue, Suite 620
Seattle, WA 98101
phone: 206.624.0551
fax: 206.624.0875
www.tlg.com

Thumbnail Creative Group
403–611 Alexander Street
Vancouver, BC V6A 1E1
Canada
phone: 604.736.2133
fax : 604.736.5414
www.thumbnailcreative.com
rik@thumbnailcreative.com

TransWorld Surf
TransWorld Media
353 Airport Road
Oceanside, CA 92054
phone: 760.722.7777
www.twsurf.com

Travel & Leisure
American Express Publications
1120 Avenue of the Americas
New York, NY 10036
phone: 212.382.5600
www.travelandleisure.com

Twelve Stars Communications
13 Chesterfield Street
London W1X 7HF
United Kingdom
phone: 44 831 801 259

Volkswagen of America, Inc.
Mail Code 4F02
3800 Hamlin Road
Auburn Hills, MI 48326

Weymouth Design
332 Congress Street, 6th Floor
Boston, MA 02210
www.weymouthdesign.com

Yoga Journal
2054 University Avenue
Berkeley, CA 94704
phone: 510.841.9200
www.yogajournal.com

Y-NOT Design
10470 Spring Run Drive
Cincinnati, OH 45231
phone/fax: 513.825.5939